D0604444

MEDITERRANEAN GRAINS AND GREENS

MEDITERRANEAN GRAINS AND GREENS

A Book of Savory, Sun-Drenched Recipes

PAULA WOLFERT

HarperCollins*Publishers*

To Frieda, Nicholas, Leila, Loretta, and Suzanne

The selection from *Voices of Marrakech* by Elias Canetti on page 16 is reprinted by arrangement with Carl Hanser Verlag, c/o Joan Daves Agency as agent for the proprietor. Copyright ©1968 by Carl Hanser Verlag München by appointment with Elias Canetti, Zurich, 1967, 1995.

Cover photograph: Tarhana Salad with Peppers, by Alison Harris

MEDITERRANEAN GRAINS AND GREENS. Copyright © 1998 by Paula Wolfert. All rights reserved. Printed in the United States of America. No part of this book may be used or reproduced in any manner whatsoever without written permission except in the case of brief quotations embodied in critical articles and reviews. For information address HarperCollins Publishers, Inc., 10 East 53rd Street, New York, NY 10022.

HarperCollins books may be purchased for educational, business, or sales promotional use. For information please write: Special Markets Department, HarperCollins Publishers, Inc., 10 East 53rd Street, New York, NY 10022.

FIRST EDITION

Designed by Joel Avirom and Jason Snyder

Library of Congress Cataloging-in-Publication Data

Wolfert, Paula.
    Mediterranean grains and greens : a book of savory, sun-drenched recipes / Paula Wolfert. — 1st ed.
      p. cm.
    Includes index.
    ISBN 0-06-017251-7
    1. Cookery, Mediterranean. 2. Cookery (Cereals). 3. Cookery (Greens).
I. Title
TX725.M35W643   1998
641.59'1822—dc21   98-10228

03 04 05 ❖/RRD 10 9 8 7 6 5 4 3

CONTENTS

ACKNOWLEDGMENTS

✳

To paraphrase a famous saying: You can never be too thin or thank people enough—especially those who've helped you.

It would be easy to simply name the people who, believing in my work, encouraged me along the way. But there're so many others—wonderful cooks who opened their doors to me, sat me down with their families, told me their stories, fed me, even invited me to move into their homes for days at a time in order to pass on the recipes, insights, and knowledge they wanted to share. Over a period of four years this adds up to a lot of people and far more recipes and material than finally made their way into this book. I must also thank the people who sent me to these sources, since a casually given name and address often led to a fantastic experience.

There were three people and groups who particularly helped me with this work. First, my very close friend, the late Arlene Wanderman. This extraordinary woman who traveled with me in Italy, Spain, France, Morocco, and Tunisia was a great source of strength and encouragement. I miss her.

Second, Oldways Preservation and Exchange Trust, the nonprofit Cambridge-based food think tank, helped me to refocus my view of Mediterranean cooking—a refocusing that led to my writing this book. I want to thank Dun Gifford, Sara Baer Sinnott, and Annie Copps for the educational opportunities they have provided through their great meetings and conferences.

Finally, there are four people—three food writers and one chef—who live around the Mediterranean and with whom I've worked and/or traveled over the past few years. These people have gone out of their way to provide me with insights into the food and culture of their home countries, as well as entrée into the homes of great cooks. I thank them for their enormous help and friendship:

Ayfer Ünsal of Turkey over the past five years has accompanied me on many trips to many regions of her country, organizing home visits, sleepovers, and cooking fests for which a thank-you is wildly insufficient.

In Greece, the Athenian food writer Aglaia Kremezi has helped me discover Greek cooking over many years. She has been a wonderful friend and teacher.

Among the dozens of Italophiles who have helped me, I must single out Faith Willinger. Her take on Italian food is astounding—intelligent, deep, informative, perceptive, and wry—just what I needed to help demystify the wonderful cuisines of relatively little-traveled parts of the country. No one I know has as much knowledge of Italian cooking or is as willing to share it.

Last but by no means least are the Tunisian chef Abdelrazak Haouari and his wife, Nabiha, who welcomed me into their new home and then, instead of teaching me chefs' cooking, showed me the wonderful home cooking of their native Djerba.

In addition, I could not have done without the help of Mirsini Lambraki, an inspired teacher on the edible wild plants of Crete.

Filiz Hösukoğlu has been a wonderful translator, always eager to help. And I'm very grateful to Dalia Carmel for her tireless researching of authentic recipes, and to Shirley Corriher for explaining to me the whys of so many things, especially chickpea leavening. I couldn't have written this book without their help.

A very special thank-you to the International Olive Oil Council and particularly Fausto Lucceti, Irfan Berkan, Linda Russo, Diane Harris Brown, and Warren Carroll for their continued support of my work.

A special thank-you to my friend Fran McCullough for giving me the title of this book.

Here, in alphabetical order, are the United States–based food writers, chefs, cooks, purveyors, producers, and editors who helped me in one way or another as I researched this book:

Colman Andrews, Arman Aroyan, Donna Bayless, Darrel Corti, Merle Ellis, Stephen Facciola, Carol Field, Janet Fletcher, Johnny Graham, Justin Guisanti, George A. Gutekunst, Barbara Haber, Suzanne Hamlin, Jessica Harris, Sally Hitchcock, Robin Insley, Dana Jacobi, Nancy Harmon Jenkins, Chef Kelsie Kerr, Peggy Knickerbocker, Corby Kummer, Paula Linton, Sheila Lukins, Zarela Martinez, Harold McGee, Rick Moonen, Molly O'Neill, James O'Shea, Michael Orlando, Russ Parsons, Charles Perry, Gayle Pirie, Sara Powers, Judy Rodgers, Julie Sahni, Joe Simone, Monica Spiller, Jeffrey Steingarten, James Villas, Donna Warner, Scott Warner, Nach Waxman, Clifford Wright, and Adrienne Zausner.

Special thanks to the editors and kitchen staffs of *Food & Wine Magazine, Saveur* magazine, and *Metropolitan Home,* where some of the recipes and notes first appeared.

I am sincerely grateful to my friend Alice Waters for allowing me to spend a day in her restaurant, Chez Panisse, where I learned more than I hoped about making polenta in the United States. I also want to thank Chef Christopher Lee, Peggy Smith, Russell Moore, Michael Peternell, Gilbert Pilgrim, Jennifer Sherman, and Mona Talbott, all of Chez Panisse, for their invaluable comments.

Thanks to Madame Houda Mokadmi, Abdelhakim Zemmel Mokadmi, Salah and Lynn Hannachi, Essid Habib, Jalloul Jabou, Khedija Ben Youssef, Rahima Methni, Aicha Rouatbi, Lola Cohen, Mohammed Melke, Taieb Dridi, Moncef Meddebeb, Fadhila Mekki, Rachida Hannachi, Najla Kahia, Safia Kahia, and Souhur Hamada for their help on Tunisian cooking.

Thanks to Vefa Alexiadou, Victoria Athanassiady, June Samaras, Eric Moscalaidis, Niki Moquist, Christoforos Veneris, Nick Metaxis, Diane Kochilas, Angel Stoyanoff, Lefteris Lazarou, and Daphne Zepos for their help on Greek and Greek-Cypriot cooking.

Thanks to Egin Akin; Mehmet Gökçek; Eren Özebeçki; Maja Biehl; Bahriye Çetinda; Günay Özal and Erminia Baydilek; Akten Köylüoğlu; Bahriye, Akten, and Fatma Hanim; Yıldız Ergun; and Gülsen Çağdas, Kezban Yavuz, Mustafa Kol, Oktay Kol, Ilhan Arslanyürek, Gülsen Hanim, Fatma Tutçuğil, Ayter Samanci, Gülsen Sözmen, Gülay Karsligil, Canan Direkçi, Meral Çavuşoğolu, Zeliha Güngören, Fatma Yazmac, and Emete Galatyal for their help on Turkish cooking.

Thanks to Barbara Temsamani, Mohammed Mhabcheb, Mohammed Zhiri, Fatima Hal, Mohammed Belhaj, Zor Ouazzani, Mohammed Boussaoud, Saad Hajouji, Abdelatif, Fatna, and Rabar for their help on Moroccan cooking.

Thanks to Chef Moshe Basson, Esther Galusko, Sara Hatan, Habib Daoud, Judy Goldman, Dalia Lamdami, Samira Zedan, Gil Hovav, and Arzit Gispan for their help on Israeli cooking.

Profound thanks to Geoffrey Weill and Pini Shani for help in arranging my trip to Israel.

Thanks to Imogena Bellucci, Rolando Beramandi, Cesare Benelli, Anna Teresa Callen, Cesare Casella, Lydia Colavita, Gianni Cosetti, Joseph Profaci, Nina Priolo, Teresa d'Errico, Felice and Rosalba Orazi, Chef Renato Piccolotto, Lidia Bastianich, Dora Ricci, Bernard Bardin, Lucio Gomiero, Bernard Bardin, Giovanne Perticone, and Anne-Marie Lombardi for their help on Italian cooking.

Thanks to Clara Maria González de Amezua, Marie Jose Sevilla, Janet Mendel, Lourdes March, Christina Salas-Porras, Nuria Juhra, Alison Turner, Chefs Pepe Peiera, Iñaki Izaguirre, Jose Antonio Valdespino and José Manuel Varo, and Tom and Betty Glick for their help on Spanish cooking. Also, special thanks to the New York office staff of ICEX for their help arranging my trip to the Spanish rice country. Thanks to Nora George, Samira Ramadan, and Rabab Tawfik for recipes and notes on Egypt and Syria, and to Randa Hmeidan for sharing her recipe for *kishk*. Thanks to Pierre Bardèche, the late Mario Ruspoli, Michel Messionnier, and Carol Robertson for their help on French cooking.

Special thanks to my copy editor, Christine Tanigawa; production editors Sue Llewellyn and Scott Terranella; director of production, Susan Kosko; the designers of this book, Joel Avirom and Jason Snyder; and my agent, Susan Lescher.

Finally, *very* special thanks to my husband, Bill Bayer, for tasting the dishes, sometimes testing them, encouraging me, advising me on the text, and doing a thousand things more to give me time and peace of mind to complete this work.

NOTES TO THE READER

Though quite a few vegetarian recipes appear on the following pages, *Mediterranean Grains and Greens* is not a vegetarian cookbook. You'll find fish, poultry, and meat in many recipes, but in many instances they are used as condiments rather than major components.

This is my fifth book about Mediterranean cooking. Many familiar grains and greens dishes will not be found here, either because I feel they've been well covered by other writers or because I've written about them myself in earlier books.

Finally, many of the recipes presented here are intended for a small family, yielding four servings as a first course or perhaps just a main dish for two. In most cases the proportions may be doubled or tripled to create a larger number of servings.

INTRODUCTION

❊

Grains and greens—there are thousands of such recipes around the Mediterranean. The nearly two hundred presented here constitute a personal selection—dishes that attract me because I love the way they taste, because there is something fascinating about the way they are made, and perhaps too because they carry a sense of adventure.

On one level this book is about meeting people, discovering places, and the good food I've eaten along the way. Ultimately, I like to think, it's about Mediterranean life itself, a prism through which I view the part of this world I love best. For example, as I was learning the secrets of a particularly challenging Cretan bread, I ended up learning too about personal integrity, mystery, "forks in the road," throwing old shoelaces on the fire—and food so demonic nuns won't consider eating it.

Over the years as I've delved deeper and deeper into the culinary arts of this region, I've come to understand how meagerly I've scratched the surface, how much more exploration remains to be done. And rather than feeling depressed by this, I've found the notion invigorating. So much more to learn! So many terrific places still to visit! Perhaps best of all, so many great women to get to know—Mediterranean home cooks, always generous with their food and knowledge, who welcome me into their homes, allow me to stand beside them at their stoves or kneel beside them at their cooking fires—people who teach and nurture me, and to whom, for that, I owe a tremendous debt. In recounting and adapting what they have taught me, perhaps I can begin to repay it.

Yes, I also learn from men, even, sometimes, from restaurant chefs. But Mediterranean cooking as I view it—the true authentic home food cooked in the countries that border the Mediterranean Sea—is ultimately a medley of cuisines prepared by women. The knowledge is passed down through generations, mother to daughter to granddaughter, women's knowledge, women's skills, women's secrets . . . and, thus, perhaps also, women's power.

The restaurant critic James deCoquet, of *Le Figaro*, is alleged to have said, "A recipe has a hidden side . . . like the moon." In every recipe there's a little something that makes it special, and, hopefully, better. It's these secrets, this power, that I try to search out, then pass on in my classes and books to my students and readers.

Even though I work hard to achieve authenticity in my recipes and never make dishes up out of my head, I don't consider myself a cultural anthropologist. Far from it. For me cooking is an art form. Instinct, inspiration, improvisation, and "taste" (visual as well as gustatory) will always be determinative.

For that reason, I always end up putting myself into my recipes. If the person who taught me a particular dish did it a certain way and it beguiled me, then I will always first try it that way too. But that doesn't mean there's only one way to prepare it, and that I'll necessarily lock myself into the method I observed. It's fascinating when two excellent cooks show me the same dish with, in each case, a marvelous result, and yet a completely different approach.

That's the fun of doing this work—solving the puzzles, sometimes only after much labor, then making the dishes for family and friends simply for pleasure. Food, after all, is ultimately about sharing. I like to think that the people who taught me these dishes did so because they knew that when I took them home I would share them too.

A few words now about grains and greens.

The food historian Charles Perry, in an extremely interesting article called "Splendors of the Grass" that appeared in the *Los Angeles Times* in November 1992, wrote as follows:

> You could . . . make a case that grain is responsible for civilization. When people settled down to farm, it was to raise grain. Now that they were living side by side with people they weren't related to, they had to outgrow tribal ways of doing things, and concepts of law and property and individual rights had to develop. Farmers had to plan ahead, so a calendar had to be devised. In Egypt and Mesopotamia, where floods often destroyed boundary markers, geometry had to be invented to re-establish field ownership when the waters receded. When writing was developed, it wasn't to record the deep thoughts of philosophers but primarily to keep track of grain sales and inventories. Because of grain, the modern world was just about inevitable.

I don't think Charles Perry exaggerates at all in his remarks about the importance of grain cultivation, so crucial in the development of the Mediterranean world. And if I were a historian, I might go on a little about the interrelation between grain cultivation and grain cookery. But since this is a cookbook, not a book of culinary history, I will simply state my belief that grains (wheat, barley, rice, and corn, which came later from the New World) are, as much as any other ingredient—as much as olive oil and wine—the foundation of Mediterranean food.

Breads, pastas, bulgur dishes, couscous dishes, Italian risottos and polentas, Spanish *arroces*, eastern Mediterranean pilafs, *köfte,* and kibbehs—the categories of Mediterranean grain and grain-based dishes are numerous and the recipes innumerable. You'll find many such dishes here, in which, often, the grain is used as a canvas. In these dishes the innate flavors of top varieties of grain serve as platforms for fascinating embellishments.

As for greens, you'll find a great many leafy greens recipes, as well as recipes for vegetables—treated as greens in a generic sense. I've placed the greens dishes into a number of chapters devoted to salads, appetizers, light meals, and main courses, and in a special chapter I call "A Bowl of Leafy Greens," I include information on choosing, handling, storing, and mixing greens.

I've also taken the opportunity to write here about wild edible greens, a long-held interest that has increased in recent years as I've literally "picked" my way around the Mediterranean, learning from a number of wonderful wise women and men how to recognize, gather, and cook with this fascinating variety of produce.

Over the years I've worked on this book, I've lived the cycle of the hunter-forager, gathering greens in Italy, Turkey, Greece, Tunisia, and Israel, with food writers, shepherdesses, chefs, and home cooks. From them I learned many secrets and two very important lessons. If you're interested in foraging for greens, follow the same rules you would follow when foraging for wild mushrooms: learn from an expert and never eat anything you don't know.

Today, in most of the places where I have foraged, wild greens are revered as the finest yield of the earth. Whether in the town of Cibin along the Euphrates in southeastern Anatolia, or an hour's drive from Heraklion on the island of Crete, or on the outskirts of Campobasso in Italy, along the Tunisian coast south of Sfax, or in an area not far from the center of Jerusalem, I foraged with people who still believe that the earth's bounty is there for the taking. Sometimes it was wild asparagus and wild garlic that they were after, or sow thistle, or nettles and mallow, or wild salsify, or wild greens far more exotic. I have seen them smile when they find these treasures, smiles that make them glow.

Everywhere I picked I was told: Put your hands into the earth and you'll be energized. I tried it and discovered it was true!

No, this is not a book that will teach you how to pick wild edible greens, but, I hope, it may inspire you to look into the matter. Everywhere around the Mediterranean, there are women who specialize in foraging. They call it "apron cooking" because of the aprons they wear, usually home-made with three pockets: one for bitter greens, one for sweet, and the third for roots or mushrooms.

It's a way of life rapidly dying out, one of the "old ways" of doing things. Perhaps I romanticize this way of life too much. All I can say is that it has inspired me, opened up a new world. In the recipes here, when I mention wild edible greens, I always provide alternatives readily available at your market. But I hope readers will consider taking up foraging, for pleasure, for health, for exercise, and as a way of discovering a natural way of living.

Throughout this book I've tried to present the great and true tastes of Mediterranean grains and greens dishes in recipes updated for the modern kitchen. Even in the few cases where the recipes are demanding, what strikes me most about these dishes is their elegant simplicity.

1

A Bowl of
Leafy Greens

TWO TURKISH FOLK STORIES

✦

The king's children were so skinny, even though they were served the best food at the palace, that the king decided to check on the children in surrounding villages. In one he met a poor woman whose children looked extremely healthy. The king asked her, "What do you feed them?" The poor woman answered, "Only greens and herbs." The king then offered the woman an exchange of food for forty days. "Send your food up to the palace, and I'll send our food down to you."

After forty days of eating greens with olive oil the children of the king became healthy. Meantime, eating the food of the palace, the poor woman's children became sick.

During the reign of sultan Abdülhamıd II (1876–1909), a doctor was appointed to a medical posting in Crete. The doctor took the assignment, but nobody turned up at his surgery claiming that he or she was sick. After a time the doctor sent a message to the palace in Istanbul: "Your Majesty, in Crete everybody is his own doctor. The people here eat only greens, herbs, and olive oil. As a result they don't need me. Please assign me somewhere else."

A MESS O' GREENS

All around the Mediterranean you find the dish—a bowl or plate, or "mess," of cooked leafy greens, usually assorted, always lovingly adorned. Though each country has its own way of preparing these dishes—as vegetables, dips, toppings, sometimes even main courses—for me the commonality cutting across national borders is more striking than the differences.

The types of leafy greens can vary widely from such common cooking greens as spinach and chard to salad greens such as arugula and watercress to wild greens gathered on hillsides such as sow thistle and mallow. One nice thing about the leafy greens recipes in this book is that the greens used are often interchangeable depending on availability and season. Yes, each green has its unique flavor, but in the following recipes I offer substitutes, which, though they undoubtedly alter the dish, still allow the recipe to retain its essence.

Aside from the greens offered in typical American supermarkets there are more than eighty different edible greens that I believe will in time be cultivated and/or foraged for consumption. Just as we now often find wild mushrooms in stores, I foresee a time when purslane, nettles, mallow, lamb's-quarters, and wild fennel will be on the produce counter along with mesclun, radicchio, *frisée*, arugula, braising mixes, and baby spinach leaves, which, though previously rare, are now thankfully commonplace.

Additions to cooked leafy greens create a huge variety of flavors. Pungent mustard greens are tamed with pomegranate molasses; braised cabbage is blended with glazed onions; meaty greens are boiled, stewed to soften, then whipped with tahini to form purées; spicy cresses are combined with crinkly spinach; bitter endives are enlivened with blood oranges; and crisp greens are smoothed out with yogurt.

You'll do well with these dishes if you commit yourself, like a Mediterranean cook, to seasonal shopping. All the ingenious spicing, saucing, or whatever won't hide old, fading, yellowed, wilted, dried-out, slippery, or mushy leaves. For all the ingenuity applied to cooking these leafy greens dishes and their embellishment with added flavorings, the recipes depend on careful selection—the greens must be of top quality, utterly fresh, then well-stored until you're ready to cook them (see page 5).

Blending Leafy Greens for Cooking Blending salad and cooking greens may sound a bit like alchemy, but if done properly it can add great depth to leafy greens dishes.

Some mixed greens formulas are quite famous. For example, in Ligurian markets in Italy, you'll find women offering their personal mixes of *preboggion,* which usually include borage, chervil, Roman pimpernel, and bladder campion. When washed, drained, and chopped, these mixes are used as fillings for the local ravioli called *pansotti,* which are then served with a walnut sauce.

In markets in Crete, women offer their gatherings of wild greens called *yahnera,* which they sell raw in bunches like bouquet garni. In Padua, in northern Italy, a friend found blanched greens mixtures formed into balls, each wrapped in plastic wrap, called *erba cotta* (cooked greens) for use in stuffing ravioli or flavoring minestrone, rice, sauces for polenta, and pasta.

I encourage you to experiment; mixing greens can be an endless pleasure. Meantime, here are some formulas that have worked well for me:

- Flat-leaf spinach leaves mixed with chard and watercress. For a change, add a small amount of bitter dandelion or endive.

- Spinach mixed with nettle tops, mustard, and chard.

- Spinach mixed with a handful of salad burnet (easily grown in a window box).

- One part each dandelion, lamb's-quarters, sorrel, purslane, and watercress. (Check whether the dandelions have turned bitter. If they have, soak them in salted water for an hour before cooking.)

Another route is to take as a starting point one of the premixed greens packages labeled "braising greens" in supermarkets, then add other greens such as chard or spinach.

Even mixtures of supermarket salad greens labeled "mesclun" or "misticinza" are a good bet for cooking, though, as the *New York Times* food reporter Marian Burros has pointed out, most combinations marked "mesclun" are not true Provençal field blends, but simply overgrown baby greens *that don't taste all that good* in salads.

When making your own greens mixtures, keep in mind the following categories:

- Sweet-tasting greens: beet greens, spinach, Swiss chard, pea shoots, orache, nettles, lamb's-quarters, and green amaranth.

- Mild, "bouncy" greens: mallow leaves, miner's lettuce, and Goldberger purslane.

- Peppery greens: arugula, cress, young mustard, radish, and nasturtiums.

- Tart-flavored greens: sorrel, vine leaves, and purslane.

- Earthy-flavored greens: mature mustard, turnips, collard greens, black or Tuscan kale, and Russian kale.

- Bitter-tasting greens: broccoli rabe, Belgian endive, curly endive, chicory, dandelion, escarole, radicchio, and wild chicory. (Please note that very bitter greens require a soaking in at least two changes of salted water. Some Mediterranean cooks leave them to soak overnight in salted water, while others blanch them two or three times.)

Storing Leafy Greens In an ideal world you'll buy your greens at the local farmers' market where the quality and selection will be so striking that, like me, you'll be tempted to purchase far more than you can use that day. Then the problem becomes how to store these beautiful leafy greens, bought in such perfect condition, until you're ready to prepare them.

Many food writers suggest keeping cooking greens unwashed in heavy plastic bags in the crisper. However, I've been steered in another direction by methods developed for salad greens by food scientist and teacher Shirley O. Corriher.

Shirley limits moisture loss by soaking her greens in cold water, spinning them dry, layering the leaves between paper towels, packing them into plastic bags, squeezing out all the air, then storing the bags in the refrigerator crisper. By this method she has sometimes extended shelf life for many weeks!

Working from her notion that you can slow deterioration by keeping out oxygen and limiting water loss, I pack layers of washed, soaked, and dried cooking greens, rolled in paper toweling, in airtight plastic boxes that have a high-humidity environment like a crisper, and store for more than a week.

For example, say I've just bought two beautiful bunches of Swiss chard. I wash the leaves, let them soak 10 minutes, drain them, shake them really dry, then remove the stems. Two pounds of Swiss chard will provide me with 14 to 20 leaves, depending on the bunch. For this amount I will need about two dozen sheets of paper toweling (which I reuse in cleanup afterward). I lay the

MEASURES FOR LEAFY GREENS

❖

Here are some approximate measurements to help you purchase or pick greens from your garden:

1 cup young shredded leafy greens =
  1½ ounces
2 loosely packed cups trimmed greens =
  1½ to 2 ounces
1 packed quart trimmed greens =
  6 ounces
1½ quarts untrimmed leafy greens =
  1 pound
1 gallon stemmed baby greens =
  1½ pounds
4 pounds leafy greens =
  2 pounds trimmed leaves
8 medium Swiss chard leaves, stemmed =
  5 ounces

NOTE: Discard thick, fibrous stems and yellowed or bruised leaves before measuring the leaves.

leaves on the toweling without overlapping, cover them with more paper towels, then roll them up tight and press them into a plastic box. A 2½-quart shallow plastic box will hold about 1½ to 2 pounds of leaves. Other greens such as arugula, baby spinach, watercress, and edible chrysanthemum can also be stored this way.

For more aggressive and sturdy greens, such as broccoli rabe, dandelions, collards, escarole, curly endive, or mustard, I immediately parboil them to tame and tenderize. After blanching and cooling, I press out all the water, press them into a pack or ball, wrap them in plastic, and store them as airtight as possible in plastic boxes in my refrigerator or freezer.

I freeze wild greens such as nettles, purslane, and wild fennel after blanching to use in soups and stews. Treated this way, nettles and purslane keep well up to four months in the freezer. Wild fennel shoots (not leaves) keep best of all.

Unless you live on the West Coast, where wild fennel grows in profusion, the only time you're likely to find this wonderful green shoot or stem, so useful in adding anise flavor to Italian, Sicilian, and Greek dishes, is during the month of March in ethnic markets (see "Mail-Order Sources"). To store: peel young shoots, blanch for just a minute, allow to cool, pack in small packets of plastic wrap, and freeze. Once frozen, they will keep their special flavor and aroma for up to a year.

Keep in mind that most greens shrink to one-quarter their size when parboiled, good news for those who don't have much room in their freezers.

With stuffing greens such as large leaves of crinkly chard, cabbage, collards, and kale, I quick-blanch, stack the blanched leaves together, press out all the water, and store them in an airtight container for a day or two in the refrigerator, or else freeze them. Tender grape leaves need only be washed and stored in plastic bags; when they defrost, they are wilted and ready to be stuffed.

Finally, Mediterranean cooks have a tradition of storing winter greens and root vegetables in cold cellars through the winter. Firm green cabbage can be kept in the crisper for two weeks, and probably longer, without harm. Very fresh Treviso-style radicchio, if wrapped in dark paper, can also be kept in the crisper for up to two weeks.

Following are some of the more popular Mediterranean methods of cooking greens. You will find others throughout the book.

Boiling Leafy Greens A Mediterranean bowl of well-cooked greens is often misunderstood. Critics speak of greens "cooked to death." Such remarks certainly don't make a bowl of well-cooked greens sound very enticing. But the critics are wrong. When leafy greens are cooked until tender, their flavor is enhanced, and healthful phytochemicals are released.

Certain strong-flavored greens, such as dandelions, collards, large turnip greens, and most wild greens, not only should be submerged in a large pot of boiling water but should be kept under water while boiling with the help of a wooden spoon. This will preserve their vivid green color, aroma, and flavor.

To stop cooking, some Mediterranean cooks plunge their greens into a bowl of icy water, while others simply scoop them out of the boiling water, drain them on a wooden board tilted into the sink, then press out excess moisture. The greens are then ready to be sautéed in olive oil, dressed with a sauce, chopped for a ravioli filling, or packed into plastic bags for storage. (If you're planning to freeze your greens, plunge them into icy water to stop the cooking immediately, drain them well, then package and freeze.)

Pan-Wilting and Sautéing Leafy Greens The method of cooking greens in a pan with just the water adhering to their leaves is excellent when dealing with tender young leaves such as baby spinach and very young chard. I always add some olive oil and flavorings to the pan before I start wilting, so that the greens will start sautéing the moment the moisture has evaporated. Once the raw taste is gone, the greens are cooked. Very soft greens such as mâche, baby spinach, and baby arugula need only a minimum touch of heat before they're "cooked."

I'm not a fan of wilting *large* leafy greens such as spinach and chard in just the water clinging to their leaves. More often than not the leaves dry out, shrivel, or even burn in a covered pan before you can save them. These leaves should be parboiled in large amounts of boiling water, cooked until al dente. Yes, waiting for a large pot of water to come to a boil is not the most interesting thing to do in the kitchen, but parboiling definitely helps with acrid, metallic, bitter, or assertive greens. And if you end up having to buy those flinty-tasting spinach leaves sold in sealed plastic bags, this method may actually make them taste sweet! See "Preparing Large Amounts of Greens for the Skillet" on page 9 for other ways to handle these greens.

Young greens such as collards, curly kale, endive, mustard, and turnip greens can be cooked by slow braising. This slow cooking can alter the texture and taste of an aggressive green into something incredibly delicious. If such greens are cooked in a small amount of fat, they will almost melt on the tongue, as in the Stewed Greens with Basturma Chips (page 297).

Every once in a while I buy a so-called bitter green such as broccoli rabe, which turns out, when I nibble on a leaf, to be not particularly bitter at all. In this case I don't blanch the green but stew it quickly in a little liquid, then sauté it in olive oil and flavorings till tender.

Another method of preparing greens is to cook them on a hot griddle. Mohammed Mhabcheb, the Moroccan chef-owner of Restaurant L'Olive in Chicago, creates a bowl of greens this way. He pan-grills raw baby leafy greens, stirring them around until just wilted, then tops them with grilled shrimps that have been soaked in a traditional marinade of fresh coriander, cumin, hot and sweet paprika, garlic, lemon, and olive oil. He says, "I love the smoky flavor pan-grilling gives to greens."

Using this method I've gotten marvelous results even with sturdy but not tough greens such as turnips and kale. I cut them first into wide strips, then cook them on a smooth iron griddle for 2 to 3 minutes, then toss them with slivers of preserved lemon in a bowl.

Steaming Greens the North African Way North African cooks use their couscous steamers for many other things besides couscous. They steam greens, all kinds of vegetables—including potatoes—chunks of lamb, whole chickens, even macaroni. If you follow my recipe for Steamed Lamb with Leafy Greens and Winter Vegetables (page 256), you'll discover how much depth of flavor can be created and vivid color retained by steaming. While assertive greens are best dropped into a pot of boiling water, most milder greens such as mallow, chard, spinach, purslane, and beet greens cook very well by being steamed.

Use a Chinese bamboo steamer or a steamer with a stainless-steel inset. If you have an aluminum inset, be sure to line your steamer with a wet cloth to keep the greens from touching the aluminum. Please note that greens you wish to serve al dente do not usually taste good when steamed, and that steamed greens always benefit from an additional sautéing or simmering to fully develop their flavor.

Cooking Frozen Greens Recently, when I visited a large radicchio farm in California's Salinas Valley, the Italian owner gave me a crate filled with huge tough outer leaves of radicchios and other chicories, telling me they'd be delicious simply blanched and then sautéed in olive oil with garlic.

A whole crate of tough greens took quite a while to clean, blanch, and pack in bags for freezing. Later, when I wanted to use them, I defrosted them, as I'd been told, directly in a deep, covered skillet set over very low heat along with some olive oil and a few cloves of garlic. When the greens were defrosted, I finished the cooking by lightly sautéing them after all the water had evaporated. This method produced a really delicious bowl of greens. I later discovered that it worked well with nearly every frozen green.

Preparing Large Amounts of Greens for the Skillet I've found that when I sauté a large amount of leafy greens, there are basically five ways to get them down to manageable size so they'll fit into my skillet: (1) hand-chop them, then let them sit awhile to wilt; (2) parboil them; (3) wilt them by the handful with just the water clinging to their leaves; (4) steam them; (5) sprinkle them with salt, then leave them in a colander for an hour while they express their liquid.

All five methods will reduce greens to about one-quarter their bulk. My favored method is the last, particularly when preparing greens for pies. If you use it, remember to rinse the leaves well to remove all the salt, then squeeze dry before cooking.

A Final Note I think of the recipes in this book as "adventures in eating"—dishes that in many cases utilize Mediterranean greens and vegetables hitherto unavailable in the United States except in small ethnic communities. Happily, as Bob Dylan put it, "the times, they are a changin'." It's so great to find such greens as radicchio, arugula, chard, and *frisée* available at farmers' markets and even in supermarket produce departments.

Still, since not every ingredient mentioned here is available throughout the country, I've tested alternatives in most of the recipes and am confident that the substitutes will work well. (See "Mail-Order Sources" for fresh produce, seeds, or live plants for *all* the greens and vegetables mentioned in this book.) Meantime, please encourage your local store to provide these wonderful Mediterranean greens. Remember: the more ardently we demand, the sooner culinary bliss will come.

2

BREADS
AND PASTRIES

BREAD

I'm looking at a famous black-and-white photograph taken by a French photographer, Willy Ronis, hardly known here in the United States but very highly regarded in France.

The shot depicts a young boy in shorts running along a sidewalk while carrying a long, freshly made baguette under one arm. His smile is brilliant. You know that sometime soon, probably the moment he reaches home, this boy will twist off an end of the long, crunchy, crusty loaf, revealing a soft crumb still moist and chewy inside, and devour it without butter, cheese, or oil—a chunk of heaven from a perfect French loaf made simply with flour, yeast, water, and salt.

Over the years I've written a lot about Mediterranean breads on the presumption that they're all wonderful, while our breads are not. Things have changed. Today I find wonderful bread all over America. Perhaps the culminating event in this change in the "balance of bread power" took place in 1997 when tall, young, blond Craig Ponsford of Artisan Breads in Sonoma County, California, won the Coupe du Monde de la Boulangerie in Paris for his baguette. In fact, this turn of the tide so alarmed the French that they started a campaign, warning that "the decline of the French baguette symbolizes the decline of French culture."

Committed American bakers today make bread with great character similar in quality to the one the little boy is carrying in Ronis's photograph—bread you can eat without embellishments. These artisanal breads are exciting news. If you can't find them near where you live, you can order them through the mail (see "Mail-Order Sources"). If you really want to splurge, you can even mail-order the famous bread made by Poilâne direct from Paris!

I lived in Morocco for seven years, and during that time we made our own bread every day from Moroccan-grown wheat. This bread went well with everything and was served with every meal.

Our housekeeper, Fatima, told me she couldn't sleep well at night if we didn't have a 100-pound sack of golden wheat in the house. Once a month we would buy such a sack, she would spend the evening cleaning the wheat, then we would take it to a particular miller, whom she trusted not to switch sacks on us, to be ground to her specifications. With this flour she would make delicious dense bread using a bit of the previous day's starter, adding top-quality green aniseed for flavor.

I published her anise-flavored bread in my first book, *Couscous and Other Good Food from Morocco* and also in *World of Food* (recently reprinted under the title *Mostly Mediterranean*). Preparing this book, I was tempted to include it again but decided finally that two publications were enough. Still, I refer interested readers to those books for the most nurturing Mediterranean bread I know.

The Italians have an expression, "*pane accompanatu*," that they apply to something that makes a good "bread companion" such as a slice of prosciutto or cheese. Many Mediterranean breads are of this type—platforms for food. And in many cases a specific bread is made to accompany a specific dish with which it is deemed to go best. There are also Mediterranean breads made not merely to accompany a dish but to become part and parcel of it. I have included all three types in this chapter: stand-alone breads, dish-accompanying breads, and dish-incorporated breads.

An example of a terrific stand-alone bread is the big, bountiful Cretan barley bread flavored with mastic, cinnamon, and cumin (page 45).

Examples of great dish-accompanying breads are: the Dense Semolina Bread from Tunisia (page 14) made for dipping in a homemade chunky *harissa* sauce (page 343), and another flakier Tunisian semolina bread (page 17) used like a warmed round of pita as a carrier for a delicious salad of crushed grilled vegetables called *mechouia* (page 115).

As for dish-incorporated breads, take a look at the demanding Cretan chickpea leavened bread (page 35) that is double-baked to make rusks that are soaked in a tomato-caper vinaigrette (page 41), a spiced barley flatbread made to be crumbled into a Tunisian fish soup (page 30), and a crunchy paper thin Sardinian flatbread moistened with a flavorful broth and layered with cheese, tomato sauce, and eggs and then baked (page 26). In these cases, I have included recipes for the dish in which the bread is to be used.

FINE AND COARSE SEMOLINA

Semolina milled from durum wheat comes in three grades: the coarsest grade used to make dense breads, steamed desserts, and delicious tahini-flavored Middle Eastern cakes; the medium grade used for pasta and stove-top breads; and the finest grade used to make delicious flatbreads and rusks. The first two grades mixed together are used to make some North African breads and also couscous (page 203). The finest grade, durum flour, is double-milled, golden and silky, and is used alone or mixed with white flour to make certain rustic breads in the eastern Mediterranean.

Fine semolina flour is available at Italian groceries, at health food stores, or by mail order. Coarse semolina, available only during the cooler months, is available at Middle Eastern groceries or by mail order. Durum flour is available through mail order (see "Mail-Order Sources").

Please remember that grains and flours should always be bought fresh. If you buy in quantity, store your grains and flours in the freezer, especially in warm weather, since spoilage may develop even in the refrigerator.

DENSE SEMOLINA BREAD (*Tunisia*)

❊

Makes two 10-inch rounds, serving 4 to 6

Aicha Rouatbi, a smiling, sunny Tunisian widow with a well-lined face, earns her living making bread for her neighbors in Sousse, a medium-size town on the Tunisian Sahel, a coastal region that adjoins a sea of olive trees.

Dressed in a black-and-blue-striped wraparound skirt, a checked blouse, and a flowery scarf around her head, she demonstrated this typical, traditional North African flatbread (called *kesra*) for me in the courtyard of her home.

When I arrived, an earthenware griddle was heating over a wood fire in the middle of the courtyard. An array of tall earthen jars, leaning against each other, were stacked in one corner, while chickens scurried about in mad circles in the other. After introductions Aicha resumed patting out her dough on a fine-mesh hoop.

She explained that the hoop kept the bread from sticking. She pierced the dough with the end of a thick matchstick at ½-inch intervals all over one side. This pricking, she told me, would allow her bread to cook evenly within.

She then placed the dough on the heated griddle, pricked-side up. After the bottom was nicely browned, she removed the bread, placed pieces of broken tiles beneath the griddle to raise it higher off the fire (her way of turning down the heat), then placed the bread back on the griddle, pricked-side down, to finish cooking.

When the bread came off the griddle she broke it into quarters, then brushed each quarter with olive oil while still hot. This bread, she told me, would be delicious with a bowl of fresh sheep's milk ricotta, with a stew of well-cooked greens such as cabbage, or, best of all, she said, with a one-minute version of *harissa*, a spicy sauce Tunisians call the "marmalade of the poor" (page 343).

Like all good North African bread makers, Aicha has her own secret leavening, which, she nicely told me, she couldn't reveal (see Leavening, page 17). But on the basis of rumors among the women in her neighborhood, I'm pretty certain she used fermented garlic.

2 cups coarse semolina

1 cup fine semolina or durum flour

¼ cup olive oil plus more for handling the dough

1¾ teaspoons salt

½ tablespoon active dry yeast softened in ¼ cup warm water

About 1¼ cups lukewarm water

Black caraway (nigella) seeds and aniseed to sprinkle on top

1. In a mixing bowl, combine the coarse and fine semolinas and ¼ cup olive oil and rub together until the semolina is well impregnated with the oil. Make a well and add the salt, yeast, and 1 cup of the lukewarm water. Use a wooden spoon to draw in the flour while mixing to a crumbly dough. Let stand 5 minutes while the semolina absorbs the water. Knead the dough, gradually adding more warm water. The dough will be softer, stickier, and fluffier than regular yeast dough, resembling mashed potatoes. Form into a ball, cover loosely, and allow to rise about 2 hours, until it appears puffed up.

2. Knead the dough *without* adding any more water until it is soft, smooth, and very moist, about 20 minutes. (This can be done in a heavy-duty mixer with a dough hook. Knead for about 10 minutes.) Work in pinches of nigella and aniseed for flavor and aroma. Divide in half and leave to rise 30 minutes.

3. Meanwhile, heat a heavy griddle and preheat the oven to 350 degrees. Oil the palms of your hands and pat each ball out to an 8-inch round. Prick the bread on one side at ½-inch intervals with the end of a match or tines of a fork. When the griddle is hot, slide the first round onto it, pricked-side up, and cook until the bread is golden brown and crusty and can easily be turned, about 5 minutes. Turn and brown the second side, then transfer to the oven to finish baking, 10 minutes. Repeat with the second round of dough. The breads are done when they feel light in the hand. Keep wrapped in kitchen toweling on a rack until ready to serve.

NOTES TO THE COOK: This bread relies on a combination of coarse and fine semolina flour. Since coarse semolina is granular, it has the ability to absorb lots of water, so the mixture of flours must be handled carefully: add the water *gradually* and then allow the dough to rest before kneading.

If you have a round, ridged Circulon-brand griddle, you won't need to do the special pricking that helps this bread bake evenly. If you use an ordinary pan, use a lattice crust wheel to make the indentations quickly.

Because this bread is quite dense, you can finish it in the oven, but only after you have developed a nice, crispy exterior crust.

*I*n the evenings, after dark, I went to that part of the Djema el Fna where the women sold bread. They squatted on the ground in a long line, their faces so thoroughly veiled that you saw only their eyes. Each had a basket in front of her lined with a cloth, and on the cloth a number of flat, round loaves were laid out for sale. I walked very slowly down the line, looking at the women and their loaves. The smell of the loaves was in my nostrils, and simultaneously I caught the look of their dark eyes. Not one of the women missed me; they all saw me, a foreigner come to buy bread. . . . From time to time each would pick up a loaf of bread in her right hand, toss it a little way into the air, catch it again, tilt it to and fro a few times as if weighing it, give it a couple of audible pats, and then, these caresses completed, put it back on top of the other loaves. In this way the loaf itself, its freshness and weight and smell, as it were, offered themselves for sale. There was something naked and alluring about those loaves; the busy hands of women who were otherwise shrouded completely except for their eyes, communicated it to them.

"Here, this I can give you of myself; take it in your hand, it comes from mine."

There were men going past with bold looks in their eyes, and when one saw something that caught his fancy he stopped and accepted a loaf in his right hand. He tossed it a little way into the air, caught it again, tilted it to and fro a few times as if his hand had been a pair of scales, gave the loaf a couple of pats, and then, if he found it too light or disliked it for some other reason, put it back on top of the others. But sometimes he kept it, and you sensed the loaf's pride and the way it gave off a special smell.

—ELIAS CANETTI, *THE VOICES OF MARRAKECH* (1967)

LEAVENING

✦

A good part of my respect for the magical process of bread making is my recent grasp of the importance of a well-developed leavening or starter to impart flavor, vigor, and aroma. These leavenings take time to make and, once made, must be cared for. The older the starter (and there are bakeries in France that claim their starters are a hundred years old!), the better your breads will be.

Nancy Silverton in her wonderful book *Breads from the La Brea Bakery* writes: "As long as you feed and maintain it, your starter will be ready to use over and over again, any time you feel like baking, for the rest of your natural life."

North Africans use interesting flavorings for their starters, including buttermilk, vinegar, lemon juice, grape must, molasses, garlic cloves, honey, and tomato juice. One of the most fascinating starter flavorings I ever encountered was one in southern Tunisia where the local cooks use *legmi,* the sap from a date palm that grows in the oasis of Gabès.

QUICK FLAKY SEMOLINA BREAD (*Tunisia*)

Makes 4 rounds

Taieb Dridi, a young Tunisian baker working in the United States, introduced me to his rapid method of making flaky semolina flatbread with and without leavening by a series of brushings with olive oil and triple folds—similar to the way one makes puff pastry.

This bread is great stuffed with seasoned ground lamb or chopped dates, or simply served with a brushing of oily *harissa* sauce or butter and honey. Try it with the chunky grilled Tunisian vegetable salad called *mechouia* (page 115), or stuff with a salad of chopped tomatoes and chopped and seeded chili peppers.

(continued)

¾ pound (about 2 cups) fine semolina
or durum flour

1 cup plus 1 to 2 teaspoons warm water

1½ teaspoons salt

Extra-virgin olive oil

1 pinch of black caraway (nigella) seeds,
sesame seeds, or crushed fennel seeds (optional)

¼ teaspoon oily *harissa* sauce or butter and
honey (optional)

1. In the mixing bowl of a heavy-duty mixer, place the semolina flour. Gradually work in 1 cup warm water to make a soft dough. Knead with the dough hook for 3 minutes on slow speed. Add the salt and 1 to 2 teaspoons warm water, raise to slow-to-medium speed, and knead for 30 seconds. The texture should be very soft and moist. Oil your palms and finish kneading briefly by hand. Shape the dough into a ball. Return to the bowl, cover, and let rest 15 minutes.

2. Begin to heat a well-seasoned griddle, preferably ridged, over medium heat. Lightly oil a work surface and the palms of your hands. Quarter the dough, knead one portion for an instant, then flatten it to make a rectangle and drizzle with a teaspoon of oil. Fold the right and then the left side of the dough over the oil. Sprinkle with a pinch of seeds, if using. Press down and begin to flatten and stretch the dough in the other direction. Brush with oil and fold in three. Pinch dough to form a round. Roll or press out the first ball into a thin 8-inch round. Immediately place it on the griddle to cook until flaky and puffed, about 1½ minutes to a side. Repeat with the remaining balls of dough. Serve at once brushed with *harissa* sauce or butter and honey, or stuff and roll. Rounds can be wrapped in cloth, packed in a plastic bag, refrigerated for one day, then reheated in the oven for a few minutes.

NOTE TO THE COOK: For an extremely flavorful bread, incorporate 3 tablespoons Garlic-Flavored Leavening (see below) into the dough in step 1. Cook an extra 30 seconds per side.

GARLIC-FLAVORED LEAVENING

To make a garlic-flavored leavening for the flaky semolina bread, combine ¾ cup semolina or durum flour and ½ cup spring water to form a dough. Stud with 4 peeled and washed cloves of garlic and place in a small jar. Cover with kitchen cloth and store in a warm place until the dough swells, 24 hours. Fold the garlic into the dough, allow to swell again, about 12 hours, then discard the cloves. Add ½ cup semolina or durum flour and ¼ cup water and let dough rise about 1 inch. To use, add 3 tablespoons sponge to the dough in step 1. Discard the remaining sponge.

Turkish *Dürüm*: My "Breakfast Biblical Burrito"

While I was doing field research for this book in that part of the Turkish countryside along the Euphrates, where so much of the Bible is set, I noticed that often when I visited homes the hostess wouldn't have any time to sit down and eat. She was too busy cooking and tending her children.

However, in one house, when we were all supposed to be napping, I saw my hostess take a whole onion, throw it into some hot embers, then later remove it, smash it, and put it on a heated round of flatbread. She spread on some hot red pepper paste thinned with olive oil and a sprinkling of dried mint, then rolled it up and sat quietly eating it with pleasure.

When she caught me watching her, she beckoned me, took my arm in hers, then stuffed a piece of the rolled bread into my mouth. It was wonderful!

"You can also add tomato and cheese to this *dürüm*," she told me in sign language. (In southern Turkey *dürüm* is the word for a round flatbread made with hard wheat flour; in other parts of the country it's called *sikme*.)

Such was the inspiration for what I have dubbed my "breakfast biblical burrito" . . . which I've been eating on and off for breakfast for the past five years. A secondary inspiration was the classic Israeli kibbutz breakfast of fresh bread with tomatoes, onions, greens, and peppers.

At home in the United States I use an old-fashioned flat toaster grill over my gas stovetop to gently heat either the semolina flatbread on page 17, a flour tortilla, or a fresh piece of lavash. Once it's heated, I slip in several chopped-up cherry tomatoes; a seeded, cored, and diced jalapeño; a little chopped green pepper; some parsley, mint, and crumbled feta cheese. I add a trickle of olive oil and a pinch of salt for flavor, then roll my "burrito" up and eat it along with a cup of coffee. Yes, it's messy . . . but *very* good!

ISRAELI-YEMENITE *MALAWEH* WITH GRATED TOMATOES, *ZHUG*, AND HARD-COOKED EGGS

Serves 4 to 8

Gaby, the owner of an Israeli-Yemenite restaurant just north of Tel Aviv, was in the midst of explaining how to make a delicious, light, flaky flatbread called *malaweh* served with various accompaniments.

". . . and then you smear each layer with butter," he said.

He smiled as I winced.

"How much butter?" I asked.

"For my recipe, which serves eight, you'll need about ⅔ cup."

I winced again. "I don't think I know eight people who eat butter."

Gaby thought a moment, then grinned as if a light had gone on in his head. "Doesn't matter!" he said, his gold tooth gleaming. "Just share a piece with your husband, then freeze the rest!"

Well, I thought, that's Mediterranean logic. But still I was delighted. *Malaweh,* accompanied by a bowl of green chilies pounded with cilantro and scented with cardamom and cumin (*zhug*), a refreshing and cooling bowl of freshly grated ripe red tomatoes, and a platter of sliced hard-cooked eggs, was one of the best meals I tasted in Israel.

My recipe is a combination of information provided by Gaby and invaluable cooking notes provided by Arzit Gispan, the jolly, middle-aged, Yemenite-Jewish housekeeper of a friend who lives in Tel Aviv. Arzit, who wears her hair in a long black braid, was most generous with advice.

You'll want your bread dough to be quite stiff, so work it until it's really elastic, then give it a long rest, preferably overnight. The dough is then rolled out until it's paper thin. The subsequent folding and brushing of each layer with butter will remind you of the method used to make classical French puff pastry.

As Gaby put it, "Fold it up and fry, flip and fry. It's as easy as that!"

Arzit, who keeps a kosher kitchen, replaces the butter with margarine, so she can serve the bread along with other nondairy dishes. Though I rarely use butter, I make an exception for this dish.

The beauty of this dish is that everything can be made in advance. The dough rounds will keep for up to two days in the refrigerator, or they can be frozen. The chili-cilantro *zhug* can be made up to a week in advance, and the grated tomato and eggs can be prepared hours before serving. The bread, which takes about 4 minutes to cook, should be served hot.

1 pound (about 3⅛ cups) all-purpose flour plus more for rolling out the dough in step 4

½ tablespoon double-acting baking powder

1 teaspoon salt

½ teaspoon sugar

1 cup lukewarm water, or as needed to make an extremely stiff dough

Vegetable oil or melted butter for greasing the work surface

⅔ cup clarified butter

GARNISH

3 large, ripe tomatoes, halved, seeded, and grated (see Note)

¾ cup *zhug* (see recipe below)

4 hard-cooked eggs, peeled, sliced, and lightly seasoned with salt and pepper

To eat, simply tear the *malaweh* into pieces, dip a piece into the relish, then heap on some grated tomato and top with slices of hard-cooked egg seasoned simply with salt and pepper. This bread is so delicious you needn't serve it with the ensemble. Israelis eat it for breakfast with a little honey.

NOTE: An approximately 20-inch-square work surface is needed to roll and stretch the dough to paper thinness.

Steps 1, 2, and 3 can be done in advance.

1. At least 24 hours in advance, make the dough. In a food processor fitted with a dough blade, combine the flour, baking powder, salt, sugar, and 1 cup water by pulsing to make a very stiff dough. It should be almost unkneadable and very rough-looking. Process the dough for about 1 minute. During this time the dough will slap against the side of the work bowl, sticking at first; then it will begin to form a mass and no longer adhere to the side. Do not overprocess, or the gluten in the flour will break into ropy strands. The kneaded dough will feel soft and pliable. Oil your palms, shape the dough into a ball, cover it with plastic wrap, and refrigerate 3 hours.

2. Divide the dough into 4 to 6 pieces. Roll one piece into a ball, flatten, then roll out into a 10-inch square and drape over the back of a chair or something free-standing, so the sheet can relax and "hang." Repeat with the remaining balls of dough. Return the first sheet to a lightly oiled work surface, brush the top lightly with clarified butter. Lift and drape the dough over your hands—palms down and fingers bent loosely underneath, so that your nails don't make any holes. Coax the dough by stretching and rotating from the center outward to paper thinness. Lay it on the work surface and trim away the thick edges and reserve. Pinch the dough where holes appear. Brush butter all over the surface, fold into thirds, and brush the top. Flatten with the palm of your hand, fold into thirds in the opposite way, and brush with butter. You should have an approximately 5-inch square with a few air bubbles. (Do not deflate; these trapped bubbles will make the bread fluffier and lighter when cooked.) Wrap in plastic and refrigerate. Repeat with the remaining balls of dough. (With the trimmings you can make another ball of dough by pressing it flat, wrapping in plastic, refrigerating, and repeating the process above when the dough is well rested.) Let all the squares rest at least 20 minutes in the refrigerator.

3. Carefully unwrap each piece on a lightly oiled work surface and roll out to the thinness of strudel dough. You will invariably get some holes, but this is not a problem. Simply pinch them together. Fold up the stretched dough to make a square in the same manner as step 2. Repeat with the other pieces, then let the dough rest 1 to 2 days in the refrigerator before cooking. *Folded dough can be wrapped and frozen. Defrost in the refrigerator before cooking.*

4. Just before serving, roll each square into a 10-inch circle on a lightly floured board. Heat two non-stick or well-seasoned skillets until almost smoking. Reduce heat to medium, slip a bread into each skillet, cover, and fry for 30 seconds. Reduce heat and continue frying, covered, until very puffy, fully cooked, and spotted a golden brown on both sides. Repeat with as many rounds of dough as needed. Keep warm in a low oven until all the *malaweh* are ready to serve. Serve immediately with the garnishes.

NOTE TO THE COOK: To grate tomatoes, halve and gently squeeze the tomatoes to remove seeds. Grate the tomato halves, cut side facing the coarsest side of a four-sided grater, or on a flat shredder. You should be left with just the tomato skin in your hand; discard. If the tomatoes are very watery, place the pulp in a sieve to drain off excess liquid.

Green Chili–Cilantro Relish (*Zhug*)

Makes 1½ cups

Israeli food writer Gil Hovav not only shared with me his grandmother's secret recipe for *zhug*, he also gave me this amusing culinary note.

"True *zhug* should not be made in a food processor," he said with a smile. "Rather, it should be made with a *mazhag*, the big, smooth, flat black stone, which a Yemeni woman always keeps near her stove. You put the ingredients on it and then mash them with another stone (smaller and preferably white), while at the same time cursing the whole world and your miserable fate!" Gil paused. "Nevertheless, the food processor version is quite good!"

10 cloves garlic (1½ ounces)

6 ounces long, green mildly hot chilies (about 10)

1 teaspoon cardamom seeds or 1½ tablespoons cardamom pods, opened

About 2 cups cilantro (4 ounces)

1 teaspoon freshly ground cumin

Pinch of salt

Pinch of black pepper

Peel the garlic cloves. Wash and stem the chilies and chop them *with* the seeds. Crush the cardamom seeds to a powder in a mortar. Put all the ingredients into a food processor and grind to a paste. Store in a clean, covered jar in the refrigerator. *Zhug* can be made up to one week in advance.

NOTE TO THE COOK: Finding the right chili is easy in the summer when farmers' markets offer a good variety of peppers with great flavor as well as substantial heat. The long, thin green chilies in Asian markets are ideal. Another good choice are New Mexican chilies or poblanos. I find jalapeño peppers unpredictable; if too hot the relish will be inedible.

For best results, buy cardamom in seed or pod form and grind just before using.

BRUMANA 6.1.28.

I have just got warm by going downstairs to see our neighbor make the flat sheets of bread I like so much. She sits on the floor with a round flattish cushion on one knee and smooths the balls of dough out on a board with her palms and fingers till they are about the size of a plate. Then she throws them with a very neat quick movement first over one forearm, then over the other. Her arms are very brown, tattooed and with twisted gold bracelets. The round of dough grows and grows miraculously till it is about two-and-a-half-feet across and almost transparent. She then tosses it onto her cushion, arranges the edges so as to make it as nearly round as possible, and throws it all in one movement, so as not to crease it, onto a little metal dome which is on the floor and has a few sticks and pine needles burning underneath it. In one minute the whole thing is cooked, and if the fire is well distributed, is nice and crisp all over, and very good. And it has the advantage of being good to eat for a week.

—FREYA STARK, *LETTERS FROM SYRIA* (1942)

Sardinian Flatbread (*Italy*)

Makes 1 pound, or twelve 10-inch rounds

There is a stunning series of photographs in Giuliano Bugialli's *Foods of Sicily and Sardinia,* showing how to make the famous Sardinian flatbread, *carta di musica* ("sheets of music paper"), so called on account of its crackling, parchmentlike texture. Thinly rolled, yeasted semolina flour dough puffs up like a giant pillow in a hot stone oven. The pillow is then removed, split sideways into two delicate sheets, then further dried in the oven. Once you have enough dried sheets, you pile them up like a stack of love letters to assemble the dish.

Those who wish to make the authentic version should follow the bread recipe in Mr. Bugialli's book. The simplified version that follows comes from Nina Priolo, who was born in the Sardinian town of Oldia. Nina, who now lives here in the United States, assures me this is an excellent substitute for authentic *carta di musica.*

1 envelope active dry yeast

1 cup plus 3 tablespoons warm water

1¼ teaspoons sea salt

1 pound (about 3¼ cups) fine semolina flour

1 cup all-purpose flour for rolling out the sheets

½ onion

Olive oil

1. In a large bowl dissolve the yeast in 3 tablespoons warm water. Allow to stand 5 minutes. Gradually mix in the salt, semolina flour, and 1 cup warm water, then beat until the dough forms a sticky mass. Cover and let stand 20 minutes, time enough for the semolina to absorb the water. Dip your hands in warm water, grasp the dough, and vigorously slam it back into the bowl by lifting the dough and slamming it down fifty times. The dough will lose some of its stickiness.

2. Turn the dough out onto a floured surface. Knead until the dough is smooth and elastic but still soft, 20 minutes. Test the dough to see if it is fully kneaded by pressing your finger into the dough; if it springs back immediately, it is ready to rest.

3. Place the dough in an oiled 3-quart bowl, cover with plastic wrap, and leave in a very warm place until the dough has doubled in volume, 2 hours.

4. Turn the dough out again onto a floured surface; carefully knock it down and knead briefly. Divide the dough into twelve pieces and roll each piece into a ball. Place on a lightly floured wooden work surface and cover with a slightly damp towel. Let rest 10 minutes.

5. Generously flour your work surface and roll out each piece into a circle 5 inches in diameter. Cover circles with waxed paper and leave to rest 10 minutes.

6. Slowly heat a smooth, well-seasoned, 12-inch griddle made of cast iron or nonstick aluminum until very hot, then adjust for steady heat. Meanwhile, begin rolling out the first round of dough to 10 or 12 inches. It need not be a perfect round, but it should be of even thinness. Dip the onion in olive oil, shake off excess oil, and rub the surface of the griddle. Immediately lift one round onto the hot griddle and cook until puffed and spotted brown. Flip and continue cooking on the second side, about 2 minutes. Adjusting heat as necessary, repeat the rolling and cooking of the rounds. You probably won't need to use the oiled onion after the first time. (The need to oil varies from griddle to griddle.) Breads should be puffy, spotted, and fully cooked. If necessary, pile them onto a baking sheet and finish baking them in a 350-degree oven for 10 minutes. Cool breads on racks. Store in a dry tin or a cloth bag in a dry cupboard; breads will keep for several months.

SARDINIAN FLATBREAD BAKED WITH CHEESE, TOMATOES, AND EGGS

Serves 2

This rustic mound-shaped dish is made up of layers of paper-thin sheets of Sardinian flatbread, a few spoonfuls of very flavorful tomato sauce, a well-degreased flavorful stock, grated cheese, and several raw eggs hidden within the bread folds. The whole is then baked together in the oven until the eggs are cooked.

1 cup homemade tomato sauce (page 342)

Salt

Freshly ground black pepper

Grated nutmeg

1 vegetable, meat, or poultry bouillon cube (optional)

5 to 6 rounds of Sardinian flatbread (recipe above)

Olive oil

½ cup ricotta cheese beaten with 3 tablespoons cool water

2½ ounces grated pecorino Sardo or Parmigiano-Reggiano

2 large farm-fresh eggs

1. About 20 minutes before serving, place oven rack on highest rung. Preheat the oven to highest setting.

2. About 12 minutes before serving, warm the tomato sauce, thin with ½ cup water, and adjust the seasoning with salt, pepper, and grated nutmeg to taste. In a wide bowl, soak the bouillon cube, if using, in 2 cups hot water; otherwise, generously salt the hot water. Break each round of flatbread into 4 or 5 pieces. Soak for 30 seconds, then drain. If some of the bread does not soften, soak longer.

3. Meanwhile, generously oil a flat baking sheet. Halve the soaked bread into two portions. Using only one-third of each portion of bread, create two 6- or 7-inch rounds. Spread ⅓ cup of the tomato sauce over the rounds; top with half the ricotta and one-third of the grated cheese. Repeat with another one-third of the bread, ⅓ cup tomato sauce, remaining ricotta, and another third of the grated cheese. Layer the remaining bread on top, make a crevice in the center of each mound, slip in a raw egg, and partially enclose it with a few folds of the soaked bread. Spread the remaining tomato sauce on top, sprinkle with the remaining grated cheese, and drizzle with a few drops of olive oil. Set in the very hot oven to bake 3 to 5 minutes, just long enough to crisp the bread and bake the eggs. Serve hot.

TUNISIAN TEN-LAYER TORN-UP BREAD

My American friend Lynn Hannachi, who's married to a Tunisian and lives in Tunis, was explaining to me the nuances of *chakhchoukhet*, a popular village bread that's served torn-up with a chicken and tomato stew, prepared all over Tunisia but rarely if ever outside the home.

"Tunisian cooks like to make things, then tear them apart to make something else," Lynn observed. "I've seen them make a sweet with this same bread. They make the bread, tear it up, knead it with soft butter, sugar, and ground nuts, then roll it into very light and incredibly delicious—and fattening—little balls."

Lynn and her husband, Salah, took me to his family's home in the town of Jendouba in northwestern Tunisia, the "family seat" of the Hannachi clan. We drove through a wild and beautiful area abutting great plains of wheat. Tunisia has been producing wheat for centuries . . . since the ancient Romans planted huge fields of it to provide grain for their legions.

There, Salah's mother and other relatives showed me some of their specialties: a delicious vegetable stew called *markat khodra* (see the revised edition of my *Mediterranean Cooking*); a flatbread stuffed with ground preserved meat flavored with sheep's tail fat; and *chakhchoukhet* as well as some other simple flatbreads.

Chakhchoukhet is made by working a semolina-based dough with extra water until it becomes elastic and smooth, then dividing the ball of dough into three smooth cylinders. Mrs. Hannachi took hold of the first cylinder and squeezed it until a perfect apricot-sized ball of dough popped out between her curved forefinger and thumb. She continued to produce balls of the same size until all the dough was used up.

After oiling her fingers, she patted down the first ball, creating a flat 8-inch disk of dough, which she then placed on a heated earthenware griddle to cook. After half a minute she flipped it. Having, meantime, flattened a second ball, she laid the second uncooked disk on the first cooked disk, waited a few seconds, then flipped the two together so that the second raw disk was now directly on the griddle. She continued in this manner until she had a stack of ten cooked disks, creating a ten-layer bread.

After creating three more ten-layer stacks, she, Lynn, and I went into action. While the bread was still hot to the touch, we proceeded to tear apart each ten-layer stack into little 1-inch pieces, which we tossed into a bowl.

Meantime, one of Salah's aunts was at the stove preparing a savory stew of chicken and tomato, flavored with garlic and spices. When the stew was ready it was poured over the top of the mound of torn bread, which we then, with much gusto, devoured.

BARLEY IN BREAD

Mediterranean barley bread is made with barley flour and semolina or wheat flour and is often spiced. (See the two barley breads offered in this chapter; though one is Tunisian and the other Cretan, both are spiced.) The Tunisians' addition of barley grits makes a heavier, nutty-flavored bread. They often use it to crumble into soups or other food in the same way that Italians in Molise crumble baked cornmeal flatbread into their greens soups. Try making the Sfaxian Soup with Crumbled Spiced Barley Bread (below) and experience the intensity of flavor that a spiced barley bread can bring to a traditional fish soup.

In southern Tunisia, unspiced barley bread, cooked on a flat iron pan, is cut into dice, then added to simple peppered salads of raw tomatoes, peppers, onions, crushed cilantro, and garlic—a Tunisian version of Italian *panzanella*.

CRUMBLED SPICED BARLEY BREAD (*Tunisia*)

1 loaf

There are certain Mediterranean breads that are not meant to be eaten alone. Rather, they're created especially to flavor, enrich, and/or thicken a soup or a stew. Here's an utterly delicious example, as well as another instance of the Tunisian trait of making something, then tearing it up in order to use the pieces to make something else.

In this magnificent recipe, barley bread spiced with anise, turmeric, and black caraway seeds and the spicy condiment *hrous* (page 344), makes a good fish soup truly memorable.

The spicy bread and the bracing *hrous* can be made in advance. The bread can even be frozen. The fish soup is easy to make if you have fish stock in your freezer.

Once you make *hrous* you'll have it on hand for a year. The recipe for soup and barley bread can be doubled or tripled.

½ cup fine barley grits (see Note)

½ tablespoon active dry yeast

2 tablespoons warm sugared water

1¼ cups barley flour

1 cup fine semolina flour

2 tablespoons olive oil (plus oil for greasing the pan)

2 teaspoons salt

Pinch of turmeric

½ teaspoon crushed black caraway (nigella) seeds

½ teaspoon crushed aniseed or fennel seeds

1. Early in the day pour boiling water over the barley grits and let stand 2 hours. Squeeze dry and keep in a cool place until ready to add to the dough.

2. About 4 hours before serving, prepare the bread. Dissolve the dry yeast in the warm sugared water in a small bowl and let stand until creamy. In a bowl or basin used for kneading dough, rub the barley and semolina flours with 2 tablespoons of olive oil until the oil is thoroughly incorporated. Make a well in the center; add the salt, yeast, turmeric, and enough warm water to make a workable dough. Gently mix for an instant, then let stand 5 minutes while the semolina absorbs the water. Work in the barley grits.

3. Knead the mixture while gradually adding more lukewarm water until the dough becomes very fluffy and light. Cover the bowl with plastic wrap and let the dough rest about 2 hours.

4. Knock down the dough; knead again until soft and smooth. Do not add any more water during this kneading. Work in the nigella seeds and aniseed and leave the dough to rise a little, then oil a 12-inch plate and the palms of your hands. Pat the dough into a 12-inch round directly on the plate and let stand while you heat a round, well-seasoned, ridged stove-top grill. On the top side only, use a sharp knife to score the bread into 8 triangles, slicing about halfway through, then prick all over with the tines of a fork. Slide the round, cut side up, onto the grill and cook until the bread can be easily turned. Cook on the second side. Continue cooking for 20 minutes, turning the bread two more times. Cool and break into ½-inch pieces. Set aside while preparing the soup. (The bread can be baked on tiles in a 425-degree oven for 30 minutes.)

NOTE TO THE COOK: Barley grits are sold at many health food stores. You can make your own by grinding hulled barley in an electric blender. If necessary, soak the hulled barley in warm water and drain well before grinding.

SFAXIAN FISH SOUP
WITH CRUMBLED SPICED BARLEY BREAD (*Tunisia*)

Serves 2 as a main course or 4 as a first course

4 cloves garlic

Coarse salt

½ teaspoon black pepper

1 teaspoon cumin

3 tablespoons olive oil

3 tablespoons tomato paste

½ pound fresh white-fleshed fish trimmings

1 tablespoon *hrous* (page 344)

1 cup fish broth

½ to 1 pound white-fleshed fish fillets, cut into thin strips

18 mussels, scrubbed and soaked in salty water for 30 minutes

1 loaf Tunisian Spiced Barley Bread (page 28), crumbled

2 tablespoons chopped cilantro

1. Pound the garlic, salt, pepper, and cumin to a paste. Place the oil, garlic and tomato paste, fish trimmings, and *hrous* in a deep heavy saucepan and cook slowly until somewhat dry. Add the fish broth and bring to a boil; reduce heat and cook at a simmer for 15 minutes.

2. Press the broth through a food mill to extract all the juices from the fish trimmings. Return to the saucepan, add 3 cups water, and bring to a boil. Add the fish and mussels and cook until the fish flakes and the mussels have opened. Correct the seasoning.

3. Scatter the crumbled bread in individual soup plates, spoon over the fish and mussels, pour over the soup, and garnish with cilantro. Serve hot.

With thanks to Mme. Fadhila Fekik Mekki of Sfax for sharing this recipe.

BLACK SEA CORN BREAD

❖

*I*t was a beautiful night in the open-air restaurant Kerasus along the Turkish Black Sea coast in the town of Giresun. We'd just finished eating a whole slew of marvelous starter dishes called *mezzes*.

"Notice how we've been influenced by Greek cuisine," said Ismail Durhan, the restaurant owner. "The Greeks lived here for hundreds of years. Their *mezzes* have become our local food."

Indeed, his well-made *mezzes* were similar to the kinds one finds in the best restaurants in Greece. One dish among them, however, stood out—a corn bread unlike any I'd ever eaten in my life.

I was beguiled by this corn bread, which, it so happened, was the only dish served to us that was not influenced by Greek cooking. Held together as if by magic, tasting of corn, crisp on the outside and very moist and flavorful within, it was a very special corn bread indeed and made without any leavening.

I met with the darkly handsome young chef, Hamid, who was thrilled to find me so enamored of his recipe. He agreed to share his secret corn preparation, he said, because I didn't live in Turkey and thus wasn't a competitor.

Hamid uses very milky corn, which he toasts and dries in a stone oven at about 170 degrees for 8 hours, turning the cobs every so often. He then cuts off the kernels.

"This is the only way to dry the kernels so they will accept the amount of water required to make this dough," he explained. "Sun-drying doesn't do the trick."

He went on, "When you touch the dough it should feel like soft yogurt. If there isn't enough water in it, it will be hard and the bread won't be crisp on the outside and moist within."

He gave me these proportions for a 5-inch round of bread, enough for 1 or 2 persons: approximately 1⅓ cups hot water gradually worked into 6 ounces of dried, coarse corn kernels along with salt to taste.

A skillet is oiled and set over low heat. With a wet hand, the dough (which should not be left to relax) is patted out onto the skillet, then cooked evenly on each side (covered at first, uncovered after being turned) until both sides are well-browned and the interior well-cooked, the process taking 20 to 25 minutes. *(continued)*

Ismail told me, "When I was growing up I only knew bread made with corn and thought wheat was something eaten by people who lived far away. My mother, who sold yogurt, dreamed of having enough money to make us bread made with wheat. She's very proud of me," he went on, "but can't understand why anyone would pay to eat corn bread in a restaurant."

Back home I tried making this bread with corn I bought at a farmers' market. Alas, the bread came out too sweet. Next I tried some delicious toasted dried corn I ordered by mail from Pennsylvania. That bread was also too sweet. Finally, the New York–based Mexican food writer and restaurateur Zarela Martinez suggested *chacales*, a dried corn kernel used in Mexican and southwestern cooking. It worked, but it lacked the incredibly fresh taste of Hamid's bread. Even when I soaked the *chacales* overnight, the taste wasn't there. I feel bad for failing to reproduce the best corn bread I ever ate. All I can do is suggest that, if you visit the fabulous Black Sea coast of Turkey, you stop at the restaurant Kerasus in Giresun and try it for yourself.

BREAD BAKED IN THE SAHARAN SANDS

❖

I once tasted a marvelously aromatic and touchingly frugal flatbread baked in the Saharan sands.

Mohammed Melke's family comes from the Tunisian Sahara. He's only thirty but already has four sons. "I'm building my own football team," he told me.

Tall, athletic, and serious about his plan for a homegrown squad of football players, he seemed an unlikely person to teach me a method of baking bread. In my idealized Mediterranean world it's the women who still make bread in the home. In Morocco and Tunisia I had observed leavened and unleavened bread being baked in the sands but never by a man.

We went into the Sahara by truck, accompanied by Mohammed's young son Ismael.

"Whenever I go into the desert to hunt for rabbits, I always take more that I can eat. Just in case, you know," Mohammed told me.

With us in the truck were tomatoes, goat cheese, a chunk of leavened dough given to us by Mohammed's wife, as well as flour, salt, and a thermos of water. On the back of the truck was a jerrican of water for washing our hands.

When we reached the sand, Mohammed prepared the dough in a wide wooden dish. He gradually worked in the lukewarm water, using his knuckles (see Technique for "Knuckling" Water into Dough).

"The water is very important for a good dough," he told me. "You need to work in as much as you possibly can. There's no other way."

As the dough was resting, he, Ismael, and I walked about, collecting pebbles and dried brush. We stopped when our stack of brush was three feet tall. This, Mohammed told me, would be enough to heat the sand beneath for baking.

He used a spade to prepare the sand, setting out a bed of small stones on one side, then piling the brush next to it. Finally he set the brush on fire.

While it burned, he returned to the dough, which had risen only slightly. He divided it into softball-size balls, worked each ball smooth, then set it beneath a wool blanket on a wooden plank.

When the brush was reduced to ashes, he dug a hole in the sand directly beneath, which by then had grown extremely hot. He then brought out the first ball of dough, which he flattened to a 1½-inch-thick disk 12 inches in diameter. He placed the disk on the hot sand, then shoveled more hot sand on top.

"The hotter sand is on top so the bread bakes from the top down," he explained.

He could tell when it was time to turn the bread by checking to see if sand stuck to the dough. When the bread was half cooked, the sand no longer clung. He scraped back the sand and ashes, flipped the disk, then buried it again. When the bread was baked he let it rest on the hot pebbles while he cooked the next loaf.

The bread that came out was flecked with black spots, perfumed by the smoke and ashes of the burning brush. We pulled it apart, spread on some *smen* (North African preserved butter) flavored with wild herbs, and ate it accompanied by mint tea.

Yes . . . it was good!

Technique for "Knuckling" Water into Dough

✦

With semolina-based breads and some other country breads made around the Mediterranean, a special method is required to enable the dough to absorb sufficient additional water. The way some bread makers approach this issue is simply to add water to the flour all at once, then wait for the drenched semolina to expand and absorb it. This works fine for most flatbreads.

However, most bread makers on the eastern Mediterranean and North African coasts take another approach, allowing them to add even more water with the object of creating moist and tender yeast breads.

The method is to add some water at first, allow the dough to rest, then knead the dough while adding more water by a method that is the opposite of our rolling up and stretching kneading technique—a method I call "knuckling in."

To "knuckle" additional water into a kneadable dough simply dip your knuckles in water, then use them to press down on the dough while gradually working the water in. Don't hurry or get overly enthusiastic; you just want to add a little more water while keeping the dough soft. If you hear squishy sounds, you're doing it right. If the dough gets too wet, simply switch to your ordinary kneading motion, which will tighten the dough, or add a low-gluten flour. To loosen the dough again "knuckle in" a few more drops of water.

It's possible to do this in a food processor or heavy-duty mixer, but I advise you to do it first by hand in order to get the feel of the dough. What you *don't* want to do is turn your ball of dough into soaking-wet gluten strands! Oiling your hands from time to time will also help.

Finally, remember that these eastern Mediterranean and North African breads don't rise as high as our European-style breads. "Knuckling in" works especially well when a dense, moist bread is desired.

CHICKPEA-LEAVENED BREAD AND RUSKS (*Greece*)

❀

Makes 2 loaves, or about 20 fat rusks

Victoria Athanassiady never lies. She tells me as much the moment we meet. "I say what I think and think what I say," she says. "If I tell you how to make a dish, you can rely on my words."

I've come to her to learn the secrets of one of the most difficult, demanding breads of the entire Mediterranean, a fermented ground-chickpea-leavened bread that has become my nemesis. After numerous failures I have been tempted to give it up, but this bread is so delicious, golden, and aromatic that I am determined to finally get it right.

The bread is made from a fermented dough of ground chickpeas flavored with aromatics. (Note: The well-known chickpea flour–based mixtures such as those used in Algerian *karántitas,* Ligurian *farinatas,* or Provençal *soccas* are different, being batters in which there is little or no chickpea fermentation.) And, interestingly, once made it's generally not eaten in bread form but turned into rusks. In a way it's the Cretan, Cypriot, and Turkish answer to the German-Mennonite zwieback but with a mouth-watering flavor all its own.

Victoria Athanassiady is middle-aged. She wears glasses, has gray hair, and comes from the town of Chania on the island of Crete. She strikes me as the kind of person who is good at whatever she undertakes. The Greek word for such a woman is *nicokeera.*

"When I was young and went to England to work as an au pair," she tells me, "the family I worked for asked me if I didn't think life was better in England than in Greece. I told them no, that I loved our traditions and ancient ways, and that frankly I thought life was better in Crete. From that moment they trusted me. Which was why, I think, Madame often asked my opinion when she brought home a new dress or lipstick. She knew I wouldn't humor her."

To meet Victoria and discuss the making of this bread is a little like going to ancient Delphi to consult the oracle. Her utterances are striking, yet there is always a deeper level. It's only when I think over what she's told me that I understand her full range of meaning.

(continued)

One of Victoria's first lessons is that the common name of the bread, *eftazimo* (kneaded seven times), is misleading. She herself thinks of the bread as *autizimo,* which means self-rising.

"It does not require seven kneadings," she says. *Good news!* I think.

I spend the day watching her make the dough, writing down everything she does. My aim is to figure out a way to reproduce the bread at home while retaining its original character. Commercial packaged Cretan rusks just don't come close.

Back in San Francisco, in the weeks following my visit, I try and fail to duplicate Victoria's results; I ponder everything she taught me, and read and reread her letters of encouragement. In an exchange of faxes, she writes, "I agree, it is not an easy bread to make. It requires much practice."

In this regard I take some comfort from a line from Diana Farr Louis and June Marinos's Ionian cookbook *Prospero's Kitchen,* in which the authors cite remarks written in 1904 by Archduke Ludwig Salvator to the effect that one should keep a black-handled knife, a red blanket, and a holy book by one's side for this bread to succeed.

It turns out that there's a fascinating aura of superstition surrounding this bread. According to Victoria, nuns in Greece never make it. "They call it 'devil's bread,'" she tells me. "The fermentation signifies boiling in anger. They won't even eat it!"

If making this bread is somehow considered demonic, that may explain the many superstitions. Village women, I learn, won't tell anyone when they're going to bake it for fear it will fail due to bad spirits and the "evil eye." For this same reason they often make it in the middle of the night so no one will smell it baking. Victoria tells me that her own mother, when making *autizimo,* would throw an old leather shoelace on the fire to make everything smell bad, so no one would know what she was doing. "If it smells good, people pass by and say, 'Ah, they're making *eftazimo* in there.' This is considered very bad luck. No one outside the family must know. Here in Crete, you understand, the 'evil eye' is a serious matter!"

Actually, this bread is not made just in Crete. I have a little church cookbook put out by a group of Albanian Greeks who make it enriched with eggs to be served on feast days with brined cheese and olives. In the Macedonian town of Florina on the old Yugoslav border, and on the Ionian island of Zakinthos in the Adriatic, this same bread is flavored with hot peppers. In southeastern Turkey it's turned into rusks to be eaten during the fasting month of Ramadan along with a cup of tea.

A few years ago I spent an afternoon with the brothers Kol in their bakery, the oldest in the Turkish town of Gaziantep. They showed me how to ferment crushed chickpeas in order to make the starter for the rusk that they called *kaak.* They told me that they made their rusks each Ramadan without any problems.

"It is not the 'evil eye' that will give you trouble," the older Kol brother told me. "Rather it's that at every step there's a crossroad, so you need to know your way. For example, a draft or a chill at the wrong time can kill the rise. On the other hand, you can store the prepared dough in the refrigerator and then return it to room temperature to bake. Also, we only partially bake the bread, so that we can slice it into strips to dry out on our stone floor in the oven fired by hardwood coals. That's our special secret."

The elder Kol apologized for not having any dough around for me to examine, but he did have some starter. He brought out a narrow jar from the warm back portion of his oven and showed me a yellowish frothy liquid, shook it for a moment, then held it to my ear so I could hear it fizzing.

"What you're hearing is fermentation," he explained. "It takes a long time to ferment and you need to pay close attention to the temperature and the flour. Too bad you weren't here last week when I went through the whole process for a Japanese television crew."

Alas, indeed! This was why I was so glad to be sitting with Victoria, watching her punch the dough and "knuckle in" the water, which had been scented with a dozen bay leaves. She bent over a wooden trough as high as her knees so her entire body was involved in the kneading. I watched as she used her fists to punch in tablespoons of bay leaf–scented brew.

"Always keep the dough moist," she instructed me amid the squishy sounds of her kneading. "Add the liquid as necessary. If the dough starts getting hard, dip your hands into the liquid, then knead like this," she said, demonstrating the "knuckling in" motion (see page 34). "If the dough gets too loose, add a little barley flour."

It took her more than half an hour to knead the dough, after which she allowed it to relax. She shaped it, made some decorative lines on top, allowed it to relax again, then finally put it in a fairly hot oven to bake. After a while it rose more than two inches. What came out was a butter-colored muffinlike bread with an incredible aroma and a special, indescribable taste. As I munched a piece in Victoria's kitchen, I knew that this was a bread I would have to master.

I took home my notes and began the marathon labor of perfecting a recipe. True to the brothers' pronouncements, there *was* an obstacle at every turn. Here are my cooking notes on each phase of the process:

The Chickpeas Buy your chickpeas at a health food store. Since you'll be fermenting them, you'll want to be sure that they weren't treated with fungicides.

My first problem was reducing the chickpeas to a gritty state. Unsoaked, they wouldn't budge in a food processor, and when I tried to smash them with a stone pestle, two out of three went flying across the kitchen. I ended up using my electric "minichopper." Or you can soak them for 30 minutes, then crush them in a food processor. Either way they should be smashed into pieces about the size of small grains of rice.

Constant Heat for the Fermentation My next problem was to find a way to maintain the proper temperature at which to cultivate the chickpeas, so they would ferment and create the proper froth. Victoria uses not only the froth and liquid but also the chickpeas in her recipe.

Recalling the Kol brothers' admonition that the most important step in the process was to maintain a constant temperature for proper fermentation, I decided to use an electric heating pad, which worked very well. Some Greek cookbook authors suggest placing the mixture in a 100-degree oven for 6 to 7 hours or until it ferments. But often the chickpeas, if not fresh, take up to 1 day to ferment.

The Flour After much trial and error, I was able to simulate Cretan country yellow flour (*kitrino*) with a combination of durum flour, barley and unbleached white flour, thereby obtaining the golden color and unique texture I so admired (see "Mail-Order Sources").

Making the Sponge I used the food processor fitted with a metal blade to make a sponge with the fermented chickpeas, a cup of durum flour, and some aromatic brew made with bay leaves and cinnamon to encourage fermentation. I then allowed the sponge to bubble in a bowl within the folds of an electric heating pad for 2 hours.

The Kneading This dough is easily made in a heavy-duty mixer with some modifications. The sponge, remaining flours, and sugar are kneaded until the dough is smooth and *stiff*, 5 minutes. Then I simulate the "knuckling in" technique (see page 34) with more brew while working in some low-gluten barley flour, which doesn't need to be fully kneaded. The dough is ready when it is firm but spongy and a small piece can be stretched without tearing.

The Rising Shape the loaves, slash deeply with a razor-sharp knife at 1-inch intervals, cover with oiled plastic wrap, and let rest in a warm place until the dough is swollen by one-third, 2 hours. For rusks, use a sharp-edged spatula to divide the loaf into 8 equal slices and reassemble in the pan.

Since you won't see much of a rise prior to baking, placing the bread in the oven is pretty much an act of faith.

The Baking Preheat a baking stone for at least 45 minutes. Place a shallow oven tray on the floor of the oven while it is heating. Just before placing the bread in the oven, throw a handful of ice cubes onto the tray to create steam. Bake the breads until well browned, turning the pan around to ensure even baking. There are two ways to check for doneness: the base will sound hollow when tapped, or insert an instant-read thermometer in the center of the loaf—the bread is baked when it registers 220 degrees.

AROMATIC BREW

6 fresh or dried bay leaves

1 cinnamon stick

½ teaspoon aniseed or fennel seeds

4 whole cloves

4 cups water, preferably uncarbonated spring water

CHICKPEA LEAVENING

½ cup dried chickpeas

Tiny pinch of salt

2 tablespoons durum flour
(see "Mail-Order Sources")

1½ cups Aromatic Brew

SPONGE

Fermented chickpeas

1 cup durum flour

½ cup Aromatic Brew

3 tablespoons olive oil

1½ cups durum flour

1 cup all-purpose or bread flour

2 tablespoons sugar

3 teaspoons salt

¼ teaspoon ground cinnamon (optional)

1 cup barley flour (approximately)

½ cup Aromatic Brew

Flour for dusting work surface

Olive oil for greasing a shallow
11-by-7-1½-inch biscuit pan

1 teaspoon sesame seeds

½ teaspoon nigella seeds

Serving the Bread The bread is fully baked. It looks good and smells terrific. Wrap in a kitchen towel to keep the crust soft.

After I felt I had pretty much achieved a good-tasting bread, I brought a sample to Christoforos Veneris, a chef from Crete whose father had been a baker. He took one look at its smooth sides and said, "You killed it! The reason you must slice the bread *before* it is allowed to rise is to make it easier to pull it apart after baking."

Traditionally the bread is torn into chunks while still warm and topped with a little olive oil or butter. It is even better after it has mellowed for about 5 hours, then toasted lightly and dipped in olive oil.

Success Happily this is a bread you can practice on with good results, since you need not discard your mistakes. Even when your first efforts aren't perfect, you can still turn them into good-tasting rusks.

Do steps 1 and 2 one day in advance.

1. Rinse the aromatics. Gently crumble the bay leaves and the cinnamon stick into a saucepan, add the remaining aromatics, cover with the water, and slowly bring to a boil; simmer 5 minutes. Strain into a measuring cup and cool to lukewarm. Discard the aromatics.

2. Meanwhile, crush the chickpeas as described on page 37. Place the chickpeas and salt in a sterile quart mason jar. Stir in 2 tablespoons durum flour and 1½ cups Aromatic Brew. Cover the jar, wrap it in a heated electric blanket, and leave until the mixture fizzles and foams, 7 to 24 hours. The chickpea mixture must ferment before you continue. It should smell pleasing and slightly yeasty; if not, discard and begin again with fresher chickpeas. Store the aromatic liquid at room temperature.

3. The following day, make the sponge. Scrape the chickpeas, foam, and liquid into the workbowl of a food processor fitted with a metal blade. Process until the texture of medium bulgur. Add 1 cup durum flour and ½ cup aromatic brew and process until foamy and well combined, 20 seconds. Scrape into the bowl, cover, and let bubble in a warm place such as the folds of the heating pad, 2 hours.

4. Scrape sponge into the mixing bowl of a heavy-duty mixer. Add olive oil, remaining durum flour, bread flour, and sugar to the mixing bowl. Begin mixing with the paddle attachment to produce a smooth, stiff dough that holds its shape. Switch to the dough hook and knead on low to medium speed for 5 minutes. Add the salt and cinnamon, if using. Increase speed to medium while adding alternately the barley flour and ½ cup Aromatic Brew in small increments until the ball of dough is fluffy and pulls away from the sides of the bowl, and a small piece can be stretched without tearing, about 3 minutes. Grasp the dough with one moistened hand and scoop it into a ball; tip it onto a lightly floured work surface and knead by hand for an instant. Dip your hands in remaining brew or water, and divide the dough in half, then gently shape each portion into a rough plump round by tucking under the edges. Leave rounds to relax for 15 minutes.

5. Dip palms into brew or water and shape each portion of dough into a smooth long pan-shaped loaf,
then tip it into an oiled pan. Use a single-edged razor or a wet thin-bladed knife to make *very deep* cuts at 1-inch intervals the length of each loaf. Cover loosely with oiled plastic wrap or foil and let them rise until one-third in size, about 2 hours.

6. About 45 minutes before baking, place an empty pan on the lowest oven shelf and a stone or tiles on the middle oven shelf. Preheat the oven to 475 degrees, then reduce oven heat to 400 degrees when ready to bake.

7. Brush the tops with a few teaspoons of cold water and sprinkle with sesame and nigella seeds. Throw some ice cubes into the pan on the lower shelf in order to create steam. Place the bread directly on the stone or tiles and bake for 20 minutes. If the tops are browning too quickly, cover with a greased piece of paper. Reduce heat to 350 degrees and continue to bake 20 minutes. Remove breads from the oven and let cool on a rack. Serve the bread warm or lightly toasted.

To Make Rusks Do steps 1 through 4. In step 5, after you have shaped the loaves, use a wet thin-bladed knife to cut each loaf into 10 1-inch-thick slices. Reform the two loaves and place them in the oiled pan. Bake as directed above for 30 minutes at 400 degrees. Bread is three-quarters cooked. Remove to cool on a rack while oven temperature reduces to 250 degrees. Break apart the slices, place side by side on the stone or tiles, and continue baking until completely dry throughout and pale golden, about 2 hours. When cold, store the rusks in tins or cloth bags.

With special thanks to Shirley Corriher for her very helpful advice on fermentation and baking.

Rusk Salad with Tomatoes, Capers, Olives, and Lemon (Greece)

Serves 2 to 4 as a snack or first course

Daphne Zepos, a Greek-born cheese expert, shared this bit of colorful advice: "Be sure," she told me, "to soak the rusks until they get to the enervating stage of a leaky faucet."

If you are daunted by the preceding recipe but still want to make this salad, you may substitute store-bought barley rusks imported from Greece called *paximadi*.

---

4 chickpea bread rusks (page 40)

⅓ cup grated tomatoes

¼ teaspoon grated lemon zest

Salt

Freshly ground black pepper

6 pitted kalamata olives, rinsed and sliced

1 cup ripe cherry tomatoes, preferably yellow or orange, halved

6 salted capers, soaked, rinsed, and drained

Pinch of dried Mediterranean oregano or hyssop

2 tablespoons roughly chopped flat-leaf parsley

1 tablespoon crumbled feta cheese

2 tablespoons extra-virgin olive oil

1 tablespoon lemon juice

¼ teaspoon red wine vinegar

2 sprigs fresh thyme

NOTE: Chickpea-leavened bread must be densely textured, or it will not make good rusks. Loose-weave bread turns soggy when moistened.

1. Soak the dry rusks in warm water until soft enough to cut with a knife. Gently shake off excess water and cut into bite-size pieces. Divide and place in the center of two small serving plates. Spoon over equal amounts of the grated tomato seasoned with sugar, lemon zest, salt and pepper. Let stand about 20 minutes, allowing the juices to baste the rusk.

2. Just before serving, decorate with olives, cherry tomatoes, capers, oregano, parsley, and feta. In a small bowl, combine the olive oil, lemon juice, vinegar, and salt and pepper; mix well. Drizzle over the garnished breads and top each with a sprig of thyme.

NOTE TO THE COOK: To grate the tomatoes, cut tomatoes horizontally in half, stem side up. Scoop juice and seeds into a strainer and press the pulp through. Grate the tomatoes, cut side down, on a rough grater. The tough tomato skin will stay on the side of your palm. Discard skin and seeds. Crushed rusks make good sturdy bread crumbs.

With thanks to Chef Rick Moonen of the Molyvos Restaurant in New York for the salad recipe.

DRUSIAN RED PEPPER, *KISHK,* AND WALNUT BREAD

❧

Makes 8 rounds

The Druse, a non-Islamic Semitic people with their own religion, are one of the few cultural or religious groups uninterested in having their own independent state. In fact, the Druse give their loyalty to the country in which they live, whether it's Lebanon, Israel, Syria, or, for that matter, the United States.

When I lived in Connecticut, I did a lot of shopping at a Middle Eastern grocery frequented by members of the local Druse community. At the store there was always a pile of freshly baked flatbreads smothered with a wonderful red-hued sauce baked right into the dough. This bread, a kind of Middle Eastern pizza, had a delicious spicy, nutty flavor due to its ingredients: Aleppo pepper, chopped walnuts, toasted sesame seeds, and finely chopped onion and tomato. But what gave it its special slightly sour quality was the addition of the nutritious *kishk.*

Kishk is a Middle Eastern version of *trahana* (see page 74) made with yogurt or naturally fermented milk and wheat flour or bulgur in a ratio of two parts milk product to one part grain. The mixture, to which salt is added, is allowed to ferment, a process that gives it a flavorful sourish taste. It is then formed into lumps and dried in the sun. It's often found in powdered or coarse flour form at Middle Eastern groceries.

Randa Hmeidan, a Druse woman from the Chouf Mountains of Lebanon who now lives in Fresno, California, gave me this recipe for Drusian paprika, *kishk,* and walnut bread.

You and I will have to purchase this wheat cereal, but every summer Randa makes her own *kishk,* starting with 20 gallons of milk, all of which she turns into yogurt, then drains for an entire week until she's left with about 60 pounds of dry yogurt cheese (*labna*). She then mixes 10 pounds of bulgur in 2 gallons of hot milk. When the grain is absorbed, she gradually stirs in the *labna* and 1 cup salt, creating a thick sticky mud. She drops small pinches of this on cloths spread out on tables in her garden, leaving them in the sun until totally dry. Later she crumbles them, then grinds the crumbs in a coffee grinder. She stores the resulting *kishk* in the refrigerator for use throughout the year in soups, in stews, as a sauce for *kibbeh,* and in this wonderful Drusian bread.

"If by chance you overcook the bread," Randa told me, "eat it right away—for then it will taste like the bread they bake in the old ovens in the Chouf Mountains. But," she added, "if you let it get cold, it will just be hard and dry." Good advice!

Bread Dough

½ package active dry yeast

1 cup warm water

3 cups whole meal flour

1¼ teaspoons salt

The Topping

½ cup finely chopped onion

¾ cup finely chopped walnuts

1¼ cups *kishk* or imported wheat cereal

¾ to 1 teaspoon sweet paprika

Extra-virgin olive oil

2 tablespoons toasted sesame seeds

½ teaspoon Aleppo or Turkish pepper, or a combination of hot and sweet Hungarian paprika

Salt

Freshly ground black pepper

1. In a large mixing bowl, soften the yeast in ¼ cup of the warm water for 10 minutes until the yeast is foamy. Add the remaining ¾ cup water and just enough of the flour to form a soft and slightly sticky dough. When dough begins to hold together, add the salt, remove the dough, and knead on a floured board for 5 minutes. Add more water or extra flour to dough as needed. Knead until dough forms a smooth, elastic dough. Let rest for 1 hour, covered with a kitchen towel.

2. In a bowl, combine the onion and walnuts until coarsely blended. Add the *kishk* and enough paprika to redden the mixture, then stir in just enough olive oil to make it spread easily. Mix in the sesame seeds and flavor with Aleppo pepper and salt and black pepper.

3. Pull off walnut-size pieces of dough and roll each in a little flour to make ¼-inch-thick rounds. Arrange side by side in an oiled baking pan. Cover with kitchen toweling and let rise in a warm place for 1 hour.

4. Preheat the oven to 475 degrees.

5. Divide the topping and spread over each round, sprinkle with sesame seeds and bake for 10 minutes. Reduce the oven heat to 375 degrees and bake 10 minutes more. Eat while hot and crunchy or cover with a damp cloth and leave to cool. Store in plastic bags at room temperature for 1 to 2 days.

THE MONK'S PIZZA WITH PAN-SEARED CABBAGE

Serves 4 to 6

So you really liked my cabbage pizza?" chef Giovanne Perticone asks. "You want the recipe? Okay, you can have it. Ever since I came to this country my mother has been scouring the Italian countryside for old cookbooks to send me ideas. This one's a 1550 recipe from Atri's Monastery in Umbria."

Never mind that I can't find mention of such a monastery, nor can anyone else! The dish is still terrific: a wafer-thin pastry dough slapped onto a hot stone or iron griddle in the oven, flipped after cooking on one side, then topped with a prepared mixture of cabbage (flavored with anchovy and a drop of vinegar) and a shaving of pecorino or pepato cheese.

You can make the dough a day in advance and prepare the cabbage an hour or so ahead. It will take a good half hour before the baking stone or griddle is heated in the oven, but actual cooking will take only a few minutes.

At one point I tried to make this dish using open store-bought pita rounds. However, I missed the crackling layers of crust, and the cabbage didn't adhere as it should.

HOT WATER DOUGH

10 ounces (about 2 cups) bread flour

1 teaspoon salt

½ cup hot water

2 teaspoons olive oil

CABBAGE TOPPING

1 small head cabbage, cored and roughly shredded

1 medium onion, finely chopped

2 cloves garlic, peeled and minced

2 anchovy fillets, rinsed and crushed

2 tablespoons olive oil

2 tablespoons dry white wine

1 teaspoon mild white wine vinegar

Salt

Freshly ground black pepper

GARNISH

Pecorino Romano cheese or pepato, freshly grated

Extra-virgin olive oil

A turn of the pepper mill for each serving

1. Place the flour and salt in a bowl, make a well in the center, and add the water. Use your index finger to work in the water, then add the oil. You can do this in a heavy-duty mixer fitted with a dough hook by combining everything at once and mixing until everything comes together as a dough. Gather the dough on a floured surface and knead into a soft ball, pushing any loose crumbs into the ball with the heel of your hand. (Try not to overwork the dough.) Wrap in plastic wrap and refrigerate at least 2 hours.

2. Set a heavy skillet over high heat and sear the cabbage for 2 minutes, stirring constantly. Add the onion, garlic, anchovy, and oil and cook, stirring, for 2 to 3 minutes. Deglaze with the wine and continue cooking another 2 minutes. Sprinkle with vinegar and season to taste with salt and pepper; set aside.

3. About 30 minutes before serving, set a baker's tile on the lowest oven rack or oven floor. Preheat the oven to its highest setting.

4. While the oven is heating, divide the dough into four or six equal balls and roll each to 6 inches in diameter.

5. Five minutes before serving, place the rounds on the hot tile and bake 2 minutes. Turn each round and spread a portion of the cabbage on top. Bake another 2 minutes, then serve at once with a sprinkling of grated cheese, a drizzle of fresh oil, and a turn of the pepper mill.

MIRSINI'S SPICED BARLEY BREAD

❧

Makes 1 large 3½-pound loaf

My friend Mirsini Lambraki from Crete is a confident cook whose dishes often probe the culinary edge. She's also blessed with an uncanny knack for discovering interesting recipes in obscure Cretan towns. When she wants to understand an unusual method she'll go straight to the source—the little old women dressed in black who live in the mountains and know the old ways of doing things.

All this is by way of introduction to what seemed to me to be a highly unorthodox method for making bread: adding barley flour to dough when it was almost fully kneaded, rather than at the start. However unorthodox, it definitely works. Mirsini believes the reason country women, lacking electric mixers, do it this way is that it makes the hand-kneading process less strenuous. I have taken this method one step further by adapting it to the heavy-duty mixer.

(continued)

The addition of spices is typical of Cretan breads, due, I believe, to the island's proximity to Arab countries. In this bread, mastic, cinnamon, black pepper, and cumin are used as flavorings.

Another unusual aspect: This bread is placed in a *cold* oven, then allowed to rise as the oven heats up. The big, brown, crusty loaf that comes out goes well with olives, cheese, and a glass of red wine—a classic Greek island lunch.

SPICED YEASTY STARTER

2 small cakes of fresh yeast, 0.6 ounce each

1 cup warm water

1 tablespoon sugar

½ cup olive oil

Pinch of salt

½ teaspoon finely ground pepper

1 small piece mastic pounded in a mortar to a powder

½ teaspoon ground cinnamon

½ teaspoon ground cumin

1 cup fine semolina flour

2 teaspoons salt

1 cup fine semolina flour

1 pound (3 cups) unbleached all-purpose flour plus 1 tablespoon for decoration

½ pound (2 cups) whole grain barley flour

About ¾ cup warm water

1. Make the yeast mixture: In a small bowl crumble the yeast with ¼ cup of the warm water until creamy. Stir in the sugar, oil, salt, pepper, mastic, cinnamon, cumin, 1 cup semolina flour, and remaining ¾ cup warm water, mixing until everything is well combined. Cover and let stand in a warm place until spongy, about 15 minutes.

2. Put the salt, semolina, and all-purpose flour into the mixing bowl of a heavy-duty mixer fitted with a dough hook. Add the yeast mixture and knead on medium speed for 10 minutes. With the machine running, gradually add the barley flour and enough warm water to form a kneadable dough. Knead this barley-enriched dough until smooth and soft, 5 minutes. Cover with a damp cloth and let rise in a warm place for 1 hour, or until doubled in volume.

3. Knock down, cover again, and return to a warm place until doubled in volume.

4. Punch down the dough, knead it briefly with oiled palms, and shape it into a large oblong loaf on a baking sheet. Slash the dough with a sharp knife three or four times and sprinkle with 1 tablespoon of white flour. Put the sheet in an unheated oven, turn the heat to 350 degrees and bake 1½ hours, or until the bread is crusty and brown and sounds hollow when tapped on the bottom. Just as you take it out of the oven, brush the loaf with water to make it even crunchier. Barley bread will keep fresh 2 to 3 days.

STALE BREAD AS A STARTER
FOR TURKISH FLATBREADS

Stale bread should be treated as an opportunity," says cookbook author and bread authority Carol Field. I agree. In fact, I think a book should be written about stale bread and what to do with it.

Perhaps the most unusual bread dough I ever ate was one from the southeastern Turkish town of Nizip in which torn pieces of stale sourdough bread are blended with whole meal flour. The mixture is then moistened and kneaded into a workable dough for a griddle bread. The dough is left to mature overnight before a second kneading and the addition of a small amount of salt. This dough can be stored in the refrigerator for use as needed for up to a week.

When ready, the dough is rolled into a round about 10 inches in diameter and ¼ inch thin, spread with a filling, folded in three, and cooked on a hot domed metal pan called a *saj*. (Indian stores sell *tavas*, which are more or less the same thing. You can also use an upside-down wok. See "Mail-Order Sources.")

These fresh, hot little breads are stuffed with all sorts of fillings, including greens stewed in olive oil (next page); cooked mashed potatoes and green onions seasoned with cumin, red pepper, and black pepper; or a combination of 1½ cups ground toasted sesame seeds crushed with sautéed onion. All make a terrific accompaniment to a soup or salad.

TURKISH GRIDDLE BREAD
STUFFED WITH GREEN GARLIC (*Turkey*)

Serves 4

Here is a simple folded griddle bread stuffed with cooked green garlic, onion, pepper, and tomato paste, then cooked over a *tava* (see "Mail-Order Sources") or an upside-down wok set over a flame.

In the absence of green garlic, pea shoots, another early spring product, may be substituted. Other greens that work well are baby spinach, lamb's-quarters, and nettles. At other times of the year substitute a handful of any tender leafy greens.

2 cups stale bread, preferably lavash or Mediterranean pita, cut into 1¼-inch or 3-centimeter cubes

1 cup whole meal, *attar,* or *chapati* flour plus more for kneading and rolling

1 teaspoon salt

GREEN GARLIC STUFFING

¾ pound green garlic stalks, untrimmed

1 cup minced onion

4 teaspoons olive oil

2 teaspoons Turkish red pepper paste (see "Mail-Order Sources")

2 teaspoons tomato paste

Salt

2 teaspoons melted butter or the rich topping from top-quality natural unflavored yogurt

1. Soak crunchy, dry cubes of bread in warm water for 20 minutes; squeeze dry. Place in a bowl, sprinkle with 1 cup flour and the salt, and gradually work in enough warm water to make a dough. Knead for at least 20 minutes, adding more water as necessary to keep the dough soft. Or you can do this in the food processor, using the dough blade and kneading until the dough is smooth, about 1 minute. Makes about 2 cups. Store in a glass bowl or jar. Cover with a wet cloth and keep refrigerated. Moisten the cloth as needed. The dough keeps for a week.

2. When ready to use, divide the dough into 4 equal parts. Flour a work surface and roll each into a smooth ball. Flatten the balls with the palm of your hand, cover with a cloth, and let rest.

3. Meanwhile, slowly heat a large, flat iron or non-stick griddle, an upside-down wok, or an Indian *tava* over medium heat until hot, about 10 minutes. Reduce the heat to medium-low to maintain a steady heat.

4. Make the stuffing: Wash the green garlic; discard the roots and dark green leaves. Finely chop the stalks to make about 5 cups. In a large straight-sided skillet sauté the onion in the olive oil until soft. Add the pepper and tomato pastes and cook, stirring, for an instant. Stir in the chopped green garlic, cover, and cook over medium-low heat until tender, 5 to 20 minutes, depending upon the age of the garlic. Leave to cool. Season to taste with salt. Makes about 2 cups stuffing.

5. On a well-floured surface, use a smooth rolling pin to roll each round into a thin 10-inch circle, flouring lightly between rolls and dusting off excess flour. Spread one-quarter of the stuffing down the center of the dough. Fold the right and then the left side of the dough over and lightly press down to seal. Repeat with the remaining dough and filling. Place the assembled breads on the heated griddle and cook until spotted brown, about 45 seconds on each side; to avoid hard bread, do not overcook. Serve hot with a light brushing of melted butter, or use the rich topping from top-quality natural unflavored yogurt on the tops of the bread.

With thanks to Gülay Karsligil for teaching me this recipe.

GREEN GARLIC

❖

Green garlic shoots, which resemble baby leeks, are immature garlic bulbs. You can find them during the spring at farmers' markets in the West and in early summer in the East. (See "Mail-Order Sources" for suppliers.) When purchasing green garlic, look for shoots with crisp green leaves. And don't cut away the stalk; the more stalk you use, the better the dish will be.

The Italians use green garlic in risottos, along with pancetta, to create a fragrant, earthy taste. In France the shoots are mashed with other spring herbs to flavor young Easter lamb. And in Spain the stalks are chopped and used to flavor all sorts of rice dishes as well as a light and delicate egg tortilla (page 162).

You can grow green garlic by inserting small garlic cloves, pointed end up, in damp soil in a sunny part of the garden. (An early November planting near rosebushes is ideal for early spring harvesting. Many gardeners claim that the roses become more aromatic, too.) I have grown green garlic on my windowsill. The 12-inch stalklike shoots were ready to harvest within 3 months.

Bread Crumb "Paella": Sautéed Bread Crumbs Served with Sausages, Green Grapes, and Fried Eggs (*Spain*)

Serves 4

Bread crumb "paella" or *migas* is a simple, delicious winter breakfast dish prepared in Andalusia. Dense, day-old, country-style white bread is crumbled, then dampened with salted milky water. This gives the crumbs the appearance of fluffy rice, which may explain why this dish is often called "paella."

There are many versions and many ways to garnish the dish of crumbs. My favorite is this spicy version with a farmhouse garnish of green grapes, chorizo, and fried eggs.

About 5 ounces stale, dense country bread with crusts, thinly sliced and torn into small chunks

⅓ cup salted water plus more when frying the crumbs

2 tablespoons milk

2 tablespoons extra-virgin olive oil

2 cloves garlic, peeled and lightly bruised

1 cup diced semi-cured chorizo sausage

4 farm-fresh eggs (optional)

Salt

Spanish paprika, preferably *pimentón de la Vera* (optional, see "Mail-Order Sources")

2 cups green grapes

---

1. At least 3 hours before serving, dump the bread into the work bowl of a food processor and pulse until the bread is the size of small chickpeas with ragged edges. Warm the water and stir in the milk.

Transfer the bread crumbs into a large plastic storage bag, dampen with ⅓ cup of *warm* milky water, and stir until all the bread is damp. Seal and let stand until ready to cook.

2. In a 10-inch well-seasoned iron frying pan or a nonstick skillet, heat the olive oil and when hot fry the garlic until crisp and brown, then discard. Raise the heat to medium-high, add the chorizo, and fry until lightly browned, then remove. Add the bread and fry, stirring and crushing with a flat spatula, until it breaks apart and gently turns a deep golden brown, about 7 minutes. From time to time, if necessary, sprinkle the bread crumbs with milky water to keep the crumbs from burning or drying out. The crumbs should be lightly browned, hot, fluffy, and light. Return the chorizo to the pan; fry, stirring, a few minutes longer, and correct the seasoning. In another pan, fry the eggs, if using, in olive oil and season with salt and Spanish paprika. Serve the eggs on a bed of bread crumbs garnished with grapes.

BRIK DANNONI:
SPICY BEEF, OLIVES, AND CAPERS IN SEMOLINA PASTRY TURNOVERS (*Tunisia*)

❁

Makes 24 pastries

*I*n Tunisia, the cooking of the capital city, Tunis, is considered the most refined in the country. One of the most famous dishes of Tunis is this pastry turnover called a *brik* (a corruption of the Turkish word *börek*), which is filled with ground beef, olives, and capers and flavored with Tunisian spices, the whole wrapped in rich pastry and fried in olive oil.

A typical Tunisian *brik*, often served at little stands on the street, is a deep-fried flaky pastry filled with an oozing mixture of egg and bits of tuna or mashed potatoes flavored with *harissa*. Such *briks* are excellent and fun to make, and I have written about them in several earlier books. But *brik dannoni*, made with a different kind of pastry, is a far finer dish.

If you don't want to make this *brik* with the meat filling, feel free to substitute a mixture of leftover *mechouia* salad (page 115), top-quality oil-packed canned tuna, hard-cooked eggs, and capers.

1. Make the pastry dough 1 day in advance. Place the semolina flour and pastry flour in the work bowl of a food processor fitted with the metal blade. Sift the flour by turning the processor on and off once. Mix ⅔ cup warm water with the olive oil, egg, butter, and salt and pour over the flour. Process with 4 or 5 short pulses, or until the mixture resembles cornmeal.

2. Place the mixture on a work surface covered with a sheet of plastic film. Gather it into a dough. It should not be too crumbly; if it is, sprinkle it with droplets of warm water—just enough to mass the dough together; it will not be very smooth. Wrap it tightly and chill overnight. Makes 1 pound dough.

3. Make the filling: Cook the beef in oil in a medium skillet for 5 minutes, stirring. Sprinkle with salt, pepper, and *tabil* and cook another minute, stirring. Remove from the heat and allow to cool slightly. Blend in the capers, olives, red peppers, crumbled egg, and raw egg; mix well. Allow to cool completely. Makes 2½ cups filling.

(continued)

The Pastry

1⅓ cups (½ pound) fine semolina flour

1 cup (4 ounces) pastry flour

⅔ cup or more warm water

2 tablespoons olive oil

2 tablespoons lightly beaten egg

3 tablespoons melted butter

Fine salt to taste

The Filling

½ pound ground beef

1½ tablespoons olive oil plus more for frying

Salt

Freshly ground black pepper

1 teaspoon Tunisian *tabil* (page 346) or ground coriander mixed with a pinch of ground caraway

2 dozen salted capers, soaked in water 10 minutes and drained (2½ tablespoons)

3 dozen niçoise olives, pitted, rinsed, drained, and chopped

1½ tablespoons chopped pickled red peppers such as cherry peppers or more to taste

2 hard-cooked eggs, peeled and crumbled

1 egg

4. Flour a work surface. Divide the dough into 4 parts. Roll one part into a thin sheet and divide into 6 equal parts. Place a heaping tablespoon of stuffing on one half of the dough and fold over. Repeat to make 24 *briks*.

5. Fill a deep saucepan to a depth of 1¼ inches with oil and slowly heat to very hot but not smoking. Immediately reduce the heat to about 350 degrees on a fat thermometer. Fry the *briks*, no more than 3 at a time, for about 2 minutes on each side, until golden brown, being very careful to keep the temperature constant. Drain on paper towels. Serve hot or warm.

NOTE TO THE COOK: Since some people are wary of eating oil-drenched food, fried stuffed pastries have more or less gone out of favor. The frying method used above reduces oil absorption to a bare minimum, which will hopefully make you want to try this recipe, which in turn will hopefully remind you how good such pastries can be. If you measure the amount of oil left at the end, you'll see how little has been absorbed.

PARSLEY, BASTURMA, AND KASSERI *BÖREK* (*Turkey*)

❧

Makes 2 rolls, serving 8

Meat böreks shall contain 250 dirhems of mutton and yufka böreks shall weigh 180 dirhems. The center must not be filled with onion. The meat shall not be a mixture of kinds but only of mutton. There shall not be excessive onion, little meat or many air cavities. The pastry shall be of fine flour, shall not contain pork fat, and any who contravene this statute shall be severely punished.

—DECREE BY SULTAN MEHMET IV, 1680

Don't worry, you won't be punished if you fail to make this *börek* . . . though of course I urge you to do so. It's from the Turkish region of Trakia near the Greek border region of Thrace. Cooks in both areas use huge amounts of parsley in their dishes and are famous for preparing pies that they call *böreks*, a Turkish word. These pies usually feature kasseri, a semihard cheese of the "pasta-filata" type that has a felicitous property—when slowly heated it melts and blends right into the pastry.

If you're tired of phyllo, either store-bought or homemade, you might try the Turkish version called *yufka*, now sold at some Middle Eastern groceries. *Yufka* is thicker than phyllo and bakes up very crunchy (see "Mail-Order Sources").

Basturma, also available at Middle Eastern groceries, is an eastern Mediterranean spicy preserved meat made during the winter with an eye-round of beef. There are two types: the Turkish or Armenian style, which has lots of flavor and also contains more fat; and the Egyptian style, which, though less tasty, is lean. Either one will do. Ask the grocer to cut it paper thin. If you don't use it within a few days, freeze it for later use, since it quickly dries out. Basturma is delicious served with a squeeze of lemon, in pilafs, in Stewed Greens with Basturma Chips (page 297), and in this delightful *börek*.

The salt of the cheese and basturma will melt into the phyllo or *yufka,* making it crunchy and crisp. These *böreks* are delicious served warm with cool drinks.

(continued)

8 sheets commercial phyllo, or 4 sheets *yufka*, halved

Olive oil

1 cup plus 2 tablespoons finely grated kasseri or Monterey Jack cheese

14 paper-thin slices basturma (about 4 ounces) or 1 cup basturma chips, soaked 10 minutes in water to remove excess salt

3 cups chopped flat-leaf parsley

Soda water or beer

1. Preheat the oven to 350 degrees.

2. Spread one sheet of phyllo or a half sheet of *yufka* on a work space. Lightly drizzle it with oil and scatter on 3 tablespoons cheese in a thin even layer. Lay a second sheet on top and sprinkle with oil and another 3 tablespoons cheese, and scatter half the basturma slices or chips in an even layer. Top with another pastry sheet, sprinkle with 3 tablespoons cheese, and pile half the parsley along one of the long edges of the pastry sheet. Top with fourth sheet and brush lightly with oil. Carefully roll into a cylinder and fold in ends. Set on a greased baking sheet; score the top and brush with oil. Repeat with the remaining ingredients. Sprinkle with soda water or beer and bake the two rolls until golden brown, about 25 minutes.

With thanks to Angel Stoyanoff for sharing this recipe.

CRETAN "SCARF" PIES WITH WILD GREENS

A warm clear spring day in Crete. Mirsini Lambraki has taken me into the hills about an hour's drive above Heraklion, to an abandoned vineyard that she has described as a paradise because it contains everything one could possibly want in the way of wild edible greens.

The place is magical—a tangle of broken stone walls, a ruined church, the remnants of neglected old grapevines just starting spring growth. We collect a gallon of greens—a mix of chard, wild carrot, Roman pimpernel, anise, salsify greens, poppy greens, fennel anise, chicory, byronia, dandelion, sorrel, purslane, and wild spinach—that Mirsini's mother will bake into the little crescent-shaped pies the Cretans nickname "scarfs."

"Our pies are always green and small," Mirsini tells me, "and are usually fried in olive oil. We mix ten or fifteen types of greens and boil them in lots of water, keeping them submerged so they'll retain their vitamins and their color. On the western side of the island, we salt the greens before putting them inside pies, while on the eastern side we stew them with onions and olive oil after boiling."

Since there's no way for me to reproduce these elaborate wild green fillings in America. I'm sorry not to be able to present a recipe. But I know I musn't let this opportunity slip by without mentioning these fabulous "scarf" pies.

Field Greens, Rice, and Pumpkin Torta (*Italy*)

Serves 6

Here is an absolutely delicious pie of "not-so-wild" edible greens from the Ligurian-Tuscan coast of Italy. The combination of greens, rice, and pumpkin gives it unusual depth.

A sinkful of greens can be daunting to shred. I use the eastern Mediterranean trick of washing the greens, salting them for an hour while they extrude a lot of moisture, then washing off the salt before shredding. I do the same with chopped leeks and grated winter squash. After everything is rinsed and squeezed dry, a gallon of raw material is reduced to a quart, ready to be sautéed in olive oil to bring up the flavor, then cooled for wrapping in pastry and baking.

Not only is volume greatly reduced, but so is any bitterness. Spring greens are peppery, sweet, or bitter. I select mostly peppery and sweet greens for this pie, choosing those with the smallest leaves such as watercress, mâche, spinach, chard, and arugula. Braising mixes offered at farmers' markets are usually excellent. If you have young borage in your garden, include that too, or else grate a little seedless cucumber into the mix to add a special flavor. If you know your wild edible greens, consider adding nettle tops and sow thistle as well.

I use a pizza pan to bake this double-crusted pie. Originally such pies were cooked in the fireplace. A covered pan called a *testo* was thrust into the coals, then more coals were piled on top, imbuing the pastry with a smoky flavor.

1. Make the dough in advance. Place the flour and salt in the work bowl of a food processor fitted with the metal blade. Sift the flour by turning the processor on and off once. Sprinkle the oil and 10 tablespoons of cold water over the flour, and process with 4 or 5 short pulses, or until the mixture resembles cornmeal. If necessary, add water, 1 tablespoon at a time, mixing well after each addition until a dough-like mixture forms. Dump the dough onto a cool work surface and gather into a ball, pushing any loose crumbs into the ball with the heel of your hand. Knead until just smooth. Divide in half; flatten each half into a 1-inch-thick round. Dust the rounds lightly with flour, wrap them in plastic wrap, and refrigerate a few hours, or better overnight.

2. Wash and stem the Swiss chard and remove any thick ribs. Place greens in a large noncorrodible colander set over a bowl. (If you don't have a noncorrodible colander, just use a large mixing bowl.) Rub with half the salt and let stand for 1 hour. Separately salt the grated vegetables and let stand for

Olive Oil Pastry Dough (¾ pound)

2 packed cups (10½ ounces) all-purpose flour

½ teaspoon salt

3½ tablespoons olive oil

Filling for a 14-Inch Round Pie

1 bunch Swiss chard

¼ pound baby spinach leaves

¼ pound watercress leaves

¼ pound mixed baby greens for braising

1 cup chopped white of leek

1 cup grated winter squash

2 tablespoons olive oil

2 tablespoons coarse salt

¾ cup grated Parmigiano-Reggiano

1 cup ricotta or grated mozzarella cheese

½ cup short-grain rice, soaked 10 minutes in hot water and drained

2 eggs, lightly beaten, plus 1 egg mixed with 1 tablespoon milk

Grated nutmeg

1 teaspoon freshly ground black pepper

1 hour. Rinse greens, squeeze dry, and shred coarse Rinse the vegetables to remove all salt and squeeze out all moisture.

3. Preheat the oven to 400 degrees.

4. In a skillet sauté the greens, leeks, and squash in hot oil until glazed, then dump into a large mixing bowl. When cool, add the cheeses, rice, lightly beaten eggs, nutmeg, and black pepper, mixing well. Taste for salt.

5. Divide the dough in 2 parts. Roll out one half of the dough to a round 14 inches in diameter. Flip the pastry onto a lightly oiled pizza pan. Roll out the second ball of dough. Spread the prepared stuffing over the pastry in the pan, leaving a 1-inch margin around the edge. Dampen the edges with water. Lift the second sheet of dough to cover, then fit the edges of the pastry snugly against the dampened margin around the bottom crust; press with your fingers to seal. Brush the top with the egg wash, score the dough with the tines of a fork, and bake in the oven until golden brown and lightly puffed, about 30 to 40 minutes. Cool the torta on a wire rack and serve warm or cool.

Adapted from a recipe in Cucina Tradizionale della Lunigiana *by Francesca Grossi.*

3

SOUPS

MORNING SOUPS

It wasn't yet the height of summer, but even at ten in the morning it was extremely hot. I was staying on the Tunisian island of Djerba in the white cubic house of Abdelrazak Haouari, a hugely talented Tunisian chef, and his wife, Nabiha. Nabiha, black-haired with vibrant smiling eyes, was dressed in her everyday garb—a pink and silvery caftan and a head scarf held down with a panama hat.

A loving, good-natured mother, she was already exhausted. Her four children, charming as they were, were wearing her down. One was doing cartwheels across the living room floor, another was curled up in a corner crying, a third was studying the Roman alphabet with me, while the fourth, deaf, was reading unconcerned amid the surrounding circus.

Nabiha glanced at her watch. "Time for *bsissa*," she announced. She was referring to a uniquely Tunisian morning soup or drink made with pan-grilled barley and spices, which she drank as her daily "pick-me-up" much the way an American or European might pause for a midmorning cappuccino.

She loved preparing the drink, or its cousin, *zomita*, made with pan-grilled wheat, serving it along with slices of cactus fruit. She took a plastic jar of powdered, spiced, pan-grilled grain down from the cupboard, mixed ½ cup of the powder with olive oil and some cold water from the house cistern, then stirred the ingredients until smooth.

"Drink it before it separates," she urged me.

Just as with strong coffee, the "buzz" or "jolt" came quickly, bringing a renewal of energy to face the exigencies of the day.

In Arabic, Nabiha called this morning soup the "spoon from God." In fact, as I discovered, the powder base for *bsissa* and/or *zomita* derives from one of the oldest methods devised for handling grains. Traditionally, in Tunisia and especially on the island of Djerba, grains are toasted in a dry skillet, then milled along with spices to make spicy flour, a method used since the earliest days of farming to preserve grains. And since no further cooking is necessary, I've come to think of these powders as the first examples of instant cereal!

This ability to preserve grain flour was extremely important, enabling one to travel with a sack of toasted flour, stopping to eat when hungry simply by blending the flour with some olive oil, rolling it into a ball, then popping it into one's mouth. Or, by adding water from a well or cistern, one could make a nourishing, refreshing drink. By adding some chopped figs, raisins, or dates, you could have a very early version of granola.

Over the years I've collected a number of formulas for flavoring toasted grains during the milling process, blending them with spices such as sesame seeds, coriander, caraway, cumin, fennel seeds, fenugreek, and green aniseed; herbs such as rue, marjoram, and wild oregano; aromatics such as dried orange peel; and other pulses such as lentils, dried favas, and toasted chickpeas. One—not a morning soup—appears in my Moroccan cookbook as a marriage dish.

Speaking of marriage, Tunisians, I recently discovered, have devised a special pick-me-up combination for *zomita* that is placed in a large bowl beside the marital bed. In the bowl, lightly grilled wheat is blended with wild oregano, rosemary, caraway, coriander, sesame seeds, cumin, black onion seeds, almonds, green anise, pistachios, pine nuts, fenugreek, honey, chickpea flour, tahini, and orange rind, accompanied by bottles of water and olive oil and two glasses for the bride and groom.

A Tunisian woman typically makes her *bsissa* or *zomita* with 20 kilos of grain, spending an entire day on the process. The following formula for *bsissa* is typical and scaled down, the derived drink is good, and the energizing effect is real.

BSISSA

On a flat griddle, toast by handfuls 1 pound barley kernels until golden, 5 minutes. Finely grind the barley in a grain mill with ⅔ cup toasted coriander seeds, ⅓ cup fennel seeds, 1 scant teaspoon ground cumin, 1 scant teaspoon ground fenugreek, 1 teaspoon sea salt, and 1 teaspoon crumbled dried orange peel. Press everything through a fine sieve. Store in a tightly closed jar. To make *bsissa*, take 2 tablespoons of the powder and mix with 1 teaspoon olive oil and enough cool water to make a smooth drink. Add sugar as desired.

El Caldero Murciano with Rice, Shrimp, Peppers, and Garlic Mayonnaise (*Spain*)

Serves 4

Traditionally a fishermen's stew made in an iron pot on board fishing boats, this delicious rice and seafood soup—eaten with a fork—has become popular in Spain as a first course. Akin to risotto in consistency, it must be served immediately after it's finished. But unlike risotto it does not require stirring, and instead of adding cheese and butter at the end you eat it along with dabs of ali-oli, garlic mayonnaise.

Three ingredients are absolutely necessary if you're to have success: a hot chili pepper, a top-quality medium-grain rice, and a savory fish stock.

One teaspoon of scraped pulp from the Murcian pepper called *ñora* gives this dish an incredible flavor. *Ñora* peppers are small, dark, and round. Though they look like Mexican cascabel chilies and are as richly sweet, they are nowhere near as hot. A top-quality New Mexican chili pepper from Tierra Vegetables may be substituted. (See "Mail-Order Sources" for both peppers.)

For this dish you will need a medium-grain rice. Spain's Calasparra rice—the name designates the region of origin—is a perfect choice because it can absorb far more stock than almost any other short- to medium-grain rice on the market. You will need an additional cup of stock, which makes the rice more flavorful. The soup is very fine when made with Spanish Valencia, American Cal-Riso or one of the Italian risotto rices such as arborio, roma, or carnaroli.

You can buy frozen fish stock or fumet at many supermarkets and most fish stores. You can also make your own with heads, skins, and trimmings of bass, snapper, or other white-fleshed fish.

(continued)

1 dried *ñora* pepper (page 61), or ½ dried New Mexican pepper

1 pound medium shrimp (20 to 25), fresh or frozen, shells reserved

1 tablespoon sea salt

1 teaspoon sugar

3½ tablespoons extra-virgin olive oil

Aromatics for the fish stock: 1 cup mixed chopped onion, parsley stems, carrots, and mushrooms

1 quart homemade fish stock (page 223), or 1 cup frozen rich fish fumet diluted with 3 cups water

1 cup chopped onion

1 teaspoon finely chopped garlic

¼ cup diced green bell pepper

1 cup diced fresh mushrooms such as cremini, portobello, brown, or white

1 cup medium-grain rice such as Spanish Valencia, Calasparra, American Cal-Riso, or Italian risotto rice

3 tablespoons homemade or top-quality tomato paste

Freshly ground black pepper

3 tablespoons chopped flat-leaf parsley

Ali-oli Sauce (page 345)

1. Stem the *ñora* or New Mexican pepper; shake out the seeds, and soak it in a small cup of warm water for about 30 minutes until soft; drain.

2. Soak or defrost the shrimp in a brine made with 3 cups water, the sea salt, and the sugar until ready to cook. If using defrosted shrimp, shell, return to the brine, and reserve the shells for the next step.

3. In a medium saucepan, heat 1½ tablespoons of the olive oil over moderately high heat. Add the shrimp shells and sauté until the shells turn pink and the oil smells fragrant, 2 to 3 minutes. Add the aromatics for the fish stock and cook, stirring, for 1 minute. Moisten with the fish stock; bring to a boil and cook for 30 minutes.

4. Meanwhile, heat the remaining oil in a heavy-bottomed medium saucepan or deep cazuela. Add the onion and garlic and cook over moderate heat until softened but not browned. Add the bell pepper and mushrooms to the pan and cook slowly for 10 minutes, stirring occasionally. Drain the dried pepper, halve, and scrape out the flesh with a small spoon to make about 1 teaspoon; set aside. Add the rice, stir, and cook over medium heat until lightly toasted and well coated with vegetables, 2 minutes. Strain the fish stock and check to be sure you have at least 3 cups. If not, add hot water. Add boiling fish stock, the pepper flesh, tomato paste, and salt and pepper and cook for 13 minutes.

5. Spread drained shrimp and the parsley over the rice, cover, and continue cooking over low heat until the rice and shrimps are cooked, about 5 minutes. Serve at once in individual serving dishes and pass a bowl of ali-oli.

With thanks to Iñaki Izaguirre for inspiring this recipe.

NOTE: Here is a reward if you purchased *ñora* peppers: a delicious, vibrant dressing devised by my friend Lourdes March, the author of *El Libro de la Paella y de los Arroces* (Allianza, 1985), to serve over poached fish fillets at another time. Poach some fish. In a skillet, gently fry an unsoaked *ñora* to soften it. Then place it in a mortar, spice mill, or food processor with 1 tablespoon each chopped garlic and chopped parsley and ½ teaspoon *pimentón de la Vera* (a mild Spanish paprika), and pound until smooth. Moisten with ½ cup fish stock and 2 tablespoons each olive oil and lemon juice, and season to taste with salt. Allow the sauce to mellow an hour or two before serving.

BLACK SEA SOUP WITH CORNMEAL, LEAFY GREENS, AND MUSHROOMS (*Turkey*)

❀

Serves 6

This soup was inspired by one that I ate on the Turkish Black Sea coast, where collard greens and Swiss chard appear in nearly every bowl of soup.

The original recipe calls for sheep's tail fat, for which I've substituted olive oil to good effect. Actually sheep's tail fat, called *kakivdak* when cooked down and crumbled, is a staple along the Black Sea, where it's used in melted form to provide a meaty richness to dishes. You'll find a jar in every home kitchen. Cooks use it to cook down greens or add a dab when preparing red or white beans for making soup. To simulate its meaty texture, I've added mushrooms to the recipe. *(continued)*

¾ cup dried white beans

½ pound small lamb neck bones

1 small carrot, peeled and thinly sliced

1 medium onion, chopped

4 garlic cloves, peeled and bruised

3 tablespoons olive oil

⅓ cup dried mushrooms

1½ tablespoons tomato paste

1 pinch red pepper flakes

Pinch sugar

4 large collard green leaves, stemmed and shredded (4 cups)

¼ cup fine or coarse stone-ground cornmeal

1 teaspoon salt

¾ teaspoon freshly ground black pepper

About 6 large Swiss chard leaves, stems and leaves shredded

1 tablespoon dried mint pressed through a fine sieve

1. Pick over the beans and soak them in water to cover overnight.

2. The following day, drain the beans and put them in a deep pot, preferably a bean pot or Chinese clay pot. Cover with 5 cups water and slowly bring to the boil, skimming carefully.

3. In a skillet gently sauté the lamb bones, carrot, onion, and garlic in 2 tablespoons of the olive oil, stirring, for 5 minutes. Add them to the beans. Bring the mixture to a boil, reduce the heat to medium-low, and simmer, covered, for 45 minutes.

4. Soak the mushrooms in 1 cup hot water for 30 minutes.

5. Drain the mushrooms; strain the soaking liquor; add both to the soup. Stir in the tomato paste, red pepper flakes, sugar, shredded collard greens, cornmeal, salt, and pepper and cook, stirring occasionally, for 20 minutes.

6. Stir in the shredded Swiss chard and 2 cups water and bring to the boil. Simmer, partially covered, for 30 minutes. Adjust the seasoning. Serve with a drizzle of mint heated in the remaining 1 tablespoon olive oil.

CREAMY FARRO AND CHICKPEA SOUP (*Italy*)

❋

Serves 4

"Farro is Farro," says Rolando Beramandi, an importer of the Tuscan cereal grain, by which he means it's a specific type of polished grain (*Triticum dicoccum Schubler*) and not, as some people will tell you, a "kind" of spelt or a "kind" of something else.

Here's how Suzanne Hamlin put it in the *New York Times:* "A grain of farro looks and tastes somewhat like a lighter brown rice. It has a complex nutty taste with undertones of oats and barley. But lacking the heaviness of many whole wheat grains, farro tastes more elegant than earnest."

Yes, if you must, you may substitute hulled barley; but if you do, please remember: don't soak it overnight.

¾ cup dried chickpeas

¾ cup farro or hulled barley

½ teaspoon sea salt

2 imported bay leaves

3 tablespoons extra-virgin olive oil plus more for garnish

½ cup chopped onion

1 tablespoon chopped prosciutto

1 tablespoon minced celery

1 quart homemade chicken stock

½ teaspoon dried marjoram

2 whiffs of freshly grated nutmeg

Freshly ground black pepper

Freshly chopped flat-leaf parsley for garnish

1. Pick over the chickpeas and soak them in water to cover overnight. Rinse the farro and soak in water to cover overnight.

2. Drain the chickpeas and place in earthenware, if possible, (beans cook more evenly in clay), cover with plenty of cold water, and bring them to a boil. Add the salt and bay leaves. Reduce heat and cook, covered, until very soft, about 1½ hours.

3. Meanwhile, in a medium saucepan, heat the olive oil and gently cook the onion, prosciutto, and celery for 4 to 5 minutes, stirring occasionally, until they are soft but not brown. Drain the farro and add it along with the stock, marjoram, and nutmeg to the onions and cook, partially covered, for about 1 hour.

4. Drain the chickpeas, discard the bay leaves, and reserve the cooking liquid. Purée the chickpeas with 1 cup reserved liquid in a food processor. Add puréed chickpeas to the farro and, if necessary, additional chickpea cooking liquid to achieve the consistency of a creamy soup. Adjust the seasoning with salt and pepper. Wait 10 minutes before serving and sprinkle each portion with chopped parsley and a drizzle of olive oil.

Farro, Leafy Greens, and Potato Soup as Prepared in the Marches (*Italy*)

❧

Serves 3 or 4

On a spring trip to the Marches (on the Adriatic coast of central Italy) I met a marvelous white-haired forager-chef-restaurateur, Felice Orazi, famous for his spring soup made with a local wild green called *bubbolino*, farro, and freshly dug potatoes.

Felice's wife, Rosalba, also uses *bubbolino* in her equally famous risottos and frittatas. Felice's restaurant, Le Copertelle, is nestled on the side of a mountain. He starts picking *bubbolino* in March, when this marvelous pealike green is barely an inch out of the ground. It's then, he says, that the plant is at its tender best. On the April day when I visited he looked out the window just before going out to forage. "Hmmm . . . the weather's weird today," he said. "I think I'll find some mushrooms, too." Then he smiled. "It's going to be a good lunch."

He returned with *bubbolino* and mushrooms, and the lunch, as promised, was good—in fact, out of this world! He told me that as spring progresses into summer he must go out earlier each day in order to climb higher up the mountain, since at lower levels the plants have matured and are too bitter for cooking.

Bladder campion (as *bubbolino* is called in English) tastes like a cross between asparagus and sweet peas—which is how I've simulated its taste in the following recipe, also adding a little arugula for texture.

When I first started searching for wild greens, I thought bladder campion would be hard to find. In fact, I found it right in the middle of my daylily patch in front of my summer home on Martha's Vineyard. Unfortunately, it was too mature to use.

If you do decide to go for the real thing, be sure to consult a reliable book on wild edible plants in your area. Otherwise you may make a mistake and cook an inedible look-alike.

½ cup farro

3 tablespoons olive oil plus more for garnish

½ cup chopped flat-leaf parsley

½ teaspoon red pepper flakes (without seeds) or more to taste

4 cloves garlic, peeled and sliced

½ pound boiling potatoes, peeled and chopped

¼ pound arugula leaves, stemmed and finely shredded

1 cup shelled peas

3 fresh asparagus spears, sliced very thin crosswise (optional)

Salt

Freshly ground black pepper

3 cups vegetable, meat, or poultry stock, simmering

Freshly grated pecorino Romano or Parmigiano-Reggiano

1. Pick over and rinse the farro and soak in tepid water overnight.

2. Drain the farro, cover with fresh cold water, and cook, covered, until tender, 45 minutes or longer, depending upon the age of the grain.

3. Meanwhile, in a heavy-bottomed bean or soup pot, heat the oil; add the parsley, red pepper, garlic, and potatoes; and sauté until soft and golden brown, about 15 minutes, mashing the potatoes in the pot, so that they begin to stick to the bottom of the pan and create caramelized areas here and there—but avoid burning.

4. Add the arugula, peas, and asparagus, if using, and stir-fry for a few minutes. Season with salt and pepper. Add the fully cooked farro and 3 cups simmering stock and bring back to a boil. Cook at the simmer for 30 minutes to cook the vegetables and blend flavors.

5. Adjust the seasoning with salt and pepper. Remove from the heat and let stand 5 minutes before serving. Serve with a drizzle of fresh olive oil and a small spoonful of cheese.

Medley of Wheat Berries, Lentils, and Rice with Fresh Herbs (*Greece*)

Serves 6 to 8

I've tasted numerous excellent combinations of pulses and grains around the Mediterranean: *maklouta* in the Middle East, flavored with cumin and hot red pepper; *mescciuà* in Liguria, which uses extra-virgin olive oil and plenty of freshly ground black pepper; pulses and grains combined with black sausage and paprika in Spain and with pigs' ears and snout in Provence. But I've never found such charming pulse and grain combinations as on the island of Crete.

This soup, which can be served as a main course, is inspired by a dish prepared for me by Christoforos Veneris, a talented, handsome, English-speaking Cretan chef. He told me, "When you mix five to six different kinds of grains, the result just has to taste good."

Christoforos calls his dish *sympetherio*, which means "in-laws"—a reference to a lot of different people (i.e., grains) living under the same roof (in the same pot). "In other words, no one can escape!" he adds as his eyebrows shoot up.

As I later discovered, there are at least three traditional names for such a soup: *psarokoliva*, a reference to fish and an ancient Greek ceremony of offering seeds and fruits to propitiate the gods of fertility and to honor the dead; *palikaria*, the eastern Cretan name for a strong young man and for a soup that includes rice, chickpeas, lentils, wheat berries, favas, and white beans; and *mayiremata*, a Byzantine dish of beans. Each year on January 7, farmers cooked this soup for their families and also for their oxen. At the same time soup was placed on the roof in the hope that the birds of the night would eat it and thus bring a good, productive year to the farm.

Mirsini Lambraki, cookbook author and forager par excellence, cooks each component separately so that each grain and bean reaches its optimum point before being combined. When the soup is lukewarm, she drizzles it with red wine vinegar and olive oil, then garnishes it with fresh wheat sprouts and pomegranate seeds.

Some Cretan cooks also add millet. Most also add snippets of dill and plenty of lemon rather than vinegar. Because lemons vary greatly in intensity, I've added a little grated lemon zest to reinforce the flavor.

This dish does not have absolute proportions. You can change the amounts of grains and pulses according to what you have on hand. This soup is especially delicious the next day accompanied by kalamata olives and crusty bread.

1 cup whole winter wheat berries,
kamut, or spelt

1 cup dried fava beans, large or small

⅔ cup dried chickpeas

⅔ cup dried navy or Great Northern beans

⅔ cup small dried pinto or cranberry beans

⅔ cup small dried brown lentils

½ cup extra-virgin olive oil
plus more for garnish

1 bunch scallions, coarsely chopped

1 teaspoon sea salt

⅓ cup medium-grain rice

1 teaspoon grated lemon rind

Juice of 2 large lemons

¼ teaspoon freshly ground black pepper

1 teaspoon flour

½ cup chopped fresh dill

1 cup kalamata olives, rinsed and drained

1. One day in advance of serving, separately soak the wheat berries and favas in lightly salted water to cover. In a third bowl soak the chickpeas, navy beans, and mottled beans in plenty of lightly salted water. Discard all beans that float.

2. The following day, about 3 hours before serving, rinse and drain the wheat berries and cook them in a large pot filled with plenty of water for 1 hour. Meanwhile, prepare the favas: Use a small paring knife to cut away the black strip on each bean.

Separately boil the favas for 10 minutes in water to cover, and remove from heat. Drain favas, add to the wheat berries, and continue cooking to finish the hour.

3. In a second saucepan, cover chickpeas, navy beans, and mottled beans with water and bring to a boil. Skim carefully, then add the chickpeas and beans to the wheat berries. Add more water, if necessary, and bring to a boil. Reduce heat and cook for 30 minutes.

4. Meanwhile, pick over the lentils, rinse, and drain. Add the lentils to the saucepan when the beans have cooked 30 minutes. Add more water if necessary to keep everything covered; salt lightly, bring back to the boil, and cook over low heat another 30 minutes.

5. Heat ½ cup olive oil in a skillet. Add the scallions and cook 5 minutes, stirring occasionally. Add the contents of the skillet, 1 teaspoon salt, rice, and more boiling water, if necessary, to keep the bean mixture covered with liquid and continue cooking until the beans, rice, lentils, and wheat berries are tender, about 20 minutes.

6. In a small cup combine the lemon rind, lemon juice, pepper, flour, and enough water to make a smooth paste. Stir the lemon rind paste into the beans' cooking liquid; correct the seasoning with salt, add half the dill, and cook at the simmer for 5 minutes. Remove from the heat and let stand until just warm, then garnish with a drizzle of olive oil and the remaining chopped dill sprinkled on top. Pass a dish of kalamata olives.

Lamb with "False Brains" and Garlic Soup

❖

I was so struck when I heard that a traditional soup from southeastern Turkey, containing a mixture of skinned wheat berries and garbanzo beans, was called a soup with "false brains" that I had to find out why. A local cook, Eren Özebeçki, explained it to me: "Sometimes it's just too tedious to break open the head of a sheep, so we use shelled wheat instead."

She went on to tell me that when this same soup is served cold in summer, some people call it soup with "dumb false brains."

Skinned Wheat Berries

❖

Skinned wheat berries (also called "hulled," "pearled," or "shelled" wheat berries) may be found at Middle Eastern groceries either whole or cracked. Wheat berries have to go through quite a lot to lose their skin. The grains are soaked, dried, then shattered with a large wooden or stone pestle—the skins that surround the kernels are thus rubbed off while the grains remain intact with a slightly polished appearance. The naked grains are washed again, then left in the sun to dry. Before cooking, usually in soups and pilafs, they are soaked again to soften and release their starches and aroma. If the grains are fresh, their texture will be creamy and their flavor superb. Even the soaking liquid can be used in desserts (see page 331) and provides a marvelous silkiness.

To keep these shelled grains from sticking to the pot, don't stir them while they cook.

RUSTIC PASTA–BASED SOUPS

In the eastern Mediterranean skinned wheat berries are crushed to make a kind of grits or groats—Armenian *gogod*, Turkish *yarma*, and Cretan *chondros*. I discovered that in central Turkey these grits are preferred to rice and bulgur in stuffings and as a substitute for bulgur in kibbeh-like confections. Turkish cooks like them for their soft texture, creamy appearance, and ability to carry other flavors, especially when poached in a well-seasoned liquid.

But for me the most interesting use of these grits in eastern Mediterranean cookery is in Turkish *tarhana*, Greek *trahana,* and Cretan *xinochondros*—dried nuggets of crushed wheat kernels cooked with sweet or fermented milk, then flavored and dried in the sun. To spare the chauvinist feelings of cooks from these three areas, I call them all "rustic pasta."

There are many versions of rustic pasta made with different combinations of milk (goat, sheep, or cow), grains (skinned wheat berries, semolina, or bulgur), and flavorings (dried mint, cornelian cherries, or *Hippomarathrum cristatum,* an unusual green herb in the dill family that grows around Izmir and is considered the ultimate).

There are formulas that add eggs and yeast to the crushed wheat, others that add buttermilk. Fresh milk makes rustic pasta sweet; buttermilk or yogurt makes it pungent and pleasantly sour. Some cooks add tomatoes and red peppers to color it. My favorite variations are the ones made with shelled wheat and yogurt (Turkish style) or lightly fermented goat's milk (Cretan style).

In Turkey the mixture of crushed wheat kernels and fermented milk is boiled until thick, with all the moisture evaporated, then the resulting dough is dropped in dollops onto large, wet sheets and left to dry in the sun. In the southeastern Turkish town of Kahramanmaras, famous for its commercial rustic pasta production, the kernels are mixed with yogurt and sun-dried for as long as a week to build up pungency.

There are various theories as to the origins of rustic pasta. The most popular is that it's the invention of people seeking a way to preserve their milk products as well as their wheat. Though in different countries the nuggets are made in different ways, the end result seems to have the same purpose—to keep milk products and wheat through the year for use in easily prepared foods.

If you like the taste of mild sourdough bread you will probably like rustic pasta. It's one of the most nourishing foods of the eastern Mediterranean. Since it is a delicious foundation for soups, I've developed an easy way to make it in a home dehydrator. (Drying homemade rustic pasta in a slow oven cooks it.) It is not useful to accelerate the drying process. Remember: the longer your rustic pasta takes to dry, the more delicious will be the dish in which you use it.

The commercial *trahana* found in Greek groceries can be used for the Spicy Lamb, Peppers, Tomato, and Rustic Pasta Soup (page 76). Otherwise, I urge you to make your own rustic pasta. I am extremely fond of the pungent Cretan-style version made with goat's milk. You can find fresh or canned goat's milk at almost any health food store.

So long as your finished rustic pasta nuggets are dry and hard as walnuts, they may be stored in cotton sacks in a cool cupboard or in a glass container in the refrigerator for up to a year.

HOMEMADE CRETAN RUSTIC PASTA (*Xinochondros*)

❧

Makes about 1 pound

My guru for all foods from the island of Crete is Mirsini Lambraki, author of a book on wild greens. One summer she kindly sent me a bag of her homemade *xinochondros*. I immediately fell in love with its exciting pungent aroma and flavor and put it to use in the recipes she also sent along.

Mirsini prepares her rustic pasta during the summer, then uses what she calls "this marvelous first material" during the winter months to prepare soups with or without meat, and potato and vegetable dishes. To use it in soups she simply drops it into the boiling liquid. In nonliquid dishes she soaks pieces in hot water for 10 minutes, then crumbles them into sautés and stews; or she soaks a lot, then serves it like a pilaf to accompany meat.

5 cups fresh goat's milk, or 1 quart canned goat's milk and 1 cup cow's milk

14 ounces to 1 pound skinned wheat, cracked (see Note)

1 tablespoon coarse salt

½ teaspoon freshly ground pepper

Step 1 must be done 3 to 4 days in advance.

1. Pour the milk into a glass bowl, cover with a clean cloth, and leave on the kitchen counter for 3 to 4 days, or until the surface is bubbling and there is a nice clean but sour aroma.

2. Shake the cracked wheat through an ordinary sieve to separate coarse and fine grains. In a heavy pot, bring the goat's milk to a rolling boil. Gradually add the coarse grains and cook, stirring constantly, over medium-high heat for 3 minutes. Add the remaining fine wheat and cook another 3 minutes, or until very thick. Makes about 1 quart. Stir in the salt and pepper and set aside, loosely covered with a cloth, for 1 day.

3. Spread dollops ½ inch thick on nonstick pans, plastic wrap, or plastic grids. Dry in a 105-degree dehydrator until bone dry on both sides, 1 to 3 days, depending upon the thickness of the *trahana*. For more even drying you can turn the pieces from time to time. If planning to keep the pasta a long time, you should raise the temperature to 145 degrees and dry out for at least 30 minutes, then reduce the temperature and dry out for up to 3 days.

4. When each pellet is as hard as a walnut and cold, store in a jar in a cool place, preferably the refrigerator. The pellets will keep up to a year. Use as directed in each recipe.

NOTE TO THE COOK: Skinned wheat is available at Armenian and Middle Eastern grocers or can be ordered (see "Mail-Order Sources"). For absolute freshness, it is advisable to buy the wheat whole but skinned. To crack skinned wheat at home, use a grain mill, or soak wheat for 2 hours. Drain well, roll dry, then crush in the work bowl of a food processor, or grind in batches in a blender.

CREAMY RUSTIC PASTA AND RED LENTIL SOUP WITH MINT AND BLACK PEPPER SWIRLS (*Turkey*)

Serves 4

*I*n the southeastern Turkish town of Cibin I watched Zeliha—a young, beautiful, Turkish-Armenian peasant woman—prepare her year's production of *tarhana*. She began with 25 pounds of cracked skinned wheat, 55 pounds of yogurt, and 1 pound of salt. She divided the cracked skinned wheat into three parts—coarse, fine, and flour—by using a series of fine and coarse strainers. This enabled her to cook the coarsest grains longer than the finer ones, holding back the strained flour for use at the end if her mixture didn't properly thicken.

She cooked the grain in a huge black pot, then quickly cooled it by ladling it into wide bowls. When it was cool enough to handle she gradually worked in the yogurt and salt, then placed dollops onto a large plastic sheet that she spread out on the roof of the house to dry in the sun for many days.

Later she showed me how to make this delicious *tarhana* and red lentil soup. After the ingredients had cooked, she took a handheld electric blender, plugged it in, plunged it into the lentils, and turned it on. In seconds the lentils and *tarhana* were churned to a beige-yellow cream. Zeliha prepared her mint and pepper oil, then stirred it into the soup, creating beautiful concentric Jackson Pollock–like swirls.

This is an ideal soup for an elegant dinner.

½ cup dried red lentils

1½ cups (about 5 ounces) crumbled homemade rustic pasta

½ teaspoon salt

3 cups vegetable, meat, or poultry stock, simmering

1 teaspoon Turkish red pepper paste (see "Mail-Order Sources")

3 tablespoons olive oil

1 teaspoon sieved black pepper

3 tablespoons crumbled dried mint, sieved to make 2 teaspoons

1. Pick over the lentils and place in a deep saucepan with 2 cups water. Bring to a boil, skim, reduce the heat, add the salt, and cook at a simmer for 5 minutes.

2. Meanwhile, soak the pasta in water 10 minutes and drain, squeezing out the excess moisture. Add the pasta, simmering stock, and red pepper paste to the soup and cook, covered, 45 minutes, stirring often. Remove and allow to cool slightly.

3. Use a slotted spoon to transfer the solids to the work bowl of a food processor and purée until smooth, then press through a strainer back into the soup. (Alternatively, use a handheld electric blender and grind until smooth.)

4. Just before serving, reheat the soup and thin with water or stock to a nice consistency. Correct the seasoning with salt to taste. In a small pan or skillet, heat the oil; add the black pepper and sieved mint; heat until sizzling. Pour over the soup in swirls. Cover, wait 5 minutes, and bring to the table.

NOTES TO THE COOK: When reheating this soup, if you notice it thickening, thin it with water and readjust the seasoning.

For best flavor, use imported Eqyptian dried mint (page 350).

SPICY LAMB, PEPPERS, TOMATO, AND RUSTIC PASTA SOUP (*Turkey*)

Serves 2

Rustic pasta can take a lot of seasoning, so when making this recipe don't skimp on the pepper. This rich satisfying soup should be served with crusty bread.

1 or 2 lamb shoulder chops (about ¾ pound), or 4 ounces ground lamb and 2 meaty lamb neck bones

½ cup crushed rustic pasta (page 71) or imported Greek *trahana*

2 teaspoons tomato paste

½ teaspoon Turkish red pepper flakes (page 351), or a dash of hot red pepper

2 tablespoons butter or oil

2 garlic cloves, peeled and finely minced

⅓ cup diced mild chili pepper such as poblano

1 large ripe tomato, peeled, seeded, and finely chopped

Salt

Freshly ground black pepper

2 tablespoons shredded flat-leaf parsley

1. Bone the lamb chops and use the bones and trimmings to make a simple broth. Boil the lamb bones for 30 minutes, skimming often. Grind the meat and set aside.

2. In a small bowl crush the pasta, then soften with the tomato paste and ¾ cup boiling lamb broth and set aside. After 10 minutes, add the red pepper and beat to a smooth purée and hold for step 4.

3. In a medium heavy saucepan, heat the butter and cook the garlic until soft but not brown. Add the ground meat and cook, stirring, until nicely browned and crumbled. Add the chili and tomato and cook, stirring, for 5 minutes.

4. Strain the meat broth; return 3 cups to the saucepan, mix in the reserved *trahana*, bring to a boil, and cook, covered, over medium-low heat for about 10 minutes, stirring often. Season to taste with salt and plenty of black pepper and serve at once sprinkled with fresh parsley.

SUMMER SORREL AND CHERVIL SOUP (*France*)

Makes 2 quarts, serving 6

Years ago, before we knew about "bad" cholesterol, I used to make a fabulous French sorrel soup using 6 egg yolks and 3 cups of heavy cream. Those were the days!

This version is a compromise, containing some saturated fat . . . but not much. Employing a culinary trick I learned from Turkish cooks (using yogurt as a thickening agent), I've cut way down on the egg yolks and cream. Had I eliminated them entirely, the soup would be too acidic.

This soup is delicious at room temperature or cold.

4 cups (32 ounces) plain yogurt without stabilizers

6 or 7 bunches fresh sorrel, washed and stemmed (1 pound)

Pinch coarse sea salt

1 tablespoon olive oil

¼ cup finely chopped scallions

1 quart degreased chicken stock

1 egg yolk

1 cup whole milk

1 tablespoon all-purpose flour

½ cup heavy cream

Freshly ground black or white pepper

4 tablespoons snipped fresh chervil

1. Drain the yogurt to 2 cups. Discard the liquid or reserve for some other purpose such as cooking vegetables.

2. Roughly chop the sorrel, place in a covered inert saucepan with a pinch of salt, and cook over low heat until broken down to a purée, about 5 minutes.

3. In a 3-quart saucepan, heat the oil; add the scallions, and cook, covered, for 2 minutes. Set aside to cool slightly. Put the sorrel, scallions, ½ cup stock, yogurt, egg yolk, ½ cup milk, and flour in the work bowl of a food processor and process until smooth. Pour back into the saucepan; add the remaining milk, cream, and remaining stock; and cook, 5 to 10 minutes, stirring constantly, until thickened and just beginning to boil. Remove from heat, thin with water to the desired consistency, and correct the seasoning with salt and pepper. Serve warm or cool with a sprinkling of snipped chervil.

CHICORY, MEATBALL,
AND PECORINO SOUP (*Italy*)

Serves 2

When I first tasted this dish at the splendid spa and hotel Il Melograno in Apulia it appeared on the menu as *Zuppa con Cicoria Seduta i Polpette* . . . meaning that the greens were "sitting" with no room to move around, since so many of them were crammed into the little serving bowls along with the meatballs, bread, and broth. In my recipe I've loosened things up a bit, but the liquid portion is still fairly small.

The meatballs are darling, tiny and light, made two by two by placing two small balls in the palm of one hand, covering them with the other hand, then gradually and steadily moving the hands in opposite directions.

If the chicory or frisée is bitter, soak in salted water for an hour or so.

This recipe will produce just enough soup for two.

Meatballs (2 dozen)

6 to 8 ounces finely ground lean veal

Salt

Freshly ground black pepper

Dash of grated nutmeg

1½ tablespoons shredded pancetta

2 tablespoons grated pecorino Romano

1 tablespoon chopped flat-leaf parsley

¼ cup stale cubes of crustless bread

2 tablespoons milk

1 egg yolk

1 teaspoon olive oil

¾ pound chicory or *frisée*, washed and shredded

1 clove garlic, peeled

2 tablespoons extra-virgin olive oil plus more for garnish

2 cups homemade chicken stock

2 stale slices country-style bread

½ cup peeled, seeded, and cubed tomatoes

½ cup grated pecorino Romano

1. Make the meatballs: In a mixing bowl, combine the ground veal with salt, pepper, grated nutmeg, the pancetta, cheese, and parsley.

2. Soak the crustless bread cubes in the milk and mash to a pulp with a flat spoon. Add to the meat with the egg yolk and olive oil. Delicately combine the mixture with your fingers.

3. Lightly oil the palms of each hand. Pinch off two marble-size bits of the meat and press each lightly to make compact. Then place both meatballs on one open palm, cover with the other palm, and move your hands in opposite directions, so that two smooth, delicate balls are obtained. Keep chilled until ready to cook.

4. Preheat the oven to 450 degrees.

5. Heat 1 cup lightly salted water in a deep saucepan, add the chicory and garlic, and cook until the greens are tender, 5 to 10 minutes. Remove the saucepan from the heat. Taste the cooking liquor; discard if bitter. Use a light stock or water instead. Discard the garlic.

6. Put 2 tablespoons olive oil in a shallow, 1½-quart heatproof serving dish and set over medium-high heat. Slip in the meatballs and cook them on all sides until they lose their color but do not brown. Spread the drained chicory and liquor or water from step 5 over the meatballs. Add the slices of stale bread, tomato cubes, and 2 cups warm stock. Sprinkle with grated cheese and a drizzle of olive oil and bake until the cheese is crusty and brown, about 5 minutes. Serve at once.

Summer *Harira* with Purslane and Spices (Morocco)

❦

Makes 3 quarts, serving 8

Since the Muslim calendar is lunar, the fasting month, called Ramadan, falls at a different time each year. But no matter the month, the fast is always broken with a soup.

In summer, the soup should be nutritious but also light. This delicious Moroccan summer *harira* is built around the delicious summer weed purslane.

Spice Mixture

½ teaspoon ground ginger

¾ teaspoon sweet paprika

¾ teaspoon ground cumin

¼ teaspoon finely ground black pepper

¼ teaspoon freshly grated nutmeg

2 cloves, crushed

Pinch crumbled saffron threads

¼ teaspoon ground turmeric

1. Combine the spice mixture well; makes 1 tablespoon. Toss the meat with 1 teaspoon of the spice mixture and set aside until ready to cook.

2. About 3 hours before serving, pick over the lentils, rinse in hot water, and soak for 1 hour.

3. Put the seasoned lamb and the bones in a 5-quart soup pot, and steam without any added fat, covered, until the meat turns light brown. Pour in 8 cups water and bring to the boil; skim; then add the onion, cinnamon stick, half the tomatoes, 1 teaspoon of the mixed spices, 1 teaspoon salt, and parsley sprigs. Return to the boil, skim once again, then simmer, covered, for 30 minutes.

4. Drain the lentils; add to the pot and bring back to a boil, skimming. Cover and reduce heat to low and cook for another 45 minutes. Discard the cinnamon stick and the lamb bones.

5. Meanwhile, rinse the rice and drain. In a second saucepan, combine the rice, remaining spice mixture, and 3 cups water. Bring to a boil and cook for 15 minutes. Add the remaining tomato, chopped parsley, cilantro, purslane, and 1 teaspoon salt and cook 5 minutes longer.

6. In a small bowl beat eggs, 2 tablespoons water, and lemon juice until foamy, about 2 minutes. Carefully add a ladleful of the meat broth to the eggs, stirring constantly. Pour the egg mixture into the simmering lentils, being very careful not to curdle the eggs. Immediately pour in the rice with its cooking liquid; stir thoroughly over gentle heat until thickened. Do not cover. Serve hot with a sprinkling of chopped cilantro, ground cinnamon, and lemon wedges.

2 lamb shoulder chops, bone in (about 1¼ pounds), trimmed of excess fat and cut into bite-size cubes, bones reserved

1 cup small dried brown lentils, preferably a mini-lentil such as Spanish pardina or Egyptian, Ethiopian, or Indian whole masoor dal

1 large onion, coarsely chopped

1 cinnamon stick

2 large juicy tomatoes, grated

2 teaspoons salt

2 to 3 sprigs fresh flat-leaf parsley plus ½ cup chopped

⅓ cup short- or medium-grain rice

¼ cup chopped fresh cilantro leaves plus more for garnish

2 cups (6 ounces) finely chopped purslane or shredded Swiss chard

2 large eggs

Juice of 1 lemon

Dash of ground cinnamon

Lemon wedges

GARLIC SOUP WITH LEAFY GREENS (*Spain*)

Serves 2

Here is a *sopa de ajo* as prepared in Valencia, a nourishing "comfort" soup that can be served year-round. Most Spanish garlic soups are simple marriages of garlic, bread, and olive oil. Here, assorted greens (spinach, chard, watercress, sometimes a little overgrown arugula) are added, their flavors harmonizing perfectly.

The sweet paprika used in Valencia is different in flavor from the smoky *pimentón de la Vera* variety recommended for other Spanish recipes in this book. But either variety will work. If you use Spanish chorizo, it, too, will impart the essential Spanish flavor.

Use any kind of meat, poultry, or vegetable broth or even water. Or, like most Valencian home cooks, use a light bouillon made with half a cube.

This simple soup of greens, paprika, and sausage is filling enough to make a light meal.

3 tablespoons olive oil

½ head garlic, separated into cloves, peeled and halved

¼ cup thinly sliced, semicured Spanish chorizo (optional)

¼ cup chopped onion or scallions

⅓ cup peeled, seeded, and cubed tomatoes

2 sprigs parsley leaves, slivered

2 cups stemmed and shredded mixed greens: chard, watercress, spinach, and arugula

¾ teaspoon Spanish sweet paprika or *pimentón de la Vera* (page 165)

2 cups light vegetable, poultry, or meat broth

Salt

Freshly ground pepper

2 farm-fresh eggs

4 strips stale peasant bread, crusts removed, toasted or fried

1. Heat the oil in a cazuela or deep skillet with the garlic cloves and chorizo, if using, and slowly fry, stirring often, until the cloves soften, 2 to 3 minutes. Transfer the garlic to a mortar.

2. Add the onions to the skillet and fry until softened. Stir in the tomato and parsley and cook until pulpy. Add the greens and cook, stirring, 1 to 2 minutes.

3. Crush the garlic to a thick paste and dissolve in hot water; add to the cazuela along with the *pimentón,* the broth, and salt and pepper. Bring to a boil and cook, stirring often, until the greens are just tender, about 10 minutes. Correct the seasoning with salt and pepper.

4. Break in the eggs and allow to poach without boiling. Sprinkle with a little paprika and serve over the toasted bread strips.

TUSCAN KALE AND BREAD SOUP (*Italy*)

Makes 8 to 10 cups, serving 6

Black kale (also called Tuscan kale and lacinata kale) is far more subtle and delicious than the common curly kale. Black-green and shaped like a palm leaf, it can be found in late autumn in farmers' markets. California farmers are now starting to grow it commercially for nationwide distribution. It's so good I'm convinced it will soon turn up in supermarkets. You can order it from Indian Rock Produce (see "Mail-Order Sources").

Collards or young red or Russian kale may be substituted, but the taste will not be quite as good.

An additional reason to make this soup is to create leftovers with which to make the famous thick Tuscan soup called *ribollita*. The wonderful Florentine version is made by bringing the leftovers to a gentle boil, adding chunks of dense stale bread, then simmering until very thick. Make it with your leftovers, or go on to the next recipe for a smashing Siennese *ribollita* with a crunchy top of crispy onions.

You can make this Tuscan Kale and Bread Soup in advance, then reheat it just before serving. Unlike many Tuscan vegetable soups, it's not normally served with grated cheese.

1 cup dried cannellini beans, Roman beans, or borlotti beans

1 sprig fresh rosemary

1½ teaspoon salt

3 large slices dried porcini mushroom

1¾ ounces pancetta, chilled or frozen

¼ cup olive oil

1 medium onion, peeled and coarsely chopped

1 small celery rib, thinly sliced

1 medium carrot, peeled and diced

1½ teaspoons minced garlic

1 pound Tuscan kale, or ½ pound tender kale and ½ pound Savoy cabbage

½ cup tomato purée

Pinch of mixed spices: nutmeg, cinnamon, and cloves

Freshly ground black pepper

12 slices dense country bread, grilled or toasted and rubbed generously with a garlic clove

A cruet of extra-virgin olive oil

1. Pick over the beans. In a large saucepan, soak the beans overnight in cold water to cover.

2. Drain the beans and cover with 2½ quarts fresh cold water. Add the rosemary sprig. Bring to a boil, lower the heat, and cook at the simmer, partially covered, until the beans are tender, about 1 hour. Midway add ½ teaspoon salt. Discard the herb sprig.

3. Wash and soak the mushroom slices in 1 cup warm water for 10 minutes. Shred the pancetta to make about ¼ cup.

4. Heat ¼ cup olive oil in a wide saucepan over medium heat. Add the pancetta, onion, celery, carrot, and garlic and cook until the vegetables are soft and golden, about 10 minutes.

5. Meanwhile, wash the kale and strip the leaves from the stems. Finely chop the leaves; add to the saucepan and cook, stirring, another 2 minutes. Add the mushrooms, soaking liquid, 1 teaspoon salt, the tomato purée, and the mixed spices and continue cooking over low heat for 10 minutes.

6. Drain the beans, reserving the cooking liquid. Push half the cooked beans through a food mill fitted with a fine blade, or purée them in a food processor. Add the puréed beans, whole beans, and about 6 cups of the cooking liquid to the saucepan; bring to a boil and simmer for 20 minutes. (The soup can be prepared earlier in the day up to this point. When cool, cover and set in a cool place until ready to reheat, 20 minutes before serving.)

7. Correct the seasoning of the soup with salt and plenty of black pepper and reheat to boiling. Place slices of grilled bread in a 3-quart soup tureen made of earthenware, stoneware, or porcelain and pour on the hot soup. Let rest for 10 minutes before serving. Pass a cruet of extra-virgin olive oil at the table.

CRUNCHY-TOPPED *RIBOLLITA* FROM SIENNA (*Italy*)

To use your leftover Tuscan kale soup to make Sienna-style *ribollita*: Place the leftovers in a shallow terra-cotta dish. Spread a layer of red onions sliced paper thin on top and brush with an aromatic and fruity olive oil. Bake in a preheated 350-degree oven until the oil begins to boil and the onions form a golden brown crust, 45 to 60 minutes. Remove from the oven and serve after a rest of l0 to 15 minutes. Accompany this version of *ribollita* with a pepper mill and a cruet of fresh olive oil.

MIDDLE EASTERN CHARD AND LENTIL SOUP (*Syria*)

❄

Makes 10 cups, serving 8

Here's a light soup for all seasons: in summer serve it cool or at room temperature to refresh; in winter serve it hot to nourish. It's delicious with grilled bread topped with crushed oily black olives and sprinkled with oregano.

This soup is even better when you add another green to the chard. In early spring I combine chard and dandelions; in summer, chard and arugula; in winter, chard and spinach.

Use any lentil you like. For me the most savory is the small Spanish pardina lentil available through Phipps Ranch (see "Mail-Order Sources") or the small brown lentils available at Middle Eastern and Indian groceries.

A potato, cut paper thin so it will dissolve, is cooked along with the lentils to thicken the soup and give it a rich creamy texture.

1 cup dark mini-lentils such as Spanish pardina or Egyptian, Ethiopian, or Indian whole masoor dal

1 teaspoon salt

2 quarts light chicken stock (optional)

1 medium potato, peeled and sliced paper thin

1 cup chopped onion

3 tablespoons olive oil

8 large Swiss chard leaves

1 pound leafy greens such as spinach, dandelions, arugula, watercress, beet greens, kale, or a mixture

¼ cup roughly chopped fresh cilantro leaves

1 tablespoon minced garlic

⅓ cup freshly squeezed lemon juice

1. Wash and pick over the lentils. Place lentils in a saucepan and cover with the stock or 2 quarts water salted with 1 teaspoon salt. Bring to a boil and skim off any foam that surfaces. Add the potato, partially cover, and cook for 20 minutes.

2. In a large skillet, slowly brown the onion in the olive oil. Meanwhile, wash, stem, and roughly shred the greens. You should have about 1 packed quart. Add the cilantro and garlic to the skillet and sauté for a minute or two, then stir in the greens and allow them to wilt, covered. Scrape the contents of the skillet, including the oil, into the saucepan and continue cooking another 20 minutes, or until thick and soupy. Stir in the lemon juice and serve hot, lukewarm, or cool.

LAMB SOUP WITH GREEN GARLIC, LEEKS, AND YOGURT (*Turkey*)

❧

Makes 3 quarts, serving 6

This dish, one of my all-time favorite yogurt dishes, has the qualities of both a soup and a stew, so rich and satisfying you probably won't need a main course to follow.

Green garlic shoots, which resemble baby leeks but in fact are unformed garlic cloves, appear at farmers' markets and in fine food stores in early spring. They're as subtly garlicky as young leeks are delicately oniony. When you combine the two you get something really special. When purchasing green garlic, look for long, firm stalks with crisp fresh leaves. (See page 49 for more details on this wonderful ingredient.)

If you have a kitchen garden and want to grow your own green garlic, separate a head of garlic that has sprouted, divide the cloves, and push each into the ground with the sprout pointing up. Don't bury them too deep. Keep the soil moist. In less than three months you'll be able to harvest fresh stalks.

I wrote extensively about yogurt soups in *The Cooking of the Eastern Mediterranean*. Home cooks in the region have taught me an unusual method of handling yogurt so it doesn't break apart during cooking, while still producing silky, creamy yogurt dishes. Step 5 below explains the technique in detail.

This soup is served with a final last-moment swirl of sizzling oil and butter and ground spices on top.

1. One day in advance, drain the yogurt to make 3 cups.

2. The following day, place the meat and 2 quarts water in a 4- or 5-quart saucepan. Bring to a boil and skim. Add the drained chickpeas, reduce the heat, cover, and simmer for 30 minutes.

3. Meanwhile, trim the root ends and remove any yellowing tips from the green garlic and leeks. Make ¼-inch slices crosswise, using approximately 9 inches of each firm stalk. You should have approximately 2 quarts. Wash and drain. When the soup has cooked 30 minutes, add the green garlic, leeks, and 1 teaspoon salt, and cook 30 minutes longer, or until the garlic shoots and leeks are meltingly tender. Remove from the heat and allow to cool. (If the meat is not tender, scoop out the greens and continue cooking. Return the greens to the soup when the meat is also very tender.)

4. Remove the meat; discard the bones and cut into bite-size pieces. Sprinkle with salt and freshly ground black pepper and return to the soup. Reheat the soup to simmering.

6 cups plain yogurt

3 small spring lamb shanks (2 pounds), or 8 ounces boneless shoulder of lamb, trimmed of all fat and cut into large chunks

½ cup dried chickpeas, soaked overnight and drained

1½ pounds green garlic, untrimmed

1½ pounds leeks, untrimmed

1 teaspoon salt plus more to taste

Freshly ground pepper

½ cup whole milk

1 whole egg

1 tablespoon all-purpose flour

1½ tablespoons olive oil

Pinch of red pepper flakes

MINT AND BLACK PEPPER SWIRLS

2 teaspoons freshly ground black pepper

3 rounded tablespoons dried mint leaves

2 tablespoons unsalted butter

5. In a second large saucepan, whisk the yogurt with the milk, egg, flour, and 1 tablespoon oil, until completely smooth. Set the yogurt over low heat and turn off the heat under the soup. Gradually stir 2 cups of the hot soup base into the yogurt in order to raise its temperature. *When the temperature of the yogurt is hotter than the temperature of the soup, pour the yogurt back into the soup and set it on medium heat, stirring, until it just comes to a boil, about 15 minutes.* Immediately remove from the heat. Correct the seasoning with salt and a pinch of red pepper flakes. Transfer to a soup tureen.

6. To make the mint and pepper swirls, press the ground black pepper and the dried mint leaves through a fine sieve directly over the soup to form a small pile. Heat the remaining ½ tablespoon oil and the butter in a small pan, bring to a sizzle, and pour over the pepper and mint. Stir gently to create Jackson Pollock–like swirls. Cover the soup and wait 5 minutes before serving.

With thanks to Ayfer Ünsal for sharing this recipe.

CARDOONS

✧

They look like enormous stalks of celery and taste somewhat similar to artichoke, and whenever they appear in markets around Christmas they're snapped up by Italian-Americans, French-Americans and North African–Americans so fast you can barely get a crack at them. The demand is there, but the quantity is small.

When cardoons are available, look for thick, meaty ribs in tight bundles of crisp stalks without fibrous insides. Since the outside two or three stalks must be discarded, buy the largest bunches you see, 3 to 4 pounds. You will need about 1½ pounds edible parts of cardoon to serve four. Avoid cardoons whose stalk interiors are spongy and pink-hued. Better to change your menu than try to make a dish with these!

At home, remove the tough outer ribs and strip any jagged leaves off the tender inner stalks. Using a vegetable peeler, pare each stalk toward the base, and cut it into pieces 3 inches long. As you work, drop the prepared cardoon and center core into a bowl of acidulated water (juice of one lemon per 3 cups water) to avoid blackening.

When working with this vegetable, keep half a lemon around to rub over your fingers to keep them from darkening. The secret to keeping cardoon pieces celadon green is to simmer them in salted water, lemon juice, and plenty of flour. Put 4 cups water in a saucepan, whisk in ¼ cup flour and 1 tablespoon salt, and bring to a boil, whisking often to prevent lumps. Add 6 more cups water, 2½ tablespoons lemon juice, and 1 tablespoon olive oil, and bring to a boil. Add the prepared cardoons and cook, covered, until tender, 30 to 45 minutes. Remove from the heat, but do not drain until ready to use. Cardoons left in their cooking water too long lose their savor as well as their unctuous quality.

Yes, preparation takes time, and when you finish cleaning you discover there's not much left. Still, cardoons are well worth the effort on account of their succulent flavor.

There are at least six varieties of cardoons found around the Mediterranean, including a smooth solid type with wide but not-too-thick stalks and pale green leaves, the long Spanish variety with large broad leaves, the kind with artichoke-type leaves but free from spines, and a type from the Monferrato region of Piedmont that the locals dip raw into their garlicky *bagna cauda*.

If you find you've bought a not-quite-perfect cardoon, you can still use the stalks in soups, slivered in risottos, or as part of the vegetable mixture in a couscous. With most cardoons, the only portions that can be eaten *raw* are the hearts—not much help if you're serving several people, since you'll need bunches and bunches to supply hearts for everyone.

All cardoons are somewhat bitter. Every cardoon I've prepared, going back to 1970, had to be blanched or at least soaked in salted water to rid it of bitterness.

To store cardoons, wrap the base end in wet paper toweling, then slip into a plastic bag and loosely close. Fresh cardoons should keep for more than a week. Don't try preparing them in advance.

The slower the cooking, the smoother the texture. Recently I read about an old Jewish-Italian technique in which cardoons are simmered 2 to 3 hours in plenty of olive oil flavored with mint to acquire silkiness.

For North African stews, cook cardoon pieces for 15 minutes in boiling salted water to remove bitterness, then drain, peel with a small knife, and finish in a long slow braise with meat and other vegetables.

FRYING CROUTONS

Here's a terrific way to make wonderfully crisp croutons without using a lot of oil. All you need is some partially stale bread cubes (not bone-dry), a little olive oil (about 2 tablespoons for ½ cup), a slotted spoon, and a nonstick skillet.

Tilt the skillet up at a 45-degree angle over the burner; warm the oil over medium heat just until it begins to spread. Add the stale bread cubes, not more than ½ cup at a time. Keeping the skillet tilted, fry the bread in the oil just until small bubbles appear around the bread cubes. Lower the heat slightly and continue to fry the bread cubes, turning them from time to time with a slotted spoon, until they are crisp and golden. Using the spoon, slide them to the other side of the skillet—the side that has no oil—and then remove them. Drain on a paper towel.

If you wish to make a second batch, take the skillet off the burner and allow the oil to cool before adding more bread cubes. If the oil is hot, too much of it will be absorbed by the bread.

And why does this method work? I consulted Harold McGee, author of *On Food and Cooking*. He suggested that heating the partially stale bread and oil together allows the bread to crisp from within as any remaining moisture vaporizes. Since there's no place for the steam to go but out, the steam pressure keeps the oil from saturating the bread. At the end, when you slide the cubes to the nonoily side of the tilted skillet, any oil remaining on the bread can run free.

PROVENÇAL CREAMY CARDOON POTAGE (*France*)

Serves 4

My late friend Mario Ruspoli gave me this recipe twenty years ago. I didn't publish it because in those days cardoons were difficult to find. Now that they're in supermarkets, the time to publish has come. This delicious celadon-colored soup makes a good introduction to cardoons. Remember not to cook cardoons in aluminum, and purée them using only stainless steel equipment, lest they oxidize and lose their color.

1 bundle fresh cardoon, 3 to 4 pounds

1 tablespoon butter

1 tablespoon extra-virgin olive oil plus more for frying

2 tablespoons shredded pancetta

¾ cup minced onion

All-purpose flour for dusting

7 to 8 cups rich chicken or turkey broth, simmering

1½ cups diced stale bread

Salt

Freshly ground black pepper

1. Clean the cardoons, and simmer them as directed above, then cut into small pieces to make about 1 quart (see page 88).

2. In a deep skillet heat the butter and 1 tablespoon olive oil; add the pancetta and onion and cook, stirring, for 1 minute. Drain and dry the cardoons, lightly dust each piece with flour, add to the skillet, and fry, turning on all sides, until just lightly golden. Stir in the hot broth, cover, and cook until tender, about 45 minutes.

3. Push the contents of the pan through the fine blade of a stainless steel food mill or purée in an electric blender and press through a stainless steel sieve. Discard any debris or strings. Return the purée to the saucepan and simmer 10 minutes.

4. In a small skillet heat olive oil to a depth of ¼ inch. When hot add the bread and fry until golden brown on all sides. Tilt the skillet to let the oil run to one side, then scoop up the croutons and drain on paper toweling. Reserve the oil for another time after straining through a sieve. Season the soup with salt and pepper to taste. Serve hot with the croutons.

VARIATION: Thicken the soup with 2 beaten eggs and 1 tablespoon lemon juice by cooking below the boil and stirring until thick and creamy. Sprinkle with chopped chervil and parsley and serve at once.

Provençal Pistou with Aged Gouda (France)

Serves 6

I'm indebted to the Provençal food writer and antiques dealer Michel Biehn for a single line in his *Le Cahier de Recettes Provençales* in which he mentions that a Dutch Edam with red annatto coloring is his cheese of choice to garnish pistou. I tried an *aged* Gouda with my own pistou recipe, instead of my usual Gruyère, with sensational results.

1 cup dried white beans soaked overnight in water

¾ pound fresh green beans, cut into ½-inch lengths

Salt

¾ to 1 pound potatoes, peeled and thinly sliced

¾ to 1 pound young zucchini, scrubbed and thinly sliced

½ cup chopped red onion

½ cup crumbled noodles such as vermicelli

¼ teaspoon freshly ground black pepper

Pistou

About 2 dozen small sprigs fresh basil

5 large cloves garlic, peeled and green shoots removed.

2 red ripe tomatoes, halved, seeded, grated, and cooked down to ½ cup

½ teaspoon freshly ground black pepper

4 ounces aged Gouda, grated to make 1 cup

⅓ cup extra-virgin olive oil

1. In a large enameled saucepan cover the beans with 3 quarts fresh water. Bring to a boil and cook 30 minutes. Add the green beans and salt and cook, covered, for another 30 minutes.

2. In a separate pot cook the potatoes, zucchini, and onions in water to cover over medium heat until the vegetables are mushy. Remove from the heat and crush with a long wire whisk. Add the beans, green beans, and pasta and cook for 5 minutes. Add the black pepper and salt to taste. Allow to cool 30 minutes.

3. Meanwhile make the pistou: Crush or purée the basil leaves with the garlic in a mortar or blender to make a smooth paste. Loosen with the crushed tomatoes, then beat in the pepper, grated cheese, and olive oil in a steady stream. Allow flavors to blend for 30 minutes.

4. Put the pistou in a deep wide dish or soup tureen. Gradually stir in some of the liquid from the soup. Fold in the vegetables and pasta. If necessary, thin with a little cool water to make about 3 quarts soup. Correct the seasoning with salt and pepper. Pistou is best served tepid.

4

Appetizers

DIPS

MOSHE BASSON'S
STEWED LEAFY GREENS WITH TAHINI (*Israel*)

Serves 4 as a mezze

This savory dish was originally made with mallow leaves, a green that grows abundantly around Jerusalem. Mallow was the green that Jews and Arabs alike ate during difficult times. In fact it was so prevalent in dishes during the austere times following Israel's independence (mallow "meatballs," mallow soup, mallow dips, stuffed mallow leaves, etc.) that people grew sick of it.

Now a brilliant Israeli chef, Moshe Basson, has reintroduced mallow with great success at his restaurant Eucalyptus in Jerusalem. Use chard, spinach, or a mixture of the two as a substitute.

1 pound young, mild-flavored leafy greens such as mallow, lamb's-quarters, Swiss chard, flat-leaf spinach, or 1 cup fully cooked mixed leafy greens, finely chopped

1 clove garlic, crushed

1 tablespoon olive oil

½ cup homemade tahini sauce (see Note)

Salt

Freshly ground black pepper

Ground sumac

1. Steam the greens until tender and drain well. Press to express all moisture.

2. In a small skillet over medium-low heat sauté the garlic in the oil until golden, 2 to 3 minutes. Add the cooked greens and cook, stirring, 1 minute. Set aside to cool.

3. In a bowl combine the greens with 5 tablespoons of the prepared tahini sauce, mixing until completely blended. Correct the seasoning with salt and pepper. Place in a shallow dish. Thin the remaining tahini with water until it is the consistency of a creamed soup. Drizzle over the greens and sprinkle with ground sumac.

NOTE: To make ½ cup homemade tahini sauce, blend 4 tablespoons tahini with 3 tablespoons lemon juice in the workbowl of a food processor. Add 3 tablespoons ice water, salt, and 1 crushed clove garlic and process until smooth. Thin with additional cold water to make ½ cup.

Parsley-Tahini-Smothered
Baby Chickpeas, Musbacha (Israel)

Serves 6 as part of a mezze or snack

The search for "the best hummus" (the classic Middle Eastern chickpea and tahini concoction) is a national passion in Israel, where the expression "let's go wipe" refers to using a piece of pita bread to wipe up this delectable dip. Israeli gastronomes will argue endlessly about such matters as whether in a proper hummus the chickpeas *must* be peeled or whether tahini sauce will be ruined if refrigerated.

Here's a story I heard from my Israeli friend Dalia Carmel. In 1997, a young Israeli journalist named Sheri Ansky was brought by a male friend to the Arab town of Beth'chanina near Jerusalem to taste a particular hummus variation called *musbacha*, a "dish of magic." As they drove to the cafe where it was served, her friend told her, "You will soon eat one of the finest renditions of hummus I have ever tasted, which will probably not be available again for a long time. In a few days demolition will begin in this sector, and who knows? Perhaps this cafe will be put off-limits."

As they passed through various checkpoints, her friend explained that he had learned of this cafe from a Palestinian journalist colleague who, taking him there, had said as a friendly taunt, "As an Israeli, you may not appreciate the magic of this *musbacha*, since you come from a culture that reduces the hummus experience to a mere 'wipe.'"

When Sheri and her friend arrived at the cafe, it was filled with customers—all Palestinian men. When the bowl of *musbacha* came, Sheri found it covered with chopped parsley and delicious beyond words. She also felt that it wasn't really a hummus dish, rather that it transcended hummus. Among other things she noticed that the chickpeas were much smaller than any she had seen before, were not mashed, and had a far spicier flavor.

Though Sheri had promised her friend that, on account of the tense political situation, she would not return to the cafe alone, she found herself over the following days yearning for the taste of this *musbacha*. So she found another friend, a fellow hummus fanatic, who agreed to take her back.

Getting lost en route to the cafe, they stopped to ask a policeman for directions. The cop advised them to turn around, but Sheri refused. After all, she told him, she was seeking a "dish of magic."

Finally, when they found and entered the cafe, the Palestinian customers stared at them with daggers in their eyes. The owner invited them to eat in the kitchen rather than in the dining room, since the political situation was now even more tense than the week before.

Though unafraid ("What would they do to me? Bombard me with chickpeas?"), Sheri agreed, thinking that perhaps in the kitchen she might learn the secret of the dish. In fact, the owner did reveal a great deal, among other things, that the flavor of these uniquely small chickpeas emerged only after five hours of cooking.

As they were talking, the owner, removing a thick layer of foam from a fresh batch of simmering chickpeas, told her more: "These are not the regular chickpeas you know but are smaller and darker with very thick skins which must be removed."

As Sheri was taking notes, a pressure cooker on the stove started to rattle, whistle, and make ominous explosive sounds. Suddenly the cafe owner stopped talking. He just stared at the jiggling pressure cooker top. Sheri stared at it too. No further words were exchanged. Sheri understood this silence as a comment by the owner on the truly explosive political situation, his way of telling her it would be best if she ate quickly and left.

Sheri Anski's conclusion: it might be a very long time before she could return to eat the dish again, so, until better days, she would have to make her own magical *musbacha* at home.

After I heard this story, I knew I too had to try to make this "dish of magic." I knew that there were several cultivars of chickpeas in the Middle East: the large succulent garbanzos and the smaller, darker, spicier thick-skinned variety called *kara mkasser* in Turkey, and *kala channa* in India. (Some cooks from the Greek island of Sifnós and on Cyprus claim that their versions of chickpea soup, *rivithia*, are superior because of the unique flavor of this smaller chickpea.)

These smaller chickpeas are, according to the Indian food expert Julie Sahni, the same type used to make the chickpea flour used in Indian puff breads, French *socca,* and Ligurian *farinata.* They differ in flavor and size because of the drier growing areas in which they are cultivated.

At an Indian store in San Francisco I searched some out and then soaked them for 24 hours, following Julie's advice to change the water often to avoid fermentation and under no circumstances to add baking soda or salt ("If you do, the peas will never soften."). I then proceeded to peel them, truly an act of faith, since these chickpeas are about one-third the size of normal plump chickpeas. I skinned the chickpeas by rubbing the soaked peas against one another under water, then removed the peels as they floated to the top. I then cooked the peas the requisite 5 hours. The resulting dish was extremely tasty, with a meaty flavor.

Every once in a while I draw a "line in the sand," rejecting a difficult method in favor of an easier one. Generally I don't like to compromise, but there comes a point when the extra work is just too much. Thus, the following recipe, which uses ordinary chickpeas. It makes a fast, fine, indeed excellent version of *musbacha*.

(continued)

1 cup dried chickpeas, soaked overnight in water to cover

6 small cloves garlic, peeled

Coarse salt

9 tablespoons sesame seed paste (tahini), stirred in the jar

Juice of 1½ lemons

3 tablespoons ice water or more to taste

1 bunch flat-leaf parsley, stemmed and finely chopped (½ cup)

1 serrano or jalapeño chile, cored, seeded, and finely chopped

Extra-virgin olive oil

Freshly ground black pepper

1. Drain the chickpeas. Simmer the chickpeas in plenty of lightly salted water for 1 hour or until tender.

2. Meanwhile crush the garlic to a purée with 2 or 3 pinches of coarse salt. Makes about 2 teaspoons.

3. In the workbowl of a food processor, combine the sesame seed paste, half of the garlic, ¼ cup lemon juice, and a good pinch of salt until blended. Add enough ice water to make the mixture the consistency of smooth mayonnaise. Fold in all but 1 tablespoon of the parsley and correct the salt. Set aside to mellow and develop flavor.

4. When the chickpeas are tender, allow to cool, then mix with the remaining garlic and lemon juice, green chili, and enough olive oil to coat the chickpeas. Season with salt and pepper. Place the chickpeas on a shallow serving dish, then spread the parsley-tahini sauce on top. Garnish with more chopped parsley and a drizzle of olive oil.

SHREDDED CABBAGE AND TAHINI DIP (*Egypt*)

Serves 2 to 4

This salad, actually a dip of shredded cabbage and tahini seasoned with ground cumin, is delicious with grilled fish steaks.

The tahini sauce should be made many hours in advance in order to have time to mellow, while the cabbage should be added at the last minute, so as not to lose its texture. To ensure crunchiness, soak the cabbage leaves in ice water for at least 2 hours before placing them in the creamy dressing.

½ small head white cabbage, finely shredded (3 cups)

1 clove garlic, peeled

½ teaspoon coarse salt plus more to taste

½ cup sesame seed paste (tahini)

¼ cup fresh lemon juice or, in season, lemon juice mixed with the juice of bitter orange

Ground cumin

1. Soak the cabbage in ice water 2 to 3 hours.

2. Make a traditional tahini sauce: crush the garlic to a purée with the salt. In the workbowl of a food processor, blend the tahini with the lemon juice and crushed garlic until the mixture is white and tightens. Add ¼ cup cold water and blend until smooth. Allow to mellow a few hours for the best flavor. Taste for salt and serve garnished with pinches of ground cumin.

3. Just before serving, combine the cabbage and tahini and spread over grilled fish.

With thanks to Nora George for sharing this recipe.

BULGUR

❖

"As an Anatolian I might say I was born with a spoonful of bulgur in my mouth," My friend Turkish food writer Ayfer Ünsal tells me, half joking. She lives in the town of Gaziantep, one of the oldest continuously populated cities in Turkey. "It's been a staple in our cuisine for thousands of years."

Though there's no particular season for eating bulgur, there is one for preparing it. When you purchase bulgur, you're buying a grain that's already cooked. Thus bulgur is a *cooked* by-product of wheat, not to be confused (as it often is) with cracked wheat, a grain that has not been cooked.

The process, Ayfer explained, begins right after the wheat harvest. "Up until fifty years ago we had a ceremony to celebrate the harvest. Everyone who wanted to make bulgur would go to a special public horse-powered mill in the countryside. The women, our grand-mothers, would stay there for two days boiling hard wheat kernels until they swelled, drying the kernels on flat roofs, then cracking and sieving them to separate the bulgur by size. During this period, when our grandmothers cooked and worked together, and everyone ate bulgur morning, noon, and night, many new bulgur dishes were invented."

Two qualities have kept bulgur popular in the eastern Mediterranean: nutritional value and flavor. In this part of the world a well-seasoned bulgur pilaf is considered worthy of being served at a wedding banquet. Bulgur is popular not only in Turkish cooking but also in Armenian, Jewish, Arab, Greek, Assyrian, and Kurdish cooking—the cuisines of all the eastern Mediterranean peoples who lived under the Ottoman Empire.

Bulgur comes in four precooked grain sizes.

Extra-coarse is used for steaming or for simmering in soups.

Large grain is used primarily for pilafs (see page 280), and dishes such as Summer Red Oil *Köfte* (page 100).

Medium grain is used to make the fermented drink *boza*, stuffings for grape leaves and vegetables, and desserts where it's cooked with a type of grape molasses called *pekmez*.

Fine grain is used in salads like tabbouleh and *kisir* (pages 154 and 156), in the *Köfte* with Scrambled Eggs, Tomatoes, and Parsley (page 104), and for all the famous *kibbehs* of the Middle East.

There's also a fifth highly exotic extra-fine-grain bulgur called *ufak simit* in Turkish, which I call "bulgur dust," not readily available in the United States. It's actually the fallout or powdery debris derived from shaking freshly ground fine-grain bulgur. This much-prized unique-tasting bulgur, which goes rancid very quickly, is used to produce texturally smooth patties made at the time bulgur is ground. See the Walnut *Köfte* (page 103) in which using fine grain bulgur simulates the qualities of *ufak simit*.

I think of bulgur as the eastern Mediterranean equivalent of Italian pasta, a tremendously versatile food that can be prepared in numerous ways. Certainly to an eastern Mediterranean cook, bulgur can do almost anything. Its graininess, earthiness, and very humbleness enable it to be pushed in numerous directions from soups to desserts. It can be the grain part of *kibbeh*, the basis of a pilaf, or a binder for greens as in a *tabbouleh*, or it can be moistened and then shaped in a great number of different ways in a whole category of round- or oval-shaped foods known as *köfte*.

In southeastern Turkey, the making of *köfte*, parallel to the Middle Eastern obsession with *kibbeh*, has reached cult proportions. *Köfte*, like *kibbeh*, can be consumed cooked or raw. Raw bulgur kneaded with chopped vegetables, oil, and spices is shaped into cylinders, triangles, or patties that make wonderful rich snacks and lunch dishes, especially in summer when they're wrapped in cooked grape leaves or pieces of romaine, then devoured like tacos.

The secret to using bulgur effectively in *köfte* is knowing how to handle it. I had always been taught that bulgur should be moistened with water and then worked, but the women of southeastern Turkey taught me ways of imbuing it with flavor by moistening it with something tasty such as the juice of fresh tomatoes.

Here are some "secrets" for altering texture and coaxing extra flavor out of bulgur when making *köfte:*

1. To soften bulgur, blend in some grated onion with or without some wet stale bread.
2. To lighten a well-kneaded mound of bulgur, laden with tomato and red pepper paste, fold in some scrambled eggs.
3. To keep thin bulgur shells from breaking when fried, work some cooked and mashed potato into the dough.
4. To keep bulgur from turning mushy (in Turkey a tiny amount of toothiness is considered correct), work in some salt.

Summer Red Oil Köfte (Turkey)

❧

Serves 4 as a snack

*T*he following *köfte* recipe comes from the town of Halfeti, built on the Euphrates River. The Euphrates! I was thrilled to be there, so near the cradle of civilization. The surface of the river seemed languid, the water a deep turquoise, but there were, my friend Ayfer Ünsal told me, strong currents beneath.

Strong political currents too. Halfeti was once an important government seat. The Armenian popes lived near here between the eleventh and fourteenth centuries. Now most of these ruins as well as magnificent recently discovered Roman mosaics will be lost when a major dam project is completed in the year 2001.

Ayfer is much involved with local efforts to excavate the mosaics before the sites are under water, for the dam project cannot be postponed, and time is running out. Just two days before my arrival, the mayor of Halfeti had a visit from the police. He had entertained a group of Armenian-Americans, visiting under the auspices of a Turkish and Armenian people-to-people program. The police wanted to know whether "these people" were merely sightseeing or had come to reclaim their family lands.

Politics are complicated here. I sat watching as Ayfer met with the mayor and town dignitaries over this latest crisis. They spoke rapid Turkish, and I couldn't understand a word, but did comprehend one thing: she was young and the only woman in the room, yet these Turkish men listened to her with great respect.

The meeting over, we adjourned to another building where two cooks, Günay Özal and Erminia Baydilek, prepared our lunch. Günay, assigned to teach me to make *köfte*, is a widow with five children living in Halfeti. Wearing the pantaloons typical of women of the Anatolian countryside and a kerchief around her head, she makes her living cooking for guests.

I found her seated on the floor with everything she needed for the lesson within reach. On one side of a tray were piles of grated onion, cubed tomatoes, garlic, and finely chopped red and green peppers, along with little piles of spices, including cumin, black and red pepper, and salt. On the other side a mound of cubed stale bread was waiting to be soaked, while in the center there was a pile of coarse-grain bulgur.

At first Günay seemed a little distant. She wanted to be sure I'm not the sort of American cook who uses powdered garlic. But after a few minutes of chat she warmed up. Then the lesson began.

She started by kneading the grated onion with the garlic and red pepper, creating a homogeneous mass. Then slowly she added some of the bulgur, then a little cubed tomato, then some pepper paste followed by spices and chopped green pepper, working the dough with her fingers as if playing a piano, feeling her way toward the proper proportions and consistency.

After soaking the bread in water, she went back to her kneading, adding a little more of this and then a little more of that, always feeling her way toward her desired result. Finally she squeezed the soaked bread, then worked it too into the bulgur, kneading for 10 minutes more.

Finally, satisfied that her bulgur had turned soft but not mushy, she added parsley, mint, and olive oil, then shaped the mixture into 1¼-inch-long cylinders.

"I know they're done when they hold their shape," she told me, confiding that the secret of the lightness of her *köfte* is her special addition of soaked bread. She patted several of the cylinders the way a mother might pat the rear of a freshly diapered baby, then added a final tablespoon of oil to coat them and make them shiny.

She told me that if the mixture is not shaped, it will keep for three days in the refrigerator. She served her *köfte* with mint and parsley leaves, hot pepper, and some boiled grape leaves for wrapping.

When I asked her why she chose to knead large-grain bulgur when she could have kneaded fine-grain with a lot less work, she responded that large-grain bulgur absorbs more ingredients and thus creates more flavorful *köfte*.

If the idea of kneading bulgur so long turns you off, you are not alone. I'm not crazy about doing so much handwork myself. Happily a heavy-duty mixer with a paddle will simulate the hand-kneading process. Don't use a food processor as you would when simulating the stone mortar-and-pestle pounding of bulgur and meat for kibbeh. Kibbeh is supposed to be crushed and blended, while *köfte* must be kneaded to stimulate the absorption of flavors and swelling of the grain.

(continued)

¼ cup grated onion

1 teaspoon garlic, crushed with ¾ teaspoon salt

¾ teaspoon mildly hot red pepper such as Turkish or Aleppo red pepper, or a mixture of hot and sweet Hungarian paprika

1 cup medium- or large-grain bulgur

1½ tablespoons tomato paste

2 teaspoons Turkish red pepper paste

3 tablespoons finely chopped fresh green pepper

1 small red ripe tomato, peeled, seeded, and cubed

1 cup soft white bread crumbs sprinkled with water to soften for 10 minutes then squeezed dry to ⅓ cup

⅓ cup chopped mixed herbs: parsley and fresh mint

About 2 tablespoons extra-virgin olive oil

Salt

Freshly ground black pepper

Boiled grape leaves or fresh Romaine leaves

In the bowl of a heavy-duty mixer fitted with a paddle, working on slow speed, blend the onion, crushed garlic, dried red pepper and bulgur until completely combined, 2 minutes. Gradually and alternately add the tomato and red pepper pastes, green pepper, and tomato cubes with the machine set on medium speed. When the bulgur forms a moist ball similar to a ball of dough, about 5 minutes, add the bread crumbs and blend 1 minute more. Work in the herbs and 1 tablespoon olive oil. Makes about 2 cups. Wait 30 minutes before correcting the seasoning with salt and pepper. Shape into 1¼-inch sausages and dab with olive oil.

WALNUT *KÖFTE*

❊

Makes about 12 sausage-shaped köfte, serving 3 to 4

In this raw *köfte* recipe very fine bulgur is used, which makes kneading easy. Chopped walnuts are worked into the dough after the *köfte* is kneaded until soft and bound with tomato, pepper paste, and spices. The *köfte* is then served with a shredded greens salad, romaine lettuce leaves, a glass of *ayran*—the thirst-quenching thinned yogurt drink of the eastern Mediterranean—and perhaps some pickles.

1 cup #1 (very fine) bulgur, or the collected "dust" by shaking 3 to 4 cups bulgur in a sieve

¼ cup grated onion

⅓ cup grated tomatoes (see step 2 in the next recipe)

½ teaspoon crushed garlic

½ teaspoon salt plus more to taste

2 teaspoons tomato paste

2 teaspoons Turkish red pepper paste

1 tablespoon olive oil

½ cup finely chopped walnuts

6 to 12 romaine lettuce leaves

1 cup finely diced green bell pepper tossed with oil and lemon juice and seasoned with salt and pepper as salad

1. In a mixing bowl, combine the fine bulgur with the onion, and use your fingers to blend until well combined. Then gradually work in the tomatoes, followed by the garlic, salt, tomato and red pepper pastes, and finally the oil and walnuts. It is properly kneaded when a small handful of *köfte* holds its shape without breaking. Let stand 30 minutes before correcting the seasoning.

2. Use a moistened palm to shape small sausages with the bulgur mixture; serve with lettuce leaves and green pepper salad.

Thanks to Gülsen Hanim and Ayfer Ünsal for sharing this recipe.

KÖFTE WITH SCRAMBLED EGGS, TOMATOES, AND PARSLEY (*Turkey*)

Serves 3 to 4

This is a simple, quick traditional dish, as much Armenian as Turkish, from the town of Birmecik on the Euphrates River. Delicious warm or cool with a chilled glass of *ayran*.

2½ tablespoons olive oil

1 medium onion, finely chopped

2 red ripe medium tomatoes (about ¾ pound)

½ teaspoon salt plus more to taste

¼ teaspoon freshly ground black pepper plus more to taste

¼ teaspoon Turkish red pepper flakes plus more to taste

½ cup #2 fine-grain bulgur

3 tablespoons butter

3 large eggs, lightly beaten

⅓ cup chopped flat-leaf parsley plus more for garnish

2 scallions, thinly sliced

3 tablespoons shredded mint leaves

NOTE TO THE COOK: When you knead the grain, work it until it's just tender but you can still feel the barest resistance "on your molars."

1. In a medium skillet heat the olive oil; cook the onion until it is soft and golden.

2. Meanwhile, halve and gently squeeze the tomatoes to remove the seeds. Grate the tomato halves, cut side facing the coarsest side of a four-sided grater or on a flat shredder. You should be left with just the tomato skin in your hand; discard. Add the tomatoes, salt, black pepper, and pepper flakes to the skillet and cook for 2 to 3 minutes on high heat, stirring.

3. Place the bulgur in a mixing bowl; pour over the hot tomato sauce and allow to cool slightly. With dampened hands, knead the bulgur so that it absorbs all the tomato sauce evenly. Cover and let stand 10 minutes.

4. Wipe out the skillet and return to low heat. Add the butter and when it is melted pour in the beaten eggs. Add pinches of salt, black pepper, and pepper flakes. As the eggs begin to stiffen, break them up with a fork, and as soon as they are cooked, tip them into the bulgur and tomato mixture. Fold in the parsley and correct the seasoning. Use oiled hands to pinch off apricot-size pieces of the bulgur mixture and shape each into a small oval. Arrange on a flat plate and garnish with scallions, mint, and parsley. Serve warm or cool.

GRILLS, SAUTÉS, AND GRATINS

ASPARAGUS À LA PARILLA WITH PARSLEY AND HAM SAUCE (*Spain*)

Serves 2

The flat iron grill plate that the Spanish call a *parilla* is used for searing fish, shellfish, poultry, and wild mushrooms, producing a pure, clean, slightly metallic taste, ideal for many tapas.

In *The Flavours of Andalucia* Elisabeth Luard describes a method of grilling asparagus that doesn't require blanching, calling the application of sizzling dry heat to fresh green asparagus "a stroke of genius." She goes on to say, "You will never want to cook it any other way; the flavor is incomparable."

I agree! The thick green asparagus are brushed lightly with oil and set on a hot griddle. The spears are then cooked until spotted black on all sides, then embellished with a sauce of chopped cured ham, garlic, lemon juice, and oil.

2 tablespoons olive oil

½ teaspoon chopped garlic

2 tablespoons (1 ounce) serrano ham or prosciutto, diced into ⅛-inch cubes

2 tablespoons stock or water

2 tablespoons chopped flat-leaf parsley

Salt

Freshly ground black pepper

1 to 2 teaspoons lemon juice

12 to 18 medium thick asparagus

½ teaspoon coarse salt

1. In a small pan heat 1 tablespoon olive oil, add the garlic and the ham, and cook, stirring, 1 minute. Add the stock and parsley and cook another minute or two. Season with salt, pepper, and lemon juice to taste and set aside.

2. Sparingly trim the stalk end of each asparagus. Lightly brush each spear with the remaining oil. Heat a well-seasoned griddle or nonstick pan and when hot sprinkle the griddle with the coarse salt. Add the asparagus, cover, and cook until lightly charred on one side. Turn and cook them, uncovered, until they are limp. Divide and arrange on serving dishes. Serve at once.

Madame Saucourt's Fabulous Ratatouille
(France)

❀

Makes 1 gallon, serving 16 to 20

My friend Adrienne Zausner, an excellent home cook, shared this recipe with me. Adrienne spends a good deal of time in Europe, frequents three-star restaurants, and knows all the great chefs. When I tasted her ratatouille, I was overwhelmed. It turned out to be the recipe of Mme. Saucourt of the famous and now defunct Hotel Mas des Serres in Saint Paul de Vence. Adrienne had loved the dish, Madame had given her the recipe, and, after I begged a bit, Adrienne passed it on to me.

Quelle recette! The verbal instructions that Madame gave Adrienne were detailed and uncompromising:

"The onions must be the fresh sugary kind you find in the summer market. Don't use red garlic, only white, and don't use an eggplant that has a purple peduncle because it will be bitter. Whatever you do, don't reduce the recipe. . . . Part of the great taste is due to the quantity. Most important, make this dish only in late summer when all the vegetables are 'sun-kissed.'"

At first glance, the recipe made me reel. My heart fell when I saw the amount of fine extra-virgin olive oil required, noted the quantities, and contemplated the time-consuming handwork. But this is absolutely the best ratatouille recipe I know, head and shoulders above any other. My theory is that when you find the holy grail of a dish, you must respect it and never corrupt it. As for the oil, at the end of cooking you'll actually get most of it back to be used again for cooking vegetables and general sautéeing.

If you're still with me, I guarantee you a great ratatouille that you can keep for up to a week in the refrigerator. Hot, it goes beautifully with roast lamb. Cold, it makes a great first course or salad. Try spreading leftovers on a sheet of pastry, crisscross with anchovies, then bake in the oven as a little tart. *Bon appetit!*

Prepare at least one day in advance, giving the ratatouille time to mellow. Note that the cooking time is 4 hours.

1. Stem and peel the eggplant. Cut the flesh into 1-inch cubes and place them in a deep kettle filled with very salty water. Keep submerged with a non-corrodible plate for at least 1 hour. Stem and peel the zucchini. Cut the flesh into 1-inch cubes and place in a deep colander. Toss the zucchini with salt and let stand for 30 minutes.

2. Meanwhile, in a very large heavy skillet or heavy-bottomed roasting pan cook the chopped onions and ½ cup of water in 1 cup olive oil until the water has evaporated and the onions are soft and golden, about

5 pounds eggplant

5 pounds zucchini

5 pounds fresh onions, peeled, halved, and thinly sliced

1 quart extra-virgin olive oil

2 tablespoons crushed garlic

2 tablespoons chopped fresh mixed herbs: rosemary, savory, peppermint, thyme, and celery

1 bay leaf

½ tablespoon sugar

1 teaspoon salt

1 teaspoon freshly ground black pepper

2 cups dry yet fruity white wine such as a Provençal Bellet

2 pounds red ripe tomatoes, cored and seeded

5 pounds red bell peppers

A few drops of red wine vinegar

3 tablespoons chopped mixed herbs for garnish: basil, parsley, thyme, and celery

30 minutes. Add the garlic, chopped herbs, bay leaf, sugar, salt, pepper, and 1 cup of the wine. Cook over medium heat, stirring often, for 10 minutes.

3. Coarsely chop the tomatoes with their skins in the work bowl of a food processor. Add to the skillet and continue cooking at a simmer 1½ hours. Whenever the onion-tomato mixture starts to stick or burn, "spot deglaze" with a few tablespoons water and scrape with a wooden spoon.

4. Grill the peppers; when cool, peel, stem, seed, and cut into small pieces. Set aside. Rinse and drain the eggplant and zucchini and lightly press dry with kitchen toweling.

5. Slowly heat the remaining 3 cups of olive oil in a wide pan or fryer until medium-hot. Add the zucchini in batches, and fry until golden on all sides. Transfer the zucchini with a slotted spoon to a colander set over a bowl to catch any excess oil. When all the zucchini has been fried, fry the eggplant in the same manner. From time to time return the "captured" oil in the bowl to the oil in the pan.

6. Spread the zucchini, eggplant, and peppers over the simmering onion-tomato mixture and pour in the remaining wine. Cover and cook at the simmer for 1½ hours. From time to time remove the cover to help evaporate some of the liquid. Place a colander over a large bowl and pour the contents of the skillet into it to drain. Stir carefully to avoid crushing the vegetables while trying to encourage any trapped oil and juices to drain. Quickly cool down the captured juices in order to remove as much oil as possible. If there is a lot of juice, boil it down until thick. Reserve all the frying oil and the oil from the vegetables for some other purpose. Pour the juices over the vegetables, taste for seasoning, add vinegar, if necessary, and carefully stir to combine. Serve hot or cold. Sprinkle with fresh herbs.

POLENTA CROSTINI

❋

*T*he Italian food writer Amedeo Sandri says that a perfect polenta slice is "as wide as the thumb of a mason" and suggests grilling it over oak or apple wood to perfume it with smoke. Much as I like the notion of using aromatic woods, I usually grill slices slowly on a ridged iron griddle set on top of the stove, so the outside crisps and browns while the interior has the consistency of a smooth custardy corn-tasting cream.

The birth of a great polenta slice, or *crostino,* begins with the mounding or shaping of your hot polenta before it cools. Rather than spreading hot polenta on a buttered sheet pan as is so often recommended, tip it into a greased loaf pan, or shape it into a high mound, or flatten and roll it up with the aid of wax paper. Use a string to cut it into slices when ready to grill, not before.

This method will provide you with freshly cut slices. Why is this important? Because when fresh-cut slices face the heat source, the surfaces brown integrally with the interiors. The usual polenta squares have a skin created when the thinly spread polenta cools and congeals; when they hit the heat, the skin separates and turns leathery. I'm so convinced of the superiority of this fresh-cut method that I no longer follow instructions in recipes for oil-patting and layering plastic wrap directly on hot polenta.

After numerous experiments I've come to the conclusion that the more slowly a slice is grilled the better the crust and the creamier the interior. It's this wonderful contrast between outside and inside that makes grilled polenta slices so terrific. By slow grilling I mean grill for at least 10 minutes per side, the exact time depending on your grill, the type of corn, and the firmness of the polenta.

I slowly heat up an oiled ridged grill, then add the polenta slices. I don't turn them until they unstick themselves—their way of telling me they're ready to be turned.

Once you have created perfect grilled slices, the question arises of what to put on top. The list is endless. In the next four recipes you'll find my favorites. (For detailed notes on making polenta, see pages 311 and 314.)

GRILLED TREVISO-STYLE
RADICCHIO ON POLENTA (*Italy*)

❀

Serves 2 to 3 as a first course

In the Veneto region of Italy there are more than a hundred ways of preparing the elongated elegant Treviso-style radicchio that are just starting to show up in American markets. This, to my mind, is one of the easiest and best of those preparations. The cooking takes a while, but with the torpedo-shaped Treviso-style radicchio, longer is better. The cooked radicchio will lose its usual attractive color, but if you're like me you won't be able to stop eating it.

Until Treviso-style radicchio reaches your market, you may substitute Belgian endive. Gardeners should look for packets of Italian heirloom seeds of "Red Treviso" available from The Cook's Garden and Shepherd's Garden Seeds (see "Mail-Order Sources").

3 heads Treviso-style radicchio or Belgian endive

Extra-virgin olive oil

Sprinkling of dried herbs such as *herbes de Provence*

Salt

Freshly ground black pepper

6 1-inch-thick slices polenta, freshly cut from a loaf or mound (see No-Stir Polenta on page 313)

A few drops of balsamic vinegar

1. Heat coals or a well-seasoned iron griddle over low heat.

2. Wash and dry the outer layer of the radicchio and discard any leaves where the white part is tinged with green. Halve or quarter lengthwise depending upon the thickness and brush lightly with oil; slowly cook over low coals or on a heated iron grid or heavy skillet until very dark and crisp on the outside and meltingly tender within on the first side, about 15 minutes. Turn the vegetable over, sprinkle with herbs and salt and pepper, and continue grilling another 15 minutes.

3. Arrange the polenta slices on the grill to slowly crisp on each side for 10 to 15 minutes.

4. Transfer the radicchio to a wooden surface, trim the root end, and cut the radicchio sideways into one-inch strips. Toss with a dash of balsamic and black pepper and pile over the crisp grilled polenta. Serve at once.

CARAMELIZED ONIONS
AND CHEESE ON POLENTA (*Italy*)

❀

Serves 4 as a first course

In May in northern Italy, cooks making this superb first-course dish search out fresh, young flattish sweet onions called *chioggias*. Our Maui, Walla Walla, and Vidalia onions are just as good when cooked until soft, caramelized, and golden.

A fine point of this dish is to cook the polenta slices on only one side, leaving light striped markings from the grill. The crust should be crackling crisp, the interior almost melting. The uncooked side should be smooth and moist, yet porous enough to take in the flavor of the onions. Serve with a handful of dressed arugula greens.

1 pound sweet onions, peeled and coarsely chopped

1 tablespoon extra-virgin olive oil plus more for grilling

Salt

3 tablespoons vegetable or chicken stock or water

2 tablespoons heavy cream

A few drops of balsamic vinegar

Pinch of ground white pepper

8 ¾-inch-thick slices of cold polenta, freshly cut from a loaf or mound (see No-Stir Polenta on page 313)

4 tablespoons finely grated aged Asiago

½ tablespoon butter

1. About 1½ hours before serving, cook the onions with 1 tablespoon olive oil and a pinch of salt in a covered skillet over medium to low heat until soft and golden, about 25 minutes. Add the stock and cream and cook, stirring, until absorbed. Sprinkle with a few drops of vinegar and white pepper.

2. Preheat the oven to 400 degrees.

3. Meanwhile lightly brush one side of each polenta slice with oil and grill, either over coals or on a ridged iron grid until crisp and nicely marked from the grill, about 10 minutes.

4. Put the polenta slices, crisp side down, on a nonstick baking sheet. Place a spoonful of the hot onion sauce on top of each, sprinkle with grated cheese and shavings of butter, and bake 10 to 15 minutes or until well browned. Serve warm.

Skillet Leafy Greens with Garlic and Anchovies on Grilled Polenta (*Italy*)

❧

Serves 2

Here's a delicious and quick first course or snack to serve over grilled polenta (page 108). Oversize arugula or any other slightly tough green will work well. Gardeners will appreciate this recipe, which also works with fresh borage leaves.

1 pound (2½ packed quarts) young leafy greens such as large-leaf arugula or borage

2 tablespoons extra-virgin olive oil

1 teaspoon minced garlic

2 to 3 anchovy fillets, rinsed and cut into small pieces

2 to 3 tablespoons water or unsalted meat, poultry, or vegetable stock

Pinch of freshly ground black pepper

Pinch of red pepper flakes

Salt

1 red ripe tomato, halved, seeded, and grated

6 ½-inch-thick slices grilled polenta (page 108) or ½-inch-thick slices grilled, stale, country-style Italian bread rubbed with garlic if desired

1. Wash, stem, and roughly shred the greens.

2. In a medium skillet over moderate heat, warm the oil. Add the garlic and sauté until just golden, about 2 minutes. Add the anchovies and crush to a purée. Gradually add the greens, allowing the first group to wilt down before adding more, then add the water or stock and cook, covered, over medium heat until tender. Season with pepper, pepper flakes, and salt. Stir in the tomato pulp and boil down, stirring, 1 minute. Divide over grilled polenta or bread and serve at once.

LEAFY GREENS "SCRAMBLED" WITH EGGS ON POLENTA (*France*)

Serves 2

Here mixed leafy greens are scrambled with eggs, then served over grilled polenta. We think of polenta as an Italian starch, but it's quite popular in France, especially around Nice, where it's used as a "landing" for stewed leeks, stewed mushrooms, game ragouts, and eggs as in this delicious dish.

I wish I could remember where I read that Provençal cooks not only like to add a bay leaf to the water in which they cook polenta, but also, if possible, stir their polenta with a stick from a laurel tree!

¾ pound baby spinach or young chard leaves

2 tablespoons olive oil

1 tablespoon minced unsmoked bacon or pancetta

¼ cup minced onion

¼ cup light stock or water

2 or 3 farm-fresh eggs, beaten

Salt

Freshly ground black pepper

4 to 6 slices grilled Polenta Crostini (page 108)

1. Wash the greens, remove thick stems, and use a rolling mincer or a knife to chop the greens into tiny pieces, about 6 cups.

2. Heat the oil and cook the unsmoked bacon and onion in a large skillet until the bacon and onion begin to turn golden and soft. Add the chopped, wet greens. Cover and cook over medium-low heat, stirring often, until greens are tender, about 10 minutes. During this time, add a few teaspoons stock to keep the greens from drying out.

3. Add the eggs directly into the skillet and immediately scramble the eggs into the greens so that the mixture thickens and resembles creamed spinach. Season with salt and pepper and serve right away with grilled slices of polenta.

GRATIN OF CARDOONS
WITH ANCHOVIES AND CHEESE (*France*)

❧

Serves 3 to 4

*I*n this delicious Provençal recipe, adapted from an old French cookbook, the delicate flavor of cardoons (see page 88) is preserved even when they are adorned with the classic Mediterranean embellishment of anchovies and cheese.

1 bundle firm, fresh cardoons (about 4 pounds)

¼ cup all-purpose flour

⅓ cup fresh, strained lemon juice

Salt

3 tablespoon extra-virgin olive oil

3 tablespoons finely chopped onion

3 anchovy fillets, rinsed, drained, and cut into small pieces

1 cup chicken broth (optional)

Freshly ground black pepper

3 tablespoons grated mild cheese such as Gruyère, Edam, or Parmigiano-Reggiano

2 tablespoons bread crumbs

1. Separate and wash the cardoons stalks. Prepare as directed on pages 88 and cut them into 2-inch lengths.

2. Put 2 cups water in a saucepan, whisk in the flour, and bring to the boil, whisking often to prevent lumps. Add 6 cups more water, 2½ tablespoons lemon juice, salt, and 1 tablespoon olive oil and bring to the boil. Add the prepared cardoons and cook, covered, until tender, 30 to 45 minutes. Remove from the heat but do not drain until ready to use in step 5.

3. Meanwhile, preheat the oven to 350 degrees.

4. Sauté the onion in 2 tablespoons olive oil in a medium skillet until soft and golden. Add the anchovies and crush to a purée. Add the chicken broth or 1 cup water and bring to a boil. Simmer for 5 minutes.

5. Drain the cardoons and dry well. Lightly oil a shallow 9-inch baking dish. Spread a thin layer of the sauce over the bottom and cover with an even layer of the cardoons. Sprinkle with the remaining lemon juice. Pour over the remaining sauce, scatter the cheese on top, and bake until golden and crusty, 30 minutes. Serve hot.

Based on a recipe in Jean-Pierre Poulain and Jean-Luc Rouyer's Histoire et Recettes de la Provence et du Comté de Nice.

ARTICHOKE BOTTOMS STUFFED
WITH CHOPPED PARSLEY AND RICOTTA (*Tunisia*)

❊

Serves 6 as a first course

This dish is typical of the refined cooking of Tunis—rich, succulent, and made without *harissa*. Quality canned tuna packed in olive oil (I particularly like the Genova brand) is a fine product; fresh tuna should not be substituted. The flavor of canned tuna that has been cooked in olive oil holds up very well in this dish against the variety of cheeses and the mildly bitter taste of the artichokes.

6 large artichokes

1 lemon

2 cups finely chopped flat-leaf parsley

1 medium onion, finely chopped

5 ounces first-quality canned tuna packed in olive oil

1 tablespoon grated Gruyère cheese

8 ounces ricotta cheese, drained overnight to remove excess moisture, makes 1 cup

1 tablespoon grated aged Gouda cheese

1 egg

Salt

Freshly ground black pepper

Grated nutmeg

2 tablespoons extra-virgin olive oil

1 clove garlic, peeled and crushed

1½ tablespoons tomato paste

1 bay leaf

1. Trim the artichokes by first snapping off the tough outer leaves near the base. Use a stainless steel knife to cut off the stems, then trim the crowns to within 1½ inches of the base. Use a melon baller to scoop out the hairy chokes and scrape around the inner sides to widen the cavity. Use a small knife to carefully trim the leaves, then pare any remaining hard green parts. As you work with each artichoke, rub it with a cut lemon to prevent discoloration. Put the artichoke bottoms in a bowl of water mixed with lemon juice. Boil or steam the artichokes until they are almost fully cooked. Allow to cool.

2. To prepare the stuffing: steam the parsley and onion until softened, 10 minutes. Cool, then mix with the tuna, cheeses, and egg, blending well with the back of a fork. Season with salt, pepper, and grated nutmeg.

3. To prepare the sauce: heat the oil in a medium-size skillet over moderately low heat. Add the garlic and cook for 30 seconds. Stir in the tomato paste with a wooden spoon until it begins to sizzle and

shine, about 2 minutes. Add the bay leaf and stir in 1 cup water until the sauce is smooth and thick.

4. Preheat the oven to 400 degrees.

5. Drain the artichokes and pat dry. Stuff the bottoms, shaping the stuffing into well-rounded domes with wet palms. Place artichokes in a shallow baking dish and surround with the tomato sauce. Bake in the oven for 15 minutes, basting two or three times with the tomato sauce. Serve warm.

MIXED VEGETABLES ROASTED IN THE EMBERS, *MECHOUIA* (Tunisia)

Makes 5 to 6 cups

This is my favorite way of preparing the famous Tunisian grilled vegetable salad, *mechouia*. The best way is not to grill the vegetables but to completely bury them in live embers, a process that cooks them evenly while imbuing them with a wonderful smoky taste. The scorched vegetables, whether grilled on the burner or cooked in embers, are then peeled and crushed one by one (heaviest first) in a mortar until puréed but still retaining some texture. If you use a food processor, pulse the mixture until chunky.

6 small onions, unpeeled (about 14 ounces)

1 whole garlic head, broken into four or five parts, unpeeled

4 fresh poblano or Anaheim chilies

8 small tomatoes (1½ pounds)

3 tablespoons extra-virgin olive oil

1 teaspoon Tunisian *tabil* (page 346)

1 teaspoon ground caraway seeds

1 teaspoon salt

Freshly ground black pepper

Quick Flaky Semolina Bread (page 17)

1. Start a wood or charcoal fire and allow the coals to turn white before cooking. You will need a supply of coals to keep a steady heat for about half an hour.

2. Do not peel the onions or garlic. Do not stem the peppers or tomatoes. Bury all the vegetables in the coals. Remove the vegetables as they become soft. Cool and peel the garlic, onion, peppers, and tomatoes. Discard all seeds. If tomatoes are excessively watery, drain in a sieve. Starting with the onions and garlic, crush the vegetables in a wide mortar or pulse in the work bowl of a food processor to achieve a chunky texture, then add the peppers and tomatoes. Scrape mixture into a bowl, whip in the olive oil to loosen, adjust the seasoning with spices, salt, and pepper, and serve warm with flaky semolina bread.

STUFFED LEAFY GREENS

❖

The following four dishes employ a variety of greens as wrappings. Turkey leads the way in the number of greens used to wrap up grain-based food. The list includes the leaves of quince, mulberry, green bean, fava bean, beet, hazelnut, cherry, grape, chard, collard, mallow, fig, sorrel, and even the stinging nettle.

If a green is to be stuffed, the grain of choice will depend upon the region: rice in France, Cyprus, Spain, Greece, and the Middle East; corn around the Black Sea; bulgur in southeastern Turkey; cracked shelled wheat in central Anatolia. Sometimes too a combination of rice with bulgur or green wheat is used—one of my favorites.

In Mediterranean countries medium-grain rice is still preferred. Though long-grain rice has many excellent qualities, traditional Greek cooks have told me its texture seems to them "like a handful of nails."

To clear up some confusion, in Turkey *sarmas* are made with leaves and *dolmas* are made with receptacle-shaped vegetables, while in Greece the word *dolma* refers to stuffed grape leaves.

Stuffed leafy greens are usually cylinder-shaped but may also be triangular or square. Some Turkish women form their *sarmas* as thin as cigarettes (especially when using fava bean, cherry, or mulberry leaves). With green bean leaves the rolls can be so thin you can see the interior filling when cooked.

KAYSERI-STYLE PAN-GRILLED GRAPE LEAVES STUFFED WITH *BASTURMA*, PARSLEY, AND ORANGE (*Turkey*)

❀

Makes 20 packages, serving 4 or 5

Jonathan Gold, writing in the *Los Angeles Times,* described the *basturma* he tasted at Sahag's, an Armenian deli in Los Angeles, as follows: "The Armenian cured beef called *basturma* may be the most powerfully flavored cold cut in the world, less a foodstuff than a force of nature sometimes, with a bit of the chewy translucence of first-rate Italian bresaola, a ripe, almost gamy back taste, and then—pow!—the onslaught of the seasoning, a caustic, bright red slurry of hot pepper, fenugreek, and a truly heroic amount of garlic that hits the palate with the subtle elegance of a detonated land mine." It must take a lot of energy to write a great paragraph like that!

20 fresh or preserved grape leaves

3 to 4 ounces basturma (spiced dried beef available at Middle Eastern groceries or by mail order)

¼ cup paper-thin onion slices

½ cup tomato, peeled, seeded, and cubed

1 small lemon, peeled, seeded, and cut into tiny cubes

½ cup orange, peeled, seeded, and cut into tiny cubes

½ cup chopped parsley

1½ teaspoons butter if the basturma is lean; omit if fatty

freshly ground black pepper

extra-virgin olive oil

In this dish from the town of Kayseri in Turkey, there's an exciting exchange of flavors among the spiced dried beef (*basturma*), tomatoes, orange, and parsley. The mixture is then wrapped in grape leaves and cooked on a ridged grill until crisp.

Basturma is also delicious served simply as a cold cut with a thin slice of lemon accompanied by a glass of anise-flavored raki.

Kayseri is famous for its *basturma*, prepared during the winter months. This preserved meat is usually made with a cut similar to an eye round of beef—first soaked in a salt brine, then dried, rubbed with a paste made with ground fenugreek mixed with paprika, garlic, black pepper, and salt with a hint of allspice and cinnamon, then hung to dry some more. Ask a Middle Eastern grocer to slice it extra thin or slice it yourself with the 1-millimeter blade of your food processor. (See also "Mail-Order Sources.")

(continued)

The fenugreek-rich paste on *basturma* is so adored by residents of Kayseri that they'll even scrape it off the meat, then blend it with a little water in order to make a creamy paste to be spread on bread.

To ensure a crackling crust, make this dish between June and September when grape leaves are fresh. Other times of the year you may substitute grape leaves in a jar, but be sure to soak them to remove all taste of brine, then carefully pat dry.

Basturma, too, should be soaked to remove excess salt before using.

1. Wash and dry the leaves. Divide the spiced beef, onion, tomato, lemon, orange, parsley, and butter, if using, evenly among the leaves. Sprinkle with pepper, wrap up, and fasten each with a toothpick. Dab with oil and set aside until ready to grill.

2. Just before serving, heat a lightly oiled ridged griddle and cook 10 packets at time, turning once, for 2 to 3 minutes. Serve hot.

VARIATION: Substitute 4 slivered hot peppers for the orange and onion.

BLACK SEA–STYLE CHARD BUNDLES FILLED WITH VEAL, TOASTED CORN KERNELS, AND FRESH MINT (*Turkey*)

❧

Makes 2 to 3 dozen rolls, serving 6 as a first course

Paradoxically, in the Islamic world one probably eats best during Ramadan, the month of fasting, when lots of specialties are prepared for the night meals that assuage the pain of abstinence during the day.

"Everyone wants to eat at Ayter Samanci's house," a friend told me as we stopped in front of the home of a woman rated as one of the best cooks in the town of Trabzon on the Black Sea coast of Turkey. "Especially during Ramadan, when she makes her *karalahana sarmasi*, delicious toasted corn and meat–filled chard rolls, nonstop."

Ayter Samanci, who looked about forty-five, was wearing the traditional kerchief worn by women in those parts to keep dust and sunlight out of their hair. A kind, warm, smiling woman, she told me she liked to work with her hands, so much so, she added, that whenever she left home she took her knitting with her.

When asked about her famous chard rolls, she laughed as she admitted that her recipe wasn't at all difficult, but that people thought it was, since the result was so delicious.

¾ to 1 cup (8 ounces) toasted corn kernels

2 2-inch marrowbones

2 tablespoons unsalted butter

½ pound ground lean veal

1 bunch scallions, white plus 6 inches green leaves (about 1 cup)

½ teaspoon red pepper plus more to taste

2 tablespoons tomato paste

2 tablespoon chopped fresh parsley

2 tablespoons chopped spearmint leaves

Salt

Freshly ground black pepper

12 large Swiss chard leaves, blanched and deribbed

"As soon as Ramadan is finished," she told me, "I'm so exhausted from all the cooking, I retreat to a spa to recuperate."

"And, of course, her knitting goes with her," her friend added.

Along the Black Sea coast the best-tasting corn dishes are made with oven-dried (as opposed to sundried) nonsweet corn. An excellent equivalent are toasted sweet corn kernels (see "Mail-Order Sources"). It's the unique flavor of toasted corn that makes the Black Sea corn dishes so exciting.

I have attempted this dish using corn grits and coarse cornmeal—even very coarse cornmeal—but nothing equaled the unique flavor of toasted corn kernels, the dominant flavor of the stuffing.

If the rolls are properly arranged in the cooking pot, when turned out they will fall naturally into a lovely flower pattern, making a nice presentation. Serve warm with plain yogurt on the side.

1. Early in the day, rinse the corn kernels, then soak in water until softened, about 2 to 3 hours. Drain well.

2. Meanwhile, pry out the marrow from the bones and soak it in salted ice water until it turns white, 2 to 3 hours.

3. Heat the butter in a medium skillet set over moderate heat and sauté the veal along with the scallions, ½ teaspoon red pepper, and tomato paste for 5 minutes, stirring often. Remove to a side dish. Deglaze the skillet with a few tablespoons water.

4. Pulse the drained corn, the veal, the pan juices, the marrow, and the fresh herbs in a food processor until well combined. Season highly with salt, pepper, and red pepper. Makes about 3 cups filling. Allow to mellow at least 1 hour in the refrigerator before continuing.

5. Pile the chard shiny side down. Cut large leaves into approximately 5-inch squares. Place a heatproof cereal bowl upside down in a heavy, shallow 3-quart saucepan. Put one leaf in the palm of one hand, top with a heaping teaspoon of filling, fold and roll to enclose. Set the rolls in the pan, pressing to make compact. Top with an inverted heatproof plate and barely cover the rolls with boiling water, about 1 cup. Cover and steam 15 to 20 minutes. Let rest off the heat, covered, for 15 minutes. Carefully turn out onto a rimmed platter. Serve warm.

Gaziantep-Style Triangles of Swiss Chard Stuffed with Green Wheat, Lamb, and Pine Nuts (*Turkey*)

Serves 6 as a main course

I never tire of Swiss chard as a wrap for Turkish preparations of meat and grains, especially in this recipe, where it envelops the preserved moist kernels of immature wheat called *freekeh*. In Turkey and the Middle East, when the stores of winter wheat have been used up, farmers gather immature wheat and set it afire for quick consumption. They burn the chaff but preserve the moist kernels, and the result is a delicious, earthy, and unique food product.

Store green wheat in your freezer to keep the nutritional value high. It takes time to clean green wheat, but there is no substitute. (See "Mail-Order Sources.")

The ingenious method of steaming the stuffed chard triangles over a bed of lamb bones and chard ribs produces an especially fine dish—buttery soft wrappings that surround a moist, tender, and extremely flavorful filling.

In one home in Gaziantep, a particularly creative cook prepared similar stuffed Swiss chard triangles, set them in a bowl along with strips of sweet red pepper and garlic cloves, then steamed the dish. When she turned it out there was a beautifully patterned hemisphere of triangular stuffed greens studded with bright red strips and creamy white garlic nuggets, a sensational and labor-intensive tour de force. The following recipe is a lot easier but no less delicious.

Serve these triangles with yogurt-garlic sauce.

2 tablespoons plus 2 teaspoons olive oil

1 cup chopped onion

1 pound ground lamb or beef

¼ cup pine nuts

1 teaspoon or more mixed spices: cinnamon, allspice, nutmeg, red and black pepper

Salt

1 cup cracked green wheat

3 bunches (3 pounds) medium to large Swiss chard leaves

2 to 3 trimmed lamb neck or shoulder bones

Juice of 1 lemon

Yogurt-Garlic Sauce (page 346)

1. Heat 2 tablespoons oil in a 10-inch skillet. Add the onion and cook, covered, over medium heat until softened. Add the ground meat and sauté until it is browned and crumbly. Add the pine nuts, spices, and salt to taste. Cook 2 minutes and set aside.

2. Place the green wheat in a sieve and shake over the sink to remove some of the grit and tiny stones. Place the sieve in a deep bowl and cover with cool water. Rub the cracked wheat kernels between your fingertips and palms vigorously to feel for stones or other foreign matter. Wash the wheat in several changes of water until the water runs clear and the kernels feel free of all grit. Let soak 2 to 3 minutes. Skim off and discard any debris that floats to the top. Drain the wheat and fold into the meat mixture, mixing well. Taste for seasoning and set aside.

3. Rinse and drain the Swiss chard leaves. Dip the leaves into simmering water until pliable, about 12 seconds, and refresh in a basin of cold water. Drain, then gently press out excess moisture. Place the leaves, smooth side down and a few at a time, on a work surface. Remove the stalks from the greens and reserve 7 or 8 of the widest ones for the cooking. Remove the center rib from each leaf to divide each leaf into irregular rectangles. Place a heaped tea-spoon of filling near a narrow end, and wrap over and over as if folding a flag, forming a small triangle. Repeat with the remaining leaves and filling.

4. In a 2½-quart saucepan, slowly brown the bones in the remaining 2 teaspoons oil. Scatter the reserved chard stalks on top. Place the Swiss chard triangles in tightly packed rows. Weight them down with an upside-down heatproof plate just large enough to fit inside the saucepan. Pour 1 cup water down the inside of the saucepan. Bring to a boil; boil hard for half a minute, cover with a tight-fitting lid, reduce the heat to low, and cook 30 minutes. Remove from heat and let stand 20 minutes before uncovering. Carefully drain off pan juices and add the lemon juice, salt, and pepper to taste and reserve. Carefully turn the contents of the saucepan into a shallow serv-ing dish. Discard bones and chard ribs. Pour over the pan juices and serve warm with sauce.

POTATO STRUDEL STUFFED WITH MIXED GREENS (*Italy*)

Serves 6 to 8 as a first course

Istrian-born Lidia Bastianich, whose Manhattan restaurant, Felidia, is one the best Italian restaurants in America, taught a similar version of this terrific first-course dish at a hands-on class.

Struccolo, from northern Italy near Trieste, is a stuffed strudel composed of potatoes, flour, eggs, and cooked greens. The strudel is poached, then sliced into individual portions, which are then brushed with a light herbed tomato sauce and baked.

Lidia's cooking hints are great: "Be sure to break up the potato—this enhances evaporation—you won't need as much flour" and "Work fast when you fold the flour and egg into the potatoes—if you take too long the dough will be heavy."

Up near Trieste cooks like to combine such greens as nettles and chard, but a combination of spinach and chard works extremely well.

1. Boil the potatoes until they are well cooked and the skins are bursting, about 40 minutes.

2. For the stuffing, place the drained ricotta on a tray lined with paper toweling. Cover with additional paper toweling and press lightly to express moisture.

3. Stem the greens, discarding any blemished or yellow leaves, and soak them in a deep pan of water to wash away all sand and grit. Blanch in boiling salted water until just cooked, about 5 minutes. Drain greens, press out all the liquid, finely chop, and leave to cool on a flat wooden board. You should have about 2 cups.

4. Heat the butter in a small skillet and soften the scallions for 2 to 3 minutes; dump onto a side dish

to quickly cool down. In a large bowl, combine the ricotta, greens, scallions, eggs, grated cheese, and seasonings; mix well. Taste for seasoning.

5. Bring a large amount of water to a boil in a fish poacher or large round pot.

6. Meanwhile, make the potato casing. Drain the potatoes and remove the skins while still hot. Force through a ricer fitted with a fine disk, a food mill, or a sieve onto a lightly floured work surface. Use a fork to crumble the potatoes. (This allows the moisture to evaporate as they cool.) When the potatoes are cool, gather into a mound; make a well in the center; add the eggs, salt, and flour; and gently but quickly work into a light, soft, well-combined dough without any stickiness.

3 large Idaho, russet, or other floury potatoes (about 1½ to 2 pounds), washed but not peeled

STUFFING

15 ounces whole-milk ricotta drained to 1 cup

2 pounds mixed mild-tasting leafy greens, including Swiss chard, spinach, and, in season, stinging nettles (use rubber gloves when handling raw nettles)

1½ tablespoons unsalted butter

½ cup chopped scallions, white plus 2 inches green leaves

1 egg, lightly beaten

8 tablespoons freshly grated *parmigiano reggiano*

Salt

Freshly ground black pepper

Grated nutmeg

POTATO CASING

2 eggs, lightly beaten

About 1 teaspoon salt

About 1¼ cups (5 to 6 ounces) sifted all-purpose flour plus more as necessary

GLAZE

5 tablespoons unsalted butter, at room temperature

1 teaspoon tomato paste

½ teaspoon dried sage leaves, crumbled, or 6 fresh sage leaves, slivered

Salt

⅓ cup grated Parmigiano-Reggiano

7. Place a double or triple layer of cheesecloth on a work surface and sprinkle with flour. Roll the dough out on the cloth to form a 12 by 16-inch rectangle. Spread the filling over the dough, leaving a ½-inch border all around. Roll the dough up, jelly roll–style, in the cheesecloth. Pinch the ends together to enclose the filling. Tie the ends of the cheesecloth with string. If your pot isn't large enough to hold it, gently curve the roll into a horseshoe shape.

8. Add about 4 teaspoons salt to the boiling water. Slide the strudel into the water so that it is submerged. If necessary, add more boiling water. Partially cover the pot and cook until the strudel is firm to the touch, about 40 minutes.

9. Put a wedge under one end of a wooden board to slant it. Lift the strudel onto the board and leave to drain. Let stand until cold before unwrapping and cutting into 1-inch-thick slices. Up to this point the strudel can be made one day in advance. Keep it refrigerated in its cheesecloth wrapping until ready to slice, heat, and serve.

10. Preheat the broiler. Place slices, side by side, on a buttered baking sheet. In a small saucepan gently melt the butter, stirring to keep it creamy. Mix in the tomato paste, sage, and a little salt to taste. Remove from the heat when smooth. Strain and brush a small amount over each slice, then top with grated cheese. Set about 5 inches from the broiler heat to reheat until slices are golden and sizzling. If desired, slices can be reheated in a hot oven for 15 minutes. Serve hot.

Escarole Stuffed with Capers, Anchovies, Golden Raisins, and Pine Nuts (*Italy*)

❧

Serves 2 or 3

There's a saying in Genoa: "At Easter every kitchen produces stuffed lettuce." I don't know if there's a similar aphorism about lettuce-stuffing in Naples, but I do know that this Neapolitan dish is a winner, bringing together the famous quartet of capers, anchovies, raisins, and pine nuts in a new and utterly delicious manner—wrapped up, then tied inside a whole head of escarole.

Serve with grilled fish and poultry.

3 tablespoons golden raisins

½ cup coarse bread crumbs from a day-old piece of white peasant bread

8 anchovy fillets, rinsed, drained, and finely chopped

¼ cup pine nuts

3 tablespoons salt-dried capers, rinsed and drained

2 tablespoons freshly grated pecorino Romano cheese

¼ teaspoon freshly ground black pepper

1 medium-large head of escarole (14 ounces)

⅔ cup unsalted chicken broth or water, simmering

1. Put the raisins in a small bowl and cover with warm water. Set aside to soak for 10 minutes, then drain.

2. In a medium bowl, combine the raisins, anchovies, pine nuts, capers, pecorino Romano, and pepper, fluffing the mixture with a fork to keep it light and airy.

3. Thoroughly wash the head of escarole, keeping it whole with the leaves intact. Drain well. Trim the core and turn the head right side up. Carefully open the leaves and sprinkle the stuffing between them. Gather the leaves and tie with kitchen string.

4. Lay the escarole on its side in a 2½-quart cocotte—it should be just large enough to hold the escarole. In a small saucepan, bring the stock to a simmer and pour it around the escarole. Bring to a boil over medium heat. Cover with a tight-fitting lid and cook, turning once, until tender, 15 to 20 minutes. Add water to the pan if it looks dry.

5. Carefully transfer the escarole to a flat dish. Remove the strings, cut the escarole into wedges, and serve warm.

SPICY LAMB- AND RICE-STUFFED APRICOTS (*Turkey*)

❀

Serves 6

*I*n Central Anatolia, where they stuff every sort of edible green, the cooks seem to have stuffings on their minds. This delicious dish of caramelized cinnamon-flavored stuffed apricots or prunes is often served as part of a large buffet.

6 ounces (about 24) pitted dried apricots or purple prunes

1½ tablespoons olive oil

5 ounces ground beef or lamb with some fat

¼ cup medium-grain rice, soaked in hot water for 10 minutes, rinsed, and drained

½ teaspoon ground cinnamon

Salt

Freshly ground black pepper

2 tablespoons granulated sugar

1½ tablespoons butter

1. Wash the dried fruit and soak in warm water for 10 minutes. Pour the soaking liquid and the fruit into a heavy saucepan and bring to a boil. Simmer 15 minutes. Drain and set aside to cool.

2. Meanwhile prepare the stuffing. In a small skillet, warm the oil, add the meat, and cook, stirring, 2 to 3 minutes. Remove from the heat and stir in the drained rice and let cool. Mix in the cinnamon and salt and pepper and knead the mixture until blended and smooth.

3. In a small saucepan bring ½ cup water and the sugar to a boil, stirring until the sugar is dissolved. Stuff the fruit, place side by side in a buttered skillet, and pour the sugared water down inside the pan. Bring to a boil, reduce the heat to medium, and cook for 5 minutes. Cover with a tight-fitting lid, reduce the heat to medium-low, and cook 30 minutes. Remove from the heat and let stand 10 minutes before uncovering.

PIMIENTOS *DE* PIQUILLO STUFFED WITH RICE AND MUSHROOMS (*Spain*)

Serves 4 as a first course

T hey're the size of two thumbs." That's how a friend describes the sublime sweet Spanish peppers called *piquillo* peppers. And if you're taken aback by the prospect of using canned or jarred pimientos, be assured that the flavor of canned *piquillo* peppers from Navarre (marked DOC on the label), slowly roasted over wood, is so extraordinary that even the three-star French chef Alain Ducasse recommends them for stuffing in his book *Méditerranées, Cuisine de l'Essentiel.*

Just as every Spanish cook has her own way of making paella, so too will she have her own approach to stuffing peppers. Preferred stuffings range from puréed salt cod and potatoes to mixtures of ground pork or veal. But for me the most interesting Spanish stuffing is this blend of rice and wild mushrooms flavored with another Spanish red pepper, dried smoky hot paprika or *pimentón de la Vera* (see "Mail-Order Sources"). The result is a great symphony of flavor in which the sweet *piquillo* pepper becomes spicy while the *pimentón* is tamed.

Triangular, bright red *piquillo* peppers from northern Spain are available at fine grocers or by mail order (see "Mail-Order Sources"). Any leftover peppers can be cut up and stirred into a sauce.

These days flour-based sauces are quite unfashionable, but don't be turned off. When properly cooked, flour will thicken a sauce without making it heavy. In this recipe it acts as a great carrier for the haunting smoky flavor of the paprika.

1 10- or 12-ounce jar or can *piquillo* peppers (12 to 16 peppers)

¼ cup medium-grain rice

6 tablespoons extra-virgin olive oil

½ cup diced onion

¾ pound brown mushrooms such as cremini, shiitake, or portobello, rinsed, dried, and thickly sliced

2 tablespoons dry Spanish sherry

2 teaspoons chopped garlic

2 tablespoons finely chopped Serrano ham or prosciutto

3 tablespoons diced green bell pepper

Grated nutmeg

Pinch of saffron

2 tablespoons flour

1 cup hot milk

½ cup hot vegetable, meat, or chicken stock

1 tablespoon *pimentón de la Vera* or sweet Spanish paprika

Salt

Freshly ground black pepper

Lemon juice

6 tablespoons chopped fresh flat-leaf parsley

3 tablespoons fine bread crumbs

1. Drain the peppers on paper toweling. Soak the rice in hot water for 10 minutes. Meanwhile, in a 10-inch frying pan, heat 2 tablespoons oil and sauté the onion until golden. Add half the mushrooms, the sherry, half the garlic, the ham, bell pepper, nutmeg, and saffron; and cook, stirring, until thick and aromatic. Drain the rice, add to the pan with 1 cup water, and bring to a boil. Cook over medium heat for 20 minutes, stirring occasionally.

2. Meanwhile, in a small saucepan heat 2 tablespoons oil and stir in the flour, letting it cook for a few minutes without browning. Whisk in the hot milk, the hot stock, and the paprika and cook, stirring constantly, until the sauce is smooth and thick. Adjust the seasoning with salt, pepper, and a few drops of lemon juice. Stir ½ cup of the sauce into the rice mixture along with half of the parsley. Adjust the seasoning with salt, pepper, and a few drops of lemon juice.

3. Preheat the oven to 400 degrees.

4. Sauté the rest of the mushrooms in 2 tablespoons hot olive oil, adding the remaining garlic and parsley, and cook, stirring, for about 10 minutes. Season with salt and pepper.

5. When the stuffing is cool enough to handle, stuff the peppers with the rice and arrange, overlapping, in a ring in an oiled, shallow 9-inch baking dish. Pile the fried mushrooms in the center. Spoon the sauce over all and dust everything with the fine bread crumbs. Place for 10 minutes in the oven. Serve hot, warm, or cold.

MUSSELS STUFFED WITH RICE, CURRANTS, AND PINE NUTS (*Eastern Mediterranean*)

❊

Serves 6 to 8 as a first course

This dish is much beloved by Armenians, Turks, and Greeks. I've tried the renditions of all three and can't find much difference among them, so I've given this recipe the default designation of "eastern Mediterranean specialty."

The mussels, which are opened raw (see "How to Open a Raw Mussel for Stuffing" on page 130), are stuffed with rice supplemented with lots of finely minced onion, currants, and pine nuts. They're then tied up and cooked the same way one cooks stuffed grape leaves.

You want to stuff the mussels while raw to preserve their meaty, moist quality, allowing them, the rice, and the spices to intermingle inside the shell.

This dish is especially delicious cold. It can be served as a main course with a salad or as part of a group of appetizers. Eastern Mediterranean hostesses will often dab the mussel shells with a little olive oil to make them shine very black on the buffet table.

Mediterranean mussels (*Mytilus galloprovincials*) are now farmed in the American Northwest. I recommend you use them if possible, since they have a true Mediterranean taste. They come jumbo-size, weighing about 3½ ounces each—a good size for stuffing. If you can't find these or other large mussels, medium-large will do. If you have to open a few extra mussels, just think of it as good practice.

1. Scrub the mussels under running water, discarding any that are not closed. Soak in salted cold water for 1 hour.

2. Heat the olive oil in a 10-inch skillet and cook the onions with 1 teaspoon salt and ½ cup water over moderate heat until soft and golden, about 20 minutes. Add the drained rice and pine nuts and sauté until the rice is dry and the pine nuts are lightly toasted. Add the currants, spices, sugar, dill,

tomato, and ½ cup water and cook over medium-high heat until all moisture has evaporated and the rice is shiny, 3 minutes. Remove from the heat, mix well, and allow to cool. Correct the seasoning with salt and spices.

3. Open the mussels as described on page 130.

4. With a small spoon, stuff the first six mussels with 2 to 3 teaspoons of the rice mixture; close firmly. Tie string around each mussel to secure.

4 to 5 pounds (2½ to 3 dozen) large mussels

Sea salt

6 tablespoons extra-virgin olive oil

4 cups minced onions (about 1½ pounds)

⅔ cup (4 ounces) short- or medium-grain rice, soaked in hot salted water for 10 minutes, rinsed, and drained

4 tablespoons pine nuts

2 tablespoons currants, soaked in hot water for 10 minutes and drained

¼ teaspoon freshly ground black pepper or more to taste

¾ teaspoon ground allspice or more to taste

¼ teaspoon ground cinnamon or more to taste

Pinch of grated nutmeg or ground cloves

1½ teaspoons sugar

3 tablespoons chopped dill

½ cup diced fresh, seeded tomato

Juice of ½ lemon

Romaine, grape, or lemon leaves for lining a 4-quart saucepan

Oil for shining the shells

Lemon wedges

5. Line a deep 4-quart saucepan with leaves and arrange the mussels in the center, hinge end down, propping them so that they support one another. Continue to stuff and tie the mussels, then place them in a circle, each resting slightly on the inner circle, always with the hinge side down. When all the mussels are in tight layers in the saucepan, weight them down using a heatproof plate just large enough to fit inside to prevent them from opening while cooking. Taste the mussel liquor accumulated while opening the mussels and dilute it until it no longer tastes salty. Add 1 cup of this liquid and lemon juice to the saucepan. Cover with a tight-fitting lid and bring to a boil. Reduce the heat to medium-low and simmer gently 20 minutes. Remove the saucepan from the heat; allow to rest 20 minutes before removing the cover and plate.

6. To serve, remove the strings and wipe each shell with oil so that it glistens. Serve with plenty of lemon wedges.

NOTE TO THE COOK: When purchasing large mussels, remember they're often heavy with mud, so check each one and discard any that seem too heavy in relation to others of similar size.

How to Open a Raw Mussel for Stuffing

✧

You see men opening raw mussels on waterfronts in Greece and Turkey. They open them so fast you can hardly believe it. It sounds hard, but it really isn't. It's just a matter of getting the hang of it.

The object is to pry the raw mussel open without damaging either mussel or shell. Some advocate microwaving the mussels for a few seconds, just long enough to make them open. Others recommend 2 to 3 minutes in the freezer. Ayla Algar, in her terrific book on Turkish cooking, suggests soaking them in warm salty water until they begin to open on their own. All three methods work, but for some reason not always for every kind of mussel.

In case none of these methods works for you, here's how an eastern Mediterranean cook does the job.

Use a kitchen cloth to pull off the beard that protrudes from the shell, then scrape off the barnacles. Working in batches of six, soak mussels in warm salted water to make them open slightly. Working over a bowl to catch the liquid, hold a mussel in a piece of heavy cloth with the rounded edge facing out. Squeeze the two parts of the shell in opposite directions to loosen. Using a triangular cheese knife or oyster knife, gently slide the tip into the opening, then work the knife around the shell toward the hinge. Don't break the hinge. Rather, pry open the mussel without separating the shells too widely. Sever the top of the mussel meat from the shell. (This preserves the neat appearance of the mussel meat.) Rinse the mussel attached to the shell in the liquor and shake out any sand. Proceed with stuffing the mussels.

5

SALADS

CHIFFONADE OF WILD AND NOT-SO-WILD EDIBLE GREENS

❖

We're all familiar with a traditional Greek salad—a mixture of large torn pieces of lettuce, chunks of tomato, and cubes of feta cheese. On the island of Crete I discovered another popular salad that is just the opposite: a dense and intensely flavorful combination of *very thinly cut* assorted young wild spring greens, providing a spectrum of colors from celadon to lushly verdant, of flavors from strong to sweet, and of textures from wiry to soft.

"There's an art to blending greens," Mirsini Lambraki tells me, as we set off to gather ingredients for this salad. We find nearly twenty kinds, each playing a different role.

The secret is to cut each leaf *as thinly as possible*, then to mix the greens ahead of time so that they wilt and become dense and the flavors intermingle. Salt is added just before serving to keep the greens from expressing too much moisture. To imagine the final texture, think of this salad as a relish you can press between slices of bread. Experiment with mesclun mixed with baby spinach, fresh leafy herbs, and even romaine.

Bulky romaine lettuce isn't usually thought of as a particularly flavorful green, but if you haven't tried it thinly shredded you're definitely in for a treat. The shredding brings out the elusive flavor of romaine. The thinner the shreds, the denser the mixture, and the deeper the flavor will be, especially when the shreds are tossed with a light vinegary dressing made with just a drizzle of extra-virgin olive oil.

In the Middle East, shredded romaine is combined with cress, cucumbers, tomatoes, and chilies for this region's version of a Greek salad. In spring, other kinds of greens, including radish leaves, young mustard, and peppercress, may be substituted.

GARDEN GREENS AND HERBS
WITH TOMATOES AND GREEN OLIVES (*Cyprus*)

❀

Serves 2

This truly lovely Cypriot version of a Greek salad is so popular that, in the words of Niki Moquist, the Cypriot-American who provided the recipe, "It is served almost every day in almost every home except in the heat of summer when it would be too hot to gather the greens."

Juice of ½ lemon or more to taste

2 to 3 tablespoons extra-virgin olive oil

Salt

Freshly ground black pepper

1 small wedge of savoy or regular green cabbage, washed, drained, dried, and finely shredded (½ cup)

1 cup washed, drained, dried, stemmed, and torn arugula leaves

½ cup washed, drained, dried, stemmed, and torn baby spinach leaves or other tasty baby greens

½ cup washed, drained, dried, stemmed, and coarsely chopped cilantro leaves

4 scallions, white plus at least 3 inches green leaves, finely sliced

8 cherry tomatoes, halved

½ cup green olives, rinsed and drained

Don't feel you need be held to the amounts below. Just try to stay within the parameters so as to create a refreshing balance, and be sure to use plenty of lemon. This salad, which has become a favorite in my house, makes a great first course.

Combine the lemon juice, olive oil, salt, and pepper in a salad bowl. Add the greens, cilantro, scallions, tomatoes, and green olives. Toss well and serve at once.

NOTE TO THE COOK: I buy a whole small cabbage and cut wedges out of it daily as needed. If well-wrapped, a cut cabbage should keep well for at least 10 days.

WATERCRESS AND TOMATO SALAD
WITH CURED TUNA (*Spain*)

❊

Serves 4

José Antonio Valdespino prepares a similar version of this dish at his restaurant, La Mesa Redonda, in Jerez.
Dried tuna or "ahi jerky" is a fairly new item in U.S. markets, similar to the prized Spanish product called *mojamma* cut from the tuna's back, then salted and air-dried. If you can't find *mojamma* and must settle for "ahi jerky," be sure to soak out the Asian flavorings, then replace them with the simpler Mediterranean flavors of olive oil and lemon.

You might want to serve an *arroz* from Alicante (see pages 217–222) after this delicious salad.

1 ounce dried tuna, finely diced to make ⅓ cup

Juice of 1 lemon

3 tablespoons extra-virgin olive oil

1 bunch (5 ounces) very fresh watercress, washed, dried, and stemmed

1 teaspoon dried savory, oregano, or *herbes de Provence*

Freshly ground black pepper

2 red ripe tomatoes, thinly sliced

1. Soak the dried tuna in a mixture of lemon juice and olive oil for at least 2 hours to soften.

2. Just before serving, mix the watercress with the dried herbs and freshly ground black pepper on a flat serving platter. Cover with thin slices of tomato and sprinkle dried tuna and its soaking marinade on top. Serve at once.

Warm Escarole and Pomegranates with Sherry and Sherry Wine Vinegar (*Spain*)

❖

Serves 3 or 4

Gentle warmth applied to cool leafy greens can have a magical effect. In this elegant and easy bitter-sweet-sour winter salad from Granada, soft green leaves of escarole are warmed at the last minute in oil, garlic, sherry, and sherry wine vinegar. The leaves, having absorbed the flavors, are then tossed and sprinkled with pomegranate seeds.

Other greens that will work well here are slivers of Belgian endive, *frisée*, or mildly bitter, yellowish-white *radicchio di Castelfranco*. When you make this salad, I suggest you follow it with the Rice with Fresh Tuna and Mussels (page 224).

1 small head escarole

2 small cloves garlic, peeled and lightly crushed

2 tablespoons olive oil

2 teaspoons sherry wine vinegar

2 teaspoons dry sherry

½ teaspoon salt

Pinch of freshly ground black pepper

½ cup pomegranate seeds

1. Thoroughly wash the escarole, separate the soft tender leaves, and dry. Tear the leaves into 1½- to 2-inch pieces and place in a wide salad bowl. You should have about 6 cups.

2. In a skillet gently warm the garlic in 1 tablespoon of the olive oil and discard the garlic. Add the vinegar and dry sherry to the oil and bring just to a boil. Pour over the greens to just warm them. Add the remaining oil, salt, and pepper and toss well. Scatter pomegranate seeds on top and serve at once.

THE CHICORIES

❖

The mother of all chicories was surely color-blind when she created this "green," which appears in numerous shades of jade, green, dark green, red, and cream. Yet I've never met a chicory I didn't like, from broadleaf and curly endive to radicchio and the fascinating coiled puntarella with its greenish-white succulent stems. Recently I counted sixteen varieties of chicory in the Cook's Garden catalog, each with its own distinctive texture and flavor. And, best of all, when cooked, they mix beautifully with other greens.

All chicories have a bitter edge that the creative cook can use to play off against such condiments as pomegranate molasses, tahini, anchovies, garlic, vinegar, tomatoes . . . and just about anything else.

If you find yourself working with a chicory that's just too bitter, use the Italian method—soak the leaves in salted water for an hour. If too sharp, tough, or intense, blanch for 5 minutes in plenty of boiling water, then press down on the leaves as they drain on a wooden board.

SLIVERED ENDIVE, FENNEL, AND BLOOD ORANGE SALAD (*Italy*)

Serves 6

The fennel bulb is shaved into super thin slices, creating tenderness without cooking. The sweet taste of the blood oranges tames the bitter endive.

This very fine salad is delicious with the Tunisian Fish Couscous with Pumpkin and Leafy Greens (page 205).

2 fennel bulbs (1 pound)

2 Belgian endives, or 6 tender celery ribs with leaves removed

Juice of 1 lemon

2 blood or navel oranges

4 tablespoons extra-virgin olive oil

Salt

Freshly ground black pepper

5 ounces watercress, washed and stemmed

¼ cup small juicy black olives such as Niçoise

2 thin slices red onion

1. Wash the fennel; remove the tops and the hard outer stalks and trim the base. Quarter and cut into very thin slices.

2. Wash the endives and cut into thin slices. Soak all vegetables in cold water and the lemon juice for 1 hour.

3. Peel the oranges and cut into small chunks.

4. In a mixing bowl, toss drained fennel, endive, and oranges with the oil, salt, and pepper to taste. Garnish with small sprigs of watercress, a few olives, and the red onion rings and serve.

Purslane and Baby Greens with Cucumber and Shredded Cabbage (*Israel*)

Serves 6

I learned this recipe from chef Moshe Basson, owner of the Jerusalem restaurant Eucalyptus and famous in Israel for his knowledge of wild native green herbs, which he features in his cooking.

"I cook the food of the land of Israel," he tells me, as we venture into the Judaean hills in search of wild greens. "I search the Bible for hints as to what's authentic."

It's spring, and the hills are carpeted with fresh wild plants. Moshe's a short, handsome, stocky guy of Iraqi-Jewish heritage. He wears his yarmulke lopsided on his head.

"I learned early about survival food," he tells me. "First I watched the goats on my father's farm, what they ate, then Arab children in our village who ate peas and beans the European Jews thought were poisonous, then old Palestinian and Druse women who collected wild plants nobody else would bother with."

Moshe refined his knowledge of wild greens during his military service. As an army cook, he constantly quizzed his fellow soldiers, asking them what they ate at home.

Shortly past Ein Kerem, birthplace of John the Baptist, we stop to collect some hyssop and extraordinary wild wide-leaf sage (*Salvia spectabilis*) that flowers in the shape of a menorah. When we return to Jerusalem, Moshe will serve me this delicious smoky-flavored green stuffed with rice, the combination heightened and held together by the addition of a little lemony sumac.

A little farther on we stop to pick wild thistles. After removing the thorns and green-white leaves, Moshe peels a stalk for me. "Please chew; notice how it quenches your thirst," he says. I find the stalk tart and refreshing. Meantime, Moshe cleans the egg-size thistle down to the size of a marble. "This has a very delicate flavor," he tells me, "more delicate than an artichoke. I often serve it at the restaurant with lamb."

Moshe's a creative cook. Sometimes he'll spend an entire day working with an ingredient, struggling to create a new recipe. "Some people think I'm crazy," he says. "Perhaps they're right. Wild greens are my passion."

We stop to pick some za'atar for a bitter salad, as well as greens for the salad bowl: river mint, cresses, wild chicory.

"The trouble with cultivated salad greens is they need too much water. I think greens must 'suffer' to develop great flavor," he says.

Back in Jerusalem, I admire his very young purslane, which has a lovely lemony flavor. "You can serve it raw only when it's very young," he tells me. "Otherwise, it's better to cook it."

"Raw or cooked," I respond, "it's one of my favorite greens. It was a favorite of Gandhi's too."

"Really?" he replies, straight-faced. "That surprises me because when Ben Kingsley was here he asked me to identify these leaves!"

Purslane, of course, is wonderful simply dressed with garlic and olive oil. Since farmers' markets usually offer purslane in small amounts, here's a delicious refreshing salad that will stretch a couple of cups of young leaves to feed six.

For a delicious summer lunch, follow the salad with a double recipe of Green Dumplings Tossed with Diced Tomato, Toasted Walnuts, and Fresh Herbs (page 200). Finish with a sorbet or fruit compote and the Black Sea Cornmeal Wafers Baked on Collard Greens (page 339).

2 cups very young purslane leaves,
(¾ pound uncleaned)

½ cup scallions, white part only, thinly sliced into rings

1 cup peeled, seeded, and cubed cucumber

1 cup shredded cabbage, soaked in salted water for 30 minutes, rinsed and drained

2 cups baby greens or mesclun

2 tablespoons fresh lemon juice or more to taste

3 to 4 tablespoons extra-virgin olive oil

Salt

Freshly ground black pepper ·

Sprigs of fresh mint, salad burnet, and chives for garnish

1. Wash the purslane and pat dry with paper toweling.

2. Combine the purslane with the scallions, cucumber, cabbage, and baby greens.

3. Separately, combine the lemon juice, olive oil, salt, and pepper to taste, mixing well. Toss with the greens; garnish with mint leaves, flowers, and chives. Serve as an accompaniment to grilled fish, lamb kabobs, or just good bread.

Purslane and Samphire Salad
with Tapenade Toasts (France)

Serves 8

Purslane and samphire are both succulent and green and both have a slightly tart flavor. When mixed together in a salad they make for a wonderful refreshing combination of puckery tastes and crunchy textures.

Samphire is the European variant for our glasswort or pickleweed, or "sea bean" as it's called in Asian and gourmet markets. You find it growing in salt marshes at low tide along both coasts, and, according to Roger Phillips in *Wild Food*, occasionally inland in wet areas of Tennessee, Kentucky, Idaho, and Ohio. Summer is the best time to gather this green, when its tender tips are perfect for salads.

½ pound fresh sea bean tips (4 cups)

½ onion, chopped

¼ teaspoon red pepper flakes

1 tablespoon hazelnut oil

2 tablespoons olive oil

¼ cup verjuice or crushed and strained grape juice reduced to 2 tablespoons and mixed with 1 teaspoon mild vinegar

4 cups trimmed purslane tips

2 cups young arugula leaves, stemmed

Salt

Tapenade Spread (recipe follows)

16 thin rounds of stale French bread, browned in olive oil and rubbed with ½ clove garlic

Along the Aegean and Turkish Mediterranean coasts, samphire is boiled and served with a taratour sauce (opposite page).

You can eat samphire raw when very tender; if tough it should be blanched in boiling water first.

1. Wash the sea beans, cut away any hard stalks, and soak for 1 to 2 hours to remove excess salt.

2. Prepare a marinade with the onion, red pepper flakes, hazelnut and olive oils, and verjuice. Blanch the beans in boiling water for 2 minutes; refresh and drain dry. Marinate the sea beans for at least 1 hour.

3. Just before serving, mix the sea beans and marinade with the purslane and arugula, add salt to taste, and arrange on individual serving plates. Serve with tapenade spread on small toast rounds.

Thanks to chefs Johnny Graham and James O'Shea for their guidance in preparing sea beans.

TAPENADE SPREAD

Makes 1 cup

1 cup oily French black olives, pitted, soaked in cold water to remove salt, then patted dry

1 2-ounce can anchovy fillets, rinsed and patted dry

3 tablespoons salted capers, soaked, drained, and patted dry

2 tablespoons lemon juice

½ teaspoon Dijon mustard

Freshly ground black pepper

1½ tablespoons dark rum

¼ cup fruity olive oil

In a food processor, combine the olives, anchovies, capers, lemon juice, mustard, pepper, and rum and blend until pasty and smooth. With the machine on, pour in just enough olive oil in a steady stream to obtain a smooth thick sauce. Let stand at least 1 hour before serving.

Variation:
PURSLANE OR SAMPHIRE WITH TARATOUR SAUCE (*Turkey*)

Serves 6

Walnuts are slightly bitter, lemon is tart, garlic is pungent, and olive oil is soothing. Put them all together and you get a thick, complex, and special sauce for greens.

This is a nice dish for early fall. In winter, you can substitute clusters of mâche for the purslane.

1 cup shelled walnuts

3 cloves garlic, peeled and green shoot removed

½ teaspoon sea salt

½ cup cubed stale bread

½ cup chilled water or unflavored soda water

Juice of 1 lemon

2 tablespoons extra-virgin olive oil

1 tablespoon finely chopped flat-leaf parsley

6 cups young green leaves, washed, drained, and patted dry

In a heavy mortar, pound the walnuts until pasty. Remove and set aside. In the same mortar crush the garlic and salt until smooth and pulpy. (Alternatively, you can do this in a food processor, but the nuts will not be as smooth.) Soak the bread in half the water and then squeeze to express all moisture. Pound the bread with the garlic and walnuts until well blended. Thin with lemon juice, 1 tablespoon olive oil, and just enough of the remaining ¼ cup water to achieve a smooth dipping sauce. Let stand 1 hour, then adjust the seasoning. Drizzle with the remaining tablespoon of oil and garnish with the parsley.

LEAFY GREENS AND POMEGRANATES
WITH CHEESE CRISPS (*Italy*)

❊

Serves 4

I was thrilled to meet Anne-Marie Lombardi, a strikingly handsome forty-something woman who's been aptly described as the "queen of Italian Molisana cooking." Blond, chic, and energetic, she caters parties for upscale families, travels the world representing Molisana cooking, and has written the only book on the food of Molise, a small, relatively unknown Italian region situated between Abruzzo and Apulia.

Twenty years ago, when white truffles were first discovered in Molise, Anne-Marie immediately found ways to incorporate them into her repertory, including a beautiful salad of young crisp arugula leaves tossed with fresh pomegranate seeds nestled in a crisp truffle-perfumed cheese wafer.

The wafer is an idea borrowed from the northern region of Fruili, where it's called *frico*. Slivers of Montasio cheese are arranged on a well-seasoned skillet and allowed to melt into a thin sheet that turns golden brown and incredibly aromatic within minutes.

Anne-Marie uses the southern Caciocavallo cheese, which she sprinkles with grated truffle as it cooks. Immediately after removing the sheet of fried cheese from the skillet, she drapes it over the back of a cereal bowl to form a charming and edible cheese wafer bowl in which to serve a simple arugula and pomegranate salad. (In the Fruilian variation below, the bowl is created to contain a slice of grill-marked polenta.)

If you have trouble finding Caciocavallo, use Montasio, or, in a pinch, young imported Asiago. (American Asiago is not the same. Also note that Asiagos are saltier and cook faster than Montasio or Caciocavallo.)

The crisp cheese wafers needn't be warm, so you can make and shape them ahead of time.

If you can't find white truffles, a few drops of truffle oil can be substituted for the olive oil to grease your nonstick skillet.

CHEESE CRISPS

4 ounces slow-melting Italian cheese such as Caciocavallo, aged Montasio, or as a last resort imported young Asiago

¼ teaspoon olive oil

1½ teaspoons grated white truffle (optional)

DRESSING

2 teaspoons extra-virgin olive oil or truffle oil

½ teaspoon *mild* wine vinegar

Pinch of salt

Freshly ground pepper

½ cup fresh or defrosted pomegranate seeds (see Note)

2 cups baby arugula leaves, washed, dried, and stemmed

1. Grate the cheese. You will need about ⅓ cup cheese to make each small cheese cup.

2. For the first cheese cup, lightly brush a nonstick 8-inch skillet or a stoneware griddle with the oil and set it over medium-low heat. Scatter one portion of the cheese in a thin even round 5 to 6 inches in diameter and allow it to melt slowly and turn golden and crisp, about 2 to 3 minutes. Flip the round, sprinkle the cooked side with one-fourth of the grated truffle, if using, and continue to cook until the *frico* is golden brown around the edges, about 30 seconds. Immediately slide it onto an inverted bowl in order to shape it into a cup while still warm. Remove and let cool. Repeat with the remaining cheese to make 3 more cheese cups. (You won't need to oil the pan after the first round. While the *frico* is cooling, blot away any excess oil.)

3. Combine all the ingredients for the dressing. Dress the arugula and sprinkle with pomegranate seeds. Serve in the cheese cups as a first course.

NOTE TO THE COOK: Buy the reddest pomegranates you can find, roll them around on your kitchen counter to soften, then break up in a bowl of water to keep juice from spurting. Drain, place skin side up in the bowl, and give each section a good bang with the back of a heavy knife to loosen the seeds. Use the seeds right away or store in a small covered container in the freezer.

Variation: LEAFY GREENS WITH WAVY FRICO AND GRILLED POLENTA (*Italy*)

Near Tolmezzo in northern Italy, not more than an hour's drive from Udine, chef-owner Gianni Cosetti presides over his Ristorante Roma, a stronghold of great cooking barely big enough to seat thirty diners. Among his dishes is one in which a cheese wafer or *frico* is used as a "bowl" in which to serve small slices of grilled polenta, the concept derived from the local custom of slicing leftover hardened cornmeal-based soup, then grilling it to serve with crunchy rounds of fried cheese.

For the *frico*, the cheese of choice is one-year-old Montasio, rather bland in its natural state but ideal for slow-melting, which is the secret of success with this dish. Grated and then spread out on a skillet to melt, it is transformed into thin and incredibly delicious crunchy wafers.

Slices of leftover polenta are grilled very slowly so that they become crisp on the outside while remaining meltingly soft within. (I should mention that Gianni Cosetti also makes an incredibly sumptuous polenta dish in which he tops a pool of the creamiest polenta with melting cheese and a cornmeal-enriched beurre noisette, topped in turn with foie gras!)

1. Make the *frico* as described on page 143.

2. For the polenta, see the grilled Polenta Crostini (page 108). Cut ½ pound cooked polenta into 12 slices, each approximately 3 inches long, 1 inch wide, and ½ inch thick; lightly brush the cut sides with olive oil and *very slowly* broil or grill until crisp on both sides.

3. Serve in the cheese bowls accompanied by slices of sausage, smoked fish, or marinated herring and a glass of wine, or with soft scrambled eggs.

Shredded Red Radicchio and Smoked Fish Salad with Polenta Crostini (*Italy*)

❊

Serves 4 as a first course

This delicious salad is made by combining finely shredded red radicchio, which is slightly bitter, with plump flakes of a rich smoked fish doused with plenty of lemon juice and seasoned with plenty of black pepper. I use smoked tuna rather than the traditional smoked herring, since the latter is difficult to find these days except in German and Russian delis. My favorite brand of smoked tuna comes from Duckworth Fish Farms (see "Mail-Order Sources"); use it and it will put this salad in a class by itself.

A similar salad is eaten by grape harvesters in Spain and Italy during picking season. They warm the smoked fish over an outdoor grill, then eat it along with wild edible greens, freshly picked grapes, bread, and wine.

I learned of this salad from an elderly Italian who sat next to me one night at dinner. He described how he'd gone into someone's home right after World War II, and, upon seeing some fish hanging from the rafters, was flooded with childhood memories. He recalled how his father would use a pole to bring down some smoked herring hanging from a beam, how his mother would soak it in milky water to remove the salt and excess smokiness, then wrap it in brown paper and grill it in the fireplace. He remembered the herring being accompanied with horseradish, raw onion, and slices of grilled polenta that had the taste of smoke . . . and how delicious it all was.

Other members of the chicory family can be substituted for radicchio, but keep in mind that many "wild" green chicories are actually more bitter than red-leafed varieties.

If desired, this salad can be lightly warmed in the oven for 5 minutes to bring up the flavors.

1. If the fish fillets are excessively smoky, soak in the milk water for 20 minutes. Drain them, rinse, and pat dry. Cut the fillets into ¼-inch dice and toss with the oil, lemon juice, and black pepper.

4 ounces skinless, boneless, smoked fillets of tuna, herring (see Note if using whole smoked herring), mackerel, or trout

⅓ cup milk mixed with 2 cups water (optional)

2½ tablespoons extra-virgin olive oil

Juice of 1 lemon

Freshly ground black pepper

4 ounces (½ head) red radicchio or other bitter green

12 to 16 rounds of sautéed Polenta Crostini (page 108)

2. Wash, drain, and finely shred the radicchio. Toss with the fish cubes and sprinkle with pepper. Let stand at room temperature 10 to 20 minutes before serving. Serve with the sautéed polenta.

NOTE TO THE COOK: If you manage to find a whole smoked herring, skin and fillet it, then discard the head, skin, and bones. If the fillets are excessively salty or smoky, soak them in milky water for 20 minutes, drain, rinse, and pat dry. Soak the roe, or creamy milt, in several changes of cold water to remove salt and excessive smokiness, drain, and cut into tiny cubes; then add to the salad.

MARINATED TREVISO-STYLE RADICCHIO WITH CRUMBLED EGGS (*Italy*)

Serves 6

This terrific salad improves with age; keep it up to a week under a thin film of olive oil. The elongated Treviso-style radicchio heads are cut lengthwise, then boiled in a solution of vinegar and water to preserve their vivid color. By the third day they're ready to be garnished with fresh hard-cooked eggs, producing a lovely magenta, white, and yellow dish.

Round red radicchio is best eaten raw, while elongated elegant Treviso-style radicchio is best cooked. During winter months, when Treviso-style radicchio comes on the market, it will keep in the refrigerator for up to 2 weeks provided it's well wrapped. Unwrapped it's likely to turn green, a sign of oxidization, which alters the taste. Always discard greenish leaves.

This salad goes well with an assortment of small salads and a plate of crisp grilled slices of polenta.

1 pound (3 heads) Treviso-style radicchio

1 cup mild vinegar such as rice or apple cider

1 clove

½-inch piece of cinnamon stick

6 tablespoons extra-virgin olive oil plus more for drizzling just before serving

Salt

Freshly ground black pepper

2 farm fresh eggs

Grilled Polenta slices (page 108)

Do steps 1, 2, and 3 three days in advance.

1. Wash the Treviso-style radicchio, discarding any green-tinged or bruised leaves. Quarter lengthwise, leaving the core to hold the wedge intact.

2. Combine the vinegar, 3 to 4 cups water—depending on the acidity of the vinegar—and the spices in a wide noncorrodible saucepan or skillet and bring to a boil. Working in batches, add the wedges of radicchio, top with a glass lid to keep them submerged, and boil for 1½ minutes. Remove and drain on paper toweling. Repeat with the remaining wedges. Discard the clove and cinnamon stick. Press radicchio gently to remove excess moisture.

3. In a glass, plastic, or ceramic bowl, stack wedges in crisscrossing layers; brushing each wedge with some of the oil; cover tightly. *Refrigerate for three days before serving.* (If properly pickled, dried, and soaked with olive oil, the radicchio will keep a week.)

4. About 1 hour before serving, bring the wedges of Treviso-style radicchio to room temperature. Slice on the diagonal into 1-inch strips. Sliver the root and sprinkle over the strips. Toss with salt and pepper and drizzle with fresh olive oil. Let stand while hard-cooking the eggs. Peel eggs when cool and rub along the side of a large-hole grater directly over the radicchio; season lightly with salt and pepper and serve with grilled polenta.

With thanks to Lucio Gomiero for sharing this recipe.

SAUTÉED YARD-LONG BEANS AND WALNUTS WITH GARDEN GREENS (*Turkey*)

❀

Serves 6

The so-called yard-long bean, readily available in Asian markets, makes an excellent substitute for asparagus beans or any of the thin, very long flavorful Mediterranean beans called *fagiolino dall'occhio* in Italy, *taze börülce* in Turkey, and *ambelofassoula* in Greece.

When buying, choose beans that are pencil thin, young (under a foot long), floppy but still firm. These beans aren't actually "a yard long"; if they were they'd be much too tough.

When young these beans are usually treated like string beans around the Mediterranean—cooked until just tender and served in salads. On the Greek island of Astapalya they're chopped with onion and fresh mint, shaped into fritters, then fried and served with a garlicky *skordalia* sauce. At the Apulian restaurant Al Fornello da Ricci they're cooked until meltingly tender, then tossed with pasta.

Long beans are extremely popular in Turkey. In the Black Sea town of Amasra, once an important port for trade with Genoa, whole potfuls of long beans are cooked until tender, then tossed with olive oil and garlic for a dish called *taze fasulye makarnasi* or "fresh macaroni-style beans." And there are other Black Sea dishes in which these long beans are diced as small as grains of rice, cooked until soft, then combined with slow-cooked onions and rice for a regional pilaf.

(continued)

1 firm bunch (1 pound) asparagus beans or Chinese yard-long beans

3 tablespoons olive oil

Salt

⅓ cup coarse chopped walnuts

½ teaspoon mildly hot red pepper such as Turkish pepper or Aleppo red pepper, or a mixture of hot and sweet Hungarian paprika

3 tablespoons mild vinegar or verjuice

2 cups torn garden lettuces

About 2 tablespoons fresh lemon juice

This Turkish long-bean recipe is from the town of Bodrum on the Aegean coast. It's a lively, refreshing salad redolent of lemon juice and is a popular *mezze*. In the words of my Turkish translator, Maja: "No matter how much red pepper you put in, there must be an equal amount of lemon. In Bodrum, where we serve this salad as a *mezze*, it must be very sour, so sour you want to pucker your mouth." Sort of like eating sushi with too much wasabi—painful and also wonderful. Diner, be warned!

Wash the beans; trim the ends and cut each bean in thirds. Heat the oil and sauté the beans for an instant in a wide, deep skillet, stirring. Add the salt and ¼ cup water. Cover the skillet and cook the beans for 3 minutes. Uncover; add the walnuts, red pepper, and vinegar; and cook until the green beans are just tender, 1 to 2 minutes. Stir in the greens and lemon juice and stir once to mix. Let stand until ready to serve at room temperature.

CACTUS, CILANTRO, AND *HARISSA* SALAD (*Tunisia*)

❧

Serves 2

Cactus came to the Mediterranean world from the Americas; its fruit is eaten throughout the region, but the only place around the sea I found cooks using cactus leaves in their dishes was in the southern Tunisian town of Gafsa. There I found this salad and also a stew of lamb smothered in cactus leaves (see page 259).

The taste of cactus pads or leaves has been described as falling somewhere between green peppers, green beans, and asparagus. I agree. When lightly blanched, cactus leaves retain their crunchy texture.

This salad is similar to cactus salads I've eaten in California, the main difference being in the hot sauce. Tunisian cooks use *harissa* (page 343), and it can be made in minutes. This is a wonderful salad to serve before a rich and satisfying Tunisian lamb stew.

2 bright green, small, firm cactus pads

1 small red onion

1 teaspoon salt

1 teaspoon *harissa* (page 343) blended with
1 tablespoon warm water

4 tablespoons lemon juice

2 tablespoons chopped fresh cilantro

1. Wear rubber gloves or use tongs when handling cactus. Use a swivel-bladed peeler or small knife to remove the spines and tiny thorns. Shave the edges of each pad and trim away any dry or fibrous areas. Cut into ½-inch dice. Soak in several changes of cold water for 10 minutes to remove any viscous fluid.

2. Drain the cactus, then simmer in salted water for 10 minutes. Meanwhile, thinly slice the onion and toss with 1 teaspoon salt. Rub the salt into the strands and let stand 5 minutes. Rinse and drain the onions. Drain the cactus; refresh to cool; mix with the onion, or diluted *harissa*, and lemon juice. Serve at once garnished with the fresh cilantro.

Leafy Greens, Garlic, Yogurt, and Red Pepper Swirls (*Turkey*)

Serves 6

Yogurt, delicately balanced between curds and whey, appears in many guises. When vigorously whipped it thins; when heated it breaks; when salted it weeps. Whenever I cook with yogurt, I first drain it in a yogurt drainer or conical sieve to make yogurt cheese.

Yogurt and garlic: this great combination is ubiquitous around the eastern Mediterranean, appearing in two sauces—Turkish *jajik* and Greek *tzatziki*—often with some minced cucumber added. In Turkey there's a special round bowl for serving this sauce called the *jajik* bowl, gaily colored to offset the white of the yogurt, which is traditionally decorated with just a few swirls of dark minted oil.

I learned about a superior variation on *jajik* in southeastern Turkey, where I'd gone to participate in the annual spring rite in which home cooks gather nourishing young leaves, roots, and rhizomes just emerging from the winter earth. These early spring greens, believed to have healthful properties, are consumed nonstop over a six-week period in a variety of recipes, many of them scattered throughout this book.

From the greens gatherers I learned about such additions to yogurt-garlic sauce as shredded blanched collards and cubed red and green peppers; cooked or raw spinach, purslane, or chard; raisins and nuts; fried slices of carrot; slivered romaine lettuce; and, for me, best of all, this perfectly balanced salad/sauce/dip of tangy greens and red pepper swirls. Never did anything so healthy taste so very good!

Make this salad in advance so the flavors have time to mingle and soften. Serve with other greens dishes for a restorative meal or as a side dish to a bulgur pilaf or fried kibbeh. And please note that in the eastern Mediterranean, fish and yogurt are rarely served together.

2 loosely packed cups leafy greens: preferably young, tangy, or assertive greens such as mustard, turnip, *shunkiyu*, kale, or collard, stemmed (1½ to 2 ounces)

1 teaspoon sea salt plus more to taste

5 Swiss chard leaves, stemmed (about 3 ounces)

1 quart (32-ounce container) plain yogurt, drained overnight to make 2 cups

2 or more cloves garlic, peeled and crushed with a pinch of salt

½ cup cold water

1½ tablespoons olive oil

1 teaspoon crumbled dried "Italian seasonings" or a mix of savory, oregano, and marjoram

1 teaspoon mildly hot red pepper such as Turkish red pepper, or Aleppo pepper, or ¼ teaspoon hot Hungarian paprika and ½ teaspoon sweet Hungarian paprika

1. Wash the greens in several batches of water and set aside to drain.

2. Bring plenty of water to a boil in a large saucepan. Add 1 teaspoon salt and the strong-flavored greens and cook, uncovered, about 5 minutes. Add the Swiss chard and continue cooking until all the greens are tender, about 5 minutes. Drain, refresh, and squeeze out excess water. Finely chop all the greens to make about ½ cup.

3. Place the yogurt in a wide mixing bowl and use a fork to gradually blend in the garlic and ½ cup cold water until creamy and smooth. Fold in the greens and salt to taste. Heat the olive oil in a small pan, bring to a sizzle, add the dried herbs and red pepper, and swirl to develop aromas. Strain over the yogurt mixture in decorative swirls. Let stand 30 minutes before serving to allow flavors to mellow. Serve the greens with yogurt-garlic sauce spooned on top.

Variation:
CRUNCHY PURSLANE WITH GARLICKY YOGURT SAUCE

Boil a handful of chopped mature purslane for 1 minute. Leave to drain until cold. Make a yogurt-garlic sauce as directed above, mixing well. Refrigerate at least 2 hours before serving. Heat 2 tablespoons oil or butter and swirl over the greens just before serving.

MOROCCAN MIXED WILD GREENS SALAD
WITH PRESERVED LEMONS AND OLIVES (Morocco)

❀

Serves 4

*I*n Morocco, this cooked dip or spread of greens is normally made with mallow leaves that grow wild in the northern part of the country. From Turkey to Morocco, mallow is the preferred green in the Islamic world.

When cooked, greens such as purslane, miner's lettuce, chard, beet, and mallow achieve a rich, springy texture and mild earthy flavor, giving heft to a salad dip, important to North Africans who like to use a wedge of dense bread to scoop it up. Preserved lemons are a great match for any and all of these greens.

If you don't have mallow, I suggest you use as great a variety of greens as possible to make your spread interesting. I've often started with a supermarket braising mix, then added chard and some miner's lettuce or winter purslane, creating a delicious dish.

When you eat this dip, the greens should melt on your tongue. If your dip isn't sufficiently creamy, you may want to beat in some additional olive oil.

This spread will keep for several days if stored covered in the refrigerator.

1 pound (6 cups) mallow or mixed leafy, mild-flavored greens (see above)

4 ounces (1 cup) stemmed flat-leaf parsley, chopped

3 cloves garlic, unpeeled

1 ounce (½ cup) cilantro leaves, roughly chopped

¼ teaspoon salt plus more to taste

3 tablespoons extra-virgin olive oil plus more for finishing

¼ teaspoon sweet paprika

Pinch of hot red pepper

¼ teaspoon ground cumin or more to taste

Juice of ½ lemon or more to taste

¼ preserved lemon (see page 347)

12 Moroccan oil-cured olives, pitted and soaked in several batches of water to remove salt

1. Wash the greens until water runs clear. Drain, stem, and chop roughly. Steam the greens, parsley, and garlic until tender, about 15 minutes. Cool the greens, then squeeze out as much moisture as possible and chop finely. Peel the garlic; place in a mortar with the cilantro and ¼ teaspoon salt and crush to a paste.

2. Heat 3 tablespoons olive oil in a 10-inch skillet, add the garlic paste and the chopped greens, and cook over medium-low heat until all the liquid has evaporated, turning the mixture often to avoid burning, about 10 minutes. Blend in the paprika, hot pepper, cumin, and lemon juice. Cool slightly, then beat in enough oil to make the texture similar to whipped potatoes. Cover and refrigerate for at least 1 hour before serving.

3. Correct the seasoning with more salt, cumin, and lemon juice if necessary; whip once more to lighten the mixture. Rinse the preserved lemon and remove the pulp, then slice the peel into slivers. Shape the greens mixture into a smooth hemisphere and decorate with slivered lemon peel and black olives.

Samira's Tabbouleh
with Parsley, Cinnamon, and Cumin (*Israel*)

❧

Makes 3 cups, serving 4

*I*n my view tabbouleh is not really a grain salad, rather a dense parsley salad that includes some bulgur. At its best it is lightly spiced, made tart with lemon or unripe grape juice and richly flavored with good extra-virgin olive oil. An Arabic linguist and food writer, Charles Perry, believes the word *tabbouleh* derives from *tewbil*, which means spices—not surprising, since most eastern Mediterranean bulgur dishes are kneaded or saturated with spices.

Judy Stacey Goldman, a Canadian-born Israeli cookbook author, took me to Oussifiya, a Druse village in the lower Galilee famous for the good cooking of the local women. Among the dishes they prepared for me were a delicious bread thrown in the air to thin out the dough, cooked over a heated concave metal tray, then served with local wild herbs; a wonderful dish of stuffed zucchini subtly scented with spices; and this very fine example of tabbouleh, more green than grain—just what I think a great tabbouleh should be.

A tall, thin woman named Samira, wearing a yellow apron and a head scarf, emerged as the principal cook among the Druse women. She had brought along her "toolbox," an old cola six-pack container, holding six plastic jars of spices. "We are rich people," she told me, "so we can afford to cook with spices."

When I peeked into the contents of the jars I found quality cinnamon, cumin, allspice, sweet paprika, and black pepper, and an extremely aromatic red pepper from the town of Yakha, where, I was told, the finest peppers in Israel are grown. Along with her six-pack of spices, Samira had packets of dried wild herbs, including hyssop, marjoram, and za'atar.

She worked like an alchemist, making a stuffing for the zucchini, seasoning the bulgur for potato kibbehs (she boiled the potatoes in an empty one-gallon olive oil can set over a brazier), then set about making her tabbouleh, which she left to rest for an hour so the flavors could blend.

The resulting dish was extraordinary, vibrant with cumin, cinnamon, and rich red pepper. Instead of adding lemon juice or vinegar, Samira added some verjuice, the filtered juice of unripe grapes, which added tartness and provided a very fruity flavor. She assured me lemon juice could also be used.

Serve this great tabbouleh salad with toasted pita bread or romaine lettuce leaves.

⅓ cup fine-grain bulgur (see Notes)

3 packed cups stemmed flat-leaf parsley, washed and completely dried

¼ cup fresh lemon, lime, verjuice (see "Mail-Order Sources"), or sour green grape juice

¾ teaspoon salt or more to taste

6 scallions, white plus 4 inches green leaves, thinly sliced

¼ teaspoon ground Ceylon cinnamon or more to taste

¼ teaspoon ground cumin or more to taste

Freshly ground black pepper

Pinch of Turkish red pepper

Pinches of sugar to taste

1 large red ripe tomato, peeled, seeded, and chopped

3 tablespoons olive oil

¼ cup finely shredded aromatic mint leaves, preferably spearmint

1 head romaine lettuce

1. Place the bulgur in a fine sieve. Shake it to remove any dust. Rinse under cool running water and drain. Let stand 10 minutes, then press out all moisture. Meanwhile, finely chop the parsley.

2. In a mixing bowl, combine everything but the mint and romaine, blending well. Cover and refrigerate for at least 2 hours before serving (it tastes even better after 24 hours). Fold in the mint, correct the seasoning, and serve. Serve with lettuce leaves.

NOTES TO THE COOK: One of the reasons some bulgur salads turn heavy is the "dust" that accompanies fine-grain bulgur. This dust doesn't plump up the way fine-grain bulgur does and will make an otherwise good salad soggy. The remedy: remove the dust by shaking the bulgur first in a fine sieve.

Turkish cooks use their accumulated "dust" (which should be stored in the freezer) to make small *köfte* balls flavored with red pepper and tomato pastes (see Walnut *Köfte* on page 103).

The texture of the salad will be superior if the greens are completely dry before being chopped.

See page 98 for a discussion of fine-, medium-, and coarse-grain bulgur wheat.

Ayfer's *Kisir*—Grain Salad
with Red Pepper Paste and Shredded Romaine
(*Turkey*)

❀

Makes 2 quarts, serving 12

My friend Ayfer Ünsal gave me this recipe with the caveat that in the Turkish city of Gaziantep, where she lives, no self-respecting woman would moisten bulgur with plain water. "If you did that no one would marry you!" she told me. "Normally you moisten bulgur with tomato or meat juices, onion juice, or spiced liquid. With the bulgur for *kisir* you use flavored water first."

In Turkish the word *kisir* means "insufficient" or "incomplete." It's considered incomplete because it's one of two or three bulgur dishes in which bulgur is served raw and cold, and not kneaded extensively with flavorings.

Kisir is Turkey's grain salad answer to Middle Eastern *tabbouleh*, both served light and loose. The primary difference is that in *kisir* the emphasis is on the bulgur, while in tabbouleh it is on the green.

For *kisir*, Turkish cooks use shredded romaine instead of parsley, and they add tomato and pepper paste as well as pomegranate molasses. *Kisir* makes a lovely summer salad piled loosely in a wide mound surrounded by boiled vine leaves or leaves of soft lettuce. You eat it by grasping up a small portion with the leafy green, shaping the bulgur into a marble-sized ball, then popping it all into your mouth.

Kisir is best made a few hours in advance so the flavors can meld. Serve as a mezze at room temperature.

2 tablespoons Turkish red pepper paste
(see "Mail-Order Sources")

2 tablespoons tomato paste

2 cups fine-grain bulgur

½ cup finely sliced scallions, white plus 4-inhes
green leaves

Salt

2 teaspoons mildly hot red pepper such as
Turkish or Aleppo pepper, or a combination
of hot and sweet Hungarian paprika

1 teaspoon ground cumin

1 teaspoon freshly ground black pepper

3 to 4 tablespoons extra-virgin olive oil

1 tablespoon pomegranate molasses
or more to taste

Juice of 1 lemon

1 cup finely chopped flat-leaf parsley

2 to 3 cups finely shredded tender romaine
lettuce leaves, ribs removed

24 tiny cherry tomatoes

8 pickled peppers (optional)

Outer leaves of romaine, or 48 boiled vine leaves
for garnish

1. In a saucepan heat the 2 cups water, add the red pepper and tomato pastes, and bring to a boil. Lower the heat and simmer for 5 minutes over medium heat.

2. Put the bulgur in a fine sieve, and shake it to remove any dust. Then place the bulgur in a wide bowl, pour the hot liquid over it, and let stand until cold. Use a fork to break up any lumps.

3. With oiled hands start mixing in first the scallions, salt, and spices; blend well. Then add the olive oil, pomegranate molasses, and lemon juice. Let stand at least 1 hour.

4. Fold in the parsley and romaine and spread out on a large serving dish. Top with cherry tomatoes and pickles, if desired, and surround with lettuce or vine leaves.

6

LIGHT MEALS

GREENS AND EGGS

Edible Wild Greens: A Visit with Sara the Goat Herder We all know the nonsense song "mares eat oats," which ends with a "a kid'll eat ivy too. Wouldn't you?" Actually, I had never been much inspired by this song. The only place I knew of in the United States where lawn or ground ivy was good to eat was Colorado, and I had never much wanted to eat in the same place as goats.

But I did last year when I went to a mountainous area called Stula in Israel's northern Galilee to meet Sara, mother of fourteen children, restaurateur, hotel-keeper, and goat herder. She'd immigrated to Israel from the Kurdish part of Iraq, arriving just after independence. She and several of her daughters settled there in what is probably, despite political hostilities, the most beautiful, quiet part of the country.

Sara grows her own wheat and produce for the Kurdish Jewish cuisine she serves at her restaurant. Now a stocky and youthful sixty-six, her eyes sparkling with warmth, a smile plastered on her mouth, she still prepares the recipes her mother taught her and also wears the same kind of clothes—peasant blouse, pantaloons with overlay skirt, a kerchief on her head to keep out the dust. She didn't seem much different from many of the eastern Mediterranean country women I've learned from over the years except that she probably worked twice as hard. Perhaps herding goats put her over the top. She has seventy goats and walks them at least twice a day.

The early spring day I came to visit, she took me out just before twilight to see what we could find in the way of wild edible greens. Before I could catch up with her I had to skip my way through a sumptuous field of overgrown thorny sow thistle—"sow thistle alley," I called it. In the last weeks of winter these thistles would have been perfect for use in stews or soups, but by the time I got to them they were far too large.

Still, since it was early spring, it was an excellent time to gather edible wild greens . . . and there were a great many underfoot, more than I'd ever seen in one place during all the years I'd gone foraging in Turkey, Tunisia, Italy, and Greece. I was delighted by the profusion and also amazed.

As we walked Sara showed me a list a naturalist had compiled for her of each season's edible greens. With the spring list in hand, she pointed out those she knew, many similar to greens that can be found in the United States (note asterisks). I counted more than thirty, including: wild mustard*, horsemint*, pennyroyal*, bergamot*, peppermint*, mountain balm, lemon balm, watercress*, thyme*, wild chamomile, verbena*, Syrian marjoram, blond psyllium, Roman hyssop, za'atar, nasturtium*, garland chrysanthemum*, cumin*, caraway*, sage*, coriander*, common cress*, dill*, purslane*, rue*, Roman pimpernel, corn poppy, sow thistle*, mallow*, and nettles*.

To find such an amazingly large number of tender leaves and shoots emerging from the earth was a wonderful experience. And I was thrilled to be with someone who could teach me how to recognize and pick them. In fact, I was in a state of bucolic exhilaration when the spell was suddenly broken. One of Sara's daughters came running out with a cell phone. Clients, she shouted, had just made a reservation for dinner!

Dinner that evening was extremely good: stuffed vegetables (grape leaves, cabbages, zucchinis), rice with fried dates, flat breads, kibbehs, eggplant salad, and pickled vegetables—all wonderful foods of the eastern Mediterranean. But in not one of them did I detect a single edible wild green! I couldn't believe it! With the greens she had shown me hours before she could have created an equally good dinner without laying out a penny for ingredients.

After the guests had gone to bed I asked Sara why. She smiled at me, then sadly shook her head. "The greens I showed you—no one wants them these days. Israelis think of them as 'survival food.' Eating them just brings back bad memories." In fact, she told me (and this was confirmed for me by several Israeli food writers), mallow and nettles had kept both Israelis and Arabs from starvation during the austere wartime period following Israeli independence.

The next morning Sara surprised me with a dish of curvy mallow leaves cooked with sautéed onions and scrambled with eggs. It was delicious!

WARM SCRAMBLED EGGS AND AROMATIC HERBS WITH BABY LETTUCES AND CRISPY CROUTONS (*Italy*)

Serves 2

Cesare Casella, formerly chef-owner of the Michelin-star restaurant Vipore in Tuscany, prepares this dish, based on a recipe he found in a historical cookbook while reading about the sixteenth-century Florentine mannerist painter Pontormo. The dish is delightfully seductive—a blend of scrambled eggs perfumed with herbs, pancetta, and baby greens, all topped with crisp, browned croutons.

RED WINE VINAIGRETTE

¾ teaspoon red wine vinegar

¾ teaspoon balsamic or sherry wine vinegar

¾ teaspoon red wine

1 tablespoon extra-virgin olive oil

Pinch of salt

⅛ teaspoon finely ground black pepper

2 tablespoons extra-virgin olive oil

½ cup finely diced stale, dense bread without crust

1 ounce finely diced pancetta (2½ tablespoons)

2 teaspoons Kittina's *Herbes de Provence* (see page 347) or a mixture of dried herbs such as thyme, savory, oregano, and lavender

5 large farm-fresh eggs

¼ teaspoon salt

Freshly ground black pepper

1½ ounces mesclun or mixed baby greens, washed and patted dry

1. Prepare the vinaigrette and set aside.

2. Place the olive oil in a 9-inch nonstick skillet over medium heat, and tilt the pan so the oil accumulates near the heat source. Heat until the oil just begins to expand in volume. Immediately add the bread and fry, stirring from time to time, until golden. Use a spatula to scrape the cubes to the other side of the pan, and remove at once to a paper towel to drain. Set the pan over medium-low heat, add the pancetta, and cook for 3 minutes, stirring. Add the dried herbs and cook another minute.

3. Meanwhile, beat the eggs in a mixing bowl with the salt and a pinch of black pepper. In a second bowl, toss the greens with the prepared vinaigrette and set near the skillet. Add the eggs to the skillet and scramble while gradually adding the prepared greens. *You will need to lift the skillet off the heat to avoid overcooking the eggs.* Divide onto two serving dishes and scatter the croutons on top. Serve at once.

ALICANTE-STYLE TORTILLA WITH GREEN GARLIC (*Spain*)

Serves 2

Unlike the dense potato-egg tortilla confection of Andalusia, this Alicante-style tortilla is light, flat, and heady with the aroma of garlic-infused eggs.

The best way to obtain the characteristic moistness of this dish is to use a 9- or 10-inch skillet, so that the eggs set very quickly. As soon as they set, they are turned out onto a prewarmed flat serving dish, which provides sufficient heat to complete the cooking process. The tortilla is then cut into wedges and served while still warm.

Skinny shoots of green garlic appear in the spring at the same time as asparagus and hops tops (see variations below). If you can't find them at your farmers' market, substitute a combination of minced garlic and lightly blanched scallions.

24 green garlic shoots

1½ tablespoons extra-virgin olive oil

Salt

4 to 5 large farm fresh eggs

Freshly ground black pepper

1. To clean the green garlic: Cut away the root ends and the tough green tops. Use all of the white part as well as the pale green stalk. Cut into 1-inch pieces. Put in a nonstick skillet with 1 teaspoon of the olive oil, ¼ cup water, and pinch of salt and cook, covered, over low heat until tender, about 5 minutes. Boil off any liquid in the skillet.

2. Meanwhile beat the eggs until well blended and season with salt and pepper. Shake the skillet so the green garlic spreads evenly. Add the remaining oil to the skillet. Add the eggs; set over medium-low heat, cover, and cook for 2 to 3 minutes, or until the top is just set. Turn out onto a 12-inch warm serving plate. (The eggs will continue to cook.) Serve hot or warm, cut into wedges.

Variation:
HOPS TOPS FRITTATA (*Italy*)

Serves 2

What do hops tops taste like? You guessed it—slightly but not aggressively bitter like beer. The texture is smooth and silky. If you know someone who grows hops to make beer at home, she'll have plenty of small, 4- to 5-inch shoots in late spring that she'll need to weed out. These will make a fine frittata.

6 to 7 ounces hops tops

¼ cup lemon juice

Salt

½ cup chopped onion

1½ tablespoons olive oil

Freshly ground black pepper

5 large farm-fresh eggs, beaten

1. Rinse the hops tops under running water; drain. Soak in water with 2 tablespoons of the lemon juice while bringing a pot of water to a boil. Add a pinch of salt and the remaining lemon juice to the boiling water (this keeps the hops green) and cook until they are crisp-tender, about 2 minutes.

2. Drain; refresh. Cut the hops tops into 1-inch pieces. Sauté the onion in the oil until wilted, add the hops tops, and fry until tender. Add the eggs and cook as above. Sprinkle with salt and pepper.

Variation: MOLISE-STYLE
FRITTATA WITH ASPARAGUS (*Italy*)

Serves 2 as a first course, lunch, or light supper

I first ate this very thin, moist, open omelet or frittata in a home in the province of Molise.

Although the dish served to me was made with deliciously bittersweet wild asparagus, the recipe is adaptable to all sorts of wild, bitter spring greens. Good candidates are nettle tops and the tart-flavored shoots of "butcher's brooms," which go deliciously with eggs. A reminder: don't eat wild greens you don't recognize.

Of course you can also substitute any fresh vegetable or wild green throughout the year: fried sliced onions and peas in summer and fried sliced potatoes in the fall or winter are excellent choices.

24 thinner-than-a-pencil asparagus

1½ tablespoons extra-virgin olive oil

Dried Mediterranean oregano

Salt

Freshly ground black pepper

5 large farm-fresh eggs

1. Trim the asparagus stalks, but do not peel. Cook in a shallow saucepan in boiling salted water until just tender, 3 to 4 minutes. Drain well and immediately transfer to a 12-inch skillet, preferably nonstick. Add the oil, oregano, a pinch of salt and pepper; sauté over medium heat for 2 minutes, stirring.

2. Beat the eggs until well blended and season with salt and pepper. Shake the skillet so the asparagus spreads evenly. Add the eggs and cook as above.

GRATIN OF LEAFY GREENS AND CRISPY POTATOES WITH SMOKY PAPRIKA AND WHIPPED EGGS (*Spain*)

❦

Serves 2

*T*he Spanish love colorful food, especially food bearing the colors of their flag—yellow (from saffron) and red (from paprika). This delicious gratin, from the Extremadura (the most rural province of Spain, near the Portuguese border) is typical of the red food of that area, where, along the lees of the Sierra de Gredos, comes the best paprika in Spain, called *pimentón de la Vera* (see "Mail-Order Sources"). It has a unique smoky flavor, the result of the slow drying of the peppers over wood fires. There are three types of *pimentón de la Vera*: sweet, bittersweet, and hot. This style of paprika is so highly valued that each can comes with a denomination-of-quality stamp and a numbered label.

Enjoy this dish on its own with some bread and wine.

2 firm, flavorful potatoes such as Yukon Gold (about ¾ pound)

8 to 10 large Swiss chard leaves or beet greens or turnip greens, washed and stemmed

3 tablespoons extra-virgin olive oil

2 large cloves garlic, peeled and lightly smashed

Salt

1 small red onion, thinly sliced

½ teaspoon sweet *pimentón* diluted in ½ cup water

2 eggs

Freshly ground black pepper

1. Preheat the oven to 400 degrees.

2. Brush a nonstick baking sheet with olive oil.

3. Peel the potatoes; slice into very thin (2-millimeter) rounds, cover the baking sheet with a layer of overlapping potatoes and set on the top shelf of the oven to bake for 15 minutes. Turn the potatoes over and bake for 15 minutes, or until the potato slices are lightly browned and tender.

4. While the potatoes are baking, cook the greens in plenty of boiling salted water until just tender. Drain greens; squeeze dry and shred with a sharp knife, about ¾ cup, tightly packed.

5. Heat 2 tablespoons of the oil in a medium heat-proof gratin pan until hot. Add the garlic and cook until aromatic and lightly browned by pressing down on the cloves with the back of a spoon. Add

the greens and a pinch of salt and fry for a few minutes, stirring. Remove from the pan.

6. Add the remaining tablespoon oil to the pan and reheat until hot, then cook the onion without browning for 3 to 4 minutes, stirring. Add the paprika-water and greens to the pan and boil for 2 to 3 minutes.

7. When the potatoes have baked for 30 minutes, remove from the oven. Reduce the oven temperature to 350 degrees. Spread potatoes over greens and onion.

8. Whip the eggs with a pinch of salt and pepper until frothy and pour over the potatoes. Set in the oven to bake until eggs are set, 2 to 3 minutes. Serve directly from the gratin pan.

YOUNG TURNIP SHOOTS AND TOPS WITH POTATOES AND SPANISH PAPRIKA

Serves 4

A bowl of simply boiled leafy greens combined with a really great-tasting potato is a much beloved dish in Spain. In Galicia, in the northwest part of the country, the dish reaches ethereal heights. It's made from special greens called *grelos* and meaty, yellow-skinned, freshly dug potatoes flavored with a local red-tinted oily sauce called *ajada*.

It took me a while to discover exactly what *grelos* were. I finally did, thanks to the food writer Janet Mendel, who is based in Spain. She e-mailed me as follows: "*Grelos* are the stems (not stalks nor shoots) of a turnip plant with an insignificant root. The stems are slightly thicker and longer than, for instance, spinach, with some greens at the top and some sprouting leaves with a flowering in the middle."

Thus, they turn out to be a Spanish version of our own common turnip greens, with the same slightly bitter flavor, and are perfect when stewed with a hunk of salt-cured ham. The new mild-tasting varieties of broccoli rabe can be used with great success.

Serve as a side dish for fish or meat.

(continued)

2 pounds turnip greens or young broccoli rabe

2 boiling potatoes such as Yukon Gold
(see Note)

Coarse sea salt

GALICIAN *AJADA* SAUCE

3½ tablespoons extra-virgin olive oil

2 cloves garlic, peeled and thickly sliced

1¼ teaspoons sweet *pimentón*

1 teaspoon red wine vinegar or more to taste

Salt

Freshly ground black peppper

Pinch of sugar (optional)

1. Wash the greens and discard any yellow or wilted leaves. Cut away any tough stems and slice tender shoots. Peel the potatoes and cut into 1½-inch dice.

2. In a deep pot bring plenty of water to a boil, place an inset over the pot, put in the potatoes and greens, cover, and steam for about 15 minutes. (Alternatively, you can boil the potatoes and greens in a large amount of salted water until both are tender.)

3. Make the *ajada* sauce. In a small skillet over low heat warm the olive oil and fry the slices of garlic until golden; then discard them. Stir in the *pimentón* and heat, stirring to make a smooth oily sauce. Add enough vinegar, salt, and pepper, and sugar if desired, and remove from the heat to avoid boiling.

Immediately drain the greens and potatoes and pour half the sauce over them. Let sit 10 minutes, then drizzle with remaining sauce and serve at once.

NOTE TO THE COOK: In an ideal world we would all have access to great-tasting freshly dug potatoes at farmers' markets. When purchasing at a supermarket, I always go for yellow-fleshed Yukon Gold potatoes and am rarely disappointed.

GREENS AND BARLEY
WITH PAN-FRIED PROSCIUTTO (*Italy*)

❀

Serves 4

*I*n the Val Colvera in the Friuli region of northeastern Italy an ancient rite of spring is still practiced today—
foraging for and cooking wild edible greens and shoots just emerging from sun-warmed forests and mead-
ows. One preparation, called *pistic,* may contain as many as fifty-six different wild plants. The valley women
sort, clean, and boil the greens, then fry them in butter with garlic and lard.

3 packed quarts mixed leafy greens: watercress,
Swiss chard, baby spinach, nettles (see Note), or
assorted tender greens such as mesclun (about ¾
pound)

Sea salt

1 tablespoon olive oil

4 slices prosciutto, bresaola, coppa, or speck

3 tablespoons butter

⅓ cup finely diced onion

¾ cup pearl barley

1 cup chicken stock, simmering

¼ cup peeled, seeded, and cubed tomatoes

¼ cup grated Parmigiano-Reggiano

Freshly ground black pepper

2 tablespoons chopped flat-leaf parsley

Close by in Carnia, not far from Udine, villagers
prepare a smaller mixture called *frite di Prât*, which
combines nettles, corn poppy, and bladder campion
and makes a superb taste-deepening addition to barley, as in this delicious first-course adaptation.

If you can't find these greens, don't despair!
The dish is still wonderful if made with Swiss
chard, spinach and watercress, or mesclun.

1. Bring a large pan of water to the boil.

2. Wash the greens, remove the hard stems, and
drain. Makes about seven cups.

3. Add salt and greens to the water and boil, pushing the greens under the water with a wooden
spoon, until tender, about 10 minutes. Drain well,
reserving 2 cups of the cooking liquid. As soon as
the greens are cool enough to handle, press them
between kitchen toweling to express as much moisture as possible. Purée to a pulp in a food processor.

(continued)

Up to this point the dish can be made up to one day in advance.

4. About 40 minutes before serving, heat the olive oil in a medium skillet until hot but not smoking. Add the slices of prosciutto and quickly fry until crisp on both sides. Remove to paper toweling and crumble.

5. Wipe out the skillet. Heat 1 tablespoon of the butter and sauté the onion until soft but not brown. Add the barley and lightly toast. Stir in the simmering stock, the reserved greens liquid, and salt. Cook, covered, over medium heat for about 15 minutes. Fold in the tomato and continue cooking 15 minutes more, stirring often. Dump into a deep bowl and fold in the remaining 2 tablespoons butter, green pulp, cheese, and salt and pepper to taste. Makes 2½ cups. Serve right away in small mounds topped with the crumbled prosciutto and chopped parsley.

NOTE TO THE COOK: When washing and stemming nettles remember to wear rubber gloves. After boiling you can handle nettles with unprotected hands. Use the dark but very flavorful boiling liquid to cook the remaining greens.

Inspired by a recipe created by Gianni Cosetti of Ristorante Roma in Tolmezzo.

CRETAN MIXED GREENS AND TOMATOES WITH BLACK-EYED PEAS (*Greece*)

❧

Serves 6 to 8

On the island of Crete, March and April are the best months to pick wild edible greens for making pies. Also in spring, in the markets of Heraklion, you'll find neatly tied-up bunches of aromatic greens called *yahnera*: a few shoots of wild fennel bunched with salsify tops, leaves of young corn poppy, Roman pimpernel, shepherd's purse, wild carrot, edible chrysanthemum, and a thick furry thistle called *eryngo*—all sweet fragrant greens nearly impossible to put together outside Crete.

The dominant flavor of a *yahnera* bunch, wild fennel, is hard to find. In spring, it grows rampantly in California; elsewhere combine supermarket fennel and some crushed fennel seeds. To simulate the other greens, I make up a mixture of three or four easy-to-find "sweet" greens (beet greens, baby spinach, Swiss chard, miner's lettuce, pea shoots, mâche, orache, nettles, lamb's-quarters, and green amaranth) to which I add just one sprig of cilantro for fragrance.

Black-eyed peas are a popular legume in many Mediterranean regions, ranging from Catalonia (where they're cooked with moist stewed wild mushrooms or a spirited blend of salt cod and wild edible greens) to Cyprus (where they're stewed with greens and served with good olive oil and lemon) to Turkey (where they're enhanced with a unique burnished red pepper, then simmered with heaps of stewed greens—see page 170).

Serve this delicious vegetable dish warm or cool for lunch along with some cheese, olives, and a glass of wine. Followed, in turn, in true Mediterranean spirit, by . . . you guessed it! . . . a nap.

1⅔ cups dried black-eyed peas

1 cup diced fennel bulb

2½ packed cups mixed tender leafy greens (see above), washed, stemmed, and roughly cut up, about 5 ounces

¼ cup extra-virgin olive oil

¾ cup chopped onion

3 scallions, finely chopped

1 sprig fresh cilantro, stemmed and roughly chopped

1 cup grated tomatoes

Pinch of fennel seeds, bruised in a mortar

Salt

Freshly ground black pepper

1. Soak the black-eyed peas according to package directions. Drain and cook in fresh water to cover until almost tender, about 30 minutes. Meanwhile, wash the fennel and the greens and let sit, dripping wet, on a plate.

2. In a 4-quart saucepan over medium heat, warm the olive oil. Add the onion, scallions, and the fennel and cook until soft, golden, and aromatic, 10 minutes. Add 1 cup water and continue to cook, stirring often, for 10 minutes. Add the greens to the saucepan along with the cilantro, tomatoes, fennel seeds, and salt and pepper and cook for another 10 minutes.

3. Drain the black-eyed peas; discard the water. Add the black-eyed peas to the saucepan along with a few tablespoons water, if necessary, to keep everything moist. Simmer another 10 minutes and correct the seasoning. Serve warm or cool.

With thanks to Mirsini Lambraki for sharing this recipe.

MUSTARD GREENS
WITH BLACK-EYED PEAS AND RICE (*Turkey*)

Serves 4

In the southeastern part of Turkey, in the town of Urfa, where I found this recipe, a unique smoky and slightly tart-flavored chili pepper is used to season *köfte*, stuffed vegetables, pilafs, kebabs, and stewed greens and beans.

Developing this recipe, I discovered that a combination of Turkish red pepper paste, smoky chili pepper such as chipotle or Spanish *pimentón de la Vera*, and black pepper simulated its special taste and stood up well to the assertive flavor of mustard greens.

I suggest serving this dish as a starter on a warmed shallow platter along with olives and cheese.

⅓ cup dried black-eyed peas

¼ cup medium- or long-grain rice

2 bunches strong-flavored mustard greens

6 ounces lean ground lamb

2½ tablespoons olive oil

½ cup chopped onion

¾ teaspoon tomato paste

¾ teaspoon Turkish red pepper paste (page 344)

Salt

¼ teaspoon mildly hot red pepper flakes

¼ teaspoon ground black pepper

4 lemon wedges

1. Soak the black-eyed peas according to package directions. Drain, rinse, and cook in plenty of water until almost tender, 30 minutes.

2. Meanwhile, soak the rice in hot water for 10 minutes and drain. Wash the greens in several changes of water; trim the stems. Chop tender stems and greens coarsely to make 4 cups.

3. Place the meat and 1 tablespoon of the oil in a 4-quart casserole. Cover and cook over medium-high heat for 5 minutes, stirring occasionally. Reduce the heat to medium, add the onion, and continue cooking, covered, 2 minutes more. Stir in the tomato and pepper pastes and ½ cup water. Bring to a boil, cover, and cook at a simmer for 20 minutes.

4. To the casserole, add the rice and the drained black-eyed peas. Simmer, covered, for 5 minutes. Stir in the greens and continue cooking over medium heat until the greens, rice, and peas are all tender, about 10 minutes longer. Remove from the heat and stir in salt to taste.

5. Heat the remaining 1½ tablespoons oil in a small skillet, add the hot red pepper and black pepper, and allow to sizzle gently. Immediately drizzle over the bean mixture and stir to combine. Tip into a shallow serving dish and serve warm with wedges of lemon.

Spinach and Chickpea Stew with Spanish Paprika (*Spain*)

Makes 5 cups, serving 4

The delicious Spanish paprika called *pimentón de la Vera*, used in this and several other Spanish recipes in this book, has a particular fragrance and smoky flavor because the peppers (sweet, semisweet, or hot) are dried over a wood fire for two full weeks. Though there's nothing quite like this *pimentón,* I'm impressed with the smoke-dried chili powder made from Anaheim peppers that is produced by Tierra Vegetables of Healdsburg, California.

Serve this truly wonderful and aromatic substantial lunch dish with rustic bread to soak up the smoky sauce and perhaps also with a simple egg salad. Or serve as a vegetable dish to accompany grilled chicken or meat.

1. Fill a pot, preferably clay, with the chickpeas, ½ onion, bay leaf, pepper, halved garlic, and salt pork rind, if using, or add a pinch of salt. Add enough water to cover by 1½ inches. Set the pot on a flame tamer and bring to a boil. Cook, covered, without stirring, over medium-low heat until tender, about 1½ hours.

2. Meanwhile, wash and drain the spinach. Drop into boiling water and cook, pushing down the leaves to keep them submerged, until tender, 5 minutes; drain and, when cool enough to handle, squeeze dry. Set aside.

(continued)

½ cup dried chickpeas, soaked up to one day in lightly salted water and drained

½ onion, plus ½ cup chopped onion

1 bay leaf

Pinch of freshly ground black pepper

1 clove garlic, halved, plus 1 large clove, unpeeled

1 small piece salt pork rind or end piece of cured ham, soaked or blanched to remove excess salt (optional)

Salt

6 cups stemmed spinach leaves

2 tablespoons olive oil

½ cup peeled, seeded, and chopped tomato

½ cup chopped green bell pepper

Pinch of pulverized saffron

1¼ teaspoons sharp or sweet *pimentón de la Vera*

3. Pierce the unpeeled garlic on a long fork and twist over stove-top flame until charred and the flesh is soft; peel and drop into a mortar. Alternatively, heat the oil and peel, crush, and fry the garlic in a medium skillet until aromatic but not brown. Remove to a mortar. If you haven't done so already, heat the oil.

4. Add the chopped onion to the skillet and cook, stirring, until softened, then add the tomato and cook another 2 minutes, stirring. Add the green pepper and continue cooking until the mixture is pastelike, 5 minutes.

5. Pound the toasted or fried garlic with salt, saffron, and *pimentón* and moisten with 2 to 3 tablespoons of the chickpea cooking liquid. Add with the spinach to the skillet, stir, and cook 2 to 3 minutes. Remove the flavorings from the pot of chickpeas and discard. Scrape the contents of the skillet into the chickpeas and simmer until flavors mingle, 5 minutes. Correct the seasoning and serve warm.

TUSCAN KALE

❖

*T*uscan kale, also called lacinata, dinosaur kale, black kale, or, in Italian, *cavolo nero*, is a vegetable success story waiting to happen, much like radicchio a few years back. In my view it's the best of all winter kales—sweet, delicious, beautifully textured, versatile, and easy to cook.

It's the secret to a great Tuscan soup such as *ribollita* (page 84); superb in risotto (page 188), as a potato cake stuffing (page 307), stirred into or used as a topping on polenta, puréed and spread on bread, or, perhaps best of all, sautéed then served with well-cooked cannellini beans (page 174).

I first encountered this winter green in the middle of summer on Martha's Vineyard. Even without the "kiss" of a good winter chill, I found it extremely good. The local grower didn't have much luck selling it at first, probably because she called it "lacinata," the name on the seed packet. Once she started calling it "Tuscan kale," sales took off.

I have fallen in love with this leafy green. It's great to grow in a kitchen garden where you can harvest what you need and more leaves will sprout. And because it resembles a small palm, it's also a landscape designer's dream.

SAUTÉED TUSCAN KALE
WITH GARLICKY WHITE BEANS (*Italy*)

Serves 2 or 3 as a side dish

This heavenly yet simple combination of beans and greens makes a delicious light meal with slices of salami and other cold cuts, or a stand-alone dish served with some good bread.

Tuscan kale is the kale of choice, perfect for this special manner of cooking. The leaves are slipped, one by one, into some hot olive oil, then water or broth is added in small amounts to keep the leaves from drying out. As the leaves cook, you juggle the lid, covering and uncovering, as the greens stew to a silky tenderness without being allowed to fry. Finally, you add beans to the pan to be reheated, then serve the two together unmixed side by side.

If you substitute another green, simply stew it in garlic-flavored olive oil before serving with the reheated beans.

12 small to medium leaves Tuscan kale
(4 ounces)

2 tablespoons extra-virgin Tuscan olive oil plus
more for garnish

1 clove garlic, peeled and thickly sliced

½ cup cooking liquor from the beans (see recipe
below)

1½ cups cooked white beans (see recipe below)

3 cloves cooked garlic, peeled and halved
(see recipe below)

Salt

Freshly ground black pepper

1. Remove the center rib from each leaf and if the leaves are long, tear each into 4- or 5-inch lengths. Wash and pat dry. In a 10-inch straight-sided skillet heat the 2 tablespoons olive oil, gradually add the leaves, and cook, stirring, until they wilt and sizzle in the hot oil, 2 minutes. Reduce the heat. Add the sliced garlic, cover, and cook the leaves until tender, about 10 minutes. Add the bean broth by the tablespoon, as needed, to keep the leaves from drying out.

2. Push the leaves to one side in the skillet; add the beans, salt, pepper, cooked garlic halves, and enough bean liquor to keep the dish juicy; cover; and simmer for 5 minutes. Serve warm with a drizzle of olive oil and freshly ground black pepper.

White Beans

Makes 3 cups

White beans make a wonderful canvas for flavorings. A combination of aromatics—fresh carrot, celery, onion, thyme, bay leaf, and peppercorns—always adds great savor. I like to cook beans in a heavy stainless steel pot, an enameled cast iron pot, or, best of all, a clay pot. I have an assortment of clay pots purchased at Asian markets just for bean cookery. (When you buy a clay pot, soak it overnight in cool water, then use it in the oven or on top of the stove with a flame tamer beneath.)

I used to salt beans right from the start of cooking, on the theory that if you salt after cooking, you're really just salting the water. If you *know* for sure that your *dry* beans are fresh, go ahead and salt the water from the start. Otherwise, add salt later, when the beans have cooked about 30 minutes.

This recipe will provide you with double the amount of richly flavored beans needed for the dish above. Store the remaining cooked beans in their cooking liquid without the garlic. Cover and keep refrigerated up to 3 days, or freeze. Use cooked beans for soups, other salads, or another bean dish.

1 cup dried white beans

4 to 5 cloves garlic, unpeeled

Aromatics Tied in Cheesecloth

1 sprig thyme

2 slices onion

1 carrot

1 small celery sprig

3 sprigs parsley

1 bay leaf

12 peppercorns

½ teaspoon salt

Pick over the beans and discard any foreign matter. Soak in water to cover overnight. Drain; place in a deep pan or clay pot with the garlic, and cover with at least 3 inches of water. Bring to a boil, skim carefully, and add the bag of aromatics, pushing it into the beans. *If you are sure the beans are fresh, add the salt now.* Simmer, partially covered, for 30 minutes, then add the salt and continue cooking until the beans are tender. (The time needed will vary, depending on the age of the beans. You can tell when they are almost done by removing one or two beans with a spoon and blowing gently on them—the skin will burst.) Simmer another 2 to 3 minutes, then remove from the heat. Allow beans to cool in the cooking liquid. Discard aromatics but not the garlic.

BEANS WITH ARUGULA AND PROSCIUTTO (*Italy*)

Serves 4

This light dish is perfect for a relaxed, informal lunch. It can be prepared ahead and assembled at serving time.

3 tablespoons chopped red onion

2 tablespoons extra-virgin olive oil plus more for garnish

¼ teaspoon crushed garlic

Pinch of grated lemon peel

3 cups cooked white beans (page 175)

½ cup cooking liquor from the beans

2 to 2½ cups arugula leaves, washed, dried, and stemmed

Juice of ½ lemon

1 tablespoon finely chopped flat-leaf parsley

Salt

Freshly ground black pepper

8 paper-thin slices prosciutto

A small chunk of Parmigiano-Reggiano

3 to 4 lemon wedges

Cruet of extra-virgin olive oil

1. In a medium skillet, gently fry the chopped onion in the 2 tablespoons oil until soft. Add the crushed garlic, lemon peel, the beans, and the cooking liquor. Cover and cook 5 minutes over medium-low heat.

2. Finely shred a small handful of the arugula and add to the skillet along with the lemon juice and parsley; stir gently. Adjust the seasoning with salt and pepper. Let stand at room temperature or in a cool place, covered.

3. Lay two slices of prosciutto on each of four individual serving plates. Season with freshly ground black pepper. Heap a spoonful of beans on top. Shred the remaining arugula and scatter over the beans. Top with a drizzle of olive oil and a sprinkling of black pepper.

4. Use a swivel vegetable peeler to pare 5 or 6 thin shavings of the Parmesan on top of each serving. Garnish with lemon wedges and serve at once with a cruet of extra-virgin olive oil.

SNAILS AND HOW TO CLEAN THEM

O n the island of Crete there's no closed season for catching or eating snails. Captured snails are fed wild greens, which give them a unique flavor, then fattened up on cooked grains such as barley. In the Cretan countryside, people still consume snails as often as three times a week. Meantime, in California, people complain that as they walk out in the morning to get their newspapers they hear the crunch of crushed snail shells underfoot.

Well, one man's scourge is another man's bounty, but I think we Americans would do well to eat more snails than we do. They're not only delicious, they're also extremely healthful. The prominent scientist Dr. Serge Renaud (he of the "French paradox") told me he believes the wild greens eaten by Cretan snails are what makes them so rich in healthful omega-3 fatty acids.

There are numerous types of snails. In Spain, in the main market in Valencia, I found three types for sale, one recommended for paellas, another for stews, the third for roasting. The snail par excellence is the one most frequently found in the United States, the *Helix aspera*, also known as the *petit gris*.

In many parts of the Mediterranean, during spring after the rainy season is over, whole families will make a day of gathering snails. When I hunted snails in Crete with Mirsini Lambraki, we found them relaxing on the large leaves of wild artichokes not too many miles outside Heraklion. We gathered them, then brought them to her aunt Stravoula to fatten up for a week, a process that makes their shells harden and a membrane develop over their openings. These membranes cause snails to stick together—a sign that they are ready to eat. (If the membranes are moist and the shells are soft, the snails are not ready and should not be eaten.)

Snail connoisseurs consider summer snails the most delicious. These snails fatten themselves in spring on young green shoots and by summer are hiding under rocks, trees, and other cool places. Summer snails are harder to find but easier to prepare in that they don't have to be fattened up.

There is a small but growing industry here in the United States, offering California and Texas snails, live and already purged, to restaurants and to certain ethnic communities. You can purchase them by mail (see "Mail-Order Sources") or buy them cleaned, parboiled, and packed in Cryovac to keep in your refrigerator or freezer. Either form is preferable to canned snails, which are usually pretty tasteless.

If you purchase live snails by mail order, handling instructions should be included. If they're not, or if you gather them live yourself, here's how they do it in Crete:

Carefully wash and clean each snail by removing the membrane with a knife, scraping off the mucus, crusty membrane, or grit that has formed on the shells. If a snail smells "bad" or doesn't stick its "nose" out when it's handled often, it's probably dead and should be discarded. Wash live snails again in clean water and rub them with coarse salt to ensure that they're clean. Rinse and drain. Place in a deep kettle and add water to cover about 2 inches. Bring to a boil, uncovered, and boil for 5 minutes, skimming carefully. Drain; "unscrew" snails from their shells using a thin skewer. Discard shells, rinse snails in acidulated water, and drain again. The snails are now ready for use in the following recipe.

Note: Live snails should be kept under cover, with holes for air, to prevent them from escaping.

STRAVOULA'S CRETAN SNAIL AND FENNEL STEW WITH LEAFY GREENS (*Greece*)

❋

Serves 4 for lunch

Pretty, sweet, middle-aged Stravoula, aunt of a Cretan friend, has been deaf since childhood. She's a jovial woman and a truly wonderful cook, who does an enormous amount of hard work yet never complains. The first time I met her she had just come in from cleaning her olive grove. She then prepared dinner for her husband, while insisting I stay for a simple lunch. Lucky Stravoula! She married the man she loved—not too common an occurrence among women of her generation. Because she's deaf, she doesn't talk easily, but her essential sweetness and sense of hospitality come through. She's always welcome at gatherings in her village. "Stravoula," people say, "always brings the sunshine."

Out in her yard I admired the rubberized cages where she keeps her snails. She eats snails as often as three times a week. Cretan cooks have literally dozens of methods for preparing them: with grapevine shoots and beet greens; fried in olive oil with rosemary and vinegar; simmered with tomatoes, potatoes, and leaf amaranth; and, my favorite, this delicious stew made with wild fennel and wild aromatic greens.

In my version of Stravoula's recipe, I've substituted a variety of domestic greens, and also added a little crushed fennel seed to simulate the original.

2 quarts mixed young greens: arugula, watercress, amaranth leaves, spinach, chard, peppercress, and any other aromatic greens

Coarse salt

24 large, shelled snails (2 cups), defrosted or fresh (see page 177 if using live snails)

½ cup olive oil

1 cup finely chopped fennel bulb

½ teaspoon crushed fennel seeds

1 cup chopped scallions, green and white part

1 pound boiling potatoes, peeled and diced

1 cup grated tomatoes (page 41)

Pinch of hot red pepper

1 to 2 teaspoons wine vinegar

Freshly ground black pepper

1. Wash the greens thoroughly; drain and cut away the stems. Shred roughly, toss with 2 teaspoons coarse salt, and leave in a noncorrodible colander for 1 hour.

2. If using defrosted snails, wash in several changes of water; rub with coarse salt and rinse again. Simmer in lightly salted water for 3 minutes and drain. If using fresh or live snails, follow the directions that accompany them or clean and prepare as directed on page 177.

3. Rinse the greens under running water to remove the salt and, working in batches, squeeze out excess moisture.

4. In a heavy saucepan, heat the olive oil over medium heat. Add the scallions and fennel bulb, and cook, stirring, 2 minutes. Add the greens and fennel seeds, and cook, stirring often, 20 minutes.

5. Add the prepared snails, potatoes, tomatoes, salt, and red pepper and ½ cup water to the pan. Cover and cook for 20 minutes.

6. If using defrosted cooked snails, add just before serving. Stir in enough vinegar, salt, and pepper to taste. Serve warm over rice or with crusty bread.

"Alexandria Quartet" of Rice, Brown Lentils, Pan-Crisped Pasta, and Browned Onions (*Egypt*)

❀

Serves 6 for lunch or a vegetarian dinner

With a tip of the hat to Lawrence Durrell, I call this version of the famous Egyptian street dish *koshary* my "Alexandria quartet" because of the way it synthesizes its four main ingredients and because it's the family recipe of my Arabic translator, Rabab Tawfik, who comes from the city of Alexandria.

Koshary, in truth, is a Cairene dish, as Rabab is the first to admit. Here's what the food writer Susan Torgersen, in her fine book on Egyptian cooking, *Flavors of Egypt: From City and Country Kitchens*, has to say on the subject:

> Throughout Cairo you will see *koshary* shops and bright-colored *koshary* carts. In these shops and from the carts, you can only buy *koshary*, a combination of protein-packed foods that are put together to form a very filling, inexpensive, delicious lunch for a large number of the Egyptian population. When I was introduced to this layered dish of rice, vermicelli, macaroni, chickpeas, tomato sauce and onions I could not imagine that this could be a winning combination, but I was very wrong.

Koshary, which literally means "messy mix," is based on the simpler Egyptian dish *megadarra*, a brown lentil and rice pilaf topped with crisp browned onions and served with garlic-flavored yogurt. *Koshary*, with its additions of cooked tube macaroni and a garlicky, vinegary tomato sauce, has a bigger, bolder flavor.

No one, least of all a Cairene, will tell you that *koshary* is a fancy dish. Rather, it's the "good grub street food" kind of dish one so often finds sold on the streets of Mediterranean cities.

Rabab told me: "The Cairene version gives me heartburn. At home we make a more subdued and aromatic dish with a touch of mastic, then present the dish with two tiers of onions—a bowl of pickled onions and crispy onion strands. It is sublime."

The method for preparing the onion is the best way I know, one I learned from an Israeli Arab. Diced onions are cooked with a little water and oil in a covered skillet until limp; then the skillet is transferred, uncovered, to a medium oven, to cook for three hours with occasional stirring until the onions turn reddish brown. At the end you recoup the oil by simply tilting the pan. Of course, you mustn't use a skillet with a wooden handle.

Make this Alexandrian version ahead, but don't prepare the raw onion slices until you are ready to reheat the lentil-rice mixture and cook it until brown and crusty.

---

2 pounds onions

⅓ cup extra-virgin olive oil

1 teaspoon salt plus more to taste

1 cup Spanish pardina, Egyptian, Ethiopian, Indian masoor dal, or any other brown lentil

½ cup white short- or medium-grain rice

¾ cup elbow macaroni

1 quart meat, poultry, or vegetable broth, or water

1 tiny piece mastic, crushed with salt in a mortar

2 teaspoons tomato paste

Freshly ground black pepper

1 teaspoon ground cumin

ONION RELISH

1 small onion, finely sliced

1 cup cider vinegar

Pinch of cinnamon

---

1. Preheat the oven to 350 degrees.

2. Peel and finely dice the onions and cook, covered, in an ovenproof, 10- or 12-inch skillet, in the olive oil, 2 tablespoons water, and 1 teaspoon salt over medium heat for 15 minutes.

3. Set the skillet in the oven, uncovered, to cook the onions until they turn a dark reddish brown and are very crisp, and the oil separates, about 3 hours. Stir often, but be careful—the handle is very hot. Tilt the skillet and remove the onions to a side dish lined with paper toweling and leave the oil in the skillet.

4. Rinse the lentils, soak in water to cover for 30 minutes, and drain. Rinse the rice until water runs clear, soak in hot water for 15 minutes, and drain.

5. Cook the macaroni in plenty of lightly salted water until just cooked. Drain and fry in the reserved oil until lightly crisp around the edges. Scoop noodles out to a side dish, leaving the oil in the skillet.

6. Add the drained lentils to the oil in the skillet and slowly fry for 5 minutes, stirring. Add the rice, stir once, cover with the broth or water, and bring to a boil. Stir in the mastic, tomato paste, pepper, cumin, and salt and cook over low heat for about 30 minutes.

7. Forty minutes before serving, prepare the onion relish. Soak the raw onion slices in the vinegar and sprinkle with cinnamon. Let marinate.

8. Stir the reserved macaroni into the lentil-rice mixture and cook, covered, until the underside is brown and crusty here and there, 5 minutes. Correct the seasoning with salt and pepper and fold in the browned onions. Transfer to a 1½-quart serving bowl. Pass the pickled onions at the table.

RISOTTOS, GRANOS, PASTAS, AND GNOCCHI

✦

*I*t's impossible to do a book about Mediterranean grains without highlighting the great grain-based dishes of the Italian kitchen—risottos, granos, pastas, and gnocchi. The diversity of these dishes is enormous. All take on numerous sauces, fats, and flavors. All require expert timing. Risottos, pastas, granos, and gnocchi are easily overcooked. (Polenta, another popular Italian grain, is easily undercooked. See page 311 for more on this delicious grain.) All require the cook to pay careful attention.

Within each category there is great variety. Risottos are made from different varieties of rice and embrace flavorings ranging from robust—beans and sausage—to delicate, cheese and wine. Pastas come in innumerable shapes and sizes and take a vast array of sauces composed of such diverse ingredients as meat, fish, seafood, vegetables, and herbs. Grano or *cranu pestatu* as it is called in the Apulian dialect, is a skinned durum wheat berry used in wonderful pilaf-like dishes served as an evening meal or first course. (See Grano with Tuna, Capers, and Cherry Tomatoes and its variation with mussels, page 199.) Polenta may be made from different grinds of cornmeal, creating subtle differences in texture ranging from undulating spreads slathered with a sauce on a wooden board to hefty mounds cut into slices with a taut string, grilled, then served with a variety of vegetable toppings.

Among the numerous preparations, one finds nearly every flavoring available in Italian cuisine. The recipes that follow constitute a brief sampling of these quintessential Mediterranean grain-based starters.

R·ICE FOR RISOTTO

Choosing the Proper Rice In Italy there are numerous varieties of rice to choose from when making a risotto. Depending upon where in Italy you ask, you'll receive a different, emotional, indeed passionate, opinion.

Since a risotto rice is not just a background ingredient but plays a decisive role in the texture, aroma, and taste of the dish, you must take care to choose the correct type and make certain the rice you choose is fresh.

Plump short- to medium-grain rice is what you want, whether the readily available *arborio*, the perfect risotto rice *carnaroli*, or the baby of the group, the smaller-grained *vialone nano*, a favorite of the Veneto.

A good general rule, followed by most Italian cooks, is to use a small-grain rice such as *vialone nano* for delicate seafood risottos, *carnaroli* for sauces containing big-flavored ingredients such as sausage, and *arborio* for anything in between.

Carnaroli has become my favorite. It can be found at numerous fine food stores and is also available by mail order. I love this rice for the way it shows off the taste of the grain and turns creamy at the finish. In fact, it continues to release starch right on the dinner plate.

A good substitute is the excellent all-purpose California-grown "Mediterranean-style" rice called Cal-Riso, as good in my opinion as imported *arborio*. Cal-Riso has choice flavor, cooks faster than Italian rices, and resembles *carnaroli*, though with less starch. *Arborio* is always good providing you find it fresh. What you don't want is a rice that's been sitting around getting dusty in an open sack.

To keep my rice fresh, I store it in a jar in the refrigerator. If you don't plan on using up your rice within a couple of months, you're probably better off storing it in your freezer. (There is no need to defrost the rice.)

Cooking a Classic Venetian Risotto with Cesare "You cook risotto by ear," Cesare Benelli tells me. This handsome mustachioed chef speaks very good English and cooks even better at his famous Ristorante Al Covo in Venice. His risottos are stunning: a brilliant pumpkin risotto with a wild duck ragout; an intense wild greens risotto with hops shoots and tops; and a family-style "butcher's choice" risotto (page 190); a Venetian classic.

Cesare is referring to the array of auditory cues one should listen for when cooking risotto—a symphony of whistles, crackles, and swishing noises along the way toward the finale.

Cesare prepares a risotto to demonstrate the sounds. He begins by preparing a small base of oil, well-softened shallots, onion, a small amount of pumpkin, and a clove of garlic that he discards when ready to add the rice.

"Too much onion at the beginning or too much cheese at the end, you end up launching onion and cheese rather than the major ingredient you want to feature—in this case pumpkin."

The base finished, he raises the heat, then adds all the rice at once so he can "toast" it in the hot oil. "When you add rice," he tells me, "you can calculate the traditional way—one handful per person. We still do it like that."

He lets the rice toast but not brown in the hot oil, wanting to coax out flavor rather than seal the grain, which would impede its ability to express starch and absorb stock.

"The rice will whistle to let me know when it's time to begin to scrape whatever's stuck onto the pan," he says. "This is the moment to deglaze with wine, giving the dish a little acidity. Let the wine evaporate completely. Then listen. What do you hear now?"

I hear crackling, the sound of the rice starting to open to release its starch.

Cesare begins to add the broth in increments so there's always just enough to cover the rice. "Don't let the rice get dry. Keep it loose during the simmering stage. You want consistency. The rice must open up slowly to simultaneously release its starches and absorb the flavorful broth."

Once all the stock has been added, Cesare takes care not to let the pan dry out, seeking a proper temperature while constantly stirring to keep the absorption process steady.

In 15 minutes the simmering phase is over. Cesare holds onto his large skillet with both hands and shakes it back and forth to bind the starches from the rice and the well-reduced flavors from the broth, with the final addition of cheese and oil or butter. (If lifting a pan and heaving the rice this way sounds daunting, you can achieve the same effect by gently mixing the rice with a wooden spoon.)

A swishing noise tells him that the finale is complete—that the risotto will hold itself together on the plate without much spreading. After correcting the seasoning the dish is done—a perfect creamy, wavy risotto in which each grain of rice, cooked but still firm to the bite at its core, is cloaked in a creamy, well-combined sauce.

USING THE PRESSURE COOKER TO COOK RISOTTO

Some risottos, particularly those that do not require the addition of ingredients midway through, can be beautifully and easily made in a pressure cooker. While a microwave ruins risotto by cooking each rice grain from the inside out, the pressure cooker works on the grains from the outside, creating well-blended creamy rice with just the right amount of chewy texture at the center.

The evenly distributed heat created by a pressure cooker allows the grains to absorb liquid at the same time that they release their starches. The pressure speeds the cooking process and eliminates the need for constant stirring—the bane of many a would-be risotto home cook. Timing is important with the pressure cooker, since there's always a chance you'll overcook the rice and end up with a gummy result. Thanks to Lorna Sass's breakthrough method, brilliantly described in her book *Cooking Under Pressure* (William Morrow, 1989), I've found that 4 minutes of pressure cooking, short though that may seem, is usually correct.

The only recipe in this book that can be made in a pressure cooker is the Black and White Risotto (page 188). To execute the recipe: Reduce the *undiluted* broth to one half to concentrate flavor. Follow step 2 and part of step 3, except use the pressure cooker. Add the reduced boiling broth. Close the cooker and bring up to pressure. Adjust the heat to maintain high pressure on medium (on some stoves this will be low) and time the cooking for 4 minutes. Immediately reduce pressure by placing the pressure cooker under cold running water to stop the cooking. Remove the cover and test the rice. If necessary, continue cooking over high heat while stirring. Add the cheese and, if necessary, a few tablespoons stock for a creamy consistency; correct the seasoning. Serve at once.

RED RISOTTO WITH RADICCHIO AND BAROLO WINE

❀

Serves 6 as a first course

*I*t was at the Trattoria Vecchia Lugano (Lugana di Sirmione) in the Lake Garda region of northern Italy that I first tasted this delicious and beautiful risotto. The chef used elongated Treviso-style radicchio instead of round radicchio, but since the latter is so easy to find, I've substituted it to good effect.

This is a risotto with true depth and multidimensional flavor due to the rich round taste of braised radicchio and the haunting savor of a rich round red Barolo wine. A lot of radicchio-based risottos turn a nasty purplish color because the base wine is white, but here a deep red wine turns the dish a beautiful magenta. When garnished with shards of good Parmesan, it's a visual stunner.

½ pound red radicchio, washed and shredded

Coarse salt

3 tablespoons olive oil

1 ounce pancetta, finely shredded (3 tablespoons)

5 cups light chicken or meat broth

2 tablespoons butter

⅓ cup finely chopped onion

1½ cups risotto rice, preferably *carnaroli*

½ cup full-flavored red wine, preferably Barolo

2 sprigs fresh thyme, minced

½ cup grated *Parmigiano-Reggiano* plus a few shards per person for garnish

Freshly ground black pepper

1. Toss radicchio with salt; let stand 5 minutes.

2. Heat half the oil and all the pancetta in a heavy saucepan until it is half melted and half sizzling.

Rinse the radicchio and add to the pan and cook, covered, until meltingly tender, 20 minutes over medium-low heat.

3. Put the broth in a saucepan, add 6 cups water and a pinch of salt, bring to a simmer, and hold. (You may not use all the broth.)

4. Meanwhile, melt the butter and the remaining 1½ tablespoons oil in another heavy, deep saucepan. Add the onion and cook until golden, 5 minutes. Add the rice and stir to coat it with the onion and fat, then allow it to "toast" for a minute. Raise the heat to medium-high, add the wine and the fresh thyme, and cook, stirring, until the moisture has been absorbed. Add the broth, 1 cup at a time, stirring constantly, adding more only when the rice has almost absorbed all the liquid. When the rice has cooked about 10 minutes, stir in the radicchio and cooking juices and continue cooking until the rice is done, another 5 to 10 minutes. Stir in the grated cheese and salt and pepper to taste. Wait 5 minutes before serving.

ARTICHOKE AND SPINACH RISOTTO

❊

Serves 3 or 4 as first course

Here's a risotto based on the old and much beloved Mediterranean "grandmotherly" combination of artichokes and spinach. Speckled with flecks of tomato, this delicious risotto is pretty too.

2 large artichokes bottoms (see Note)

1 lemon, halved

Coarse salt

Juice of ½ lemon

2 tablespoons flour

6 cups chicken or vegetable stock

4 tablespoons olive oil

2 tablespoons finely chopped onion

1 clove garlic, peeled and finely chopped

1 pound fresh spinach, washed in several changes of water, stemmed, and finely shredded

1 cup risotto rice

¼ cup dry white wine

1 red ripe tomato, peeled, seeded, and cubed

½ teaspoon finely ground black pepper

½ cup freshly grated *Parmigiano-Reggiano*

1. Trim the artichokes and rub with a lemon half. Bring a small pot of water to the boil; add ½ teaspoon salt, juice of ½ lemon, and flour; and whisk to combine. Simmer the artichoke bottoms in the liquid for 5 minutes, then remove and leave to cool. Thinly slice the artichoke bottoms. Artichokes can be prepared 3 to 4 hours ahead to this point; cover and refrigerate.

2. In a separate pan, heat the broth with 5 cups water and a pinch of salt to simmering; hold over low heat.

3. Heat the olive oil in a deep heavy saucepan, add the onion, and cook over medium heat, stirring, until soft. Add the artichokes, garlic, and half the spinach and cook, stirring, for 3 minutes. Add the rice and stir to coat it with the artichokes and oil, then allow it to "toast" for a minute. Raise the heat to medium-high, add the wine, and cook, stirring, until the moisture has been absorbed. Add the broth, 1 cup at a time, stirring constantly, adding more only when the rice has *almost* absorbed all the liquid.

4. When the rice has cooked about 10 minutes, stir in remaining spinach, tomato, and black pepper. Cook another 5 to 10 minutes. Stir in half the cheese and correct seasoning with salt and pepper. Wait 5 minutes before serving. Dust with remaining cheese.

NOTE TO THE COOK: To make artichoke bottoms, first snap off the tough outer leaves near the base. Use a stainless steel knife to cut off the stems, then trim the crowns to within 1½ inches of the base. Use a melon baller to scoop out the chokes to widen the cavity. Use a small knife to carefully trim the leaves, then pare any remaining hard green parts.

BLACK AND WHITE RISOTTO

Serves 3 or 4 as a first course

Here's a stunning risotto combination featuring "black" or Tuscan kale and creamy white beans. Originally this dish was made with polenta, but it works just as beautifully with rice. (For more information on black Tuscan kale see page 173). This variety of kale is particularly desirable for this risotto because of its rich, round, pure, clean flavor, and because, when cooked, it maintains its dark attractive color.

To avoid using canned beans, soak and cook white beans as described on page 175. Refrigerate the surplus, then use within a few days.

4½ cups (approximate) unsalted vegetable or poultry broth

Salt

⅓ pound black Tuscan kale or any soft kale or young collard greens, washed and stemmed

2 tablespoons olive oil

2 tablespoons finely shredded pancetta

1 thinly sliced leek

¼ cup finely chopped onion

Freshly ground black pepper

1 cup risotto rice

⅔ cup cooked and drained white cannellini beans

⅓ cup freshly grated *Parmigiano-Reggiano* plus more to serve at the table

1. Heat the broth with 5 cups water and a pinch of salt in a saucepan and keep at a low simmer. (You may not use all the broth.)

2. Cut the leaves into ribbons to make about 3 packed cups.

3. In a 10-inch straight-sided skillet, heat the olive oil. Add the pancetta and cook, stirring, over medium heat until the shreds melt. Add the leek and onion and sauté until softened and lightly golden. Add salt, pepper, and the rice and continue to sauté, stirring, until all the grains are well coated and lightly toasted, about 2 minutes. Stir in the kale and sauté until wilted. Continue to cook, stirring constantly, until all the liquid in the skillet has been absorbed by the rice or evaporates. Raise the heat to medium-high and begin to ladle in enough of the simmering broth to completely cover the rice, then stir well. Cook, stirring, until *almost* all the broth is absorbed. Add another ladleful of simmering broth and continue until the rice has cooked about 15 minutes.

4. Fold in the beans and continue cooking and gently stirring until the rice is creamy and tender—but still firm to the bite. Stir in the ⅓ cup cheese and season highly with black pepper. Taste for salt. Serve at once with additional grated cheese at the table.

BROCCOLI RABE RISOTTO WITH PORK

Serves 8 as a first course

This superb risotto tames the slightly bitter and often aggressive flavor of broccoli rabe with a combination of tomatoes, garlic, and pork . . . a marvelous dish wrought out of extremely simple ingredients.

Cesare Casella, an inventive and lighthearted Tuscan chef, shared this 17-minute recipe with me and encouraged me to use the variety of rice called *carnaroli*. "It'll make creamy risotto whether you want it to or not!" he assured me.

¼ cup extra-virgin olive oil

2 medium shallots, peeled and finely diced

2 cups risotto rice, preferably *carnaroli*

5 tablespoons dry white wine

2 garlic cloves, chopped

Pinch red pepper flakes

5 ounces trimmed tenderloin of pork, finely diced

½ cup chopped Roma tomatoes

3½ cups simmering vegetable broth

3 cups washed and shredded broccoli rabe

Salt

Freshly ground black pepper

1 tablespoon unsalted butter

2 to 3 tablespoons grated *Parmigiano-Reggiano* plus shards of *Parmigiano-Reggiano* for garnish

1. Heat the olive oil in a heavy, wide saucepan, add the shallots. Sauté over medium heat for 1 to 2 minutes, or until transparent but not brown.

2. Add the rice, stir, and cook over moderate heat 2 minutes, or until the rice is lightly toasted and well coated with oil.

3. Add the wine and allow it to evaporate. Then add the garlic and red pepper and sauté for 1 minute. Stir in the pork and allow it to brown lightly.

4. Add the tomatoes and enough of the simmering broth to cover the rice by ½ inch. Cook, stirring often, until all the liquid is absorbed, about 7 minutes.

5. Stir in all the broccoli rabe and the remaining broth and cook over medium-high heat, stirring occasionally, until the rice, pork, and greens are cooked, about 8 minutes. (The rice should be a little firm to the bite.)

6. Remove from the heat and correct the seasoning. Immediately stir in the butter and grated cheese and swirl the pan to create a creamy, well-combined sauce that coats each grain of rice. Let rest 2 minutes before serving. Decorate each serving with a few shards of cheese.

THE BUTCHER'S CHOICE RISOTTO
AS PREPARED IN VENICE

❉

Serves 4 as a first course

When Cesare Benelli, chef-owner of the famous Ristorante Al Covo in Venice, was talking to me about risotto, he mentioned a version made with beef.

And not just any piece of beef! "This is a homestyle Venetian dish which is hard to make unless you have a very good rapport with your butcher. You want to use what the Venetians call *secole*, the juicy stuff around the upper spine going toward the shoulder, the very part the butcher keeps for himself unless you're a very good client and he gives it to you. It makes the most succulent and delicious risotto, especially in winter."

The sad truth is that here in the United States it's even harder to get these morsels than in Italy, since, even if your butcher likes you, most meat these days is precut before it even gets to his shop. In San Francisco, I found an Italian butcher who knew the dish and tried to be helpful, suggesting I cook a piece of "flatiron"— a cut from the foreleg portion of the chuck striated with gelatinous ribbons. It is perfectly described in Merle Ellis's *Cutting Up in the Kitchen* (Chronicle Books, 1975): "On one side is a small triangular shaped muscle called, by most butchers, the 'Flatiron.' This is a tender little morsel that is usually sliced into steaks, which are dubbed 'Butter Steaks' or 'Petite Steaks' or some other cute and tender-sounding name."

Ask for a meat cut from the top side of the blade portion of chuck. You won't need very much, since very little meat is used in proportion to rice, but you want a tasty, well-marbled piece that will permeate the rice with its flavor.

I found that scraps from the short ribs work well, too, if you cook them the way Turkish cooks prepare tough pieces of meat to extract maximum flavor. Cut the meat into small bits, then cook slowly in a covered pan until the meat throws off all its moisture, then uncover and brown lightly so the meat "reabsorbs" the juices. You'll probably have to add occasional douses of water before the meat becomes soft enough to break up with a wooden spoon. The method works, with all the flavor still intact and ready to perfume your rice.

This is a soupy risotto, so the best rice for it is *carnaroli*, which has the ability to stay creamy for a long time. If unavailable use Cal-Riso and shorten the cooking time by 3 minutes.

If you're worried that your meat will be disappointingly tasteless, buy some bone marrow, soak it, and add to the risotto midway through. I have also occasionally added one or two finely chopped cherry tomatoes to bring up the meat flavor. You might also add a little meat glaze, such as the veal-duck glaze sold under the D'Artagnan label. But whatever you do, don't use a bouillon cube!

Cesare's suggestion: About 3 minutes before the end of cooking, when the rice still has some bite, add a dash of brandy when you swirl in the cheese and oil. This will give a nice "shot" to the dish. He goes on: "Don't forget to top this risotto with a good aged cheese such as a two-year-old *parmigiano reggiano*, which will have great rapport with meat."

This kind of soupy risotto, unlike most risottos, goes beautifully with a good young Chianti, since the tannins in the wine will add a welcome degree of acidity.

5 ounces prime or choice flatiron (see above), scraps from the back of the rib, or 1 pound short ribs, bone in

4 tablespoons olive oil

Salt

Freshly ground black pepper

1 quart homemade very light meat or vegetable broth

1 large clove garlic, peeled and bruised

2 large shallots, peeled and minced

1 *rounded* cup (8 ounces) risotto rice, preferably *carnaroli* or Cal-Riso

3 tablespoons dry white wine

1 inch bone marrow, soaked, scooped out, and thinly sliced (optional)

2 tablespoons chopped flat-leaf parsley

2 cherry tomatoes, halved, seeded, and chopped

⅓ cup grated aged *Parmigiano-Reggiano*

1 tablespoon brandy

1. Cut the meat into 1-by-1-by-¼-inch pieces. Discard the bone if using short ribs. Put meat and 1 tablespoon of the oil in a small heavy-bottomed pan and cook, covered, over medium-high heat for 5 minutes. Uncover and boil off the liquid in the pan, stirring often. Allow the meat to gently brown in the fat, stirring often. Add a few tablespoons water, cover, and cook over low heat for 1¼ hours, stirring from time to time and adding tablespoons of water as needed. The meat is ready when it is soft enough to cut with a wooden spoon. Sprinkle with salt and pepper and set aside.

2. Heat the broth, add a pinch of salt and 3 cups water, and bring to simmering; hold over low heat. (You may not use all the broth.)

3. Heat 2 tablespoons of the oil in a heavy, wide saucepan, add the garlic, and sauté until golden, then discard the garlic. Add the shallots and cook, stirring, until they turn golden. Add the meat and all its fatty juices and the rice. Cook, stirring, over moderate heat until the rice is lightly toasted and well coated with sizzling meat juices. Deglaze the pan with the wine and allow it to evaporate. Raise the heat to medium-high; add enough of the broth to cover the rice and cook, stirring, until it is *almost* absorbed. Gradually add the remaining broth. The cooking should take 17 to 20 minutes. Midway, taste the liquid and, if desired, stir in the sliced marrow for added flavor. About 3 minutes before the rice is cooked but still firm to the bite at the core, add the

parsley, tomatoes, cheese, brandy, and remaining tablespoon of oil and immediately swirl the pan to create a creamy, well-combined sauce that coats each grain of rice. Taste for seasoning, adding a good pinch of black pepper and serve.

HANDKERCHIEF PASTA WITH WILTED GREENS AND WILD MUSHROOMS, *MANDILI DE SEA*

❧

Serves 4

These *mandili de sea* ("silk handkerchiefs") are a Ligurian specialty—shimmering, ghost-white handmade pasta noodles, the size of handkerchiefs, served slightly disheveled with sauce hidden within their folds. They're served in a pile on a central platter, then each diner cuts out a section, as if taking a piece of pie.

The classic sauce for these noodles is pesto, brushed onto each sheet after cooking. Equally if not more delicious is a light sauce made of wild mushrooms and quickly sautéed young greens. That is how I first tasted the dish at the marvelous Ligurian-inspired Rose Pistola restaurant in San Francisco.

You can substitute steamed dandelions or other less tender greens and braise until tender.

1. Remove the pasta from the freezer (if frozen) and bring to room temperature. Do not unwrap until ready to cook. Bring a large pot of water to a boil.

2. Meanwhile, carefully strain dried mushrooms and place the mushrooms, soaking liquid, and chicken stock in a small saucepan and bring to a boil. Clean, trim, and thickly slice the fresh brown mushrooms. Place in a skillet with a pinch of salt and cook, covered, over medium heat for 5 minutes, then scrape

into the saucepan with the dried mushrooms and simmer all together until almost all the liquid has evaporated or been absorbed, 10 minutes. Season with salt, pepper, and the lemon juice.

3. Over medium heat, deglaze the skillet with a few tablespoons water. Add 2 tablespoons of the olive oil, pancetta, garlic, sugar, and dried herbs, and sauté until the pancetta is slightly crisp, the herbs are sizzling, and the garlic is pale golden. Add all the

The Wilted Greens and Wild Mushroom Sauce

½ ounce dried cèpes, soaked in water for 10 minutes

½ cup chicken stock

½ pound fresh small brown mushrooms

Freshly ground black pepper

Coarse salt

A few drops of fresh lemon juice

3 tablespoons olive oil

1½ tablespoons minced pancetta

2 large cloves garlic, minced

Pinch of sugar

2 teaspoons dried herbs such as herbs de Provence or Italian seasonings

3 ounces (3 cups) mixed baby greens, washed and roughly shredded

2 tablespoons butter

A bowl of freshly grated *Parmigiano-Reggiano*

10 5-inch squares of homemade, fresh, or frozen handkerchief pasta

greens and cook, covered, for 3 minutes. Uncover, sprinkle lightly with salt and pepper, and cook, stirring, for another 2 minutes.

4. Reheat the mushrooms in the saucepan, add the butter, swirl to create a sauce, and pour over the greens in the skillet. Correct the seasoning and keep warm.

5. When the water has just come to the boil, reduce the heat slightly, and add salt, the remaining 1 tablespoon olive oil, and half the pasta. Cook until the pasta rises to the surface, about half a minute if your pasta is very thin; more time is needed if it is thicker. Use a wide, deep strainer to scoop out the pasta. Shake to remove excess water and place the sheets of pasta in a wide, heated serving bowl. Spread half the greens and mushrooms over the pasta. Repeat with the remaining pasta and sauce and serve at once with a bowl of grated cheese.

NOTES TO THE COOK: Use a mixture of fresh mushrooms such as portobello, shiitake, and oyster, or, if available, wild mushrooms such as porcini or chanterelles. Because mushrooms are often quite wet, I salt them lightly, then sauté them quickly in a nonstick skillet, stirring constantly until their moisture is exuded and boiled off, a process that intensifies the mushroom flavor. After cooking, they'll keep up to 2 days in the refrigerator.

HAND-ROLLED LIGURIAN PASTA

Makes about 1½ pounds, enough for 2 recipes

With so many terrific types of fresh pasta on the market, I wouldn't ordinarily suggest making your own. But this type, not otherwise available, is unique and well worth the effort.

"We Ligurians are frugal, frankly—too cheap to use lots of eggs in our pasta!" says the Ligurian food expert Darrel Corti. For this reason you'll find the slippery texture of these noodles more Asian than you'd expect, without the bite of egg noodles or firm semolina pasta. These noodles are the opposite of noodles made in neighboring regions of Italy, where sometimes a dozen eggs are used to make a kilo of pasta.

Please note: You don't need a pasta machine to make these sheets. Most machines are way too narrow to produce 5-inch-square sheets, and in any event it's very easy to roll the sheets out, then let them dry on kitchen toweling for a short time before cooking fresh or wrapping and storing in your freezer.

When chef Scott Warner of Rose Pistola told me I would need only 5 eggs to make 7 pounds of noodles, I knew his recipe was authentic. But it took a bit of juggling to scale down his recipe for home use.

"Don't forget to use a dry white wine such as a sauvignon blanc," Scott told me. "It'll give the dough a slightly acidic edge and keep the pasta light, so there'll still be room for a main course." For a great first course, figure on using two pasta sheets per serving.

Because this pasta is so tender, light, and fragile, there's an art to cooking it. Cook two or three sheets at a time. Once you add the pasta to the water and the water returns to the boil, lower the heat, then cook for literally 10 to 25 seconds! Otherwise the sheets may fall apart. All the better if you have a pasta colander insert. Otherwise do as I do: use two large skimmers to remove 2 or 3 sheets at a time from the water so they don't break up and will look good on the plate.

1 pound all-purpose flour plus ½ cup for dusting

1½ farm-fresh eggs, lightly beaten

⅓ cup dry white wine

½ teaspoon fine sea salt

Lukewarm water, about 9 tablespoons

1. Put a mound of flour on the pastry board and press a hollow in the center to form a well. Add the beaten eggs, wine, and salt to the well. Using a fork, little by little mix the flour into the center. Then little by little add the water to form a ball of dough. Continue to knead the dough for about 10 minutes or until very smooth, firm, and elastic. (If desired, you can use a heavy-duty mixer fitted with a dough hook to knead the dough. Set to a slow setting and mix for 5 minutes or until the dough is soft and silky.) Finish by hand, kneading the dough on a lightly floured board, then wrap in plastic and let stand 30 minutes.

2. Cut the dough into ten equal parts and keep nine wrapped while working the first. Roll out to a large rectangle, 6 by 12 inches. The dough will stretch easily if you push it with the rolling pin, dust it often with flour, and lift it often in order to make half turns and keep the rectangular shape. When it is thin enough to be translucent, cut it in half to make two squares, trim away about 1 inch from all sides, and place the sheets on floured paper toweling to dry while repeating the process with the remaining nine portions of dough. Makes twenty 5-inch squares.

To store the pasta sheets, layer them between paper toweling, roll them up, then pack them in a plastic bag. They will keep in the refrigerator 2 to 3 days or in the freezer for a month.

PASTA WITH BITTER GREENS AND TOMATOES

✿

Serves 2 or 3 as a first course or light supper

Here's an easy, light pasta dish from Molise, the "Cinderella" region of Italy. "Nobody knows how beautiful it is here," the locals keep saying. Molise cooking is similar to cooking in the surrounding regions of Apulia and Abruzzi. This recipe, from the restaurant Antici Trattoria da Tonino in Campobasso, uses long wavy strips of pasta called *lagane*, but any good wide semolina noodle such as *pappardelle* can be used.

What's special here is the treatment of the tomatoes. They're halved, dried in the oven in their skins, then chopped and simmered in olive oil with red pepper and garlic. The resulting sauce is unusually flavorful.

The greens are cooked the traditional southern Italian way, in a huge amount of water. While boiling they're kept submerged with the back of a wooden spoon so they cook evenly and retain their beautiful color. After they're removed and drained, the water is brought back to the boil and used to cook the pasta.

1 pound ripe Roma tomatoes, halved and seeded

½ pound bitter greens: dandelions, Belgian endive, curly endive, homegrown or wild green chicory, or escarole

2 tablespoons extra-virgin olive oil

½ cup chopped red onion

3 cloves garlic, peeled and halved

Freshly ground black pepper

¼ teaspoon red pepper flakes

Salt

½ pound long, wide, flat noodles such as *pappardelle* or *lagane*

¼ cup grated pecorino Romano

1. Preheat the oven to 350 degrees.

2. Spread the tomato halves on a lightly oiled baking sheet and bake for 1½ hours, turning them midway. Meanwhile, wash the greens in several changes of water until clean. Soak for 1 hour in salted water to help remove some of the bitterness.

3. Put the oil and onion in a 10-inch skillet and cook over low heat until the onion is soft, sweet, and golden, about 10 minutes.

4. Remove the tomatoes from the oven, cool, and chop finely. Add the tomatoes, garlic, black pepper, and red pepper to the skillet and continue cooking 10 minutes longer. Remove from the heat and allow to cool.

5. Purée the tomato sauce in a food processor or press through a food mill. Adjust the seasoning with salt and pepper. Return the tomato sauce to the skillet.

6. Bring a large quantity of salted water to a boil. Add the drained greens and cook until they are tender but not mushy, 5 to 10 minutes. Remove the greens with a slotted spoon; roughly chop and stir them into the tomato sauce.

7. Cook the pasta in the same boiling water until al dente. Add about 2 tablespoons of the pasta cooking water to the skillet (to dilute the sauce). Drain the pasta; add to the skillet and mix well. Cook over low heat for 30 seconds. Serve directly from the skillet or a shallow bowl. Pass the cheese at the table.

RADICCHIO *PASTICCIO*

❁

Serves 6 as a first course

Here's a vegetarian *pasticcio* (sister to lasagna) from the Italian Veneto—a terrific winter pasta dish of slightly bitter radicchio leaves shredded and sautéed, then enrobed in a béchamel sauce flavored with *Parmigiano-Reggiano* and brightened with a few leaves of escarole.

You can make this dish two days in advance, but I never do, since it takes but ten minutes to prepare, ten to bake, and (very important) a final ten to rest before serving. If you make it with the elongated Treviso-style radicchio starting to appear in markets, you'll really have something special.

In the original recipe, long radicchio leaves are grilled leaf by leaf over a hot grill. In this adaptation devised by Lucio Gomiero, an Italian-born, California-based grower, you simply sauté all the radicchio in a skillet and drop it into the béchamel sauce.

Béchamel? You bet, the old warhorse itself, so long out of fashion, makes its reappearance here to great effect. This is a great old-fashioned dish.

(continued)

2 cups milk

1 small onion, peeled and studded with 2 cloves

1 teaspoon salt

4 fresh lasagna sheets, approximately
9 by 12 inches (⅓ pound)

¼ cup unsalted butter plus more for greasing
the baking dish

¼ cup all-purpose flour

¼ teaspoon freshly ground black pepper

¾ pound red radicchio or Treviso-style radicchio

2 tablespoons olive oil

Heart of 1 escarole, trimmed and cut into
½-inch strips (1½ cups)

1 cup (4 ounces) freshly grated *Parmigiano-Reggiano*

1. In a small saucepan, heat the milk with the onion and simmer for 15 minutes; discard the onion.

2. Meanwhile, bring a pot of water to a boil, add ½ teaspoon of the salt and the noodles, and cook for 1 minute. Transfer to a bowl of cold water to stop the cooking, then shake off excess moisture and let cool on kitchen toweling.

3. In a 3- or 4-quart saucepan, melt the ¼ cup butter, add the flour, and stir over medium heat for 1 minute. Gradually add the milk, whisking to keep the mixture smooth. Cook, stirring, until it just begins to boil and becomes thick, about 2 minutes. Reduce the heat, stir in the remaining ½ teaspoon salt and the pepper, and cook 5 minutes more.

4. Meanwhile, wash, halve, core, and thinly slice the radicchio. In a wide skillet over medium heat warm the oil, add the radicchio and escarole, and sauté until tender and lightly browned, 2 to 3 minutes. Scrape into the béchamel and immediately remove from the heat; add the cheese and stir everything until well mixed.

5. Lightly butter a 9 by 12-inch baking dish. Smear the bottom of the dish with 3 to 4 tablespoons of the prepared mixture and cover with a sheet of lasagna. Smear one-quarter of the remaining mixture evenly over the pasta and cover with another sheet of lasagna. Repeat, finishing with a layer of the prepared mixture. At this point the dish can be covered and refrigerated up to 2 days. Return to room temperature before continuing.

6. About 30 minutes before serving, preheat the oven to 450 degrees. Bake the *pasticcio* for 10 minutes or until bubbling and golden on top. Wait 10 minutes before cutting into squares and serving.

GRANO WITH TUNA, CAPERS, AND CHERRY TOMATOES (*Italy*)

❀

Serves 2

Grano (skinned durum wheat berries) is a specialty of the region of Apulia and used in wonderful pilaf-like dishes served as an evening meal or a first course.

The texture of grano is creamier than that of unskinned wheat berries, and the flavor, though less nutty, makes a great backdrop for strong flavors. A half century ago, an Apulian home cook would have skinned them herself, using a deep long narrow stone or wooden mortar. She'd use a stone or wooden pestle to rub off the husk, leaving them shiny, with an off-white color. Grano is available at fine food stores or can be ordered by mail (see "Mail-Order Sources"). To keep grano fresh, store in the freezer.

This dish relies on good-quality tuna packed in olive oil and fragrant, in-season, soft-skinned cherry tomatoes. The better the tuna and tomatoes, the better the dish.

½ cup grano (skinned durum, or "hard," wheat berries) or skinned white wheat berries

Sea salt

1 (3½-ounce) can solid tuna packed in olive oil, preferably "Genova" brand

1 tablespoon extra-virgin olive oil

3 tablespoons chopped flat-leaf parsley

1 large clove garlic, peeled and chopped

1 pinch of hot red pepper flakes

1¼ cups (5 to 6 ounces) thin-skinned ripe cherry tomatoes, halved

12 salted capers, soaked in water and drained

Salt

Freshly ground black pepper

One important rule when cooking skinned wheat berries: Never stir. Stirring makes them stick to the bottom of the pan.

1. Rinse the grano under running water and drain. Bring 2 quarts water to a boil and add the grano; boil for 5 minutes. Remove from the heat and let soak 1 hour.

2. Bring 6 cups salted water to a boil in a heavy saucepan. Drain the grano, add it to the boiling water, and cook 25 minutes, skimming often. (If using soft-shelled wheat berries, soak overnight to soften. Drain, cover with 6 cups fresh water and cook for 25 minutes, skimming as necessary.)

3. When the grano is almost cooked, drain the oil from the tuna into a 10-inch skillet. Add the olive oil, 1 tablespoon of the parsley, and the garlic and cook over medium heat, about 2 minutes. Add the pepper flakes and the cherry tomatoes, cover, and steam for 3 minutes.

4. Add the tuna, flaking it with a fork, then add the capers and cook, uncovered, for 1 minute more. Add the drained wheat berries and ¼ cup of the cooking liquid and boil over high heat for 1 minute. Add the remaining parsley and salt and pepper to taste. Use a slotted spoon to divide servings on wide plates. Boil the pan juices down to napping consistency and pour over each serving. Serve at once.

Variation: SKILLET MUSSELS WITH WHEAT BERRIES

Omit the capers and tuna. Wash, soak, and clean 2 dozen mussels. Separately, steam open the mussels, shell, and add in step 4 with the pepper flakes.

Adapted from Luigi Sada's classic book on Apulian cooking, La Cucina Pugliese.

GREEN DUMPLINGS TOSSED WITH DICED TOMATO, TOASTED WALNUTS, AND FRESH HERBS (*Italy*)

❧

Serves 2 or 3 as a first course or lunch

These delicious, light, easy-to-make dumplings are flatter than most gnocchi and fluffier, too, because they use very little flour. But lightness and fluffiness can be a two-edged sword: Unless properly handled these gnocchi can fall apart when they hit boiling water. It's best to roll them the day before, then chill them overnight.

Various sauces can be used to top these light delicious dumplings. Try the lightly herbed tomato sauce from Potato Strudel Stuffed with Mixed Greens (page 122) or this Ligurian-inspired version made with chopped walnuts, tomatoes, and fresh herbs.

¾ **pound young "sweet" leafy greens such as stemmed spinach, lamb's-quarters, beet greens, chard, or a mixture of the above plus a few borage leaves**

Fine sea salt

1 tablespoon unsalted butter

¼ teaspoon freshly ground black pepper

Grated nutmeg

½ cup ricotta cheese

6 tablespoons freshly and finely grated *Parmigiano-Reggiano*

1 egg plus 1 egg yolk

All-purpose flour

SAUCE

5 tablespoons unsalted butter, melted and clarified to make 3 tablespoons

3 tablespoons chopped fresh walnuts

4 tablespoons coarsely chopped fresh tomatoes

2 to 3 tablespoons chopped mixed herbs: parsley, marjoram, and dill

1½ tablespoons freshly and finely grated *Parmigiano-Reggiano*

1. Wash and cook the greens with a pinch of salt for 3 to 4 minutes in a boiling salted water; drain well. Chop them very fine and squeeze to remove excess moisture. In a large skillet, heat the butter and fry the greens until glossy but dry. Season with ½ teaspoon salt, pepper, and a pinch of grated nutmeg.

2. Push the ricotta cheese through a sieve; pour off any liquid. In a medium-large bowl combine the greens, ricotta, cheese, egg, and egg yolk, mixing well with a wooden spoon until well combined. Add just enough flour to hold the mixture together, about 3 tablespoons. Correct the seasoning. If the mixture is sticky and difficult to handle, chill it before continuing.

3. With well-floured hands pinch off a tablespoon of dough and place on a well-floured cloth spread over a baking sheet. Repeat until all the mixture is used up. Gently indent each piece with a floured thumb. Leave to dry, uncovered, at room temperature for 1 hour before cooking. Or refrigerate, uncovered, until ready to cook. Makes about 2 dozen dumplings. This recipe can be prepared one day in advance up to this point. Cover and refrigerate.

4. About 20 minutes before serving, preheat the oven to 325 degrees.

5. Bring a wide pan of water to a boil. Add salt to the boiling water and slide in half the dumplings. Cook until they rise to the surface, about 1 minute. Let them boil another 30 seconds, then remove with a slotted spoon to a buttered, shallow baking dish. Keep warm in the oven. Repeat with remaining dumplings.

6. Spoon the warmed butter over the dumplings and scatter the walnuts, tomatoes, and herbs on top. Return to the oven for a minute or two. Serve with a small sprinkling of grated cheese.

7

MAIN COURSE DISHES

COUSCOUS

Couscous is usually made from granules of semolina, though barley, millet, corn, and even dried bread crumbs are also used. The granules or grains are steamed until separate and tender, then doused with herb-scented butter or fragrant olive oil and tossed with a flavorful sauce. When properly cooked, couscous is the great "grain" dish of North Africa. It's also the most maligned.

Let me begin by dispelling some myths about couscous.

Myth 1: Couscous is a grain. Yes, couscous is granular, but the substance we normally think of as couscous is made from semolina flour, a product of durum wheat. Thus, wheat is the grain. (Of course, if you make a couscous-type dish with barley, corn, or millet, then you actually will be working with a grain.)

Myth 2: Couscous is dried pasta. Not true! Pasta is made by kneading semolina and water to make a strong dough that can be stretched and cut to specific sizes and then boiled. As food expert Charles Perry wrote in the *Los Angeles Times*: "If you boil couscous (especially handmade couscous), it turns into a porridgy mess. If you steam it, though, it fluffs up into something completely lacking the chewy quality of gluten—something amazingly tender, practically ethereal."

Myth 3: There's real couscous sold out of sacks in health food stores and an inferior product called "instant couscous" sold out of packages at supermarkets . . . and never the twain shall meet. Not true! Nearly all commercially sold couscous, whether labeled "instant" or not, is virtually the same, since all factory-made couscous is partially precooked. Truly raw couscous, that's been rolled and dried without any steaming, is nearly impossible to find outside of private sources. If you want really good couscous that's fluffy and light, you have two alternatives: make your own (which is easy and fun; see page 210) or purchase packaged or loose couscous and steam it the proper way. If you do this, you will get a yield more than twice and sometimes triple what you would get if you followed the instructions on the couscous package. On the other hand, if you follow the box instructions, the couscous you prepare will swell up in your stomach rather than in the steamer as it should. Great for people who like to feel full, I suppose, but for couscous lovers a disaster.

Myth 4: You should line the perforated bottom of your steamer top with cheesecloth to keep the couscous from falling into the broth. Not true, because, with steam rising, the grains won't fall through . . . except perhaps an inconsequential ½ teaspoon's worth before the steam takes over.

You can always tell when couscous is fully cooked. It changes color, turns pale blond, and becomes bouncy and light. That is the moment to turn it out into a large bowl, moisten it, and let it rest, covered, for at least 10 minutes before serving.

Anyone who's ever tried to find coarse semolina in summer will immediately understand why a method was needed to preserve the semolina part of the hard wheat, which quickly goes bad in warm weather from weevils or spoilage. I don't know when couscous was invented (Charles Perry believes it was in the eleventh or twelfth century), but I believe it was created just like pasta as a way to preserve semolina throughout the year.

TUNISIAN COUSCOUS SALAD

There's a famous ad on Tunisian TV showing women sitting in a group making couscous, a once-a-year ritual, taking place over several days, during which a year's supply of couscous is rolled, steamed, sun-dried, then sewn into sacks.

Suddenly this well-depicted pastoral scene is broken by a severe summer shower. The message to the viewer is clear. "Don't go to all the trouble to make your own couscous, folks; instead, buy it ready-made at your local grocery." This ad, run by a consortium of couscous manufacturers, has been so effective that every year fewer and fewer Tunisian women make their own couscous.

Still, some do. Communal food preparation remains an important part of life in traditional Tunisian villages. When these women took a meal break from their task, I watched as they prepared a quick tasty "salad" of undried fresh couscous simply steamed and lightly dressed. Jerked meat called *kadid*, boiled with a few dried anchovies and mixed with Tunisian spices, fresh tomatoes, peppers, snipped dill, parsley, and chopped onion lightly salted "to kiss away the harshness," was placed in an earthenware mortar, then crushed with a smooth stone. This "dressing" was then mixed with some freshly steamed couscous, left to rest until it reached room temperature, then eaten accompanied by glasses of cold buttermilk. Afterward, refreshed and nurtured, the women, including me, went back to work.

TUNISIAN FISH COUSCOUS
WITH PUMPKIN AND LEAFY GREENS (*Tunisia*)

❖

Serves 8

"With couscous there are a thousand possibilities," chef Abdelrazak Haouari tells me. Nothing proves this better than his stunning fish and pumpkin couscous.

This wonderful homey dish from the island of Djerba combines chunks of white fish, winter vegetables, and subtle spicing. The unique Djerbian way of steaming fish (or meat) is a three-tier process. Broth bubbles in the bottom compartment; fish, greens, and pumpkin steam in the middle; couscous steams on top. When the fish is ready it's easily removed and held warm without any disturbance to the couscous. You end up with moist, flavorful fish; meltingly soft vegetables; fluffy tender couscous; and a richly flavored broth.

TOMATO-AND-GREEN-PEPPER-FLAVORED BROTH

⅓ cup extra-virgin olive oil

½ cup minced onion

1 tablespoon crushed garlic

2 teaspoons ground cumin

1 teaspoon sea salt

½ cup tomato paste

2-inch cinnamon stick

½ teaspoon dried mint

2 teaspoons homemade *harissa* (page 343)

1 green bell pepper, cored, seeded, and finely diced

2 cups concentrated fish stock

You can easily execute this dish with a roomy steamer. Just place an additional steamer top or colander on top. Or use a three-tier Chinese steamer. If neither solution is feasible, you can still make this dish (see Note below).

The fish portion can be just one type or a combination of up to four types of dense-fleshed fish such as swordfish, Chilean sea bass, halibut, and tilefish. For the winter squash my first choice would be nutty-flavored cabocha, since, on account of its dense flesh, it won't break up during cooking.

In this recipe you don't sliver the greens until just before using lest they throw off their moisture in advance. By slivering them at the last moment, then tossing them with the fish, you not only impart flavor, you provide the fish with insulation against overcooking. *(continued)*

This is a really good party dish, since it can be prepared in advance through step 4. A half hour before serving, simply steam the couscous for the second time and cook the fish until just tender. Try serving with the Slivered Endive, Fennel, and Blood Orange Salad (page 137).

1 pound medium- or small-grain couscous (2½ cups) or substitute "Roll Your Own Couscous" (page 210), steps 1, 2, 3, and 4.

2 pounds boneless, thick fish slices

1 teaspoon crushed garlic

4 teaspoons homemade pepper paste such as *harissa* (page 343)

4 tablespoons tomato paste

1 cup sliced onion

2 tablespoons olive oil

1 pound small carrots, pared and cut into 1-inch lengths

¾ pound small purple-topped white turnips, pared and quartered

2 boiling potatoes (1 pound), pared and cut into 1-inch dice

¾ pound winter squash, peeled, cored, and cut into 1-inch dice (2 cups)

1 bunch Swiss chard, or 12 ounces flat-leaf spinach, washed and stemmed

2 bunches flat-leaf parsley, washed, stemmed, and chopped

3 tablespoons unsalted butter

Sea Salt

Freshly ground black pepper

1. Make the Tomato-and-Green-Pepper-Flavored Broth: In a medium soup pot or the bottom of a couscous cooker, heat the olive oil and sauté the onion over low heat until lightly colored. Add the garlic, cumin, sea salt, and tomato paste and stir for 1 to 2 minutes, until smooth and glossy (this softens the acidic and metallic taste of tomato paste). Add the cinnamon stick, dried mint, *harissa,* green pepper, and 1 cup water. Cook, stirring, until thick and the peppers are meltingly tender. Add the fish stock and 7 cups water, bring to a boil, and cook at the simmer over medium heat for 10 minutes.

2. Meanwhile, rinse the store-bought couscous in a sieve under running water, spread it on a flat dish, and let it sit until grains swell, 5 to 10 minutes. Wash the fish, cut into 1½-inch chunks, and toss with garlic, *harissa,* tomato paste, onion, and olive oil. Keep in the refrigerator, loosely covered.

3. Break up any lumps by raking the store-bought couscous through your fingers. Lightly oil the inside of the perforated top or colander and fasten it onto the couscous cooker or pot; seal the two containers, if necessary, with a strip of wet floured cheesecloth. When steam is rising through the perforated holes, pile the store-bought or homemade couscous into the top container. Cover and steam the couscous for 20 minutes.

4. Transfer steamed couscous to a shallow wide dish. Gradually break up lumps with a long fork while sprinkling couscous with 1 teaspoon salt and 1 cup cold water. When the couscous is cold enough to handle, break up any lumps with moistened fingers. Cover with a damp towel. Remove the broth from the heat and keep in a cool place. *Up to this point the dish can be prepared 3 hours in advance.*

5. About 1 hour before serving, reheat the broth in the large pot, add the carrots and turnips, and bring to a boil; fasten on a steaming tray or a Chinese bamboo steamer. Place the potatoes and squash in the steamer, set the second steamer or colander on top, add the couscous, cover, and steam 10 minutes.

6. Roll the leafy greens into a tight coil and cut into hair-thin shreds. Toss the greens and parsley with the fish. Lift up the couscous basket; add the greens and fish to the potatoes and squash. Return the basket of couscous, cover, and steam until just tender, about 15 minutes.

7. Tip the couscous into a wide serving dish. Add the butter and fluff the couscous with a fork. Set the fish and its garnish on the side, covered, to keep warm. Taste the cooking liquid in order to correct the seasoning with salt and pepper. Gradually moisten the couscous with 2 cups of the stock. Toss lightly, cover with a large plate or foil tent, and let stand 15 minutes to swell. Arrange the fish chunks and garnish on top. Surround with carrots and turnips and serve at once with the remaining broth on the side.

NOTE TO THE COOK: If you have only one steamer or colander, you can still make this dish: After steaming the couscous for the second time and removing it to the serving dish, steam the potatoes and pumpkin in the same colander or steamer for 10 minutes, then add the fish and steam 15 minutes longer. The couscous will hold its heat if well moistened and covered.

MOROCCAN BERBER COUSCOUS FOR SPRING (Morocco)

❀

Serves 8

Back in the late seventies, the great American food writer James Beard asked to visit me in my home in New York to interview me for an article he was writing about Moroccan couscous.

At that time I'd published only two books, *Couscous and Other Good Food from Morocco* and the original edition (since completely revised) of *Mediterranean Cooking*. Excited about Mr. Beard's impending visit, I wanted very much to present him with a new and exciting couscous dish that wasn't in either of my books.

I called an old friend, the Moroccan ambassador Abselam Jaidi, who suggested I speak to his wife. She told me that on a recent trip back to Morocco she and Abselam had eaten one of the most delicious couscous dishes of their lives. She had no idea how it was made, but promised to try and find out. Days passed. No word came from Mrs. Jaidi. Perhaps she'd forgotten or had been unable to unearth the secret.

Since it was late spring, I decided to make a slightly new version of the Berber couscous in my book, and went off to buy the ingredients. The night before Beard's visit, Mrs. Jaidi called. She had the secret! Milk! All I had to do, she said, was toss the couscous with milk instead of water after the first steaming . . . and the couscous flavor would come alive.

I knew Berbers sometimes added milk to their couscous sauce, but was worried that wetting the couscous down with milk would cause it to lose its fluffiness. So I decided to make my Berber couscous in two batches, the first the traditional way, the second utilizing the "secret."

I couldn't get over the difference, and neither could Mr. Beard. We agreed that the addition of milk really made the couscous "sing." I've made my spring couscous this way ever since.

1. Place the meat, chicken, 3 tablespoons of the butter, quartered onion, herbs, salt, cinnamon stick, black pepper, and saffron in a 5-quart Dutch oven. Heat over a low flame, swirling the pan once or twice to let the contents mix gently. When the butter is melted, add 3 quarts water, bring to a boil, and cook, covered, at the simmer, 30 minutes.

2. Fill a deep pot with water and bring to a boil. Meanwhile, place couscous in a fine strainer and rinse under cool running water. Dump into a bowl and let stand until grains swell, 10 minutes. Break up any lumps with your fingers. Place the perforated top into the deep pot and check that it is a tight fit. If the fit isn't perfect, use padding. Dampen a long strip of cheesecloth, twist it into a strip the length of

1 pound veal or lamb shank

1 pound chicken thighs

8 tablespoons butter

1 large Spanish onion, quartered

8 sprigs each parsley and cilantro tied together with a thread

3½ teaspoons salt

1 cinnamon stick

2 teaspoons freshly ground black pepper

1 good pinch pulverized saffron

1½ pounds couscous

2 cups milk

10 white baby onions, peeled

1 pound very small purple-topped white turnips, or very fresh red radishes, well scrubbed and trimmed

¼ cup golden raisins

1½ pounds small zucchini, trimmed and halved lengthwise

2 pounds fresh fava beans

2 large red ripe tomatoes, halved, seeded, and grated

1 fresh green or red chili pepper, stemmed and seeded

1 cup heavy cream

2 tablespoons olive oil

½ cup snipped cilantro leaves

the circumference of the pot top, and tuck it between the two parts, to make sure the steam rises only through the perforated holes. Lightly oil the inside of the perforated top. There should be some room between the boiling water and the bottom of the perforated top. Pile in the dampened couscous and steam, uncovered, 30 minutes.

3. Remove the chicken when cooked and strip away bones, fat, skin, and gristle. Season with salt and pepper and wrap in foil to keep moist. Refrigerate if preparing in advance. Continue cooking the meat until fork tender.

4. When the couscous has steamed for 30 minutes, dump it into a roomy pan and gradually sprinkle with the milk. Use a long pronged fork to break up any lumps. Toss with 1½ teaspoons salt and set aside. Aerate the grains from time to time by raking them with your fingers. Let rest until 45 minutes before serving.

5. When the meat is fork tender, remove the broth from the heat and cool quickly. Skim off the fat that rises to the top. Bone the meat and season with salt and pepper. Wrap up meat, quickly chill broth, and refrigerate both. *Up to this point the dish can be prepared many hours in advance.*

6. Forty-five minutes before serving, repeat steaming of couscous, as directed in step 2, for 30 minutes. Reheat the broth to boiling. Add the baby onions, turnips, and raisins and cook, partially covered, 20 minutes. Add the zucchini and continue cooking. Blanch the favas and peel away the second skin. When the vegetables are tender, add the favas, tomatoes, chili pepper, and cream and bring to a boil. Continue cooking until the vegetables are *very* tender. Remove from the heat and correct the seasoning.

7. Dump the couscous onto a very wide serving dish and toss with remaining butter and strain over 2 cups of broth. Toss, cover and let stand 10 minutes.

Meanwhile, reheat the meat and chicken: In a covered skillet, sauté the meat and chicken in hot oil until well browned on all sides. Spread out the couscous and form a well in the center. Put in the contents of the skillet, top with the vegetables, and serve with the remaining broth on the side.

ROLL YOUR OWN COUSCOUS

Serves 8

I know! Just the thought of making your own couscous gives you a headache, but in fact it's easier than making your own pasta or bread and delivers the same satisfaction: superior taste and a sense of wonder at the magic of it all.

I don't know why it took me so long to start teaching homemade couscous. Once I did, putting on a show costumed in pantaloons and sitting on the floor the way North African women do, I remembered how much fun it was and how astonishing the results were. Now, spurred on by terrific feedback from my students, I demonstrate couscous making whenever I get the chance.

When making couscous you'll need two horsehair, wire, or plastic sieves of different calibers through which to shake the rolled beads of semolina. You'll also need a couscous cooker or deep kettle with a colander that will sit snugly on top. And, of course, you'll need some fresh coarse semolina and fine semolina flour purchased by mail-order or from a good Middle Eastern store. With these items in hand, you'll be able to make enough fine-grain couscous to serve eight in less than 1 hour.

When making your own couscous, you must use coarse semolina, not couscous, as the "magnet" for fine semolina flour.

To make a sublime dessert with couscous, see page 335.

This recipe can be halved to serve 4.

1 cup coarse semolina

⅓ cup cold water (approximately)

1 cup fine semolina flour

Pinch of fine sea salt

1 teaspoon olive oil

To Flavor the Couscous

2 tablespoons butter or olive oil

2 cups strained meat, fish, or poultry broth

1. Spread the coarse semolina on a large, preferably round tray. Sprinkle a few tablespoons of salted cold water over the coarse semolina and, at the same time, rotate the palm and fingers of one hand in wide circles (in one direction only) to create tiny spheres.

2. After two or three rotations, begin to sprinkle the semolina flour and about ¼ cup cold water alternately on the spheres while continuing to rotate. As the spheres absorb the flour and water they will turn into tiny couscous "beads" more or less the same size. You may need another 1 to 2 tablespoons of water.

3. Shake or lightly press the couscous "beads" through an everyday wire or plastic 10-mesh strainer in order to standardize their size. Place in a finer sieve to shake and remove excess flour. (You may discard or use the flour, as North Africans do, to start the next batch.) Makes about 3¼ cups uncooked fine couscous.

4. Bring plenty of water to a boil in the bottom of a deep kettle or couscous cooker. Pile the freshly rolled couscous into a lightly oiled colander or top container. Fit the top onto the bottom, checking for a tight seal. Partially cover and steam 15 minutes.

5. Dump couscous onto a tray and break up lumps with a large fork or whisk. Sprinkle with ½ cup salted cold water and rake the grains to keep them separate. Gradually add another ½ cup water and 1 teaspoon olive oil while raking the couscous. When the couscous has absorbed all the water repeat the steaming for 15 minutes.

6. Dump couscous onto a tray, gradually work in another cup cold water, and rake the grains to keep them separate. Allow to rest, covered, for 15 minutes. Fluff up the couscous and loosely cover with a damp towel. *Up to this point the couscous can be prepared a few hours in advance.*

7. Thirty minutes before serving, bring water back to a boil. Return the couscous to the colander or top container and steam, uncovered, an additional 10 to 15 minutes. *Couscous lightens in color when fully cooked.* Dump couscous onto a wide shallow serving dish and toss with oil or butter; then gradually moisten with broth. Let stand, covered, for 10 to 15 minutes. Gently fluff the couscous, pile in a mound, and decorate with meat or fish and vegetables.

BARLEY FOR COUSCOUS

No Mediterranean country uses as much barley as Tunisia. There's even a museum in Sfax celebrating barley and its national culinary uses. Small illuminated boxes portray the different stages of processing from seed to grain and all the diverse products Tunisians make from barley along the way. Not surprising, since barley is probably the oldest cultivated Mediterranean grain.

Barley is still grown in great quantity in the southern part of the country and on the islands of Kerkenna and Djerba for use in soups, breads, and couscous. On Djerba I've seen it planted in groves of olive and palm trees. When the spring rains are good, the barley truly looks magnificent, ready for harvest around the first of May.

When toasted, barley is lighter than most grains and easier to digest, especially when made into couscous. Barley couscous comes in two sizes: large, similar to cracked Scotch barley, and small, similar to barley grits. Both are available at well-stocked health food stores and can be used interchangeably in my recipes. Simply add a few extra minutes of steaming if you use the larger size. (If your health food store doesn't stock barley grits, pulse hulled barley or cracked Scotch barley to the size of grits in a spice mill or electric blender . . . but not a food processor).

Cracked barley is used to make hearty dishes such as a festive couscous that includes lamb's head, carrots, and turnips, or simply steamed and topped with chopped fennel, mallow, or turnip greens and chickpeas.

The smaller barley grits are used to make a richly favored couscous, such as the Tunisian Barley Couscous with Swiss Chard, Lamb, Chickpeas, and *Hrous* (page 214), or they can be added to soups.

Barley is even turned into bulgur in Tunisia. It's boiled, cracked, sieved, then dried in the sun. Fine-grain barley bulgur is used in soups.

For me, the most interesting process is the one whereby immature barley grain is made into *frik,* the Tunisian version of Middle Eastern *fireek* or green wheat. The immature barley is steamed, dried, slowly toasted on earthen plates over embers, then cracked by hand. The largest pieces are used to make a special couscous called *azenbu*, the smaller ones for soup, while the very finest are turned into flour used in the preparation of the soup-drink *bsissa* (page 60).

In my cookbook *Couscous and Other Good Food from Morocco*, there's a description of *azenbu*:

This couscous, made with barley shoots or green barley, is considered one of the most delicious in Morocco, though it is available only in the Rif and in the Souss. Admired for its purity and utter simplicity, it is the ultimate country dish. Immature barley is grilled in a pan with za'atar [oregano], then cracked and sieved. The smaller grains are used in soup, and the larger grains are steamed over boiling water, placed on a platter, buttered, and served with a bowl of cold milk or buttermilk in the Berber style.

In the Tunisian Souss, I learned how to roll the most unusual couscous I've ever seen. Barley grits, instead of coarse semolina, were used as the "magnet" for fine semolina flour; the two grains were rolled together creating a fascinating double-level couscous, combining the deep full taste of semolina with the nutty warm flavor of barley. This couscous, which must be steamed fresh, is so fragile that it isn't tossed with sauce; instead, it is simply placed on a plate with the sauce poured on top. If you're interested in making it, follow the directions on page 210 for making hand-rolled couscous, substituting barley grits for the coarse semolina, then steam twice.

TUNISIAN BARLEY COUSCOUS WITH SWISS CHARD, LAMB, CHICKPEAS, AND *HROUS* (*Tunisia*)

❧

Serves 4

This peppery couscous is from the town of Tozeur in southern Tunisia, where cooks use finely shredded greens to thicken their sauces. I like to make this dish in fall, when farmers' markets sell thin-stemmed chard and early turnips.

The cooking method for the sauce is unusual, one of the most interesting I've encountered in over thirty years spent studying Mediterranean cuisines. In this recipe, two pounds of leafy greens are cooked with a handful of root vegetables without water over very low heat for about ten minutes with constant stirring and crushing. The object is to cook away all the expressed moisture. Next, the meat and a little oil are added, then the whole is cooked slowly so that the meat, vegetables, and greens fry in the fat. Assorted flavorings are added and also a potato in order to absorb any residual moisture. This unusual method yields a delicious intense "sauce" for the meat and the barley.

This dish was served to me accompanied by plain steamed barley couscous, one of the few times in my years in North Africa I've been served couscous separately from a sauce.

For best results, prepare the sauce in advance and reheat while steaming the barley couscous.

1. Drain the chickpeas; place in a 5-quart heavy casserole, preferably nonstick and set aside. Wash and stem the chard. Pile the chard leaves and shred as fine as possible, then cut in half. Makes about 10 packed cups.

2. Add the chard, carrots, and turnips to the casserole and set over medium heat to cook. Stir and crush the greens constantly with a wide wooden spoon for 10 minutes to avoid burning. Add 1 teaspoon of the salt to draw out moisture and continue to cook, stirring and crushing, 5 minutes. Add the lamb and 2 tablespoons of the olive oil and stir-fry everything for 5 minutes. Stir in the tomato paste, paprika, garlic, hot pepper paste, and potato and cook, stirring and crushing from time to time, for another 15 minutes.

3. Add 3 cups water, cover, and cook over medium to low heat until the meat and chickpeas are tender, about 1½ hours. Makes 5 to 6 cups sauce.

4. Meanwhile, soak the barley grits in just enough salted hot water to cover; leave for 15 minutes without stirring. If using hulled barley, use a spice or grain mill to grind barley to the size of grits.

⅓ cup dried chickpeas, soaked overnight in water to cover

2 pounds Swiss chard leaves (about 3 bunches)

2 small carrots, pared, trimmed, and halved lengthwise

2 small white turnips, scrubbed, trimmed, and halved

1½ teaspoons salt

¾ to 1 pound boneless lean shoulder of lamb, trimmed of excess fat and cut into 1-inch cubes

2½ tablespoons olive oil

2 tablespoons tomato paste

2 tablespoons sweet paprika

2 cloves garlic, peeled and sliced

1 tablespoon *hrous* pepper paste (page 344)

1 large potato, quartered

1⅔ cups barley grits or 2 cups hulled barley, 12 ounces

5. Fill the bottom part of a couscous pot with water and bring to a boil. If you don't own a couscous pot, a deep kettle and a snug-fitting vegetable steamer or colander will do. If the fit isn't perfect, use padding: Dampen a cheesecloth, twist it into a strip the length of the circumference of the kettle top, and tuck it between the two parts to make sure the steam rises only through the perforated holes. Lightly oil the inside of the steamer. Don't let the perforated top touch the boiling water below.

6. Stir the barley grits under water with your hands to soften and separate. Rinse, drain, and steam for 30 minutes, covered, then fluff the grits with a fork, toss with the remaining ½ tablespoon of olive oil and ½ teaspoon salt, and steam 20 minutes more, uncovered.

7. Tip the barley into a wide dish. Sprinkle the grains with 1 cup cold water and fluff with a fork. Pile the barley back into the perforated top, cover and continue steaming 15 minutes. Makes about 1 quart barley grits.

8. Tip tender barley into a shallow serving dish, fold in 1 cup of the meat sauce, and serve the remaining sauce on top.

SARDINIAN *FREGULA*, SICILIAN *CUSCUSÙ*, ISRAELI *COUSCOUSOU*, SYRIAN AND LEBANESE *MOGRABIYAH*, JORDANIAN *MIFTOOL*, TUNISIAN *MHAMMAS*, AND TURKISH AND GREEK *KUSKUS*

Query: If it's round, hand-rolled, made with semolina, and at least as small as rice grains, is it couscous? Answer: Very likely.

It didn't surprise me to hear that there was a form of couscous on the island of Sardinia. After all, you can find couscous in Sicily and even in parts of mainland Italy. However, I was surprised by how different and charming the Sardinian version turned out to be.

Called *fregula* or *freula sarda*, it is hand-rolled, made with fresh coarse semolina, fine semolina flour, and water like North African couscous, then sun-dried. Though the pellets are larger than the North African variety (about the size of small peas) it's the next step that makes *fregula* unique: the pellets are baked, giving them a toasty flavor and making it possible for them to be simmered in broth or salted water just like pasta, while retaining the incredible lightness of couscous.

In Sicily they make a variant of North African couscous called *cuscusù*. After steaming, the couscous grains are left in fish broth to "cure," then steamed again. This way, the fish flavor is imbued into the grains during steaming, rather than at the end when the grains are sauced. *Cuscusù* is usually served with a "short" sauce.

Two varieties of couscous have recently shown up in American Middle Eastern groceries (or through mail-order from Kalustyan): *couscousou* from Israel, which is toasted and about the size of peppercorns, and a large pasta-like Syrian and/or Lebanese couscous called *mograbiyah* (or, in Jordan, *miftool*). American chefs are cooking both to the consistency of risotto—tender but slightly chewy.

Tunisian *mhammas* starts out as semolina couscous, but ends up larger, shinier in appearance, and firmer in texture, as a result of an unusual second rolling after sun-drying in flat bowls filled with wet, salted sliced onions. The grains are then pressed through a sieve to make them uniform, then dried again. Since it's a huge job, taking up to two weeks, *mhammes* is usually purchased in shops rather than made by hand at home. Tunisians steam it and then boil it. "It never breaks down that way . . . and it absorbs lots of flavor," a Tunisian chef told me. It is not available in the United States.

Turkey and Greece have their own versions of couscous called *kuskus*. I was staring at some couscouslike grains in a store window in the northern Greek town of Ceres one day, when a passerby, noting my curiosity, stopped to explain their use. She told me, "We boil hard wheat berries, then crack them the same way we crack bulgur. We next pass the grain through a strainer to get even sizes, then clean it, take away the bran, roll it into dough balls using warm water and flour, toast it in a pan, then dry it and store it in a cloth sack. We use it in stews, throwing it in so it releases its starches and makes for a creamy sauce."

Turkish *kuskus* is simply an egg-rich dough, made with semolina, formed into tiny balls that are boiled and served with tomato sauce.

AN INTRODUCTION TO SPANISH RICE DISHES

A well-made paella Valenciana will always be a great dish, but unfortunately too many paellas are pedestrian. Beyond paella, there's a whole world of Spanish rice dishes called *arroces*, which are equally fabulous but aren't nearly so well-known.

"The Valencianos are stuck with their tradition; they spend an inordinate amount of time arguing about what is the 'true' Paella Valenciana," writes Pedro Nuño, a Spanish gastronome and specialist on the cuisine of Alicante province. "Here in Alicante our cooks are free to be more imaginative. We can take some garlic, a little fish, an onion, a pepper, some greens and good-quality rice and make something so good it'll make you suck your fingers!"

Alicante cooks, he goes on, "free of the yoke of Valencian paella, have created over a hundred types of rice dishes." Then he adds, "Everyone is entitled to be creative, of course, but not to create a mess!"

These words were what led me to Alicante, halfway between Valencia and Murcia along the Spanish Mediterranean coast, to discover what Alicante rice cookery was all about. Along the way

I learned dozens of fine recipes for seasonal Spanish *arroces*. The six that follow range from an apparently simple yet extraordinarily tasty and truly delicious *arroz,* in which the rice, cooked in an aromatic fish stock, is served adorned with tuna and mussels (page 224) to an elegant, complex *arroz negret,* as "black rice" is called in Alicante, which in my opinion surpasses paella Valenciana in depth of taste as well as visual splendor (page 226).

The Sofrito is the base for a great *arroz.* Josep Pla, a Catalan food authority, once said, "So long as the *sofrito* is well-made, the *arroz* will become monumental no matter what else you put into it."

I'm not sure he didn't exaggerate, but I certainly agree that the *sofrito,* the initial stew of vegetables and flavorings, is the foundation of a great Spanish *arroz,* just as a *soffritto* is the foundation of a great Italian risotto, and a *sokaric* the foundation of a great eastern Turkish pilaf.

In each case, finely diced vegetables are slowly stewed in fat to accentuate their flavors. In Spain, the *sofrito* is most often made of onions, tomatoes, peppers, both dried and fresh, and garlic. These ingedients are blended in the pan, then reduced to a thick, rich, flavorful, jamlike consistency, ready to receive and enhance either liquid or rice—whichever, according to the particular recipe, is first to go into the pot.

The Liquid Though plenty of good Spanish cooks use ordinary heated tap water when making their *arroces,* I always use a homemade stock. Typical ingredients of such a stock might be a selection of aromatics along with simmered bones and skins of poultry, or monkfish skins, heads and frames of bony fish, or simply shrimp shells and frozen fish fumet, along with vegetable trimmings. Spanish cooks will also use duck or eel skins to provide flavorful gelatin-rich stocks for *arroces.*

Characteristic Spanish flavorings include garlic, the Spanish paprika called *pimentón,* red peppers, saffron, and, if possible, wood smoke produced by cooking over an open fire.

Burt Schoenfeld, writing in *Saveur* magazine, reports on the importance of water in making paellas. "Is the water really all that important to a good paella?" he asked the acting president of the *Tribunal de las Aguas* in Valencia. "Only as important as blood to a person," the president replied.

Later in Mr. Schoenfeld's story another interviewee states, "Water is water. What's important are the hands that make the paella. The genius. The inspiration."

Spanish cooks who use water say that the cooking time varies, depending on whether the water is hard or soft.

"Be sure to allow up to a half hour for Calasparra-type rices if your water is soft," advises Rafael Navarro, the controller at the Calasparra station up in the hills above the town of Murcia. "On the other hand if your water is hard, it will only be fifteen to eighteen minutes."

The Rice When Señor Pla wrote about the importance of the *sofrito,* he assumed his readers knew the importance of choosing the proper type of rice—a squat Spanish rice with a starchy inner core and high absorption characteristics—its thickness and hardness allowing it to incorporate flavorful broth without becoming mushy.

Spanish Calasparra rice (the name designates the region of origin) can absorb far more stock than almost any other short- to medium-grain rice on the market. Under the umbrella of Calasparra, the most coveted rice is Bomba, which you can order through The Spanish Table (see "Mail-Order Sources"). Bomba absorbs even more liquid than other Calasparra types, but any Spanish short- to medium-grain rice will make a fine *arroz.*

Italian medium-grain rices as well as the California short-grain rices do not cook the same way. Still, since we live in an imperfect world, it may be necessary to substitute them with the understanding that though the result will still be good, adjustments will have to be made. Many food writers suggest using Italian risotto rices such as *arborio, Roma,* and *carnaroli,* but in the words of Maria Jose Sevilla, author of numerous books on Spanish food, "the dish will be 'Spanish-style,' not true Spanish *arroz.*"

Other short- to medium-grain rices such as the American Cal-Rosa and California Pearl should be avoided. These rices are very starchy, which causes them to break down and turn sticky when infused with the large amount of liquid used in Spanish rice cookery. The best American substitute I've found is the "Mediterranean-style" Cal-Riso (see "Mail-Order Sources"). And there are other, less expensive Spanish rices on the market that work perfectly, though they absorb less liquid than rices of the coveted Calasparra group.

The ability to absorb liquid is the key. A cup of Bomba rice will absorb *up to* 3½ cups liquid. A cup of most other Calasparra rices will absorb 2¾ to 3 cups liquid. However, a cup of nearly all other short- to medium-grain rices will absorb only 2 cups liquid . . . and therein lies the difficulty. If you use one of these other rices, please remember to adjust the amount of liquid in accordance with instructions given in the recipes. Otherwise you'll get a poor result.

The Cooking Vessel The pan in which you cook your rice will affect its flavor and consistency. For example, oven-baked rice dishes such as the Golden Rice (page 230), which are cooked in shallow earthenware casseroles, which are often drier than soupier rice dishes such as Caldero Murciano (page 61), which are cooked in deeper cazuelas on top of the stove.

Paella Valenciana is always cooked in the classic two-handled shallow sloping pan that holds the rice, liquid, and garnishes to a depth no higher than a thumb. Hence the need for a wide pan to provide room for the rice, stock, and other ingredients to cook together properly. Paella pans, in sizes serving from two to sixty people, may be purchased through The Spanish Table. Classic paella pans are superb for *arroces*, especially those prepared over a wood fire, when the aroma of the smoke becomes a component. (You can cook paellas in the fireplace, over a campfire, or over an outdoor grill.) If you're not cooking over a wood fire, larger paella pans are often impractical, as they must straddle several burners.

Some of the following recipes call for a paella pan, either the small, 12-inch rim-to-rim size that will hold up to 2 quarts of food and will serve 3 to 6 people, or the 18-inch size that will hold up to 5 quarts of food and will serve 8 to 12 as a main course. I use a 9 by 21-inch cast-iron grid (comal) to straddle two burners, then set my paella pan on top. Though you don't need to do this, it does help create a wonderful brown crust, called the *quemada,* or *soccarat,* on the bottom of the rice as it rests after the initial cooking.

All the recipes can be made in an earthenware cazuela, but please remember to adjust the liquid and use a flame tamer under the casserole.

The Fire As romantic and delicious as it is to prepare an *arroz* over burning wood, the process can be fraught with anxiety. A wood fire is difficult to control, and much moving of the paella pan up and down, and even occasionally off the grill, may be necessary to ensure that the liquid doesn't boil off too fast.

A friend, Tom Glick, a professor of Spanish history and American paella expert par excellence, was present on one occasion when my husband and I worked furiously to salvage an *arroz negret* that was quickly boiling down to a black glaze. "Ah!" he said, as we fumbled with the hot pan, "the open-hearth paella is a harsh mistress!"

I still recommend an open fire to courageous cooks who are in pursuit of the ineffable delights of a smokey *arroz,* and who understand that precise timings do not apply, that open-fire cooking is always a matter of "feel."

For those who would rather work at a stove without straddling burners yet still make an *arroz* in large quantities, I'm happy to pass on a technique I learned from Spanish-based American food writer Janet Mendel, author of four Spanish cookbooks. Instead of using two skillets, as is usually recommended, Janet uses a deep flat-bottomed two-handled rolled steel *perol.* Similar to a wok, 7 inches across the bottom and approximately 14 inches from rim to rim, it is readily available in the United States. She brings the *sofrito* and liquid to a brisk boil, stirs for a few minutes, adds the rice, then lowers the heat and never stirs again, though she will occasionally give the pan a brisk shake. She then serves the rice spooned out onto plates the way Italians serve risotto.

Cooking the Rice In traditional Spanish rice cookery, done over an open wood fire, the liquid goes into the pan before the rice. This is because the liquid must be boiling when the rice is mixed with it, and outdoors there is only one fire.

Old-time cooks still determine the amount of liquid by filling a broad flat paella pan with hot stock to the top of the two screws on either side that hold the handles. They sprinkle in rice while making the sign of a cross over the pan, flare the rice out with the back of a wooden spoon, stir it just once, then gently shake the pan. They then cook the liquid and rice at a fast boil over very high heat for approximately 10 minutes, gradually reducing the heat (by moving the coals) as the rice continues to cook and absorb the bubbling stock. The minute the rice is tender almost to the core, they remove the pan from the heat, cover it, then leave it to continue to cook in its residual heat 5 to 10 minutes more.

The rice of a good *arroz*, when properly cooked, whether over a fire, on top of the stove, or in an oven (as in Crusty Rice with Chicken and Pork Sausages, page 234), should be plump with flavor yet still slightly firm. Each grain should be separate, what the Spanish call *en su punto*, when removed from the heat. Then, as it cools down, it continues to cook to perfect creamy tenderness.

SPANISH RICE DISHES: A FEW HELPFUL DOS AND DON'TS

1. *Don't* wash the rice. If the rice looks dirty or dusty, simply place it dry into a sieve, then shake it over the sink.
2. *Don't* stir. Actually, you may stir *just once*—when you add rice to the boiling stock or when you add boiling stock to the rice.
3. *Do* keep extra simmering water on hand. Rapid boiling causes rapid evaporation, so you may need to add liquid to keep the rice moist during the first 10 minutes of cooking.
4. *Don't* set a hot cazuela on a cold surface and *don't* add cold liquid to a hot cazuela. The cazuela will break.

AROMATIC FISH STOCK FOR FISH-BASED *ARROCES*

❊

Makes 3 quarts

Spanish cooks have a saying: "A good fish stock should be the nectar of the sea." To which I would add, in connection with rice cookery: A good fish stock should, when reduced, bind to starchy rice, creating a caramelized crust on the bottom of the casserole.

I urge you to make this aromatic fish stock in advance, then freeze it. Doing so will cut down on work time the day you make your fish-based *arroz*. Stock will keep several months in the freezer. You can also freeze discarded lobster and shrimp shells from another meal, saving them until you're in the mood to make your stock.

3 tablespoons extra-virgin olive oil

2 pounds fish trimmings: small rockfish, bass frames, monkfish skins, shrimp shells, or lobster shells, washed and drained

1 red bell pepper, cored, seeded, and finely chopped

1 clove garlic, peeled and sliced

1 teaspoon paprika, preferably Spanish *pimentón*

Sprig of fresh rosemary

1 tablespoon tomato paste

½ cup chopped green scallion tops

Pinch of hot red pepper flakes

Pinch of ground cinnamon

1. Warm the olive oil in a large pot over moderately high heat and cook the fish trimmings until the oil smells aromatic, 2 to 3 minutes. Reduce the heat, and at one-minute intervals, add the chopped bell pepper, garlic, paprika, rosemary, tomato paste, scallion tops, red pepper flakes, and ground cinnamon in that order.

2. Increase the heat and cook until almost all the moisture evaporates, 1 to 2 minutes. Add 12 cups water and bring to a boil. Partially cover and simmer for 45 minutes. Force through a sieve or purée in a blender or food processor and return to the pot. Simmer 15 minutes longer, strain, and reserve. Dilute the liquid to make 3 quarts.

RICE WITH FRESH TUNA AND MUSSELS

❀

Serves 3 as a main course

This wonderfully delicious *arroz* uses a combination of garlic, peppers, tomatoes, Spanish paprika, and cubed artichokes for the underpinning of the *sofrito*. The Spanish food authority Lourdes March told me with a wink—as if imparting a big secret—that cooking artichokes in an iron or steel paella pan accentuates their bitterness, thus balancing the sweetness of the *sofrito* and the rice. It also helps blacken the rice without the need for squid ink.

For this dish I suggest you use a 12-inch rim-to-rim paella pan to serve 3 as a main course. You can use the same size paella pan to serve 6 by simply doubling the ingredients.

1. Scrub the mussels. Soak them in a bowl of lightly salted cold water for at least 30 minutes, so they purge themselves of sand.

2. Meanwhile, rinse, dry, and cut the tuna into 1-inch cubes. Lightly sprinkle with sea salt and let stand 30 minutes.

3. Seed the dried pepper and soak in hot water until softened, 30 minutes.

4. Place the diced tomatoes, paprika, saffron, sugar, and salt and pepper in the work bowl of a food processor and hold.

5. Heat 2 tablespoons oil in a small 12-inch paella pan or a wide skillet until hot but not smoking. (If you have a comal or iron grid set over two burners, place paella pan on top and heat before continuing.)

6. Add the garlic and artichokes to the pan and fry until golden. Transfer the garlic to the workbowl.

7. Add the diced red pepper and drained chile pepper to the pan and fry, stirring, for 5 minutes. Scoop up the bell pepper and chile and add to the work-bowl and process to a chunky mass, the *sofrito*. Return the *sofrito* and 1 tablespoon olive oil to the pan and continue to fry with the artichokes over medium heat for 5 minutes more. *Up to this point the dish can be prepared in advance. Reheat the contents in the pan before continuing.*

8. Toss tuna with seasoned flour in a sieve; shake off the excess, and quickly fry on all sides to brown. (The chunks of tuna will be lightly tinged with the *sofrito*.) Remove tuna to a side dish.

9. Stir shredded greens into the pan and sauté until they wilt, about 5 minutes.

10. Meanwhile, open mussels by steaming, and strain the mussel liquor directly into the fish stock. Heat the stock to a simmer. Wrap the mussels to keep warm.

36 small mussels (1½ pounds)

¾ pound 1-inch-thick slice fresh tuna, preferably ahi

Coarse sea salt

1 mild dried New Mexican pepper, or 2 Spanish *ñora* peppers

¾ cup diced flavorful tomatoes (out of season, use canned Muir Glen)

1 teaspoon sweet or sharp paprika or Spanish *pimentón*

Pinch of crumbled saffron threads

Pinch of sugar

Freshly ground black pepper

Extra-virgin olive oil

5 cloves garlic, peeled

1 cup fresh or frozen diced artichoke bottoms

¼ cup diced red bell pepper

Seasoned flour for dredging

2 cups stemmed and roughly shredded Swiss chard or spinach leaves

2 to 4 cups homemade fish stock (page 223), or 1 cup frozen fish fumet diluted with water

1 cup Spanish rice, or any medium-grain rice as discussed on page 219

1 roasted red pepper, cored, seeded, and cut into long strips

2 tablespoons chopped flat-leaf parsley

Lemon wedges

11. Measure the stock. You will need 2 cups for ordinary medium-grain rice, a scant 3 cups for Calasparra, and almost 3⅓ cups for Bomba. Add stock to the pan and bring to a rolling boil. Scatter the rice on top and stir once and cook, uncovered, over lively heat for about 8 minutes. Slip in the chunks of tuna and gradually reduce the heat during another 5 minutes. When the rice has absorbed most of the liquid, push the mussels and roasted red pepper strips into the rice and continue cooking over gradually reduced heat for another 5 minutes. Be sure to rotate and shake the pan in order to cook the rice evenly. Turn off the heat, cover with a sheet of paper toweling and an inverted pizza pan, and let rest for 5 minutes before serving. Serve directly from the pan decorated with parsley and lemon wedges.

Inspired by a dish served at the Cavia Restaurant in Campello, Alicante.

BLACK RICE WITH MUSSELS AND SHRIMP

Serves 6 to 8 as a main course

*B*lack paella, or *arroz negret,* as it's called in Alicante, is colored not by additions of squid ink but rather from the *sofrito*—a blend of caramelized onions, crushed sausage, chopped squid, roasted tomatoes, and dried red chilies cooked down to a jam that eventually turns a rich dark chocolate color without burning. This is similar to the way one makes a Creole gumbo. Using several packets of squid ink will also deepen the color and add saline flavor, but this is unnecessary, especially since these packets can cost up to five dollars each.

This wonderful dish can be prepared in the fireplace or out of doors, giving it a delicious smoky flavor. But even made on top of the stove or in the oven, the dish will still knock you out. For this version you will need an 18-inch rim-to-rim paella pan. You can use the same size paella pan to serve 12 as a main course by scaling up all the ingredients and using 5 cups (2 pounds) of rice.

1. Peel the shrimp, reserving the shells. Toss the shrimp with coarse sea salt and soak in water to cover until needed.

2. Prepare the fish stock on page 223 using the peels from the shrimp for added flavoring. If using canned *calamares en su tinta,* squeeze the solids through cheesecloth to extract as much "ink" as possible. Discard the solids, add "ink" to the stock, and bring to a boil. Reduce the heat and keep at a simmer, if continuing through to the final step. If preparing the stock in advance, cool, cover, and refrigerate until 1 hour before serving.

3. Heat 3 tablespoons oil in a skillet and fry the onions with a pinch of salt over medium heat until deeply browned but not burned, 30 minutes. Add the sausage and squid and cook, covered, until all liquid has evaporated, 10 to 15 minutes. Add a few tablespoons stock and continue to cook the squid until fork-tender.

4. Meanwhile, combine the tomatoes, garlic, drained peppers, paprika, parsley, saffron, and a few spoonfuls stock in the workbowl of a food processor and grind to a purée. *Up to this point the dish can be prepared in advance.*

5. Scrub the mussels and soak them in salted water for 1 hour.

6. About 1 hour before serving, reheat the stock and keep it at a simmer. Have a second pan of simmering water as a backup. Steam the mussels open, discard top shells, and strain juices through cheesecloth and add to the stock. Discard any that remain closed. Season mussels with pepper and a few drops of olive oil and moisten with a few tablespoons stock. Keep moist and covered.

1½ pounds fresh or defrosted frozen shrimp, unpeeled

6 to 10 cups Aromatic Fish Stock (page 223), depending on the rice you use (see page 219)

Sea salt

1 or 2 cans *calamares en su tinta* (optional)

½ cup extra-virgin olive oil

1 medium onion, peeled and chopped

1 small, flavorful fresh pork sausage (4 ounces), skinned and crushed with the side of a fork

1 pound fresh or defrosted frozen squid, cleaned, skinned, and cut into bite-size pieces

3 red ripe tomatoes, halved, seeded, and set skin side up under the broiler and cooked until soft

4 large cloves garlic, unpeeled, broiled until soft, then peeled

2 dried sweet red *ñora* peppers, or 1 dried New Mexican pepper, cored, seeded, and soaked in hot water

1 teaspoon sweet Spanish paprika, preferably *pimentón de la Vera*

2 tablespoons chopped flat-leaf parsley

½ teaspoon saffron threads, dried and crushed with a pinch of salt

2 pounds fresh small mussels

Freshly ground black pepper

3 cups Spanish rice or other medium-grain rice as discussed on page 219

Lemon wedges

Ali-oli Sauce (page 345)

7. Heat 5 tablespoons olive oil in an 18-inch paella pan and fry the tomato mixture until it glistens. Add the squid and a few tablespoons stock and stir rapidly to make a homogeneous mass, and until all moisture evaporates and mixture begins to turn dark brown, 10 minutes. Add hot stock and bring to a boil. Scatter the rice on top and stir once. Cook over moderately high heat for about 10 minutes. Gradually lower the heat, slip shrimps and mussels into the rice, and cook another 8 minutes or until the rice is almost cooked through.

8. Remove from the heat, cover the rice with kitchen toweling and an inverted pizza pan, and let stand 5 minutes until the rice finishes cooking. (If the rice is very liquidy, place in a medium oven for 5 minutes more.) Serve with lemon wedges and ali-oli sauce.

NOTES TO THE COOK: If planning to make this dish out-of- doors, or in the fireplace, or over a barbecue, start your fire about an hour before serving. (The fire should be quite hot but not smoking. Don't forget that you will need to push the wood or coals around a bit to keep an even heat.) Otherwise plan to prepare this over a stove top using a large flat griddle for even heat, or use the wok method outlined on page 221.

ARROZ A BANDA

Serves 6 to 8 as a main course

*I*n this recipe the rice is cooked and served in an 18-inch-rim-to-rim paella pan without garnish, but with two sauces . . . and what glorious rice!

There's an amusing story about this dish: A gourmet from Valencia, tasting it for the first time, burst into tears. "Why are you crying?" his friends asked. "Because I'm forty years old, I never tasted this dish before . . . and now I'm thinking about all the time I've lost."

Strangely, there is controversy about this dish among gourmets, though *not* about its flavor. Some experts believe it has been around for centuries, while others say it was recently concocted by fancy restaurants as a way to use up their bony fish frames and skins while still charging customers a lot. I say no matter which theory is correct, the diner wins.

Serve all the shellfish with the rice, or afterward as the Spanish do.

1. Peel the shrimp, reserving the shells, toss with coarse sea salt, arrange on skewers, cover, and refrigerate.

2. Heat 1 tablespoon of the oil in a deep saucepan, add the peels, and slowly fry until rosy. Add the fish stock and bring to a boil. Keep simmering if continuing through to the final step. If you are doing this step in advance, simmer the shells for 10 minutes, strain the stock, and leave to cool. Store covered in the refrigerator until ready to use.

3. Make a dense tomato sauce: Heat 2½ tablespoons of the olive oil in a medium skillet and cook the onion until it starts to soften but not change color. Raise the heat, add the green pepper, and continue cooking over moderate heat for 3 minutes or until the pepper begins to soften. Add the tomatoes, sugar, and

salt and cook, stirring often, until the sauce has thickened to a creamy and homogeneous compote, 20 minutes. Add the paprika and saffron and quickly "toast," while stirring madly to avoid burning, then immediately remove from the heat. Divide the compote; reserve half as a condiment and mix the rest with the minced squid, garlic, and salt and pepper in a second dish. Cover both dishes and refrigerate. Up to this point the dish can be made in advance.

4. Make the ali-oli as described on page 345.

5. Optional: If planning to make this dish out of doors over wood, or in a deep fireplace with a large Tuscan-type grill, or over a kettle barbecue (see Note to the Cook), begin the fire about 1 hour before serving. Slowly heat wood or coals until quite hot but not smoking. You may need to push the

2 pounds fresh or defrosted frozen large shrimp, unpeeled

Coarse sea salt

8 tablespoons olive oil

6 to 10 cups Aromatic Fish Stock (page 223), depending on the rice you use (see page 219)

1⅓ cups finely chopped onion

½ cup finely chopped green bell pepper

2 medium red ripe tomatoes, peeled, seeded, and finely chopped

1 teaspoon sugar

½ teaspoon Spanish sweet paprika

½ teaspoon saffron threads, dried and crumbled, preferably La Mancha

¼ pound fresh squid, cleaned and finely minced by pulsing in the workbowl of a food processor to make ½ cup

1 teaspoon chopped garlic

Freshly ground black pepper

2 cups Ali-oli Sauce (page 345)

1 cinnamon stick

2 cups simmering water

3 cups Spanish rice or other medium-grain rice as discussed on page 219

coals around a bit to keep an even heat. Otherwise plan to prepare this over a stove griddle, or use the wok method outlined on page 221.

6. About 1 hour before serving, reheat the stock and keep it just below the simmering point. Have a second pan of simmering water as a backup.

7. To prepare the dish on top of the stove: Preheat the oven to 300 degrees. Place a paella pan measuring 18 inches across the rim on a heated flat griddle or use the wok method. Heat the remaining 2½ tablespoons olive oil with a cinnamon stick. Stir in the squid-tomato compote and cook for 2 to 3 minutes, stirring, until fragrant. Add the stock and bring to a boil. Sprinkle the rice over the stock and use a spatula to gently press grains into the bubbling stock. Correct the seasoning with salt and pepper. Cook over high heat 8 to 10 minutes, moving the pan as needed to keep a general overall steady boil. If liquid boils away too fast during the first 8 to 10 minutes, add spoonfuls of simmering water. Then gradually reduce the heat as the rice cooks another 8 minutes. The rice should be slightly al dente when all moisture has been absorbed. Remove from the heat, cover with kitchen toweling and an inverted pizza pan, and let stand over a flame tamer or an electric flat griddle set at low heat, or hot tiles in a slow oven. Let the rice develop a nice bottom crust, 10 minutes. For this dish the rice should be fairly dry to the touch. *(continued)*

8. Brush shrimp with the remaining oil and grill close to the embers (or fry or broil) until firm. Brush with a little of the ali-oli and broil for 1 to 2 minutes longer, until fully cooked. Serve the rice directly from the pan. Pass the grilled shrimp, the reserved dense tomato sauce, and a bowl of ali-oli.

NOTE TO THE COOK: To prepare the dish out of doors, place a paella pan measuring 18 inches across the rim on the hot coals. Heat the remaining 4 tablespoons olive oil with a cinnamon stick. Stir in the squid and cook for 2 to 3 minutes, stirring, until fragrant. Add the stock and bring to a boil. Sprinkle the rice over the stock and use a spatula to gently press grains into the bubbling stock. Correct the seasoning with salt and pepper. Cook over high heat for about 10 minutes, then push the coals to the sides away from the pan in order to help reduce the heat. Continue to cook another 5 to 10 minutes. Rice should be slightly al dente. Push aside any live coals, cover the rice with a pizza pan and let rest over very low coals for about 10 minutes in order to develop a good bottom crust and finish the cooking. Rice should not be too wet.

This recipe was inspired by two very famous recipes for this dish: Chef Pepe Peiera's world-famous version served at his restaurant El Pegoli in Denia, and the recipe of the paella champion Vincent Esteve Albert.

GOLDEN RICE

Serves 6 to 8

Rice sautéed in hot olive oil until golden, then smothered in a delicious saffron-tinted boiling fish broth, "is simplification carried to its ultimate limits," wrote Catalan author and food authority Joseph Pla. Pla continued, "Each grain has to be tied with the others but still have its own personality."

Actually this superb dish isn't all that simple, at least the way I serve it, since it requires a Catalonian almond-based fish stock, so the aromatic fish stock suitable for the Alicante *arroces* cannot be used. I've also embellished the original concept with a number of richly flavored additions: slices of monkfish, slices of potato, fresh tomato, and a side serving of ali-oli sauce.

If you use the correct rice, one that can absorb all these flavors, such as Bomba or Calasparra, no matter the embellishments, the rice will still be the king of the dish.

Serve as a first course or part of a buffet.

For this dish I suggest you use a 10- to 12-cup capacity cazuela or eathernware flameproof dish.

1 pound monkfish tail, skinned
(reserve skin for stock)

Sea salt

3 dried *ñora* peppers or 2 mild New Mexico
peppers, stems and seeds removed, or 2
tablespoons Spanish *pimentón* (use in step 3)

RICH FISH STOCK

1 tablespoon extra-virgin olive oil

1 cup finely chopped onion

1 ripe tomato, peeled, seeded, and chopped

1 tablespoon chopped garlic

3 sprigs parsley

1 bay leaf

18 lightly toasted blanched almonds

½ teaspoon salt

⅛ teaspoon dried and crumbled saffron threads

3 quarts fish stock or water, or 2 cups frozen
fish fumet and 2½ quarts water

Fish skin, preferably monkfish (optional)

3 medium-size Yukon Gold potatoes, peeled

Freshly ground black pepper

3 tablespoons extra-virgin olive oil

1 green bell pepper, cored, seeded, and finely
chopped (1 cup)

2 cloves garlic, peeled and chopped

1 thick slice red ripe tomato

2⅓ cups (1 pound) Spanish rice or other
medium-grain rice (see page 219)

Ali-oli Sauce (page 345)

1. Rinse the fish, then drain, dry, sprinkle with coarse sea salt, cover, and refrigerate.

2. Tear the chili peppers into small pieces, soak in hot water for 15 minutes, and drain.

3. Make the rich fish stock: In a deep saucepan, heat 1 tablespoon of the olive oil over medium-low heat. Add the onion, a pinch of salt, and a sprinkle of water and cook, stirring occasionally, until onion is melting and golden, about 10 minutes. Add the tomato and cook 10 minutes longer, or until dry. Stir in the garlic, parsley, bay leaf, almonds, and drained chili peppers, and cook until all the excess moisture evaporates and contents are sizzling, 10 minutes.

4. Scrape contents into the workbowl of a food processor, add the ½ teaspoon salt, saffron, and paprika, if using, and purée until smooth. Scrape back into the saucepan, add 3 quarts stock or water, the monkfish skin, if using, and the peeled whole potatoes. Bring to a boil over high heat and cook until the potatoes are tender, then remove and continue cooking the stock 20 minutes more. Cool, strain, measure, and adjust the stock if necessary to make 5 to 10 cups (depending on the rice you are using, see page 219).

5. Make the ali-oli as directed on page 345 with two of the potatoes. Thickly slice the remaining potato, pat dry on paper toweling, season with salt and pepper, cover, and hold. *Up to this point the dish can be made in advance.*

6. About 30 minutes before serving, preheat the oven to 450 degrees. *(continued)*

7. Slowly heat the olive oil in a cazuela set over a flame tamer. Reheat the stock to simmering.

8. Cut the fish into ½- by 1-inch strips and pat dry with paper toweling.

9. Sauté the green peppers and garlic in the oil until aromatic, then push to one side. Add the cold potato slices and fry on each side until just golden, remove, and reserve. Add the tomato slice and fry for an instant, remove, and reserve. Add the monk-fish slices and sauté for 2 minutes on each side. Add the rice and stir until fish, peppers, garlic, and rice are well coated with oily juices and everything is sizzling. Add 4⅔ cups to 7 cups hot stock and cook briskly for 10 minutes, then place the tomato slice in the center on top of the rice and surround with golden potato slices. Bake, uncovered, for 10 minutes. Remove from the oven, cover loosely and let rest 5 minutes before serving. Serve the rice directly from the cazuela. Pass a bowl of ali-oli.

ALICANTE-STYLE RICE WITH PIG'S HAND, SAUSAGE, AND CELERY

Serves 8 as a first course or part of a large buffet

*I*n Valencia," the Alicantinos say, "they use red peppers to decorate their paellas, while here we use them twice, in both our stocks and our *sofritos,* which is why our *arroces* are so delicious."

Pig's hand is much meatier than pig's foot. You can find pig's hand in Asian markets. A pig's foot can be substituted. This dish is ideal for a large buffet table in winter.

Do steps 1, 2, and 3 the day before serving.

1. Soak the chickpeas in water overnight.

2. Scrub the ham hocks and pig's hand and place in a 6-quart pot with plenty of cold water to cover, and slowly bring to a boil, skimming carefully. Add the onion stuck with cloves, salt, 1 cup celery leaves, bay leaf, 6 peppercorns, and dried chilies and cook, covered, until tender, about 1½ hours. Remove the meats when tender, cool, then cut away fat, bones, and gristle. Cut skin and flesh into ¼-inch dice and season with salt and pepper. Strain the cooking juices into a tall container. Pick out and reserve the red chilies. Cover chilies, meats, and cooking juices and refrigerate.

3. Wash and string all the celery stalks and cut them into 1½-inch lengths. Place wet celery in a non-

¾ cup dried chickpeas

2 ham hocks

1 pig's hand or foot, split lengthwise
(1½ pounds)

1 onion, peeled, stuck with 3 cloves

Salt

1 bunch celery, plus 1 cup celery leaves,
plus 3 celery sprigs for garnish

1 bay leaf

6 peppercorns

2 *ñora* peppers or 1 New Mexican chili pepper,
previously seeded

Freshly ground black pepper

2 tablespoons lemon juice

1 teaspoon sugar

5 tablespoons extra-virgin olive oil

Pinch of saffron

3 large cloves garlic, peeled and sliced

½ cup thick tomato sauce, preferably homemade
(page 342)

1½ cups Spanish rice or other medium-grain
rice discussed on page 219

¼ to ½ pound Spanish *morcilla* sausage or
French- or Italian-style black sausage in natural
casing (see "Mail-Order Sources")

Lemon wedges for garnish

metallic saucepan. Add the lemon juice, sugar, pinch of salt, 1 tablespoon of the oil, and 2 tablespoons water and add to the celery. Bring to a boil, set an upside-down plate on top of the celery, and cover with a tight-fitting lid. Cook over low heat 20 to 25 minutes. Uncover the pan, remove the plate, and reduce the pan juices, stirring to glaze the celery on all sides. Cool, cover, and refrigerate.

4. The following day, drain the chickpeas, rinse well, place in a saucepan, preferably earthenware or stainless steel, cover with fresh water, add ¼ teaspoon salt, bring to a boil, and cook at the simmer, covered, about 1 hour, or until tender. Bring the meat to room temperature and wipe away any congealed fat. Skim off the fat from the stock.

5. Reheat 3 cups of the reserved broth with 1½ cups chickpea cooking liquor, add the crushed saffron, and bring to a boil. Keep at a low simmer. If using medium-grain rice use 3 cups of the mixed liquid. If using Calasparra use about 4 cups of the mixed liquid. Correct the seasoning with salt and pepper.

6. In a medium-size cazuela set over a flame tamer, fry the garlic in the remaining 4 tablespoons olive oil until golden. Add the tomato sauce and the reserved cooked chili peppers and fry until thick. Add the drained chickpeas and the drained meats and fry until lightly crisp. Pour in the simmering stock and scatter the rice on top, stirring once. Bring the mixture to a boil and cook over high heat, moving and shaking the pan for even cooking over 10 minutes.

(continued)

7. Meanwhile, with a thin-bladed knife cut the sausage into 12 even slices. Slowly brown them in a small nonstick skillet 3 to 5 minutes, until crisp. Remove to paper toweling to drain.

8. Gradually reduce the heat under the rice. Push the glazed celery around the outer rim of the rice, spread sausage slices in the middle in an attractive design, and continue cooking 8 minutes. Remove from the heat; cover with a sheet of paper toweling and a wide tray or other object, which will help hold in the heat. Let the rice rest 10 minutes. Serve warm, garnished with the sprigs of fresh celery and lemon wedges.

NOTE TO THE COOK: To ensure a light rice, make the stock at least a day in advance, then remove the fat.

Inspired by a recipe created by Chef José Manuel Varo of the Restaurant Delfin in Alicante.

CRUSTY RICE WITH CHICKEN AND PORK SAUSAGES

❀

Serves 6

This unusual *arroz* is baked, then served in wedges like a cake. It's a challenging dish to bring off because it requires a top crust made by adding whipped eggs to the nearly cooked rice, then allowing the eggs to brown. If the rice isn't sufficiently cooked or the oven isn't sufficiently hot, the eggs will tend to fall between the grains, making the dish heavy and dense.

Frederico Angelis Domingo, chef at the restaurant El Elche in Barcelona, told me, "Be sure to use at least two kinds of sausages so that there'll be lots of complex flavor. If you just use chorizo the dish will lack interest and harmony."

You'll need a 2½- or 3-quart cazuela or shallow flameproof serving dish to make this dish, or substitute an iron skillet if presentation isn't an issue.

Serve this *arroz* as a main course along with a sharply flavored salad.

1 pound mixed uncooked sausages such as chorizo and pork or veal sausage

2 ounces unsmoked streaky bacon, pancetta, or blanched lean salt pork

1 pound chicken legs and thighs

1½ tablespoons commercial or homemade meat or chicken glaze (optional)

3 cups assorted vegetables for the stock: chopped carrots, turnips, Swiss chard leaves, green beans trimmings, parsley stems, onion trimmings, and garlic cloves

½ teaspoon peppercorns

Salt

Freshly ground black pepper

5 tablespoons olive oil

1 large onion, finely minced

4 cloves garlic, finely minced

1 cup tomato sauce

1 tablespoon tomato paste

Pinch of sugar

1 cup cooked chickpeas, drained and tossed with olive oil, parsley, and salt and pepper

1 good pinch pulverized saffron threads

½ teaspoon Spanish *pimentón*

4 tablespoons chopped flat-leaf parsley

2 cups Spanish rice or other medium-grain rice as discussed on page 219

6 eggs, lightly beaten

½ teaspoon grated lemon rind

¼ teaspoon freshly grated nutmeg

1. Early in the day, cover the sausages, bacon, and chicken with 3 quarts water. Slowly bring to a boil and skim. Add the meat or poultry glaze, if using, the stock vegetables, and peppercorns. Skim off any scum that surfaces, then partially cover and cook, removing poultry and meats to a work surface as they become tender. Continue to cook the stock for another hour, then strain and reduce or dilute to 2½ quarts. Discard the vegetables.

2. When the meat and poultry are cool enough to handle, cut away all fat, skin, and other debris and dice the flesh. Season with salt and pepper, then fry in 2 tablespoons of the olive oil until crispy on all sides, moistening with spoonfuls of stock until the cubes of flesh are moist, burnished, and syrupy. Cover and refrigerate. Return to room temperature to use in step 7.

3. Prepare the *sofrito* in the cazuela set over a flame tamer. Heat the remaining 3 tablespoons olive oil, add the minced onion, and cook slowly until it is soft and golden brown. Add the garlic, tomato sauce, tomato paste, and sugar and cook, stirring, until thick and creamy. In a small pan reduce 2 cups of stock to 3 tablespoons syrupy glaze, mix with the seasoned chickpeas, and hold for step **6.** *Up to this point the dish can be prepared 5 to 6 hours in advance.*

4. About 45 minutes before serving, place oven racks in the upper and middle positions. Preheat the oven to 425 degrees.

5. Measure the amount of stock needed for the rice that you are using (see page 219) and bring to a boil. Reheat the *sofrito* in the cazuela, add the saffron, *pimentón,* 1 tablespoon of the parsley, and the rice, stirring rapidly. When the rice turns slightly translucent, add the boiling stock. Set on the middle rack and bake until the rice has absorbed most of the liquid, 12 minutes.

6. Raise the oven heat to the highest setting. Spread the prepared chickpeas in an even layer over the rice and return to the upper shelf to glaze, 5 minutes.

7. Meanwhile, in a bowl mix the glazed meat, pinch of salt, eggs, grated lemon rind, ground pepper, and grated nutmeg. Whisk until frothy. Remove the cazuela from the oven, immediately spread the meat and egg mixture over the chickpeas tilting for an even layer. Return to the upper shelf and cook 5 minutes. (This final cooking can be done under a broiler for a crustier topping.) Let cool 5 minutes before serving.

FISH

BRAN-CRUSTED BARBECUED WHOLE FISH WITH CHARD STEM TAHINI SAUCE (*Egypt*)

Serves 2 to 4

Nora George, author of *Nora's Recipes from Egypt,* shared this recipe with me when I asked her if Egyptian cooks do anything special with wheat and fish.

"We certainly do," she told me. "I spent all my childhood summers in the seaside resort of Damietta in the North of Egypt. We used to take the local mullet, wrap it in wheat bran, and grill it. The wheat bran kept it incredibly moist and delicious."

Though I knew well the Mediterranean method of baking fish in sea salt to keep it moist and bring out flavor in the flesh, I just couldn't imagine how wheat bran would stay in place during grilling.

Nora explained that the bran attaches itself to the fish's scales while the fish is grilled over coals until black on both sides. Once grilled, the fish is dipped in salted cold water, which causes the bran to wrinkle and soften. The fish is then placed on its side and peeled. The skin, scales, and bran come off easily together. Fish cooked this way are served with a tahini-based sauce made with parsley, cauliflower, or Swiss chard stems.

"Nowadays there are barbecue stands all over Cairo that prepare fish this way. After cooking, they wrap the fish up in paper so you can take it home."

2 (1½-pound) whole white-fleshed fish, preferably gray mullet, striped mullet, or striped bass

1 clove garlic, peeled and crushed with ½ teaspoon sea salt

½ teaspoon ground cumin

¼ teaspoon freshly ground pepper

1 cup fine, almost powdered, wheat bran (available at health food stores)

2 tablespoons salt

Juice of 1 lemon

Lemon wedges as garnish

Chard Stem Tahini Sauce (recipe below)

1. Heat coals in a barbecue.

2. Rinse, drain, and gut each fish through the gills, but do not remove the scales. Season the belly with the crushed garlic, cumin, and pepper. Pat the fish dry, then roll it in the fine wheat bran to coat completely and press down with your palms to help the bran adhere. Brush the grill with oil and barbecue the fish 12 minutes to a side. The bran will become coal black on all sides, but the flesh of the fish will be moist, white, and tender within.

3. While the fish are cooking, dissolve the salt in 3 quarts cold water in a wide and shallow basin. When the fish are cooked, immediately transfer them to the water bath and let stand 1 minute. Turn both fish and let stand 1 minute more. Tip the basin to pour off some of the water; peel away the softened and wrinkled black skins, which should come off in large

pieces. If desired, leave the head and tail of each as decoration. When each fish has soaked for 1 minute on the second side, transfer to a work surface or serving dish, blackened-skin side up, and peel away remaining skin. Sprinkle the flesh with the lemon juice and serve whole surrounded with lemon wedges. Pass the tahini sauce at the table.

NOTES TO THE COOK: If using scaled fish, wash, dry, and brush with olive oil before coating with bran.

In Egypt the fish is grilled with the intestines and is therefore not spiced; seasoning is simply from the soaking in salty water.

CHARD STEM TAHINI SAUCE

Makes about ⅔ cup

8 thick Swiss chard stalks

1 clove garlic, peeled and crushed with ¼ teaspoon salt

3 tablespoons tahini paste, stirred

2½ tablespoons lemon juice

2½ tablespoons cold water

Reserve the chard leaves for some other purpose. Wash and peel the stalks and cut into fine dice. Steam until just tender, 5 minutes. Drain and set aside. Place crushed garlic, tahini paste, lemon juice, and water in the work bowl of a food processor and process until the mixture becomes a smooth creamy sauce. Scrape into a bowl and fold in the cooked chard stalks. Let mellow at least 1 hour in the refrigerator before serving.

GRILLED FISH STUFFED WITH SEAFOOD, MOROCCAN *CHARMOULA*, AND SPICES

❧

Serves 4

On a recent trip to Tangier I found an eating place unlike any other. Called simply Mohammed Belhaj (the name of its owner-chef) it bills itself as Morocco's "first health food restaurant."

The food here is excellent and also interesting . . . as is its impassioned owner. Mohammed is quite a character, smiling and flapping his arms while talking a blue streak about the healthful properties of his food. As one regular customer confided, "If you don't enjoy his theater, he really doesn't want you in the place."

I was especially impressed by two of his fish dishes. The first was a delicious tour de force, which Mohammed calls *Tagine de Poisson de Rif*, consisting of five types of seafood and fish marinated with spices and sautéed with chopped herbs and vegetables, to which two eggs are finally added to cook off the fire in the residual heat.

The second, offered below, is an equally delicious dish of spiced grilled fish stuffed with shrimps and cubes of swordfish. Though an original creation of an accomplished chef, it's fairly easy to make and brims with traditional Moroccan flavorings, including the Moroccan marinade called *charmoula*—a generous mixture of cilantro and parsley, cumin and paprika, oil and vinegar or lemon juice, plus celery, ginger, garlic, and turmeric.

I recommend that you serve this splendid dish with a simple rice pilaf.

2 whole, meaty white-fleshed fish (2½ to 3 pounds each), cleaned and scaled, such as striped bass, blackfish, snapper, sea bass, or rockfish

1 tablespoon plus ½ teaspoon coarse sea salt

1 tablespoon extra-virgin olive oil

2 teaspoons fresh lemon juice

¼ teaspoon ground white pepper

STUFFING

2 tablespoons olive oil

1 tablespoon lemon juice

¼ teaspoon hot red pepper

½ teaspoon sweet paprika

¼ teaspoon ground cumin

⅓ cup finely chopped fresh flat-leaf parsley

2 tablespoons finely diced celery

⅓ cup finely chopped fresh cilantro

4 ounces raw swordfish, cut into ¾-inch cubes

4 ounces raw fresh shrimp (about 12), shelled, deveined, and cut in half

TOPPING

¼ teaspoon salt

¼ teaspoon ground white pepper

¾ teaspoon ground cumin

¼ teaspoon ground ginger

Pinch of ground turmeric

2 to 3 tablespoons fresh lemon juice

1. Rinse the fish, then rub each fish inside and out with 1 tablespoon salt. Let stand 20 minutes. Rinse again and pat dry with paper towels.

2. Preheat grill or broiler.

3. Mix the olive oil, lemon juice, ½ teaspoon salt, and white pepper in a small bowl. Brush the fish inside and out with this mixture. Score the fish cross-wise, being careful not to cut through to the bone.

4. Combine the ingredients for the stuffing in a medium bowl and mix well. Divide and stuff the cavity of each fish with the stuffing and brush the outside with any remaining liquid mixed with an additional tablespoon olive oil. Place in an oiled double-hinged fish rack to keep the stuffing inside when turning. (If you lack such a rack, wind string around the body of the fish to hold stuffing in place.) Grill or broil until skin is crisp and flesh is firm, about 8 minutes each side.

5. To prepare the topping, combine the salt, white pepper, cumin, ginger, and turmeric in a small bowl. Sprinkle the cooked fish with the spices and drizzle the lemon juice on top. Serve with a cruet of olive oil.

MIDDLE EASTERN FISH PLATTER
WITH SPICES, CARAMELIZED ONIONS,
AND RICE WITH ONION-TAHINI SAUCE (*Lebanon*)

❋

Serves 4 to 6

This presentation of white-fleshed fish is popular in the Middle East from Syria to Egypt. There are small differences from country to country; the only place I ever found a major difference was in Aleppo. (See my *Cooking of the Eastern Mediterranean* for that city's version of this dish, prepared with bulgur instead of rice and topped with a spicy tomato salsa.)

In most parts of the Middle East the fish is showered with browned pine nuts, and then presented on a bed of rice that has been cooked with caramelized onions and spices. This is one of the great fish dishes of the Middle East.

½ cup olive oil

½ cup pine nuts

3 large onions, peeled and coarsely grated in the food processor (3 cups)

ONION-TAHINI SAUCE

4 onions

½ cup tahini paste

½ cup lemon juice

1 teaspoon salt

Do steps 1 and 2 at least 4 hours before serving.

1. Preheat the oven to 350 degrees.

2. In a 10-inch straight-sided skillet, heat the oil and quickly fry the nuts until pale golden. Use a slotted spoon to remove and reserve for garnish. Add the grated onions to the skillet, and fry, turning them over from time to time, until they turn soft and pale golden, 10 minutes. Scrape all but 2 tablespoons into a jelly roll pan, spread out, and set in the oven to cook down to a dark reddish brown, 2 to 3 hours. Leave the 2 tablespoons onions in the skillet to use in step 6.

2 pounds thick white-fleshed fish fillet such as bass or snapper, with the skin on

Sea salt

Freshly ground black pepper

Juice of ½ lemon

1¼ cups long-grain rice

¼ teaspoon ground cinnamon

1 tablespoon ground cumin

¼ teaspoon ground turmeric or crushed saffron

2½ cups boiling water

Ground cinnamon for garnish

3. To make the sauce, cut the onions into small pieces and boil for 15 minutes in salted water. In a food processor combine the tahini, lemon juice, salt, and 1 cup cold water and process until smooth. Drain the onions and add to the tahini, pulsing once to combine. The sauce should remain chunky. Adjust the seasoning. Allow to mellow at room temperature.

4. Meanwhile, clean and wash the fish; season with salt, pepper, and the juice of ½ lemon; and refrigerate for 1 hour.

5. Wash the rice in three changes of water, rubbing the rice with your hands to remove excess starch. Drain well.

6. About 35 minutes before serving, push the reserved 2 tablespoons onion to one side in the skillet, place the fish, skin side down, on the other side and cook over high heat for 1 to 2 minutes to crisp the skin. Reduce the heat to medium, sprinkle the rice around the fish, and cook, stirring occasionally, 3 minutes. Add the spices, salt, pepper, and the boiling water. Bring to a boil and stir once. Simmer, covered, until the liquid has been absorbed, about 18 minutes. Carefully lift out the cooked fish, cover, and keep warm. Place a folded paper towel over the rice, cover the skillet, and let rest, with the heat turned off, 10 minutes. Cut the fish into bite-size pieces and season lightly with salt, pepper, and cumin.

7. Spread the hot rice on a long platter, arrange the fish on top, and sprinkle with the oven-browned onions and pine nuts. Dot with ground cinnamon and serve with the onion-tahini sauce.

Adapted from Lamya Al-Jabri's recipe for sayadiah samak in her Delicious, Good-Tasting.

FISH FILLETS ATHENS–STYLE WITH WILD CELERY AND AVGOLEMONO (*Greece*)

Serves 3 or 4

This is a lovely Athenian soup/main course dish that will serve 3 or 4. Any thick, white-fleshed fish fillet will work. The fish is cooked by half poaching and half steaming in aromatic broth, then finished with a light, airy lemon-egg sauce.

The essential flavoring here is wild celery, which is nothing more than Mediterranean "soup" celery, a thin-stalked dark leafy green that still grows wild throughout the region. It's known here as "cutting celery." Since its aroma is twice as pungent as the cultivated variety, you won't mistake it. Look for it in Asian markets in the autumn, where it is called *kun choi* or *kin tsai*. Whenever I find it I buy more than I need, then blanch and freeze the remainder for future use. And while you're at the Asian market you might want to buy your fish there too—it is usually extremely fresh.

If you grow your own wild celery, you can cut the leaves and more will grow back. Shepherd's carries the seeds (see "Mail-Order Sources").

2 bunches cutting or "wild" celery (about 1 pound)

3 or 4 white-fleshed fish fillets (1 pound)

Sea salt

¼ cup extra-virgin olive oil

1 small onion, peeled and cut into thick slices

1 carrot, pared and cut into thick slices on the diagonal

1 bay leaf

1 large egg

3 tablespoons fresh lemon juice

Freshly and finely ground black pepper

If you can't find wild celery, substitute 2 quarts of the leafy greens and tender stalks of the cultivated variety as well as some tops of celery root and a small pinch of crushed celery seed. The dish will be good, but not as aromatic as the original.

1. Wash the celery leaves and tender stalks. Blanch 1 minute in boiling water, then drain. When cool enough to handle, squeeze out excess water and cut into 2-inch lengths.

2. Rub the fish fillets with sea salt and let stand until step 4.

3. Heat the olive oil in a wide pan and cook the onion, carrot, and bay leaf over medium heat 2 minutes. Add ½ teaspoon salt and 4 cups water, bring to

a boil, cover, and simmer for 10 minutes. Remove the bay leaf, add the celery, and cook 10 more minutes.

4. Reduce the heat, slip in the fish fillets, and cook, covered, until the fish is just done, about 7 minutes. Using a slotted spoon, transfer the fish onto a shallow serving dish.

5. In a medium mixing bowl, beat the egg until thickened, then beat in the lemon juice. Gradually add 1 cup hot (not boiling) broth to the egg mixture, beating well after each addition. Remove the soup from the heat. Slowly pour the egg mixture into the remaining soup while stirring with a spoon.

Gently reheat in order to cook the egg, stirring constantly for about 10 seconds. Do not boil or the soup will curdle. Season the soup with salt and pepper. Pour over the fish and serve.

NOTE TO THE COOK: The lightest, foamiest, and whitest avgolemono is always made with whole eggs. Some cooks use a little flour to stabilize the soup, but if you beat the eggs sufficiently (you can do the first two parts of step 5 in a food processor if you like) and add the hot soup carefully, you shouldn't have any trouble or produce unsightly egg white strings.

MOROCCAN *BISTEEYA* WITH SEAFOOD, SPINACH, AND NOODLES

❋

Serves 6

*I*n the late 1970s, some years after I published my first cookbook, *Couscous and Other Good Food from Morocco*, I started hearing rumors of a fabulous new dish, a seafood *bisteeya*, that was appearing on private Moroccan tables in place of the traditional very rich pigeon pie *bisteeya*, in my opinion the *pièce de resistance* of Moroccan cookery.

I long wanted to obtain a recipe, but was never served a version I liked. Then I heard that the world-famous Mamounia Hotel in Marrakech had a great recipe in which spicy noodles replaced the buttery almond that holds traditional *bisteeya* together. I was eager to learn the recipe.

I tracked Mohammed Boussaoud, former executive chef at the Mamounia, to the luxurious Jerusalem restaurant Darna ("Your House"), where as chef he prepares a kosher version of the dish he once cooked so famously in Marrakech.

(continued)

Tomato-Flavored *Charmoula*

3 tomatoes, peeled, seeded, chopped,
and lightly fried in oil until reduced to ½ cup

1 tablespoon crushed garlic

¾ cup torn leaves of fresh cilantro

¾ cup torn leaves of fresh flat-leaf parsley

1½ teaspoons sweet paprika

Pinch of freshly ground black pepper

½ teaspoon mildly hot red pepper

1 teaspoon ground cumin

1 teaspoon salt

3 tablespoons fresh lemon juice

½ cup olive oil

5 ounces dried fidelini noodles, broken into
1-inch lengths

1 pound mixed firm fish such as cod, halibut,
monkfish, swordfish

1 preserved lemon (page 347; optional)

½ pound commercial phyllo

Olive oil for brushing the phyllo

½ pound shelled large shrimp

1 pound spinach, washed, stemmed, cooked,
drained, squeezed to make 1 cup, divided into
3 equal parts, and shredded

¼ cup club soda

An Arab Moslem Moroccan chef working at an Israeli restaurant! Well, why not? In fact, I was delighted, for it gave me a chance to meet with him on a recent trip to Israel and learn how to make his original nonkosher version.

Mohammed explained that the seafood and fish (shrimp, monkfish, and other thick-fleshed fish) are sandwiched between two layers of noodles and spinach leaves, which enables them to cook at very low heat to a point of perfect moistness.

1. In a blender or work bowl of a food processor, combine the ingredients for the *charmoula* and blend until smooth. Makes about 1¼ cups.

2. Boil the fidelini for 2 minutes; drain and immediately put to soak in ¾ cup of the prepared tomato-flavored *charmoula*. Leave to cool.

3. Thinly slice the fish; mix with remaining ½ cup *charmoula*. Rinse the preserved lemon, if using, discarding the pulp, and quarter. Mix with the slices of fish and the *charmoula*. Cover and refrigerate until ready to use. Can be prepared 2 to 3 hours in advance.

4. About 1 hour before serving, preheat the oven to 350 degrees.

5. Unroll the phyllo pastry leaves, keeping them under a damp towel to prevent them from drying out. Brush a 10- or 12-inch pizza pan with oil, then cover the bottom with two-thirds of the phyllo, one on top of the other so they overlap the edges, quickly brushing oil between each layer. Spread out half the prepared noodles in one even layer over the pastry, then cover with a layer of fish, lemon peel, if using, shrimp, and spinach. Top with the remaining noodles. Fold the overlapping leaves up and cover with the remaining leaves, quickly brushing oil between each layer and fold under the pie (like tucking in sheets). Score the top, brush with oil, sprinkle the top with soda water, and set in the oven to bake until golden brown and crisp, about 30 minutes. Serve hot.

SQUID LIGURIAN–STYLE SMOTHERED IN AROMATIC GREENS (*Italy*)

❈

Serves 6

Sauces composed of leafy greens pop up all around the Mediterranean. Each country seems to have its own way of using them to create deep, earthy sauces to smother fish, meat, poultry, and vegetables. In Provence, slow cooking turns greens into an unctuous sauce to enrobe artichokes. Tunisian and Egyptian cooks reduce greens to a paste, then rehydrate it to make a velvety sauce, as in the Jewish wedding dish on page 275. In Morocco, greens are cooked until thick and savory to enrobe chickpeas, while in northern Greece they're melted down to a thick cream to embellish lamb chops. Spanish cooks enrich their sauce greens with ground toasted almonds, while cooks in southeastern Turkey thicken theirs with just a few grains of rice or bulgur to serve as a platform for braised meat.

One of the most stunning of all leafy greens preparations is Tuscan *in inzimino*, which is made at Ristorante Cibreo in Florence for a delicious homestyle dish of braised cuttlefish, specks of hot pepper, fragrant wine, and rich earthy greens.

Since the Cibreo recipe is so well known, I present here a Ligurian variation, which employs cucumber-flavored borage, some sorrel, and other greens as well as the standard chard and spinach. Slow cooking changes each green's qualities: the spinach gives off a tinge of metal and the chard a deep earthiness; the borage or its pretender, grated cucumber, adds a touch of fresh, clear vibrancy. To this I add cress leaves for pepperiness, a little sorrel for acidity, and a few yellow raisins for sweetness.

This wonderful squid dish is even better made a day in advance of serving. Just gently reheat until warm.

(continued)

1½ pounds small squid, cleaned

3 tablespoons vinegar

3 tablespoons extra-virgin olive oil

1 cup mixed vegetables: onion, celery, and carrot, finely diced

⅓ cup chopped flat-leaf parsley

⅓ cup dry white wine

1 clove garlic, peeled and lightly crushed

¾ cup tomato purée

Salt

Freshly ground black pepper

¾ pound Swiss chard

⅔ pound baby spinach leaves

A handful of mixed aromatic greens: mint, borage, salad burnet, cress, sorrel

¼ cup golden raisins

2 pinches of red pepper flakes without seeds

1. Wash the squid and soak in a bowl of water with some vinegar for 15 minutes. Rinse, drain, and cut into bite-size pieces.

2. Heat the olive oil in a deep 5- or 6-quart saucepan, and cook the onion, celery, and carrot with 3 tablespoons water and the parsley over medium heat until soft and golden, about 10 minutes.

3. Add the squid and cook until the water produced evaporates; continue cooking until the pieces begin to turn golden, about 10 minutes. Add the white wine, garlic, and tomato purée and season with salt and pepper. Cover and simmer for 15 minutes, or until the contents of the pan are well reduced.

4. Meanwhile, wash, stem, and roughly cut up the greens; you should have 1 packed gallon. Sprinkle with salt and set in a noncorrodible colander for 30 minutes to release moisture. Wash off the salt and squeeze out the moisture. Add the greens, raisins, and pepper flakes to the pan, adding a little water if the sauce is too thick. Slowly bring to a boil, cover, and simmer for 45 minutes, or until the squid is tender and the sauce is moderately thick. Increase the heat and boil to reduce the sauce. Correct the seasoning and remove from the stove. Let cool and allow the flavors to mellow.

5. Reheat to warm and serve with crusty bread and a glass of Chianti.

Deep-Dish Leafy Greens and Clams with Potatoes À la Importancia (Spain)

Serves 4

À *la importancia* means "to presume to be more important than you are." Potatoes are given that kind of importance here by special treatment. They're boiled, sliced, rolled in seasoned coarse bread crumbs, then pan-fried with clams. As the potatoes brown, a wonderful crisp crust develops, due to caramelization with juices released by the clams. The dish is then served around a heap of peppered greens.

Accompany this very briny flavorful dish with a simple tomato and cucumber salad.

1½ pounds fresh flat-leaf spinach or mixed braising greens, washed, stemmed, and drained

Coarse sea salt

1½ pounds (24 pieces) small littleneck clams

2½ to 3 pounds Yukon Gold potatoes or other firm-flesh potatoes

1 cup coarsely ground dry bread crumbs

Freshly ground black pepper

5 tablespoons extra-virgin olive oil

½ tablespoon minced garlic

3 anchovy fillets, soaked in milk, rinsed, and drained

Pinch of crushed chili flakes without seeds

3 tablespoons meat, poultry, or vegetable stock

Tiny pinch of grated nutmeg

2 tablespoons chopped flat-leaf parsley

2 tablespoons pine nuts

1. At least 2½ hours before serving, cut the greens into 1-inch-thick ribbons and toss with the sea salt. Let stand in a colander to wilt.

2. Rinse the clams under cool running water and scrub away any traces of sand. Soak in lightly salted water for 1 hour and drain well.

3. Wash and scrub the potatoes and boil until barely tender, 6 to 10 minutes, depending upon size. Drain the potatoes, reserving 2 cups of the potato water, and set aside.

4. Season the bread crumbs with salt and freshly ground pepper and place in a deep bowl. When potatoes are cool enough to handle, peel them and slice into ¼-inch disks. As you slice, dip each potato into the bread crumbs and place on a paper-towel-lined tray, slightly overlapping, to dry.

5. Rinse the wilted spinach to remove the salt; squeeze the leaves dry. Heat a tablespoon of the olive oil in a small skillet and sauté the garlic until golden, about 1 minute. Add the anchovies and crush to a purée. Stir in the red chili flakes, greens, and stock. Cook, covered, over medium heat until tender. Season with grated nutmeg, black pepper, and salt to taste. Keep warm in a double boiler or over low heat, partially covered, until ready to serve.

6. You will need two large nonstick skillets for this step. Divide the drained clams and the remaining 4 tablespoons olive oil between the two skillets and heat. Cook clams 1 minute, add the potatoes and parsley in one layer, surrounding the clams, loosely cover the skillets, and cook 3 to 4 minutes, adjusting the heat so as not to burn the potatoes. Remove clams to a side dish as they open. When potatoes develop a golden brown crust flip them over, add

the pine nuts, and continue to cook, loosely covered, until potatoes brown on the second side and pine nuts begin to turn golden brown. If the potatoes absorb the pan juices too quickly and start to burn, sprinkle with a few teaspoons of the reserved potato water.

7. Place the greens in the center of a warm serving platter and surround with potatoes, clams, and pine nuts. Add a little potato water to each skillet and quickly deglaze, then pour juices over the greens. Serve at once.

With thanks to chef Joe Simone for sharing this wonderful recipe from Spain.

CHICKEN AND SQUAB

Sweet Garden Greens and Toasted Bread Cubes with Roast Chicken

Serves 2 to 4

Is there anything left to say about roasting chicken? Possibly not, but there is still something important to remember: allow a resting period so the juices and flesh relax before being cut. Actually all roasted meat, game birds, and poultry benefit from a good rest.

Judy Rodgers, chef and co-owner of the celebrated Zuni Restaurant in San Francisco, agreed to trade recipes with me. She'd serve my Purée of Salt Cod, Potatoes, and Walnut Oil from my book *The Cooking of South-West France* as a special in return for allowing me to include her marvelous Italian-inspired Greens and Bread Salad with Roast Chicken in this book. Naturally we each made subtle personal changes in the other's recipe. Here's my version of Judy's great dish.

3 to 3½ pounds chicken—kosher or other top-quality chicken

1 sprig rosemary or oregano, chopped

2 teaspoons crushed garlic

Salt

Freshly ground black pepper

4 cups stale, country-style, dense white bread with crusts removed, cut into 1-inch cubes

4½ tablespoons verjuice or cider vinegar

1 tablespoon currants

6 cups (8 ounces) baby greens (in winter use mâche, in summer any mild baby greens)

1 tablespoon olive oil

½ bunch scallions, finely sliced

1 teaspoon chopped garlic

Steps 1 through 4 can be done early in the day.

1. Wash and dry the chicken. Combine the rosemary, 1 teaspoon of the garlic, and salt and pepper. Rub the chicken with the mixture inside and out and under the breast skin as far down as your fingers can reach. Wrap in paper toweling and a sheet of plastic wrap; refrigerate until 2 hours before serving.

2. Heat the broiler and lightly toast the bread cubes on all sides. Place in a large 18 by 9-inch ovenproof serving dish; cover lightly with paper toweling and set aside.

3. In a bowl combine ½ tablespoon verjuice with 1 tablespoon water, add the currants, and let soak.

4. Wash and dry the greens, wrap in paper toweling, and refrigerate.

5. About 2 hours before serving, remove the chicken from the refrigerator, unwrap, and bring to room temperature.

6. About 1¼ hours before serving, preheat the oven to 450 degrees.

7. One hour before serving, place the chicken, breast side up and untrussed, on a rack in a roasting pan. Roast the chicken in the middle of the oven for 30 minutes, then turn over and continue roasting 20 minutes longer. Chicken should cook a total of 50 minutes. Remove the chicken from the oven and let stand, covered, 10 to 15 minutes. Do not turn off the oven.

8. While the chicken is resting, toss reserved bread cubes with a mixture of the remaining 3½ tablespoons verjuice, the olive oil, ½ teaspoon salt, and a dash of pepper. Place the bread cubes in the hot oven for 5 minutes. Pour off all but 1 to 2 tablespoons fat from the roasting pan. Set the pan over medium heat, add the scallions and garlic, and cook, stirring and lifting the brownish bits stuck to the bottom. Stir in the currants and soaking liquid and bring to a boil. Remove from the heat.

9. By this time the bread should be ready to remove from the oven. Turn off oven heat and pour the contents of the roasting pan over the bread, then stir in *most* of the greens and toss well. Return the bread and greens to the oven to bake in the receding heat for 5 minutes.

10. Carve the chicken into 8 pieces. Remove the bread and greens from the oven, fold in the remaining greens, top with the chicken, and serve at once.

CHICKEN CAMARGUE–STYLE WITH RICE AND BLACK AND GREEN OLIVES (*France*)

✿

Serves 4

*I*t was probably in the fifteenth century that men first planted rice in the marshy wilderness south of Arles, the area known today as the Camargue. Because of the high salt content of the water this early attempt at growing rice was not a success. It wasn't until after World War II that there was a revival of interest in rice growing in the region. New paddies were created, irrigation programs were instituted, and now Camargue rice is big business. Unlike their Italian and Spanish neighbors, who produce short-grain rice for their risottos and *arroces*, the French planted long-grain Carolina rice, which they prefer.

A dozen or so years ago, they started planting a rice hybrid developed from an indigenous red wild grass, producing a delicious, nutty, very light rice called "red rice," much prized by French and British chefs.

This rice, chicken, and olive dish reflects the recent impact of North African gastronomy upon southern French cooking. It is made in a completely different way from the vast array of North African chicken and olive dishes, but matches such dishes in intensity of flavor. Chicken skin is always a problem when cooking with rice and vegetables. To maintain an attractive skin, I wash and dry the chicken early in the day, then leave the legs and thighs, skin side up, on paper toweling to thoroughly dry out. This seems to encourage the skin to crisp when browning and to keep a good appearance even after being cooked in a closed pan.

2 pounds chicken, legs and thighs (4 of each)

Salt

Freshly ground black pepper

2 tablespoons olive oil

1½ cups chopped onions

1 tablespoon chopped garlic

1 large green bell pepper, cored, seeded, and finely diced (1½ cups)

2 ripe tomatoes, seeded and pressed through a sieve or puréed (1 cup)

½ cup blanched slivered almonds

½ cup black raisins

1 teaspoon ground ginger

1 teaspoon ground coriander

Pinch of red pepper flakes without seeds

1 cup medium- or long-grain rice

½ cup French black olives, preferably Nyons, rinsed and pitted

½ cup green olives, rinsed and pitted

2 tablespoons chopped flat-leaf parsley

1. Season the chicken with salt and pepper.

2. Heat the oil in a 10- or 12-inch straight-sided, heavy-bottomed skillet and in it place the chicken, skin side down. Brown over high heat for 7 minutes. Lower the heat, turn the chicken, and continue browning for another 3 minutes. Remove from the skillet.

3. Pour off all but 2 tablespoons fat from the skillet and add the onion. Cook, stirring, 3 to 4 minutes. Stir in the garlic, bell pepper, tomatoes, almonds, raisins, and spices. Cook over medium-low heat, stirring often, for 10 minutes. Return the chicken to the skillet, skin side up, cover, and cook for 10 minutes more. Carefully remove the chicken to a side dish.

4. Stir up the caramelized vegetables and their juices in the skillet. Add 1½ cups water and bring to a boil. Sprinkle the rice in an even layer over the vegetables, then top with the chicken, skin side up. Cover tightly and continue cooking until the rice and chicken are tender, 18 minutes. Five minutes before serving, stir in the olives and correct the seasoning. Sprinkle with the parsley just before serving.

Rice and Chicken with Glazed Carrots, Chestnuts, and Pistachios (*Turkey*)

❀

Serves 6 as a main course

*I*n this recipe an assortment of garnishes—glazed carrots, chestnuts, and pistachios—take a basic molded chicken and rice pilaf to new visual and gastronomic heights. Whenever I make this dish, I borrow a symmetrical design inspired by one of my husband's kaleidoscopes. When I find a design I like, I simply steady the kaleidoscope, then copy the pattern visible in the tube, using pistachios, currants, walnuts, pine nuts, almonds, and chestnuts. The result is always visually beautiful.

Serve this delicious rice pilaf with a refreshing vegetable salad made with cucumber, tomato, parsley, spearmint, and green chili, all chopped very fine and mixed with lemon juice, olive oil, and just enough cold water to make it slightly soupy.

1. Cover the rice with hot water and stir in 1 tablespoon coarse salt. Let stand at least 30 minutes (some cooks soak the rice as long as 2 to 3 hours.) Rinse under running water until water runs clear; drain.

2. Meanwhile, cut the chicken and/or lamb into pieces the "size of a bird's head," about 1¼-inch cubes. Toss with salt, pepper, and cinnamon.

3. Make a broth with 2 quarts water and the aromatics. Add the seasoned chicken and cook until tender, skimming often. Strain the broth and reserve 4½ cups for the rice.

4. In a nonstick straight-sided skillet, heat a teaspoon each of oil and butter over medium-low heat. Add the pistachios, stir to coat, and cook until just shiny; remove to drain on paper toweling. Add the

almonds and cook until golden. Repeat with the pine nuts and the walnuts. Keep all the nuts in separate piles on paper toweling.

5. Add 3 tablespoons of a combination of butter and oil to the skillet, add the carrots and fry gently until the oil turns a beautiful orange color. Add the rice and stir constantly for 1 minute.

6. Heat the reserved broth in a saucepan. Pour over the rice and carrots, bring to a boil, cover, and cook over medium heat 10 minutes. Lay a sheet of paper toweling under the lid and continue cooking another 5 to 10 minutes or until the rice is tender and fluffy. Correct the seasoning of the rice. Scrape all the rice into a bowl. Do not rinse the skillet.

7. Garnish the bottom of the skillet with a design of nuts, carrots, currants, and chestnuts. Press an even

3 cups medium-grain rice such as *baldo*, Cal-Riso, or pearl

Coarse salt *

1½ pounds boneless chicken thighs or leg of lamb or a mixture of chicken and lamb

Freshly ground black pepper

Finely ground cinnamon

Aromatics for making a broth: onion, carrot, celery, bay leaf, parsley stems, and 2 cloves

Olive oil

Butter

½ cup shelled, blanched, and peeled pistachios, preferably green (see Notes)

½ cup shelled, blanched, and peeled whole almonds, coarsely chopped

¼ cup pine nuts

½ cup shelled walnuts, coarsely chopped

2 cups thin-sliced rounds of fresh carrots

½ cup currants, soaked in warm water for 10 minutes and drained

1½ cups shelled and crumbled chestnuts, or 1 (12-ounce) jar steamed chestnuts (see Notes)

NOTES TO THE COOK: Turkish pistachios are vivid green, and need only be glazed in hot butter and oil for a second. If your pistachios are beige, you may want to "color" them with parsley water. To do this: Pound parsley in a wooden mortar until pasty, wrap in cheesecloth, and squeeze out the liquid onto a small plate. Soak dried peeled pistachios for a half hour, then pat dry. Do not fry the "colored" pistachios; simply roll them in a bit of oil to make them shiny.

Steamed chestnuts: Recently, plump, peeled, and cooked chestnuts, packaged under the Compagnie du Mont Lozère label, have become available at upscale markets. These have an incomparable flavor and sweetness; I highly recommend them. It's also quite easy to prepare a small amount of chestnuts at home for this dish. To prepare chestnuts: Make a slit on the flat side of each with a sharp knife. Boil the chestnuts until tender, about 3 minutes. Remove them to a covered dish to keep them hot and steamy. One by one cut away the shell and skin together. If the inner skins are difficult to remove, return the chestnuts to hot water for a instant to help loosen their skins. If the inner skins still resist, spread the chestnuts out on a baking sheet and place them in a slow oven to dry. Once bone dry, they can be rubbed with a coarse cloth.

layer of lamb and or chicken on top and spoon the rice over it. Press gently to make everything compact. Set the skillet over a wider and deeper pan of boiling water, cover, and steam for 15 minutes. Remove from the heat and allow the contents to settle without lifting the lid for 5 minutes. Then carefully invert onto a wide serving plate. You should have a beautiful mosaic topping for your rice.

A chestnut knife, with a short, slightly hooked pointed blade set into a 4-inch wooden handle, is the ideal instrument for slashing and peeling chestnuts. See "Mail-Order Sources."

Adapted from a recipe created by Mrs. Gülsen Çağdas of Gaziantep.

EGYPTIAN-STYLE SQUAB BAKED
WITH GREEN WHEAT, GARLIC, AND LEMON

❧

Serves 2

*I*n this recipe squabs are served on a bed of green wheat flavored with cinnamon, cloves, and mint (see page 120 for information on green wheat). If green wheat is unavailable, you can substitute coarse bulgur.

Since cleaning green wheat is truly a "labor of love," you should probably love the person you're cooking for when you make this dish. My suggestion: make it for your loved one on Valentine's Day, then see if he or she appreciates your good work!

1. Early in the day, combine the spice mixture, blending well, and rub the squabs with about ½ teaspoon of the mixture. Keep birds in the refrigerator until 45 minutes before serving.

2. To make a simple broth, cover the necks, onion, and spices with 4 cups water and cook for 1 hour; strain, reduce to 2 cups and reserve. Keep the giblets for step 4.

3. Clean the green wheat by washing it in a sieve under running water until water runs clear. Soak the wheat for 30 minutes and remove all debris that rises to the top of the water. Rub wheat through your fingers to remove any fragments that are sharp or hard. Drain the wheat thoroughly.

4. In a small saucepan, heat the butter, add the shallots and pigeon giblets, and cook 2 to 3 minutes, stirring. Add the garlic, wheat, remaining spice mixture, and salt and cook, stirring, for an instant. Moisten with 1½ cups of the reserved pigeon broth and bring to a boil; cook 10 minutes. Set aside to cool. *Up to this point the dish can be prepared early in the day, up to 12 hours before serving.*

5. About 1½ hours before serving, bring the squabs to room temperature. Loosen the breast skin and slip about 2 tablespoons wheat mixture between the skin and the flesh.

6. Place the birds, breast side up, in a deep, heavy-bottomed dutch oven. Add ¾ cup water, cover with crumbled parchment paper or foil and a tight-fitting lid, and cook over low heat 45 minutes.

Egyptian Spice Mixture

¼ teaspoon *each*: cinnamon, cardamom, coriander, black pepper, red pepper, and cumin

Pinch of ground cloves

Pinch of oregano

¼ teaspoon salt

½ teaspoon dried mint

2 squab pigeons (1 pound each), with gizzards, livers, and hearts washed and finely chopped

2 cups pigeon broth made from the necks, onion, and a cheesecloth bag with 6 peppercorns, 1 stick cinnamon, 4 whole cardamom, and 1 piece mastic

½ pound *freekeh* (green wheat) available at Middle Eastern groceries or coarse bulgur (see "Mail-Order Sources")

3 tablespoons butter, or 2 tablespoons oil

2 large shallots, chopped

1 teaspoon crushed garlic

½ teaspoon salt

Juice of ½ lemon

Olive oil

Lemon wedges

7. Add the remaining ½ cup broth to the wheat and finish the cooking. Cover with a paper towel and a lid, and cook over lowest heat until tender. There should be a crunchy brown crust on the bottom of the pan. Correct the seasoning, adding just enough of the lemon juice to give a pleasant tart flavor to the grain.

8. When the birds have cooked 30 minutes, preheat the oven to 400 degrees. Remove birds from the pan, drizzle them with oil, and place in the oven to brown. Meanwhile, reduce pan juices to ½ cup. Add lemon juice to taste and correct the seasoning. Serve browned birds over the green wheat, pour the pan juices on top, and surround with lemon wedges.

With thanks to Clifford Wright for providing the details for making this delicious dish.

STEAMED LAMB WITH LEAFY GREENS AND WINTER VEGETABLES (*Tunisia*)

❀

Serves 4

Mediterranean cooks use all kinds of thickeners for their sauces—flour and butter, yogurt, ground nuts. Tunisian cooks use extremely thin shreds of spinach or chard. Because of the way these greens are cut, they become plump and buoyant, thickening a sauce, instead of sinking to the bottom and lying flat.

The unusual and delicious methods of thickening sauces with finely shredded greens are unique to Tunisian cooking. See Tunisian Barley Couscous with Swiss Chard, Lamb, Chickpeas, and *Hrous* (page 214), Tunisian Fish Couscous with Pumpkin and Leafy Greens (page 205), Tunisian-Jewish Wedding *Pkaila* with Spiced Beef (page 275), and the following steamed lamb. In each case the thickening is achieved in a different manner.

When Houda Mokadmi, who comes from the town of Gabès, where the cooking is very fine, demonstrated this recipe for me, she added a dozen indigenous Tunisian truffles to the stew, creating an extremely aromatic dish. These light brown truffles are not as potent as the truffles of France, Spain, or Italy. They also cost about one-third as much. If you want to try them in this dish, you can find similar Moroccan truffles in cans under the Aicha brand in some Middle Eastern groceries.

This dish is extremely good without them. I suggest adding a handful of small fresh shiitake mushrooms instead.

When you've prepared this dish, consider saving the boiling liquid to make a light soup with barley and snipped dill.

3 to 4 pounds young lamb shoulder, cut into 1¼-inch chunks

1 medium onion, finely chopped

2 heads garlic, peeled, plus 2 tablespoons crushed garlic

1 tablespoon hot red pepper paste such as *hrous* (page 344), *harissa* (page 343), or imported Turkish hot pepper paste

2 tablespoons tomato paste

1 cup chopped cilantro leaves

1 cup chopped flat-leaf parsley leaves

½ teaspoon turmeric

⅓ cup olive oil

1 pound young spinach, washed, stemmed, and very finely shredded to make about 2 packed quarts

Sea salt

Freshly ground black pepper

1 fennel bulb, cut into thick slices

3 large leeks, roots trimmed and cut into 1-inch pieces, or 12 boiling onions, peeled

12 small boiling potatoes, scrubbed

3 winter carrots, pared and cut into 1-inch pieces

1 dozen fresh, small shiitake mushrooms, or 1 can imported Moroccan truffles, drained

¼ cup coarsely chopped fresh herbs for garnish: dill, cilantro, and parsley

Pinch of crushed fennel seeds

Step 1 can be done one day in advance.

1. Trim the meat of excess fat. Place the onion, half the garlic cloves and crushed garlic, red pepper and tomato pastes, herbs, turmeric, and olive oil in a large noncorrodible mixing bowl. With a spatula blend thoroughly, then stir in the meat and the shredded spinach and mix again. Cover and refrigerate until ready to cook. (For easier storage, pack the marinated meat in small plastic boxes or bags.)

2. About 1½ hours before serving, bring the meat mixture to room temperature. Choose a deep kettle that will hold a large vegetable steamer or colander snugly on top. Fill with 3 quarts water and set the colander or steamer on top. If it doesn't fit perfectly, pad it with a long strip of moistened cheesecloth, twisted into a strip the length of the circumference of the kettle top, and tuck it between the two parts, to make sure the steam rises only through the perforated holes. Put the meat and marinade into the colander, sprinkle with 1 tablespoon salt and 1 teaspoon black pepper, and mix. Cover tightly and steam for 30 minutes.

3. Add the fennel, remaining garlic cloves, leeks, potatoes, carrots, and mushrooms; cover tightly; and steam until the meat and vegetables are tender, about 25 minutes. Serve with a sprinkling of crushed fennel seeds and fresh herbs.

TUNISIAN SPRING LAMB STEW WITH FRESH FAVAS (*Tunisia*)

Serves 4

There are many variations of this rustic stew. This one's my favorite on account of the addition of twice-peeled fava beans.

You may have heard there's an easy way to remove the inner peel around favas—drop them into boiling water, wait a minute, drain, rinse, then pinch off their skins. Yes, this technique's easy and quick, but it works only if you use the beans within the hour. If you peel your favas this way too far in advance they will turn slimy and lose their texture. That's why, if you want to prepare your favas early in the day, I suggest you peel them "dry."

2½ tablespoons olive oil

2 pounds shoulder lamb chops, trimmed of excess fat and cut into ¾-inch pieces

1 medium onion, chopped

1½ tablespoons tomato paste

1 tablespoon *harissa* (page 343)

2 cloves garlic, peeled and crushed

Pinch of ground curry spices

Salt

Freshly ground black pepper

3 pounds fresh unshelled fava beans, or about 3 cups shelled fava beans

2 bunches Swiss chard, washed and stemmed

1 cup chopped flat-leaf parsley

Chopped fresh cilantro for garnish

Abdelrazak Haouari, the Djerbian chef who taught me this dish, suggested it be accompanied by bread baked in the *tabouna*, an oven similar to a tandoori. Lacking a *tabouna*, you can serve it with lavash or commercial pita quickly toasted on an open stove-top flame to warm and aromatize just before serving.

1. In a 4-quart heavy casserole, combine the oil, lamb, and onion, and cook over medium heat, stirring often, until meat turns light brown, about 8 minutes. Add the tomato paste and *harissa* and stir until they glisten and coat the meat, about 2 minutes. Add the garlic, curry spices, salt, and pepper and ¾ cup water, cover, and cook over medium-low heat for 1½ hours.

2. Meanwhile, shuck the beans and discard the pods. Peel the favas by dropping into boiling water and cooking for half a minute, then drain. Rinse under cool running water and peel off the skins. Cover with plastic wrap and hold up to one hour.

3. Cut the Swiss chard as thinly as possible, then cut into 1-inch lengths.

4. Add the Swiss chard to the casserole and continue cooking 20 minutes. Stir in the favas and parsley and cook 10 minutes longer. Correct the seasoning with salt and pepper and present decorated with cilantro leaves. Serve at once.

LAMB STEW SMOTHERED WITH CACTUS (*Tunisia*)

Serves 2

This easy and unusual recipe comes from a small town near Gafsa, where it's eaten along with bread made in a beehive oven called a *tabouna*. I found the original recipe in a pre–World War II cookbook written by a Frenchman and adapted it. A long, gentle simmer in a closed pan makes the cactus pads buttery.

8 ounces (6 small) cactus pads

1 tablespoon olive oil

10 ounces lamb shoulder, cut into 1½-inch chunks

1½ cups chopped onion

½ cup top-quality canned tomato purée

Salt

Freshly ground black pepper

½ teaspoon red pepper

A few drops of lemon juice (optional)

3 tablespoons fresh cilantro leaves, roughly chopped

1. Wear rubber gloves when washing the cactus pads. Scrape off the needles with a sharp knife. Trim the hard edges and soak in several changes of cold water for 1 hour.

2. Place the olive oil, lamb, onion, tomato purée, salt, black pepper, and red pepper in a small, heavy-bottomed casserole. Cover and cook for 45 minutes, stirring occasionally.

3. Drain the cactus pads and place over the meat. Place a crumbled piece of wet parchment paper or foil directly on the pads, cover the casserole, and cook over low heat for 45 minutes. Regulate the heat so the meat and juices do not burn but develop some caramelization, which is important for a deep flavor.

(continued)

When ready to serve, carefully transfer the cactus pads to a flat surface to avoid damaging their shape. Allow the meat to brown in the caramelized pan juices. Correct the seasoning and sprinkle with a drop of lemon juice. Place meat in serving dish, arrange the pads slightly overlapping on top, and decorate with cilantro leaves. Serve at once.

Adapted from a recipe from La Cuisine Tunisienne d'Oummi Taïabat *by A. Bernaudeau.*

BLACK SEA–STYLE LAMB SMOTHERED WITH NETTLES AND LEEKS

Serves 3 or 4

*T*his is a hearty dish from northern Turkey in which leeks and nettles are stewed with lamb and tomatoes, the result then garnished with a drizzle of yogurt-garlic sauce. I serve this dish with creamy mashed potatoes.

Be sure to wear rubber gloves when handling nettles until they've been blanched. Though raw nettles are prickly, they lose their "sting" when cooked.

1. In a wide, heavy casserole set over medium-high heat, heat the oil and brown the lamb on all sides. Add the onion, reduce the heat, and slowly cook to a deep brown. Add the tomato purée, salt and pepper, and 1 cup water, and cook, covered, 30 minutes.

2. Prepare the leeks. Peel away the coarse outer leaves of the leeks. Wash well to remove all sand and cut the white and pale-green parts into ½-inch slices. Add to the casserole.

3. Prepare the nettles. Wear rubber gloves when handling raw nettles. Wash the nettles in several changes of water and remove the stems. Drop the leaves into plenty of boiling salted water and cook for 3 minutes, then drain on a slanted wooden board. When cool, gently squeeze the nettles to remove as much water as possible; finely chop to make about ¾ cup. Add to the casserole. Continue to cook the lamb and vegetables until the meat is very tender, about 1½ hours total cooking time.

1½ pounds lamb shoulder, trimmed of fat and cut into 1-inch cubes, plus bones

2 tablespoons olive oil

⅓ cup minced onion

¾ cup top-quality canned tomato purée, preferably Muir Glen

Salt

Freshly ground black pepper

3 or 4 long white leeks

¾ pound (12 cups) nettle tops

1 cup plain yogurt

3 cloves garlic, peeled and crushed with ½ teaspoon salt

2 sprigs fresh mint, stemmed and slivered

4. Meanwhile, blend the yogurt and minced garlic and let mellow in the refrigerator for at least 1 hour.

5. Use a slotted spoon to arrange the meat, nettles, and leeks on a warm serving dish. Correct the seasoning of the cooking juices and pour over the meat and vegetables, then drizzle some of the yogurt-garlic sauce in concentric circles on top. Decorate with fresh mint. Pass the remaining yogurt-garlic sauce at the table.

Inspired by a recipe in Evelyn Lyle Kalças's Food from the Field.

TURKISH–CYPRIOT MOLOKHIYA WITH LAMB AND TOMATOES (*Turkish Cyprus*)

Serves 6

I came to Mersin on the Mediterranean coast of Turkey in spring to attend a conference on Mediterranean food and also to pick greens and learn about them from Emete Galatyal, a Turkish-Cypriot teacher of nutrition.

A kindly, bespectacled woman, she walked me through a lush valley, pointing out all sorts of greens that grow wild along the Turkish coast. Though somewhat stocky and middle-aged, she had the vitality of a youngster, jumping from rock to rock, spotting greens with her eagle eye, excitedly teaching me about them.

Later that day, she prepared this delicious lamb stew with molokhiya leaves (see Notes), which became the hit of the conference.

¼ pound dried molokhiya leaves

4 tablespoons olive oil

3 cups chopped onions

2 pounds boneless lamb shoulder lamb, trimmed of excess fat and cut into 1-inch cubes

3 cups chopped red ripe tomatoes, or 1 (28-ounce) can

2 teaspoons salt

12 large cloves garlic, peeled and thinly sliced

Juice of 4 lemons

¾ teaspoon Turkish red pepper (page 351) or more to taste

1 teaspoon freshly ground black pepper

1. Place dried molokhiya leaves in a large strainer set in a large bowl. Use your fingers to rub the leaves to crush and remove any dried stems. Cover dried molokhiya with warm water and let soak for 20 minutes. Lift the strainer in order to leave any sediment in the water. Wash the leaves in two or three changes of water until clear. Squeeze out excess moisture and set aside.

2. Place meat in a 5-quart casserole and sear without fat for 10 minutes, stirring often, until all the juices are absorbed. Add the oil and onions and cook until golden, 5 minutes. Stir in the tomatoes and continue cooking 3 minutes longer. Stir in the salt, garlic, molokhiya, lemon juice, and 2 cups water. Bring to a boil, cover, and cook at a simmer until tender, about 1½ hours.

3. Add the red pepper, black pepper, and salt to taste. Serve in individual soup bowls on a bed of rice or bulgur pilaf.

NOTES TO THE COOK: When I lived in Connecticut my local Middle Eastern grocer sold molokhiya seeds each spring to members of the Middle Eastern community who wanted to plant their own for late summer harvest. I chose not to grow this green because of the difficulty of removing each leaf from the stalk without releasing the substance at the joint that creates gooiness. In this recipe, I recommend the purchase of dried molokhiya leaves by mail (see "Mail-Order Sources") or at a Middle Eastern grocery. Please note that sometimes dried leaves are dusty; if so, they should be shaken in a sieve before use. Look for whole dry leaves, avoiding those that are crushed—nicknamed "birdfeather" on account of their appearance.

The fresh or frozen leafy green called molokhiya provides a much prized viscous texture to soups and stews made with chicken, rabbit, or meat. The texture of molokhiya is similar to that of okra and wild mallow, a quality people either love or hate. If you enjoy gumbo you'll probably enjoy adding molokhiya to your repertory of greens. In some Middle Eastern dishes the leafy greens are simmered with a captivating mixture of cinnamon, cardamom, mastic, and garlic in a rich chicken broth.

HARPOUT KÖFTE WITH FRESH MINT AND EGG SALAD

❀

Makes 3 to 4 dozen dumplings, serving 4

When I heard that there were sixty-four types of bulgur and wheat-based *köfte* in the central Anatolian town of Malayta of course I knew I had to go there and see what all the fuss was about. After eating my way through quite a few *köfte*, I moved on to the town of Elazig to check out the competition. Here I found my hands-down cooked *köfte* favorite . . . which, thankfully, put an end to my quest.

"I'm not surprised you chose this one," Bahriye Çetindağ told me, "it's one of the most popular dishes in the region." A good-natured, chunky Turkish woman with a bandana around her head, she went on to explain that *harpout*, the name of this *köfte*, means "little mountain," formerly the village of an Armenian community renown for its cooking.

"In the old days," she told me, "they stuffed it with fat and onion which made the juices flow in your mouth. For health reasons I don't make it that way."

Traditionalists may well raise their eyebrows at this deliberate reduction in richness. I can only say that this is Bahriye's version, and that though it is undoubtedly less luscious than the original, it's still very delicious.

Bahriye served me these delicious *köftesi harpout* with a hard-cooked egg and fresh mint salad (recipe below) along with plenty of good Turkish bread to mop up the tasty broth.

1. Place the dry bulgur, meat, onion, red pepper flakes, basil, spice mixture, parsley, and salt in the work bowl of a heavy-duty mixer fitted with a paddle and knead until completely blended. Add the ice water and knead on medium speed until well mixed and similar to a soft dough, 5 minutes.

2. Place the meat mixture on a work surface and set a bowl of cold water next to it. With moistened hands pinch off a piece of dough the size of a large cherry; squeeze into a smooth ball. Then, if you are right-handed, slip the ball in your wet left hand in between the thumb and forefinger and with the wet fingers of your right hand reshape the sphere into a

flat round, about ¾ inch by ¼ inch. Use your thumb to make a small indentation on one side. Repeat with the remaining dough. Can be made many hours in advance up to this point. Cover and keep refrigerated.

3. Prepare the poaching liquid: In a wide saucepan, heat the oil with the tomato and pepper pastes and cook, stirring, for 1 minute. Add the fresh tomatoes, salt, and 2 quarts water and bring to a boil. Simmer for 10 minutes. Drop 6 *köfte* at a time into the simmering broth. Cook until the *köfte* float to the surface, about 2 to 4 minutes. Remove to a shallow serving

1 cup fine bulgur

1 cup ground lamb or beef

1 small onion, cut into small pieces

½ teaspoon red pepper flakes

¾ teaspoon crumbled dried basil, preferably opal basil

½ teaspoon Elazig *Köfte* Spice Mixture (recipe below)

2 tablespoons flat-leaf parsley

1¼ teaspoons salt

Ice water, about ¾ cup

POACHING LIQUID

2 tablespoons olive oil

2 tablespoons tomato paste

1 tablespoon homemade or imported Turkish pepper paste

2 fresh tomatoes, halved, seeded, and grated

1 tablespoon coarse salt

3 tablespoons chopped herbs: parsley and dill (optional)

dish. Quickly reduce the broth to about half. Taste for seasonings. Spoon about 2 cups broth over the *köfte*, sprinkle with herbs, and serve at once with a platter of fresh mint and egg salad. Reserve the remaining broth for a soup or freeze for some other purpose.

ELAZIG *KÖFTE* SPICE MIXTURE

1 cardamom pod

2 cloves

½ teaspoon ground allspice

½ teaspoon Turkish red pepper flakes

¼ teaspoon ground cinnamon

1 teaspoon black peppercorns

Mix all the spices. Grind to a powder and sieve. Store in a tightly closed jar.

FRESH MINT AND EGG SALAD

When I make a chopped egg salad, I peel hard-cooked eggs, then rub them along the large holes of a grater, a quick effective technique.

½ to 1 cup slivered mint leaves (amount depends upon the intensity of the mint)

½ cup finely sliced scallions

1 teaspoon Turkish red pepper flakes

2 hard-cooked eggs, peeled and rubbed on a coarse grater

Juice of ½ lemon

1 tablespoon olive oil

Salt

Mix the mint, scallions, red pepper, and eggs in a bowl. Dress with a mixture of the lemon juice, olive oil, and salt. Chill until ready to serve with the warm *köfte*.

KIBBEH

✦

In my last book, *The Cooking of the Eastern Mediterranean*, I devoted a good deal of space to the making by hand of kibbeh, which I called "the masterpiece of Middle Eastern cuisine." I described fifty kibbehs and gave recipes for twelve. That chapter was popular: I've since had spirited correspondence with numerous readers. I refer those interested in kibbeh to that book.

Many readers requested the recipe for the kibbeh of raw lamb bound with bulgur. Concerned about the possible consequences of eating raw meat, I decided not to send out the recipe. I recently discussed the health consequences with Samira Zedan, a Druse woman cook I met in Israel. She told me she freezes her lamb for a week before making the dish, believing freezing will kill any germs. She may be right for her "homegrown" lamb, but I still hesitate to pass along recipes using raw meat.

While in Israel I met with Kurdish and Iraqi Jews who make a kibbeh-style dish called *kubbah* with ground rice instead of bulgur. They soak short-grain rice in water for an hour, then, after draining, grind it in a food processor with turkey breast, season the combination with salt, then gradually work in semolina or farina to make a strong dough. They then stuff this dough with a mix of cooked beef, onion, celery, paprika, turmeric and chicken soup powder, then poach the *kubbah* in a tomato soup made with such vegetables as okra, pumpkin, and Swiss chard. Other cooks poach *kubbah* in a soup made with beets, beet greens, zucchini, and garlic. As much as I liked these dishes, I never really got turned on to the texture of rice *kubbah*. I refer readers interested in recipes to Claudia Roden's terrific *The Book of Jewish Food.*

White Turnip Rounds with Bulgur, Rice, and Lamb with Yogurt–Garlic Sauce and Sizzling Tomato and Mint (*Turkey*)

❀

Serves 4 or 5

This main course dish comes from the eastern Turkish town of Erzurum, an area of long hard winters, where people gorge themselves on pickled cabbage and turnips, preserved greens in salt, meat preserved in its own fat, and, contrary to our understanding of Mediterranean cooking, lots of fresh butter! They also consume lots of tea with lemon—often twenty-five glasses per person per day, which, they claim, "thins" their blood and "melts away the fat." I certainly don't advocate their diet, but here's one dish they make that's truly splendid.

Slices of white turnips (you can substitute celery root) are softened by a light salting (no blanching required). Half of the slices, placed in the baking pan as a bottom layer, will become wonderfully caramelized during cooking, while the top turnip layer becomes crusty and brown. Meantime, seasonings in the interior meat, kneaded with rice, onions, and parsley, provide complexity to the dish. Because the meat is partially exposed, some fat is required to keep it from drying out. In this adaptation, if the meat is too lean I use some well-drained yogurt. You'll need yogurt anyway because the dish is served with a garlicky yogurt sauce topped with a final sizzling swirl of tomato and mint oil. If you like, finish the meal with black tea "to cut the fat."

(continued)

1/3 cup medium-grain rice

Coarse salt

4 large white turnips (2 pounds)

14 ounces ground beef, preferably chuck

1 cup minced onion

3 tablespoons fine-grain bulgur

1/2 teaspoon Elazig *Köfte* Spice Mixture
(page 265)

1/3 cup mixed chopped herbs: parsley
and fresh mint

1 teaspoon dried mint

1 tablespoon tomato paste

Freshly ground black pepper

1/2 teaspoon Near East pepper

1/3 cup drained yogurt (optional)

TOPPING

1 cup lightly drained yogurt mixed with
3 cloves garlic, peeled and crushed to a pulp
with a pinch of salt

4 tablespoons sweet butter mixed with oil

1 tablespoon tomato paste

1 tablespoon dried mint, pressed through a fine
sieve to make about 1 teaspoon

1. Soak the rice in hot water with a pinch of salt until ready to use, about 25 minutes.

2. Trim and peel the turnips and cut into 1/3-inch rounds. You should have about 32 to 40 rounds. In a mixing bowl, toss them with 1 teaspoon coarse salt and let stand 15 minutes or until limp. Rinse to remove the salt and leave to drain.

3. In a food processor, combine the meat with the onion, bulgur, spice mixture, herbs, dried mint, tomato paste, salt, pepper, and red pepper. Process until well combined.

4. Drain the rice and add, pulsing once to combine. Fold in the drained yogurt if the meat seems too lean.

5. Divide the mixture into 16 to 20 equal parts; roll each flat, to resemble a coin.

6. Lightly oil a 12-inch deep skillet (or a shallow heatproof pan), and arrange half the turnips in one layer. Top each with a "coin" of meat and another turnip round. Press down to adhere. Add 1/2 cup water to the pan and bring to the boil. Cover tightly and cook over reduced heat for 40 minutes.

7. Make the topping. Have the yogurt-garlic sauce ready in a serving bowl. Tilt the skillet and remove 1 tablespoon of the cooking juices to a side dish. In a small skillet, melt the butter and oil mixture and tomato paste, stirring, until it sizzles. Add the sieved mint and let sizzle, then stir in the reserved table-spoon cooking juice to stop the butter from over-heating. Swirl the mixture over the yogurt and serve with the stuffed turnips.

Provençal "Meat Loaf" with Cabbage, Artichokes, Chard, Spinach, and Ground Pork (France)

Serves 8

1 chopped onion

2 leeks, trimmed and chopped

2 tablespoons extra-virgin olive oil

2 artichoke bottoms, blanched for 10 minutes, then thinly sliced

¾ pound ground pork

2 bunches Swiss chard leaves, cooked and chopped

1 bunch stemmed spinach, cooked and chopped

2 ounces pork sausage, skinned and shredded

2 ounces cured ham such as prosciutto, shredded

1 teaspoon salt

½ teaspoon freshly ground black pepper

⅔ cup chopped flat-leaf parsley

¼ teaspoon grated nutmeg

¼ teaspoon ground allspice

1 tablespoon crushed garlic

3 cups stale crustless bread, torn into small pieces

1 medium green or savoy cabbage (2½ pounds)

¼ cup bread crumbs

This delicious Provençal "meat loaf" will easily feed eight. I like to prepare it for four, serving it warm along with pickles, salad, and mashed potatoes, then prepare the leftovers the following day by slicing it, dusting the slices with flour, and frying them in extra-virgin olive oil until brown and crunchy on all sides. This second-day preparation goes beautifully with the home-style tomato sauce on page 342, thinned with a half a cup of water and the seasoning corrected.

1. One day in advance of serving, fry the onion and leeks in the olive oil in a small skillet until softened. Cool, then mix with the artichoke bottoms, pork, greens, pork sausage, ham, salt, pepper, parsley, spices, garlic, and dried bread in a bowl; blend well. Cover and refrigerate overnight to allow flavors to develop.

2. The following day, preheat the oven to 350 degrees.

3. Discard outer leaves of the cabbage. Wash the cabbage, discard inner core, and cook in boiling salted water for 30 minutes. Drain cabbage well.

(continued)

4. Line a 6- to 8-cup oiled gratin dish with half the cabbage leaves, overlapping. Place the filling in the center, flatten slightly, and cover with the remaining leaves to completely enclose. If the cabbage and its filling rise above the sides of the dish, gently pat down to make them more compact. Brush the top with oil and sprinkle with bread crumbs.

5. Fill a roasting pan with water and set it in the oven. Place the dish in the center and bake for 1 hour. Remove the water bath and finish baking until brown and crusty, 1 hour more.

STUFFED SWISS CHARD ON A BED OF TARO ROOT OR POTATOES (*Cyprus*)

Serves 4

Mrs. Niki Lazaridou Moquist, a Cypriot now living in central California, generously shared this and several other delicious homey Cypriot recipes.

In Cyprus, these rolls, called *koupepia*, are served as a main dish, made with Swiss chard in fall and winter, with grape leaves in summer and spring.

In this wonderful dish, taro root or potatoes work equally well. Serve with a bowl of yogurt and a plate of fresh radishes with their inner green leaves still attached.

1. Prepare the Swiss chard rolls. In a mixing bowl, combine all the ingredients for the *koupepia* except for the Swiss chard, blending well. Boil the Swiss chard leaves a few at a time in salted water for 30 seconds, remove, and drain in a colander. Cut away the thick center stem. If the leaves are unusually large divide into three parts. Use about 1 heaping tablespoon filling in each leaf and roll up. (The rolls should be approximately 2 inches long.) Makes about 36 rolls. *Up to this point the rolls can be made one day in advance.*

2. About 1½ hours before serving, cook the *koupepia*. In a 4-quart heavy saucepan, sauté the onions in the olive oil until transparent.

KOUPEPIA

1 pound ground meat (a combination
of veal and pork)

Marrow from 1 veal bone, or 2 tablespoons
olive oil

1 tablespoon finely chopped flat-leaf parsley

⅓ cup short-grain rice

¼ cup grated Roma tomatoes

1 teaspoon finely crumbled dried mint

½ teaspoon ground cinnamon

½ teaspoon freshly and finely ground
black pepper

½ teaspoon salt

16 to 18 large Swiss chard leaves, or substitute
36 large grape leaves

2 medium onions, thinly sliced

2 tablespoons olive oil

1 pound taro root, scrubbed and thoroughly
dried with a kitchen towel (see page 272),
or 3 or 4 boiling potatoes, washed

1 cup grated Roma tomatoes

Juice of 1 lemon

¼ teaspoon salt

⅛ teaspoon freshly ground black pepper

3. Meanwhile, peel and "chip" the taro root (as described on page 272), or cut the potatoes into ¼-inch-thick slices and add to the pan. Sauté for another 5 minutes, then add the grated tomatoes and enough water to cover, about 1 cup. Pour over the lemon juice and add the salt and pepper. Bring to a boil and simmer until the taro root is soft enough to break in half when pierced with a fork, about 45 minutes for the taro root and 30 minutes for the potatoes.

4. Remove the pan from the heat and place the prepared Swiss chard rolls on top in layers. Set an upside-down heavy plate on top to hold them in place; cover the pan and return to the stove to continue cooking for another 30 minutes. Remove from the heat without lifting the lid and let stand 20 minutes before arranging tubers and rolls attractively in a serving dish. Pour over the pan juices. If there is more than ½ cup liquid in the pan, boil it down, then pour over the rolls. Serve hot.

HANDLING TARO ROOT

✦

Before the sixteenth century, when the potato was introduced to the Mediterranean from the New World, brown-skinned taro root, a slightly sweet-tasting starchy tuber, was as prevalent in cooking as the potato is today. Taro roots are still eaten widely in Egypt in a dish called *oulaas,* as well as in Cyprus and along the Turkish Mediterranean coast. You can easily find them fresh in fall and winter in Asian markets, either in the small 2- to 3-inch size or the larger variety 7 to 8 inches long. Both sizes taste the same. You can also buy them frozen, imported from Egypt, at Middle Eastern stores. Just ask the grocer for *kolokassi* or *culcacia.*

Taro root probably went out of fashion in most regions because it easily turns slimy. Here's a method for slicing it that prevents this unpleasant texture: Scrub the taro roots under running water, dry them well, then peel. Next cut them into ¼-inch-thick chunks, but just before you finish cutting, turn the knife so that the piece "chips," or snaps off. (If substituting frozen taro root simply use frozen and do not slice.)

STUFFED CABBAGE (*France*)

Serves 6

This rustic-style French dish of cabbage rolls stuffed with a rich, sumptuous mixture of leafy greens, veal, chicken, and pork, flavored with garlic, nutmeg, cognac, and wine, was inspired by a dish made by an old friend in Paris, Pierre Bardèche. I have been visiting his bistro, Aux Charpentiers, on rue Mabillon, since the seventies, and I always organize my visit so I can go on a Saturday to enjoy the lunch special of stuffed cabbage.

In Pierre's recipe he uses the leftover meat from Thursday's *pot au feu* as well as *lard gras*, fatty pork neck, and cream. He cooks the stuffing twice, first in a covered pan, after which he pours off all the fat, and then again when it is stuffed inside his cabbage leaves.

1 bunch scallions, thinly sliced, trimmed with white and enough of the green leaves to make 1 cup

3 tablespoons olive oil

3 tablespoons dry white wine

1½ cups torn pieces dried bread, without crusts

⅔ cup cold stock or milk

4 large cloves garlic, peeled

4 allspice berries

1 teaspoon sea salt

10 ounces lean pork, finely chopped or ground

4 ounces ground veal

4 ounces ground chicken breast

¼ teaspoon grated nutmeg

1 cup blanched spinach mixed with 2 chard leaves, finely chopped

6 tablespoons chopped flat-leaf parsley

2 eggs, beaten

½ teaspoon freshly ground pepper

1 tablespoon Cognac

1 large savoy or green cabbage (about 3½ pounds)

Salt

Freshly ground black pepper

2 ounces pancetta or blanched salt pork

2 tablespoons olive oil

½ teaspoon sugar

1 small chopped onion

1 large chopped carrot

1 large chopped celery rib

¼ cup dry white wine

In the following adapted version, I use leaner meat, thus eliminating the need to double-cook.

You can prepare the rolls several hours in advance; keep them moist in their cooking juices. The stuffing is better if made a day in advance and allowed to mellow, and the cabbage rolls are also better when reheated.

1. Early in the day or a day in advance, sauté the scallions in the hot oil until golden, then deglaze with the white wine and reduce to a glaze. Scrape into a mixing bowl and leave to cool.

2. Soften the bread with the cold stock and squeeze dry. Add to the mixing bowl.

3. Crush the garlic with the allspice berries and salt. Add to the bowl along with the remaining ingredients for the stuffing; blend well. Cover and refrigerate to allow flavor to develop.

4. The following morning, remove outer leaves from the cabbage, remove core, and drop the whole cabbage into a pot of simmering salted water and cook, covered, 1 hour, or until the leaves separate easily; drain. Cool, then pull back leaves and separate. Shave away all hard ribs. (This makes it easier to roll neatly.) Cool leaves; divide into 12 even piles mixing large and small leaves. Season each pile with salt and pepper.

5. In a heavy 4- or 5-quart casserole or large straight-sided skillet, lightly brown the pancetta in the olive oil. Add the sugar, onion, carrot, and celery and cook, stirring, until golden brown. Add the white wine to deglaze. Pour in 2½ cups water and boil for 5 minutes. Remove from the heat and allow to cool.

(continued)

6. Meanwhile divide the stuffing into 12 portions. Set a portion in the center of each pile of cabbage leaves. Lift one pile into the palm of your hand; use a method of cradling and rolling the leaves to enclose the stuffing. Repeat until all the rolls are ready to place, seam side down, in the liquid in one layer. Weight them with a heatproof, upside-down plate just large enough to fit inside the pan and cover with a tight-fitting lid. Return to a boil, reduce heat to very low, and cook for 1¼ hours. Remove from heat and let stand 30 minutes. (The rolls will be better if left undisturbed a few hours.)

7. About 20 minutes before serving, tilt the casserole and pour off almost all of the juices. Carefully reheat the rolls, allowing them to caramelize in the remaining pan juices, 10 minutes. Strain the pan juices through a sieve directly over the cabbage and reheat until hot.

With special thanks to Pierre Bardèche for sharing his recipe.

TUNISIAN-JEWISH WEDDING *PKAILA* WITH BEEF AND GREENS

❦

Serves 6 as a main course or 12 as part of a banquet

*I*n Tunisia, women collect leafy greens, shred them, then cook them in a pan over medium heat until no further moisture can be expressed, and the greens turn nearly black without being burned. (If the leaves burn, they turn bitter.) They know the leaves are cooked when they hear them crackling, a sound similar to what you hear when you walk on dead leaves in autumn. The leaves are then fried in oil, pounded to a paste, and preserved in a jar.

When the cook wants to use this paste in a recipe, as in this delicious spicy traditional Jewish wedding dish, she opens the jar, takes out a few tablespoons of paste per person, dilutes it with meat broth, then cooks her ingredients in the blackish liquid.

This may not sound very good, but in fact it's delicious if you make the paste properly. The problem with most recipes for this dish is that they encourage you to hurry up the paste-making process, in which case the unique richness is lost. Below I describe how a Tunisian-Jewish cook made this dish. The recipe that follows is a simplified version of what she did. However, the one thing I didn't change was the slow preparation of the paste, an essential flavoring.

I first tasted this dish in a suburb of Tunis, where it was taught to me by a retired schoolteacher, Lola Cohen, who assured me that if only her single daughter learned to make it she'd have no trouble finding a husband. It's just that good. she said.

"We consider green a lucky color," she told me, "which is why we serve this dish at weddings. And of course we accompany it with our ice-cold *boukha*, a fig liqueur that makes you want to dance on the table!"

Lola demonstrated the dish for me in her apartment kitchen, which overlooked the ruins of ancient Carthage.

She already had her jar of blackish green paste. While I watched, she prepared a stew of beef short ribs, soaked white beans, mint, cinnamon, fresh cilantro, a veal foot, and ½ pound broiled and scraped beef skin (not shin). She also made two sausages called *osban*: one large and thick in which ground lamb and herbs were encompassed in a beef intestine casing, the other thin and fragile in which tripe, beef liver, lamb, and other ingredients were encompassed in a lamb casing. Having prepared the parts, she added some of the oily paste to flavor, color, and thicken the bean-enriched meat stew. She then served the whole dish at the table in an electric frying pan to keep it warm as we slowly ate our way through its many components.

The following recipe is a modified version of this sensational dish, in which I leave out the veal foot and beef skin, and the two *osbans*. It's still fine eating! However, for enthusiasts who want to go the whole nine yards, you'll find recipes for the two *osbans* Lola made in the Notes to the Cook that follow the recipe.

Claudia Roden, in her brilliant *The Book of Jewish Food*, observes that this was the traditional sabbath dish of Tunisian and Algerian Jews, and that it is now a popular dish in France. See her recipe for *T'fina Pkaila*, a meat stew with beans and spinach, for another way to use this paste.

4 pounds fresh young Swiss chard leaves or chard mixed with some fresh flat-leaf spinach

⅓ cup olive oil

1 cup dried small white beans

2½ pounds short ribs, partially trimmed of excess fat and cut into 6 pieces

1½ pounds beef shank

⅓ cup chopped red onion

1 cinnamon stick

1 tablespoon crushed garlic

½ teaspoon freshly ground black pepper

Salt

½ cup chopped cilantro leaves

3 cloves garlic, crushed with ½ teaspoon aniseed

1 teaspoon dried mint

Do steps 1 and 2 one day in advance of serving.

1. Wash, stem, and shred the greens. Wilt the leaves in a heavy casserole and continue cooking until the leaves are dry and begin to stick to the bottom of the pan. Use a wooden spoon to work in the olive oil. Continue sautéeing and pressing down on the greens so their structure breaks down to a smooth paste. This takes about 45 minutes of almost constant stirring without burning. The greens are ready when they turn very dark and feel slightly like fabric yet are oily. You should have about 1½ cups. Discard any rib "strings" remaining in the paste. Store the paste in a jar.

2. Wash, pick over, and soak the beans overnight in cold water to cover.

3. The following day, combine the meats, red onion, cinnamon stick, crushed garlic, pepper, and 3 quarts water in a heavy casserole. Bring to a boil, lower the heat, cover, and cook 2 hours. Do not salt at this time.

4. Meanwhile, drain the beans; put them in a small saucepan and cook with lightly salted water until barely tender. Set aside.

5. When the meat is just cooked, remove to a side dish and cut away bones, fat, and gristle. Season the meat with salt and pepper.

6. Pound the prepared greens in a mortar to a smooth paste or process in a food processor. Add the chopped cilantro, crushed garlic with aniseed, and dried mint and process until well combined. Carefully add enough of the meat broth to make a smooth creamy sauce. Scrape into a clean saucepan; add the drained beans, the boned meats, and just enough skimmed broth to cover. Partially cover and cook over medium heat for 1 hour or until all the meats and beans are fully tender, and the only liquid left is a fluffy green oily sauce. Keep hot in a low oven until ready to serve. The dish can also be kept hot in a chafing dish.

NOTES TO THE COOK: The traditional wedding banquet preparation of this dish often includes two sausages, one small, the other large. If you wish to include the two sausages as well as a cracked veal foot, and ⅓ pound beef skin, previously broiled and scraped clean, add everything at step **3.** Be sure to add enough water to cover.

To make the small *osban*: grind together ¼ pound beef liver; ¼ pound ground beef; ¾ cup raw rice; 1 cup diced, blanched tripe; ¼ cup chopped cilantro leaves; 2 tablespoons chopped flat-leaf parsley; 4 large Swiss chard leaves, stemmed and shredded; ¼ cup chopped mint; 1 teaspoon crushed garlic; ½ tablespoon hot red pepper; some dill; and enough olive oil to moisten. Stuff into lamb casings and tie at 4-inch intervals. Add to the meat broth when it first comes to a boil in step 3 and remove when tender. At serving time, cut into 1-inch pieces and reheat in the sauce.

To make the large *osban*: Combine 7 ounces ground lamb or beef; 1½ tablespoons chopped flat-leaf parsley; 1 teaspoon crushed garlic; ½ cup chopped cilantro leaves; ¾ cup chopped fresh mint leaves; ⅓ cup snipped fresh dill; salt and freshly ground pepper; and 1 tablespoon olive oil. Stuff into a large beef intestine casing, add at step 3, and boil 3 hours. Serve sliced in the sauce.

HONEYCOMB TRIPE STEW
WITH CELERY, PARSLEY, AND SARDO CHEESE (*Italy*)

Serves 4

This Sardinian stew is especially delicious served on a bed of soft polenta.

1. Wash the tripe in vinegared water; rinse well and drain. Cut into ¼-inch strips, about 2½ inches long. Place tripe and salt pork in a deep saucepan, cover with cold water, and slowly bring to a boil. Simmer 15 minutes; remove the salt pork to a cutting board. Continue boiling the tripe 30 minutes. Cut the salt pork into small cubes to make about ⅓ cup.

2. In a heavy 3-quart casserole, slowly cook the cubed salt pork, olive oil, and onion until onion turns golden, 5 minutes. Add the garlic and allow it to turn golden. Add the carrot, celery, celery leaves, 1½ cups of the parsley, and the pepper flakes; raise the heat and cook, stirring, until all the moisture has evaporated. Stir in the drained tripe, cover, and allow it to absorb flavors, 5 minutes. Stir in the wine, salt, black pepper, and ⅔ cup of the stock. Bring to a boil, lay a crumbled piece of wet parchment directly over the contents of the casserole, cover with a lid, and cook over low heat 2 to 3 hours, stirring from time to time and adding spoonfuls of reserved stock as necessary to keep the tripe juicy. When the tripe is fork tender, and the cooking juices are very aromatic, remove from the heat. *The dish can be prepared 1 to 2 days in advance to this point.*

1½ pounds ready-to-cook tripe

3 tablespoons vinegar

2 ounces salt pork or fatback

3 tablespoons olive oil

½ cup minced onion

1 teaspoon minced garlic

½ cup minced carrot

1 cup minced celery

2 teaspoons minced celery leaves

2 cups chopped flat-leaf parsley (2½ ounces)

Pinch of red pepper flakes

½ cup dry white wine

1 teaspoon sea salt

1 teaspoon freshly ground black pepper

About 1 cup homemade meat or chicken stock

⅓ cup grated pecorino cheese, preferably Sardo

3. Reheat the tripe and its cooking juices in a small saucepan over gentle heat; add the remaining ½ cup parsley and simmer 10 minutes, uncovered. Serve very hot with a light dusting of grated cheese.

8

SIDE DISHES

RICE AND BULGUR PILAFS

Since I wrote a lot about rice and bulgur pilafs in *Cooking of the Eastern Mediterranean*, I won't cover the same ground here. But I would like to demonstrate, with a couple of quotes and aphorisms, the importance of rice pilafs in Turkish daily life.

There's a Turkish expression used to define a well-made rice pilaf: "One should be able to count the rice grains one by one." Or, put another way: "Each grain should fall easily from the spoon." Both sayings refer to the importance of texture. To achieve the right texture, Turkish cooks will soak their rice in salted water, wash it to remove surface starch, and then, after it's cooked, slip toweling under the lid of the rice pot to capture any excess moisture.

There's an eastern Mediterranean porridge-style rice dish called *lapa* in Turkey and Greece, quite similar in texture to Italian risotto. Though it's appreciated, especially by someone who is sick, a Turk might say derisively of a soupy and thus failed rice pilaf, "Oh, dear! Her pilaf didn't turn out very well, so she turned it into *lapa!*"

A good rice pilaf can be made either with short to medium stubby rice such as Turkish *baldo* (similar to Italian *arborio*), or with elegant long-grain rice such as Persian or basmati. Some Turkish cooks now use long-grain American rice if they can afford it, since it doesn't require soaking.

In the old days, before supermarkets came to Turkey, women would buy *baldo* and spend hours cleaning it of stones and debris, then sieving it to separate whole kernels from broken. The whole kernels were used for pilafs and the broken for rice stuffings such as *dolmas*. To keep their rice from becoming moldy, they'd add a lot of salt to the sack. And before cooking they'd soak it for as long as three hours in salted water.

Turkish *baldo* (available by mail order from Kalustyan) is still popular, but for me it doesn't have the taste of the long-grain basmati. Still, most of the Turkish home cooks I stayed with soaked their rice whether long or short in salted warm water, claiming that the salt keeps the rice from softening too much during cooking, while still absorbing a maximum amount of liquid.

Whatever kind of rice is used (and there are thousands of varieties in the world), an eastern Mediterranean cook will commit herself to getting the starch out of each and every grain.

Bulgur is popular in Arab, Armenian, Assyrian, Cypriot, Greek, Jewish, Kurdish, and Turkish cooking. Two qualities have kept bulgur popular in the eastern Mediterranean: nutritional value and flavor. In this part of the world a well-seasoned bulgur pilaf is considered worthy of being served at a wedding banquet. For more information on bulgur see pages 98 and 266.

RICE PILAF WITH LEEKS AND DILL (*Greece*)

❊

Serves 4 as a side dish

*I*n northern Greece, leeks, collected at the end of September, are piled at the end of the garden, covered with ferns, then left to be covered by the October snows. Stored this way through the winter, they're retrieved as needed . . . for use, for example, in this terrific rice pilaf.

Serve with feta cheese, with a Greek salad, or with grilled poultry or fish.

1 pound young leeks, white part plus pale green shoots, trimmed, split, washed well, and drained

3 tablespoons extra-virgin olive oil

½ cup chopped onion

½ cup chopped carrots

½ teaspoon salt

¼ teaspoon freshly ground black pepper

2 tablespoons snipped dill

1 cup unsalted chicken broth or water, simmering

½ cup long-grain rice

1. Cut the leeks into ¾-inch lengths, place in a colander, and rinse under cold running water. You should have about 1 quart.

2. Heat the olive oil in a 10-inch straight-sided skillet. Add the onion, cover, and cook over medium heat 5 minutes. Add the carrots, leeks, salt, pepper, and 1 teaspoon of the dill. Cover and cook 5 minutes more. Add the simmering broth or water and bring to a boil. Stir in the rice and cook, covered, at a simmer for 15 minutes. Place a paper towel over the rice, cover the pan, and place it over a flame tamer to continue cooking another 10 minutes. Gently fluff the rice, adjust the seasonings, and sprinkle with the remaining dill.

GREEK-STYLE RICE WITH SPINACH, FETA, AND BLACK OLIVES

❀

Serves 4 as a side dish or supper with crusty bread

This dish of spinachy rice with feta and black olives is extremely simple . . . and therein lies its elegance. Some people simply don't get it. "It's just so humble," they say. To which I respond, "That's what I like about it!"

2 pounds fresh spinach, washed and tough stems removed

Coarse sea salt

4 tablespoons extra-virgin olive oil

½ cup thinly sliced scallions

¾ cup finely chopped onions or leeks

½ cup fresh tomato purée reduced by boiling to 3 tablespoons

½ cup long-grain rice

¼ cup chopped dill

Freshly ground black pepper

Oily black olives for garnish

Chunks of feta cheese or spoonfuls of thick yogurt for garnish

1. Wash the spinach and tender stems until the water runs clean; drain. If leaves are large and crinkly, sprinkle lightly with salt and mix well. Let stand in a colander 15 minutes; rinse and squeeze out excess moisture. Shred the spinach to make about 3 cups.

2. Heat 3 tablespoons of the olive oil in a 10-inch straight-sided skillet. Add the scallions, onions, a pinch of salt, and ¼ cup water and cook, covered, over medium-low heat for 10 minutes. When the water evaporates, slowly let the onions turn golden, stirring occasionally. Add 1 cup water, the reduced tomato purée, and rice. Cover and cook for 10 minutes.

3. Spread the spinach and dill over the rice, cover, and cook 10 minutes longer. Remove from heat, mix, then place a double thickness of paper toweling over the rice, cover again, and let stand until cool. Adjust the seasoning with black pepper and salt and drizzle with the remaining tablespoon olive oil. Serve at room temperature garnished with black olives and feta cheese or yogurt.

Armenian Green Bean and Bulgur Pilaf (*Turkey*)

❁

Serves 6

The best string beans for this dish are big fat ones, to be quartered lengthwise. Remember: you're *not* trying to turn thick string beans into French *haricot verts*; rather, you want to open them up so they'll cook more thoroughly, while releasing their flavor into the grain. Instead of knocking yourself out trying to cut the beans lengthwise by hand, consider getting a Kiske cutter, which slices beans lengthwise and removes strings at the same time. Available at most hardware stores, it's a nifty gadget.

In the time-honored tradition of the Mediterranean (and the American South) thick green beans are considered more delicious when well cooked. Forget fashionably crunchy vegetables. When cooked slowly in their own moisture with onions and tomatoes, the beans will turn soft and buttery.

Serve with yogurt and garlic sauce (page 346).

¾ pound fresh green beans

3 tablespoons extra-virgin olive oil

1 large onion, peeled and chopped

1½ tablespoons tomato paste

1½ tablespoons Turkish red pepper paste (see "Mail-Order Sources")

1 cup fresh or canned chopped tomatoes

Salt

1 cup coarse-grain bulgur

½ teaspoon freshly ground black pepper

¼ teaspoon Turkish red pepper flakes (see "Mail-Order Sources")

Pinch of sugar

1. Wash and trim the beans and cut them into quarters, lengthwise, then into 1-inch lengths.

2. In a 3-quart casserole heat the oil, add the onion, and cook until soft and translucent. Add the tomato paste and pepper paste and cook for 1 minute, stirring. Add the string beans, tomatoes, and 1 teaspoon salt and cook, covered, over low heat until the string beans are meltingly tender, about 1 hour.

3. When the green beans are ready, stir in the dry bulgur, black pepper, red pepper flakes, and 1⅓ cups water, and bring to a boil, stirring once. Cover the pan, and cook over very low heat for 20 minutes, or until almost all the liquid has been absorbed. Place a folded paper towel over the bulgur, cover tightly, and cook another 5 minutes. Turn off the heat and let stand at least 15 minutes, or until the bulgur is completely swollen and all the liquid has been absorbed.

Winter Squash Pilaf with Bulgur (*Cyprus*)

Serves 4 to 6 as an accompaniment to roast chicken

Niki Moquist, a California home cook born in Cyprus, gave me this terrific bulgur and squash pilaf recipe. Akin to rice pilafs with pumpkin, it combines red winter squash, raisins, and spices.

Now that earthy, mildly toasty coarser grains of bulgur are available in Middle Eastern and health food stores, this dish is a cinch to make. It is perfect with grilled poultry or meat.

Choosing a good winter squash is important. I've had success with banana squash, butternut, and especially the hybrid called red kuri. Also, remember that winter squashes are not actually grown in winter. They're called that because they're hard-shelled and thus can be easily stored to develop flavor and sweetness.

2 pounds banana, red-kuri, or butternut squash or pumpkin

¼ cup salt (not a mistake! see Note)

1 medium onion, diced

⅓ cup extra-virgin olive oil

1 cup large-grain bulgur

1½ tablespoons sugar

1 cup golden raisins

½ teaspoon ground Ceylon cinnamon

¼ teaspoon finely ground black pepper

1. Peel and finely dice the squash. You should have about 3 cups. In a bowl, toss the squash with the salt; let stand for 3 to 4 hours. Transfer to a large sieve, wash thoroughly, and let drain. Pat dry with kitchen toweling.

2. In a wide skillet, sauté the onion and squash in the olive oil until soft and golden. Meanwhile, place the bulgur in a fine sieve; shake to remove dust but do not wash. Add the bulgur and 1½ cups boiling water to the skillet, bring to a boil, stir once, cover the pan, lower the heat, and cook 20 minutes, or until all the liquid has been absorbed. Stir in the sugar, raisins, cinnamon, black pepper, and salt to taste. Remove from the heat and let stand 5 minutes before serving.

NOTE TO THE COOK: Pumpkin and winter squashes should be salted to draw out excess moisture and intensify flavor. Please don't skip this step. Remember to wash off all the salt before cooking the fruit.

TURKISH *HOSHAFS* AND *JAJIKS*

✦

Throughout Turkey and Greece, main-course pilafs, being relatively dry, are presented with moist accompaniments, similar to the way North African couscous is served with bowls of broth, Spanish paellas are accompanied by garlic mayonnaise, and numerous Indian dishes are accompanied by raitas.

In Turkey today these accompaniments might include: pickles; a glass of the thinned yogurt drink *ayran*; a peppery radish-type salad; a bowl of caramelized onions; or the yogurt-garlic dip called *jajik* (page 346) served in gaily colored vessels called *jajik* bowls.

Another popular accompaniment to pilafs, also served in *jajik* bowls, are *hoshafs*—sweetened compotes made with dried fruits, sour cherries, sour apricots, prunes, apples, pears, sour grapes, or cooked-down mallow leaf jam.

Pilafs aren't the only dishes that get this treatment. I ate a particularly delicious *hoshaf* in a home in the northern Turkish town of Edirne, where my hostess served me the local specialty, a rich cheese pie with a billowy phyllo pastry crust, accompanied by a golden raisin compote scented with rosewater. The mild brininess of the cheese and the sweet syrupy golden raisins made for a great combination. The following recipe includes an adaptation of that *hoshaf*, excellent for accompanying any number of bulgur pilafs.

ZELIHA GÜNGÖREN'S SCALLION BULGUR PILAF WITH GOLDEN RAISIN *HOSHAF* (*Turkey*)

❈

Serves 4 to 6 as a side dish

Make this dish in late spring when scallions are at their thickest, using only the white portion. It is excellent served with grilled fish and a spoonful of Golden Raisin *Hoshaf*.

2 tablespoons olive oil

1½ cups thinly sliced white part of very fat scallions

1 tablespoon tomato paste

1½ cups simmering water

1 teaspoon salt

¾ teaspoon Turkish red pepper (see "Mail-Order Sources") or a mixture of hot and sweet Hungarian paprika

¼ teaspoon freshly ground black pepper

1 cup coarse-grain bulgur

Golden Raisin *Hoshaf* (recipe follows)

1. In a saucepan, heat 1 tablespoon of the oil over medium heat, add the scallions, and fry, stirring often, until glazed and soft. Add the tomato paste and cook, stirring, 3 minutes over reduced heat. Add the simmering water. Bring to a boil, stir in the salt, ½ teaspoon of the red pepper, the black pepper, and the dry bulgur. Bring back to the boil, reduce the heat, cover, and cook until the bulgur absorbs all the liquid, 20 minutes. Place a double layer of paper toweling or a kitchen towel on the grains, replace the cover, remove from the heat, and let stand 10 minutes before transferring to a serving dish.

2. Heat the remaining tablespoon oil; add the remaining red pepper and let sizzle. Pour over the bulgur and serve.

GOLDEN RAISIN *HOSHAF* (*Turkey*)

Makes about 1 cup

1 cup sugar

2 cloves

1 cup golden raisins, washed

2 drops of lemon juice

⅓ teaspoon rosewater

Put the sugar, 1 cup water, and cloves in a saucepan and cook, stirring, until the sugar is dissolved. Remove the cloves, add the raisins, bring to a boil, and remove from the heat. Wait 2 minutes, then return to medium heat and bring back to the boil. Use a slotted spoon to transfer the raisins to a clean jar. Boil the syrup with the lemon juice for 2 minutes, then pour over the raisins. When cool add the rosewater and cover. Store in a cool place.

Bulgur Pilaf with Fresh Tomatoes, Thick Yogurt, and Fried Onion Strings (*Greece*)

❉

Serves 3 or 4

*I*n this pilaf, inspired by a soup created by chef Christoforos Veneris, who teaches cooking on the island of Crete, takes the dish one step further: freshly grated tomato is cooked down to the point where its natural sugars caramelize. Suddenly a workhorse dish is lifted far above the mundane.

"Onion strings," the traditional topping for many pilafs in the region, are simply long thin onion strands fried until golden.

1 cup plain yogurt

⅓ cup extra-virgin olive oil

1 medium onion, peeled, thinly sliced, and patted dry

1 medium onion, peeled and finely chopped

2 large red ripe tomatoes, halved, seeded, and grated on a coarse grater

1 cup large-grain bulgur

1½ scant cups boiling chicken, vegetable, or meat stock

Salt

¼ teaspoon freshly ground black pepper

Pinch of red pepper

1. Drain the yogurt in a cheesecloth-lined sieve (½ cup).

2. Heat half the oil in a 9- or 10-inch skillet. Add the sliced onions to the skillet; cook over medium heat, stirring often until golden, about 10 minutes.

Tilt the skillet to separate oil from onions and with a slotted spoon, remove the onions and set aside to cool. Add the chopped onions to the skillet and cook, stirring, over medium-low heat until golden. Add the tomato pulp and cook, stirring, until thick and lightly caramelized, about 10 minutes. Add the bulgur to the skillet and continue stirring for an instant. Then add the heated stock, salt, and black and red peppers, mixing well. Cover and cook at a simmer over low heat until all the liquid has been absorbed, about 20 minutes.

3. Remove the skillet from the heat, stir in the remaining olive oil, and place a folded kitchen towel over the pilaf. Cover tightly and set in a warm place for 15 minutes, or until the bulgur is completely swollen. Serve warm with a dollop of yogurt and garnish with reserved onion strings.

LEAFY GREENS

HORTA

Greeks and Cypriots eat a dish called *horta*, a bowl of greens par excellence—simply boiled greens dressed with vinegar or lemon juice and best-quality olive oil. Some cooks will add a little *rigani* (a type of oregano) or thicken the greens with some grated zucchini or garnish them with a few crumbles of briny feta cheese, but no matter the variation the dish retains its elegant simplicity.

Horta is also a generic term used to describe a mix of bitter, tangy, sharp, or mild edible wild greens of the Grecian countryside in their raw state. Since these greens are wild, one cannot always count on finding a specific mix. Some *horta* mixes are truly superb. Nettles, spinach, and wild chard, for example, is a great combination not only for a dish of *horta* but also for stuffing pies and for use in soups and pilafs. Other mixtures might include three or more of the following: very young dandelion, wild fennel, arugula, mustard, chicory, nettles, radish sprouts, pea shoots, escarole, curly endive, spinach, lamb's-quarters, and amaranth.

In a typical household in the countryside on the island of Crete, a simply dressed bowl of *horta* might well be served every day.

AUTUMN *HORTA* WITH EDIBLE CHRYSANTHEMUM, VINEGAR, AND OLIVE OIL (Greece)

Serves 4

On a recent visit to Crete, I tasted an aromatic green incredibly pure in flavor, tasting a little like a spicy asparagus but with far more bouquet. It took me a while to realize that this was the same dark green used in chop suey served in Chinese restaurants in Brooklyn when I was a kid. It's called crown daisy, or garland chrysanthemum, and is readily available in Asian markets; ask for *tun ho* or *shunkiyu*.

Joy Larkcom, writing in her definitive book, *Oriental Vegetables*, explains the connection between the humble chop suey greens and the Mediterranean:

> The edible chrysanthemum (*Chrysanthemum coronarium*) originated in the Mediterranean, spreading throughout Europe and into Africa and Asia, often becoming naturalized in the wild. Strangely it has only been adopted as a vegetable in China, Japan and south-east Asia. In the West it is grown as an annual garden chrysanthemum.

In the eastern Mediterranean there are two types of edible chrysanthemum: the fresh young leaves of the crown daisy and a look-alike called corn marigold (*Chrysanthemum segetum*). To cook these young leaves, boil for 10 minutes, then stir into soups or stews at the last minute, or cool and fold into thick yogurt or a strong vinegar–olive oil dressing.

Serve the following bowl of greens as a side dish or part of a large-scale mezze table.

2 pounds young edible chrysanthemum leaves, unsprayed

2 tablespoons mild red wine vinegar or fresh lemon juice, or more to taste

4 to 5 tablespoons extra-virgin olive oil

Sea salt

Freshly ground black pepper

1. Discard the long stems as well as old, yellowed, or thick leaves. Wash the greens well until the water is clear. Cook, uncovered, in boiling salted water until leaves are just tender, about 10 minutes. Do not overcook. Leave them to drain on a slanted wooden board in the sink, or in a colander. Press down with a spatula to extract excess moisture and roughly chop.

2. Place in a serving dish; use a fork to loosen the leaves and dress with a well-beaten mixture of the vinegar or lemon juice, oil, salt, and pepper. Serve warm or at room temperature.

TENDER GREENS AND SHEEP'S MILK CHEESE

❁

Serves 3 to 4

In late spring Greeks make delicious *hortas* with garden greens and seasonal cheese. One of my favorites is a combination of amaranth and sheep's milk cheese. Delicious and healthful amaranth, which often grows spontaneously in gardens, is readily available in Asian markets. Ask for Chinese spinach.

Finely grated Greek sheep's milk cheeses such as sharp, salty *kefalotyri* and mild, smooth *kasseri* melt beautifully when mixed into a bowl of freshly cooked leafy greens. If these cheeses are not available, substitute any other good-quality sheep's milk cheese from your local cheese store.

Serve as a part of a mezze or as an accompaniment to grilled lamb.

1 pound young garden greens such as amaranth or lamb's-quarters, or a piquant salad mix of arugula, mustard, cress, curly endive, and radish sprouts

A few lovage leaves if available (optional)

Sea salt

1 cup meat or chicken stock

2 to 4 tablespoons freshly grated sharp sheep's milk cheese such as *kefalotyri*

2 to 3 tablespoons freshly grated mild sheep's milk cheese such as *kasseri*

2 tablespoons Greek extra-virgin olive oil

Freshly ground black pepper

1. Wash the greens and remove all wilted or bruised leaves and hard stems. Rub with 3 teaspoons salt and let stand at least 30 minutes. Wash in several changes of water to remove all salt; cut away any thick stems. You should have about 4 cups.

2. Bring 1½ cups water and the stock to a boil, add the greens, and cook until tender, about 10 minutes. Drain and immediately mix with half the cheese and the olive oil. Depending upon the flavor of the greens add more cheese as needed. Correct the seasoning with salt and pepper. Serve warm.

MIXED GREENS WITH GARLIC AND BALSAMIC VINEGAR (*Italy*)

Here's an Italian variation on the Greek *horta* dish above.

When making your own greens mixtures, keep in mind the following categories: sweet-tasting greens such as nettles, chard, borage, and spinach; tart-flavored greens such as sorrel; pungent-flavored greens such as mustard; and bitter-tasting greens such as escarole.

4 types of young leafy greens (see page 288)

2 tablespoons extra-virgin olive oil

1 clove garlic, peeled and minced

1 tablespoon good-quality balsamic vinegar

Salt

Freshly ground black pepper

1. Wash, drain, stem, and roughly shred the greens.

2. In a wide skillet, heat the oil and add the greens; sauté until softened. Stir in the garlic and vinegar and cook, covered, for 2 minutes. Remove from heat and serve hot or warm.

"DRAGGED" GREENS WITH POTATO, GARLIC, PEPERONCINO, AND ROSEMARY (*Italy*)

Serves 2

Use all kinds of leafy greens in this dish, the more variety the better," urges Beatrice Evans, coauthor with her husband of *La Cucina Picena*, a terrific book about the cooking of the Italian Marches. When I ask her to name a few, she replies, "Chard, the leaves of broccoli rabe, corn poppy, spinach, cress, and you can also use the braising mix at the supermarket." *(continued)*

Along with the greens, potatoes in their skins are added to the boiling water. Keep the greens submerged while boiling so they don't lose color. When cooked, the greens and potatoes are drained, the moisture is pressed out, the greens are shredded and spread out on a wide wooden board to cool down, the potatoes are peeled, both greens and potatoes are crushed together, then the mix is cooked with pancetta, rosemary, garlic, and red pepper for a few minutes over a hot fire. The result is a fabulous vegetable "hash."

Serve this dish with salami and ham slices, or alone as a light meal. Or add some eggs and turn it into a frittata.

1 pound mixed leafy winter/spring greens (see suggestions above), or 1 bunch broccoli rabe, hard stems removed

1 medium boiling potato, preferably Yukon Gold, unskinned (about ⅓ pound)

Salt

2 tablespoons extra-virgin olive oil

1¾ ounces very lean pancetta, rinsed, patted dry, and finely shredded to make about ¼ cup

1 teaspoon fresh rosemary or more to taste

½ teaspoon minced garlic

Pinch of red pepper

Freshly ground black pepper

Pickled green peppers for garnish

1. Bring a large saucepan of water to a rapid boil. Meanwhile strip the greens and discard the stems and any tough parts, then wash the leaves in several changes of water. If using broccoli rabe, cut into 1-inch chunks to make about 10 cups. Add salt to the water, then add the greens and potato and cook until both are tender, about 10 minutes. Drain in a colander; press on the greens to express moisture. When the potato is cool enough to handle, peel and crush it with 1 teaspoon of the olive oil with the back of a fork. Finely chop the greens, or crush the broccoli raab with the back of a fork.

2. Heat the remaining olive oil and pancetta in an 8-inch nonstick skillet and cook very gently until the pancetta melts or at least becomes softened. Add the rosemary, garlic, red pepper, greens, and potato and cook over medium-high heat, turning the contents often with a spatula, so they blend as they are "dragged" through the oil, about 5 minutes. Season with salt and pepper. Serve hot with a sprinkling of coarse salt and freshly milled pepper on top. Pass a dish of pickled peppers.

Best-Ever *Bugulama* (Turkey)

Makes about 6 cups

*B*ugulama is the Turkish word for steamed food. In this "best-ever" preparation of greens and bulgur, the water content of the chopped young greens is used to moisten and flavor large-grain bulgur . . . with a little help from such friends as red pepper, onion, and a load of garlic. The ingredients are very well mixed. Some cooks even knead the bulgur with the greens before cooking to get the vegetable-flavored moisture into the grain as soon as possible. The whole mixture is cooked, covered, over very low heat, then served hot or cold.

Certain greens will make for a distinct and intensely flavorful *bugulama*, while others will only impart blandness. The trick is to know which greens to use. Puckerish young grape vine leaves (stemmed) have little moisture but will impart a vibrant tart flavor that I find very appealing. A wild edible such as corn poppy, which you can grow from seed and harvest *before* it flowers, will impart a sweet buttery flavor with undertones of hazelnut. In southeastern Turkey, it's the green of choice for this dish.

I use Russian kale. When cooked, its thin leaves literally melt into the bulgur. Other greens that work well are Swiss chard, beet, and turnip greens.

Originally, this was a dish for poor people, who would roll it in a thick doughy round of flatbread called a *dürüm*. In recent years it's become rather fashionable in southeastern Turkey, where it's served as a side or lunch dish sometimes wrapped in thin warm bread.

In traditional Turkish cooking, many bulgur dishes were served with fruit compotes or what were called "sweet soups." Others were served with yogurt or yogurt soups. When I first tasted the tart vine leaf version of *bugulama*, I felt a craving for something sweet. Perhaps this is why raisins or currants are often added to stuffed vine leaf dishes. When I retested the dish I served it accompanied by a plate of lightly sugared, poached dried apricots. The combination was delicious.

(continued)

1 head of garlic, peeled and finely crushed with 1 teaspoon salt

1 pound onions, peeled and finely chopped

1 pound Russian kale, Swiss chard, beet and turnip greens, or blend of sweet and bitter greens, washed, stemmed, and finely slivered

1 cup coarse-grain bulgur

4 tablespoons olive oil

2 to 3 teaspoons Turkish or homemade pepper paste (page 344)

½ teaspoon freshly ground black pepper

¼ teaspoon Turkish red pepper flakes or more to taste (see "Mail-Order Sources")

Salt

Fresh scallions, roots trimmed and curled, for garnish

Lemon wedges

Variation: BEST-EVER BUGULAMA WITH BITTER GREENS

Some Turkish cooks, especially in the village of Nizip on the Euphrates, prefer bitter greens, such as dandelions or young chicory, in their *bugulama*. If you want to take that route, don't add the onions to the mixture. Rather, slice them thin, fry until golden brown and sweet, then sprinkle over the bulgur and greens just before serving.

Since bitter greens are soaked in water to remove their bitterness, they have a high water content. Therefore you won't need more than ⅓ cup water to execute this recipe. Bitter greens such as dandelion or young chicory should be torn into pieces, placed in a bowl of cold water mixed with coarse salt, then left for an hour. Drain, rinse, and finely shred before using.

In a large deep saucepan, combine the garlic, onions, greens, bulgur, olive oil, pepper paste, black and red peppers, and salt to taste. Work in ½ cup water until well absorbed. Lay a sheet of paper toweling over the mixture, cover the pan, and set over medium-low heat to steam for 30 minutes. Serve hot or cold garnished with scallions and lemon.

With thanks to Mrs. Gülay Karsligil of Gaziantep.

PICKING MALLOW LEAVES

❖

Mallow, called *khobbeiza* throughout the Middle Eastern and North African worlds (except in Morocco, where it's called *beqquoula*), has a soft creamy quality similar to okra when cooked. It's such an outstanding culinary green, and so rampant in gardens everywhere in the United States, that it's worth learning how to recognize it and pick it.

Though no members of the malva family are known to be poisonous, some are definitely tastier than others. My suggestion is to seek the advice of someone in your area well versed in wild edible greens.

Picking shiny, wavy mallow leaves and tender shoots isn't difficult. Pick only the tender leaves that grow on stems no taller than 12 inches; leaves on larger and longer stems will be too tough. Avoid blemished leaves and leaves that have yellowed. As for mallow shoots, cut into them to see if they're white at their centers. If so, the shoots will be dry and tough. As soon as mallow plants flower, the leaves lose their flavor.

Mallow leaves should be carefully stemmed, since it's the stems that can make a dish gooey. And remember that these greens should not be cooked in the usual quick stir-fry fashion but are best treated with steaming.

Mallow Leaves with Tunisian Spices (*Tunisia*)

❀

Serves 5 or 6

Tunisian cooks tell me there are three steps to making a great bowl of *khobbeiza* (mallow greens): steam the leaves; pound them; beat the greens with oil and hot water until they turn creamy. When spices are added, the dish becomes extraordinary.

It's delicious with a piece of Dense Semolina Bread (page 14) or Quick Flaky Semolina Bread (page 17).

---

2 quarts stemmed young mallow leaves (about ¾ pound) or miner's lettuce (winter purslane), purslane, chard, or beet greens, well washed

3 large cloves garlic, unpeeled

Salt

½ teaspoon homemade *harissa* (page 343) or Turkish pepper paste (see "Mail-Order Sources")

¾ teaspoon ground coriander

⅔ teaspoon ground caraway seeds

2 tablespoons extra-virgin olive oil

1 tablespoon lemon juice

---

1. Steam the trimmed greens and garlic cloves until tender. Press out all the moisture.

2. Peel the garlic.

3. Combine the garlic, greens, salt, *harissa*, and spices in the work bowl of a food processor. With the machine running, add the olive oil and just enough hot water to make the mixture slightly soupy—for dunking Dense Semolina Bread (page 14). Correct the seasoning and add lemon juice to taste.

STEWED GREENS WITH BASTURMA CHIPS

❧

Serves 4

My favorite basturma, spicy preserved meat, comes from New Jersey and is available by mail order. Many Middle Eastern shops sell it thinly sliced. Since recipes call for only a small amount, freeze the remaining slices. Armenians and Turks serve it sliced with slivers of orange peel and scrambled eggs for breakfast, or with a wedge of lemon and a shot of raki as a mezze. Personally, I like it best when used as a flavoring in, for example, the Parsley, Basturma, and Kasseri *Börek* (page 53), the Kayserie-Style Pan-Grilled Grape Leaves Stuffed with Basturma, Parsley, and Orange (page 117); and in this stewed greens recipe.

It was in Gaziantep from Turkish home cook Kezban Yavuz that I learned to make this dish, using rehydrated dried and crumbled madimak leaves that Kezban had collected and dried the preceding spring. Working up a recipe of my own, I substituted young turnip greens, spinach, beet greens, purslane, chard, or a combination of the above for the wild edible madimak so beloved in Turkey. Serve as a side dish or first course.

1½ tablespoons extra-virgin olive oil

3 tablespoons basturma (available at Middle Eastern groceries)

½ cup chopped onion

1½ pounds fresh leafy greens (see above), stemmed and finely shredded

2 tablespoons tomato paste

3 tablespoons fine-grain bulgur

½ teaspoon ground fenugreek

1 cup vegetable, meat, or poultry stock

Yogurt-Garlic Sauce (page 346)

Fried or grilled hot green chilies for garnish

Heat the olive oil in a deep saucepan and sauté the basturma until aromatic and softened. Add the onion and cook another minute. Stir in the greens, tomato paste, bulgur, fenugreek, and stock and cook, covered, 20 minutes. Serve with a bowl of yogurt-garlic sauce, some grilled green peppers, and flatbread.

DRIED GREENS

❖

*I*n northern Greece I met cooks who dried spinach, sorrel, chard, and mustard greens for use in their winter pies. When they wanted to use these dried greens (which are usually very intense in flavor), they poured boiling water over the leaves, drained them, then simmered them, or just crumbled them into soups.

For all my efforts I was never successful making a dish called *avloukia* as described to me in the northern Greek town of Veria. In this dish, dried sorrel greens are rehydrated, simmered, then whipped with garlic and oil to make a kind of "black caviar." To paraphrase Senator Lloyd Bentsen's comment to vice presidential candidate Dan Quayle in their famous 1988 debate: "You, sir, are no kind of caviar!"

Despite its very thick leaves and stems, green early summer purslane is dried by Turks for use in soups, and yellow late summer purslane is dried for use in winter pilafs. Turkish cooks tell me that dried and rehydrated purslane is even more delicious than purslane that's been freshly cooked.

A friend who was sailing around the Peloponnese told me that in late winter in the village of Kyparissi, in southeastern Greece, people gather, dry, and smoke wild bitter greens to use in summer, when, on account of the dry weather, there aren't any fresh wild greens to be found. He tasted these boiled smoked greens and found them delicious.

◆

LEAFY MIXED GREENS FLAVORED WITH LAMB (*Turkey*)

❧

Serves 4 to 6

*I*n spring in the northwestern Turkish village of Sivas, women pick seven kinds of wild greens (mallow, sorrel, nettles, shepherd's needle, purslane, salsify tops, and lamb's-quarters), which they wash, shred into large pieces, then sauté in a mixture of butter and oil in which ground meat, onion, red pepper, tomato paste, and salt have previously been cooked. Sometimes a little rice or bulgur is added as well.

The resulting country dish isn't a pilaf or stew; it's just a bowl of greens—a *yemek* (which, literally, means simply "food")—served with bread for dunking. Or better yet, it can be a good first course before grilled or roasted kabobs.

3 quarts mixed greens: a good mix might be ½ quart young mustard greens, ½ quart fresh flat-leaf spinach, 1 quart miner's lettuce or chard, and 1 quart arugula leaves

1 tablespoon olive oil

½ cup chopped onion

5 ounces lean ground lamb

½ tablespoon tomato paste

¼ teaspoon freshly ground black pepper

¼ teaspoon ground allspice

Salt

2 tablespoons medium- or long-grain rice

1. Trim all the greens and discard any yellowed leaves. Wash the greens well, then place in a deep pot with ½ cup lightly salted water. Cover and cook over low heat for 5 minutes. Drain, reserving 1 cup of the cooking water (if necessary, add water to make 1 cup). Allow the greens to cool, then squeeze out excess moisture. Roughly chop the greens to make about 3 cups.

2. Heat the oil in a large heavy skillet, add the onion, and sauté until soft over moderate heat, about 2 minutes. Add the lamb and cook, breaking up the meat with a fork, until lightly browned, about 3 minutes. Add the tomato paste, pepper, allspice, and salt to taste. Cook, stirring, 2 to 3 minutes.

3. Stir in the chopped greens, reserved cooking liquor, and the rice. Reduce the heat to low and simmer, covered, until all the rice is fully cooked. Adjust the seasoning with salt and pepper. Serve warm.

GREENS WITH GOLDEN RAISINS, PINE NUTS, AND SHERRY VINEGAR (*Spain*)

Serves 6

2 tablespoons olive oil

1 pound thinly sliced red onions

1 clove garlic, peeled and bruised

1 pound young spinach or tender Swiss chard

1 anchovy fillet, rinsed and cut into small pieces

⅓ cup pine nuts

⅓ cup golden raisins, soaked 10 minutes in hot water and drained

2 teaspoons sherry wine vinegar

1 teaspoon sugar

Freshly ground black pepper

Though this delightful dish is well known, I include it here because it's a personal favorite.

You can use either spinach or Swiss chard. The dish makes a perfect first course or side dish adorned with crisp triangles of grilled or fried garlic-rubbed bread.

1. In a 12-inch straight-sided skillet, heat the oil. Add the red onions and garlic and cook, covered, until all the moisture has evaporated and the onions begin to caramelize, about 20 minutes. Meanwhile, wash and stem the greens, drop into salted boiling water, and cook 2 minutes. Drain well and shred.

2. Add the anchovy fillet to the skillet and sauté, crushing to a purée. Lightly brown the pine nuts; then add the raisins, the greens, vinegar, sugar, and pepper and cook, covered, until the greens are tender, 5 to 10 minutes. Serve warm.

Swiss Chard

Recently I asked a number of American friends which leafy green they thought was most popular around the Mediterranean. Almost everyone chose spinach. In fact, the answer is Swiss chard, possibly because it's gentler, softer, and can resist more heat, an important factor in warm Mediterranean countries. Also, of course, it's easy to clean and one of the best greens to use as a base for an intriguing greens mixture, as well as being excellent when served alone.

There are two primary types of Swiss chard: the big crinkly kind with thick crunchy stalks, and the finer kind with small smooth-textured leaves sprouting from thin stems. If you have a kitchen garden, you can get excellent Swiss chard seeds, including those for a tasty French variety called Paros, which bears delicious stalks and leaves.

Young Mustard Greens with Pomegranate Molasses (*Syria–Lebanon*)

Serves 2

In this Syrian-Lebanese dish, mustard greens, probably the strongest flavored of all Mediterranean greens, are tempered with the sweet and sour flavor of pomegranate molasses.

4 cups mustard greens or young dandelion leaves

2 tablespoons olive oil

1 clove garlic, sliced

1 teaspoon pomegranate molasses diluted in 2 tablespoons water

Salt

Freshly ground black pepper

1. Set a large of quantity of water to boil.

2. Wash and stem the mustard greens; drop into boiling salted water and cook 2 minutes. Drain well.

3. Heat the olive oil in a wide skillet, add the garlic, and cook, stirring, for 30 seconds. Add the greens and cook until tender. Stir in the diluted pomegranate molasses and boil for an instant. Taste for salt and pepper, and serve warm as a side dish.

WILD GREENS AL POMODORO (*Italy*)

Serves 4

*I*nspired by an Apulian recipe that calls for wild chard stewed with tomatoes and garlic, I've substituted a combination of curly endive, beet greens, and Swiss chard—a combination neither too bitter nor too harsh, full of flavor, and tasting of the earth. The curly endive is quite bitter when raw but when cooked becomes an excellent blending green . . . as does the broadleaf variety, which may also be used.

In winter, when fresh tomatoes are out of season, I recommend Muir Glen canned organic tomatoes for best flavor.

2 medium-size curly or broadleaf endives

4 large Swiss chard leaves

Handful of beet greens

2 tablespoons olive oil

1 clove garlic, peeled and sliced

1 small dried red pepper, crumbled

2 medium red ripe tomatoes, peeled, seeded, and chopped (¾ cup)

Sea salt

1 bay leaf

1. Cut out the core of the endives and stem the chard and beet greens, if using. Wash the greens in several changes of water, shake off excess water, and set on a flat plate until ready to cook.

2. Heat the olive oil in a medium-size skillet and sauté the garlic with the crumbled red pepper for 30 seconds. Add the tomatoes, a pinch of salt, and the bay leaf and cook over medium heat for 10 minutes. Add the still wet greens and continue cooking over very low heat until tender, about 10 minutes. Serve warm.

PROVENÇAL TIAN WITH CREAMED SPINACH (France)

Serves 6

Christopher Lee, chef at Chez Panisse in Berkeley, California, gave me this terrific recipe, which combines hand-chopped young spinach with lots of stewed onions, enriched with a creamy béchamel-style sauce. The result: one of the most luxurious presentations for a bowl of spinach. Christopher serves his version in a pastry shell; I bake and serve mine in an earthenware pan called a tian.

Serve as a first course or as a side dish with roasted chicken.

4 quarts young flat-leaf, stemmed spinach leaves

5 tablespoons butter

3 cups chopped onions

1½ cloves garlic

Salt

Freshly ground black pepper

1½ tablespoons flour

1 cup milk, heated

Grated nutmeg

¼ cup grated bread crumbs

1 teaspoon olive oil

1. Wash the spinach thoroughly; discard the stems and bruised leaves and drain in a colander.

2. Heat 3 tablespoons butter in a 12-inch saucepan until bubbling. Add the onions and cook, covered, over medium heat for 10 minutes. Meanwhile, roughly chop the spinach.

3. When the onions are soft but not brown, stir in the spinach, garlic, and salt and pepper to taste. Raise the heat a little and cook for 10 minutes while stirring, until the spinach has expressed its moisture and is very liquidy. Cover the skillet, tip the pan, and drain the liquid into another pan. Reduce the liquid to one-half and reserve.

4. Melt 2 tablespoons butter in a heavy saucepan. Stir in the flour and cook for 1 minute without browning. Pour in the reduced liquid and stir vigorously with a wooden spoon until the mixture is creamy and smooth. Gradually stir in the hot milk and nutmeg, and bring to a boil, stirring.

5. Preheat the oven to 375 degrees.

6. Place the spinach in an oiled 10-inch earthenware cazuela or tian, sprinkle with bread crumbs, and drizzle with oil. Bake for 20 minutes, until the crumbs are browned and the tian is bubbling. Cool for 15 minutes and serve warm.

TENDER YOUNG GREENS
WITH TOMATO AND ONION (*Greece*)

Serves 4

This very simple, uncluttered dish is terrific stuffed into warm pita bread or simply spread on a shallow plate as an accompaniment to grilled or panfried fish.

For this dish I prefer pea shoots that are no longer dewy and young, available at Asian and upscale food markets. I don't mean old tired shoots, just shoots that aren't too fragile, so they can take a decent amount of cooking. It is also good with baby spinach, orache, baby beet greens, or any other young green.

1 quart stemmed pea shoots or a mixture of tender greens: baby spinach, orache, baby beet greens, lamb's-quarters, miner's lettuce

Sea salt

2 tablespoons extra-virgin olive oil

½ cup minced onion

2 cloves garlic, peeled and minced

½ teaspoon dried spearmint

½ teaspoon dried Mediterranean oregano or *herbes de Provence*

⅛ teaspoon hot paprika or more to taste

1 medium red ripe tomato, peeled, seeded, and chopped

1. Wash and coarsely slice the greens. Place still wet in a covered skillet with a pinch of salt and steam until tender, about 2 minutes. Transfer to a side dish.

2. Heat the olive oil in a medium-size skillet. Add the onion, garlic, and dried herbs; sauté until the onion is soft, about 2 minutes. Add the paprika, tomato, and greens and cook until the greens are well combined with the seasonings, stirring often. Allow to cool to room temperature and correct the seasoning.

Variation: PEA SHOOTS WITH TOMATO AND EGG (*Turkey*)

Serves 1 as a quick lunch

¾ pound pea shoots

2½ teaspoons olive oil

1 small onion, peeled and grated

½ teaspoon tomato paste

1 farm fresh egg

Salt

Freshly ground black pepper

1. Wash and coarsely chop the pea shoots. Put in a skillet while still wet with 1 teaspoon of the olive oil and sauté until wilted. Remove to a side dish.

2. Sauté the onion in the remaining 1½ teaspoons oil until golden. Stir in the tomato paste and the chopped greens and cook another minute. Break in the egg and scramble until just set. Season with salt and pepper, stuff into warm pita, and serve at once.

SICILIAN SQUASH TENDRILS

On a recent trip to Sicily, which took place during late summer, a Sicilian friend advised me, "Be sure to try soup with *tenerumi*."

Tenerumi, which in Sicilian literally means "rags," are the side shoots of a kind of huge vine zucchini with a rather nondescript flavor. The buds, tendrils, and curly tips are used along with garlic, tomatoes, and broken pasta in a soup I can only describe as bland. In fact, Sicilians will tell you with great enthusiasm how refreshing and light it is, with, they add, so little flavor that after they've finished off a bowl they barely remember having eaten it! To which I say that there must be something in the collective unconscious of Sicilians that makes them so fond of this ever-so-subtle soup.

Since I found the dish so tasteless, I wasn't too interested in pursuing it. Then I came across a recipe in Giuseppe Coria's excellent and exhaustive *Profumi di Sicilia* in which he uses a huge amount of these same tendrils to produce a thick bowl of greens. Coria describes discovering that if you finely chop these greens, boil them until just al dente, then finish them off in a light tomato sauce, they make a quite wonderful *contorno* or vegetable accompaniment.

I tried his recipe and was thrilled with the result. In his dish I was at last able to appreciate the soft, velvety texture of *tenerumi*, due, no doubt, to their sheer density and the fact that the dish is best served at room temperature, generously drizzled with heady olive oil. Since then I have served it as a dip for bread, as part of an antipasto, and as an accompaniment to veal, poultry, and fish. In fact, I've decided that the dish is not only tasty enough to be remembered but even tasty enough to be enjoyed!

I purchased my first bunches of *tenerumi* at the Union Square Greenmarket in New York, where a few farmers carry it in late summer. If you have a kitchen garden, Shepherd's sells the seeds under the name *Zucchetto Rampicante* (see "Mail-Order Sources").

BRAISED CABBAGE WITH GLAZED ONIONS AND SAUTÉED MUSHROOMS (France)

❀

Serves 4 to 6

leave out pancetta — don't like the aftertaste at all

Cabbage is a vegetable flattered by every method of cooking. Whether flash-cooked, well-cooked, or overcooked it's always delicious. In this excellent ragout, the cabbage is "cooked to death," turning meltingly soft while losing its original color. No matter! When it's smothered with sautéed mushrooms and glazed onions, you won't notice how brown it is.

This delicious side dish goes well with a bowl of steaming polenta and is terrific with grilled pork chops.

1. In a small dutch oven heat 1 tablespoon of the oil, add the aromatics and the sliced onion, cover, and let sweat for 5 minutes. Add the wedges of cabbage, salt, ½ teaspoon of the sugar, ½ cup of the stock, and the white wine and cook, covered with parchment paper and a lid, over low heat for 1 hour. (This can also be cooked in a 300-degree oven.)

2. Meanwhile, sauté the pancetta in another tablespoon of oil in a 9-inch skillet over medium heat until nicely browned, adding spoonfuls of stock whenever necessary to keep the slivers moist. Add the small onions, the remaining ½ teaspoon sugar, another ½ cup stock, salt, and pepper and cook, covered, for 30 minutes. Continue cooking the onions, uncovered, until well glazed and brown. Add to the cabbage, cover, and continue cooking over low heat.

3 tablespoons olive oil

AROMATICS

1 bay leaf

1 clove garlic

5 sprigs thyme

1 onion, thinly sliced

2 pounds cabbage, washed, bruised leaves removed, cored, and cut into 2-inch wedges

½ teaspoon salt

1 teaspoon sugar

1½ cups chicken, meat, or vegetable stock

⅓ cup dry white wine

1½ ounces pancetta, slivered

12 small red or white pickling onions, trimmed, blanched and peeled

Freshly ground black pepper

½ pound assorted fresh mushrooms (oyster, hedgehog, cremini), cleaned and thickly sliced

2 cloves garlic, finely chopped

2 tablespoons chopped flat-leaf parsley

Sprig of thyme

3. Add the remaining tablespoon olive oil to the skillet and slowly sauté the mushrooms and garlic, adding spoonfuls of stock to keep the skillet moist, 20 minutes. Stir in 1 tablespoon of the parsley and the thyme sprig and cook for 2 to 3 minutes. Pour the mushrooms over the onions and cabbage, cover, and cook until the cabbage is meltingly tender. Correct the seasoning with salt and pepper. Tip the contents of the dutch oven into a shallow serving dish, boil down any pan juices, and pour over the vegetables; sprinkle with the remaining parsley and serve.

POTATO CAKE STUFFED WITH TUSCAN KALE AND TALEGGIO CHEESE (*Italy*)

Serves 4

This delicious rustic "cake," excellent with roast lamb, is similar to the leek and potato pie in my book *The Cooking of South-West France*. Here, stuffed between the outer layers of crusty potato shreds, is a lovely soft mixture of cooked Tuscan kale and melted cheese.

Though I think Tuscan kale (see page 173) makes the best stuffing, you can use any green or mixture of greens.

1 pound Tuscan kale, 2 dozen 12-inch long leaves or 4 dozen 6-inch long leaves

Sea salt

1 clove garlic, chopped

Freshly ground black pepper

1 pound boiling potatoes

1 tablespoon white vinegar (optional)

Extra virgin olive oil

5 ounces sliced semisoft cheese such as imported Taleggio, Fiore Sardo, or Fontina

1. Wash and stem the kale. Cook in boiling salted water until just tender, about 10 minutes; drain. When cool, coarsely chop. Season with salt and pepper and mix in the garlic. (If desired, you can stew the greens after parboiling in some olive oil to make it even richer in texture.)

2. Meanwhile, peel and shred the potatoes, easily done using the fine julienne blade fitted over the work bowl of a food processor. Rinse the potatoes in several changes of water; drain. To keep the potatoes for up to a half hour, store in vinegared water to keep them from turning brown. Rinse and drain well before using. *(continued)*

3. Twenty-five minutes before serving, heat the olive oil in a 9-inch seasoned or nonstick skillet. Spread half the potatoes to cover the bottom of the skillet. Spread half the kale over the potatoes, leaving a 1-inch margin around the edge. Spread the cheese over the kale and cover with the remaining kale and potatoes. Pat to form a compact cake. Cover and cook 5 minutes over medium heat, shaking pan often to keep potatoes from sticking. Lift the cover off to allow steam to escape. Wipe the inside of the lid dry. Cover and cook 5 minutes longer, shaking the skillet.

4. Tilt the skillet and spoon off any excess oil; reserve. Invert the potato cake onto the lid. Return the oil to the skillet and reheat; slide the potato cake back into the skillet, browned side up. Continue cooking, uncovered, over medium-low heat 10 to 15 minutes or until the potatoes are tender and browned. Slide onto a serving dish, sprinkle with coarse salt, and serve at once, cutting the cake into wedges.

SORREL, SPINACH, AND ARTICHOKE RAGOUT (France)

❀

Serves 4

Plum-sized artichokes weighing less than 1¼ ounces each are available in the spring. Young enough to be eaten whole, because they don't have a formed choke, these baby artichokes are simmered with extra-virgin olive oil, sliced onion, garlic, carrot, cubed lardons, and a dash of dry white wine in a tightly closed earthenware pot. When the artichokes are half cooked, heaps of shredded sorrel and spinach are piled on top, and the cooking continues until the artichokes are fork tender. The reduced rich green sauce has a definite tartness with a hint of anise, and the artichokes develop a delicate almost sweet flavor.

If medium-size artichokes are substituted, they will have to be quartered, hollowed out, and very well trimmed.

Serve as a first course or as a side dish.

24 baby artichokes (about 1½ pounds; see Notes)

3 tablespoons lemon juice

3 tablespoons extra-virgin olive oil

1 cup thinly sliced onions

⅔ cup thinly sliced carrots

½ cup (2 ounces) diced fatback or salt pork, blanched 5 minutes, drained, rinsed, and patted dry (see Notes)

5 whole cloves garlic, peeled

3 tablespoons dry white wine

Salt

Freshly ground black pepper

8 ounces young spinach leaves, stemmed

4 to 8 ounces sorrel leaves, depending upon the strength of the sorrel

2 tablespoons finely chopped dill, chervil, or tarragon

1. Slice off the tips of the leaves of each artichoke, trim the stem, and pull away two or three layers of thick leaves until you reach the tender ones. Soak in acidulated water until ready to use.

2. Gently heat the olive oil in an enameled-lined casserole, earthen *daubière*, or *cazuela*. Add the onions and allow to turn golden. Stir in the carrots, *lardons*, and garlic and sauté gently for 5 minutes. Add the white wine and boil down to a glaze.

Arrange the drained artichokes, side by side, over the vegetables, sprinkle with a few pinches of salt and pepper, cover with a sheet of crumbled wet parchment and a lid, and cook over low heat until artichokes are almost tender but still resistant to the prongs of a fork, about 45 minutes.

3. Meanwhile, wash the leafy greens in several changes of water. Remove and discard all the stems and yellowed and blemished pieces. Roll the leaves and cut into ½-inch-wide ribbons. Makes 6 to 8 cups.

4. Spread the shredded greens and 1 tablespoon of the chopped herbs over the artichokes; cover the pan and cook over low heat until the artichokes are meltingly tender and the rich green-hued sauce is well reduced, about 45 minutes more. Place the artichokes and sauce on a warmed serving dish and top with the remaining chopped herbs.

NOTES TO THE COOK: To substitute 4 to 6 medium artichokes, remove the hard, outer leaves of each artichoke, cut off the stalk and tops, and trim off all hard green parts around the base. Halve each artichoke and use a melon scoop to remove the pink leaves and the choke. Scape away any fibrous and prickly material. Wash artichokes; rub all cut surfaces with lemon, then soak in cool acidulated water (1 quart of water to the juice of 1 lemon) until the leaves soften, 10 minutes. Drain well before adding to the pan. Add 20 to 30 minutes cooking time in step 2.

Pancetta, if substituted for the fatback, does not need to be blanched.

PROVENÇAL BRAISED CELERY HEARTS WITH SCALLIONS (*France*)

❁

Serves 4 as a side dish

*T*his excellent approach to celery hearts requires time spent at the stove but is actually not all that much trouble. The recipe, an old one from southwest France, is adapted from one of my favorite French cookbooks, André Marty's *Fourmiguetto: Souvenirs, Contes et Recettes du Languedoc*. The cooking method allows you to skip blanching. By just cooking a little longer than usual, your celery hearts will come out meltingly tender.

This dish is excellent with grilled or roast chicken or meat.

2 celery hearts

Juice of 1 lemon

1 tablespoon olive oil

½ cup finely sliced scallions, whites plus 3 inches green

1 tablespoon flour

⅓ cup minced pancetta (2 ounces)

½ teaspoon crushed garlic

1 tablespoon tomato paste

Salt

Freshly ground black pepper

1. Wash the celery hearts and cut into 1½-inch lengths to make about 6 cups. Soak in acidulated water for about 1 hour.

2. In a wide, heavy-bottomed saucepan, heat the oil. Add the scallions and flour, and stir until well blended. Add the pancetta, garlic, and tomato paste and cook 2 minutes, stirring. Drain the celery without patting dry and add to the pan. Top with an upside-down plate or crumbled wet parchment and a tight-fitting lid and cook over low heat 40 minutes. Check after 15 minutes and add a few tablespoons water, if necessary. Just before serving, correct the seasoning and serve warm.

POLENTA

Polenta, I've discovered, is not everybody's favorite around the Mediterranean. A Greek friend, pointing to a beautiful photograph of the stuff, exclaimed, "Cornmeal mush! You've got to be really hungry to eat *that*." He went on to explain that as a teenager during the Greek Civil War he had eaten nothing but polenta three times a day for nearly a year and hoped never to dip his spoon into a bowl of it again.

But to others polenta is a gift from God. As Luigi Merotto, a driver from Veneto, put it to me, "Polenta is our bread. We cannot imagine a meal without it."

Northern Italians understand it best—as a culinary canvas, a soothingly textured dish with a unique flavor that they then embellish with other food. As Italian food expert Darrel Corti explained to me, "Italians admire those who make something special with polenta. In the Marches they put a rich sauce of livers and meat on it; in Venice they make a crunchy addition like deep-fried baby shrimp over white cornmeal; in the Piedmont they fatten it up with cheese, cream, butter, and eggs . . . and so it goes."

I'm sure many readers, like myself before I started on this book, are put off by polenta, figuring that the amount of work required—all that constant hand-stirring—is barely worth the candle. Well . . . give polenta a chance. It can be a lot easier than you think, and once made there are marvelous things you can do with it.

For me the turning point was my discovery of a new way of preparing it, a way of making polenta as good as it gets with virtually no stirring. Italian polentaphiles will no doubt scoff. But read on.

I went through a rite of passage to learn this method, learning much more about polenta along the way. The no-stir method here is the *only* method I now use. It's ideal for the home cook but not for a restaurant cook who needs to feed a large number of people.

Let me tell you first what the no-stir recipe does *not* require: no stirring the traditional way; no sputtering from the pot; no steamy taste and instant polenta flavor from the covered-dish-in-the-oven method; no loss of aroma from the steaming-in-a-double-boiler method; no seizing-up or gumminess because your cornmeal cooked too fast; no raw corn flavor due to undercooking; no more worries that if you add too much water after thickening you'll lose creaminess; no more worries about starting the emulsion process and then keeping it going; and no more worries that your polenta will get too dry.

The downside: Cooking polenta using the no-stir method will take twice as long as the traditional method—an hour and a half instead of forty-five minutes. But the entire cooking process requires absolutely *no* work.

And wait till you see and taste your result: a well-cooked polenta with an appetizing sheen—glossy, soft, tender, and fluffy, with the voluminous "bosomy" quality a well-made polenta should have. No excessive grittiness under the teeth from undercooking, nothing tasteless or gummy. Just the fresh taste and aroma of good corn. No, there are no absolutes with polenta, but this method brings you as close as any.

And where did I discover this wondrous no-stir process? Believe it or not, on the back of a bag of Golden Pheasant brand polenta, a product distributed by the Polenta Company of San Francisco to the northern California market. (A similar recipe appears in Michelle Anna Jordan's book *Polenta*.) Though it was news to me, the recipe is not at all new; it has appeared on bags of Golden Pheasant polenta for the last twenty years!

"It's an old *paesan*'s mother's recipe from Tuscany," Ed Fleming, owner of the Polenta Company, told me when I called to inquire where he got it. (Golden Pheasant is available from Corti Brothers by mail order.)

Buying Polenta A good bag of polenta or stone-ground cornmeal should smell bright and sweet. A bad bag has a stale old smell and a cardboard taste. If you can't find good polenta in your market, see "Mail-Order Sources."

Not all cornmeal is the same: Quality of meal is the most important factor in making a delicious polenta. Polenta or cornmeal comes in fine, medium, medium-coarse, and coarse grinds. The texture varies, depending upon how and where the corn was milled. Some varieties of cornmeal such as Moretti Polenta imported from Italy absorb more water than others. I've tried to standardize all the recipes in this book for medium- to coarse-grind cornmeal, or a combination of coarse and fine grind.

Keeping Polenta Keep fresh cornmeal in a dry cupboard up to a few months to avoid rancidity. If it's been ground with the germ (the label will tell you) store it in the freezer, since refrigerated cornmeal can turn moldy.

No–Stir Polenta

Serves 6

Here's the basic no-stir method used for all the polenta recipes in this book.

I cook polenta in a 12-inch nonstick, heavy-gauge aluminum "Peking" pan developed by Joyce Chen. Originally designed for stir-frying, it has a long handle that makes it easy to turn the polenta out onto a wooden peel or into an oiled mold. Because of its exceptional width and rounded sides, it exposes a larger amount of cornmeal to oven heat, which I find coaxes more flavor from the corn by "toasting" it as it cooks (see "Mail-Order Sources"). A 4-quart ovenproof saucepan can substitute. When you make a very soft creamy polenta (*polentina*) to be served with, say, a stew, simply pour the polenta into a deep, warm serving bowl where it will hold its heat, then top it with the stew. Or else serve the stew, vegetable, or whatever on the side. Chefs call this kind of steaming-bowl-of-polenta presentation a "landing."

2 tablespoons butter or oil

2 cups medium-coarse or coarse-grind cornmeal, preferably organic stone-ground cornmeal

7, 8, 9, or 10 cups water (see Notes)

2 teaspoons salt

1. Preheat the oven to 350 degrees. Grease a 12-inch-wide, heavy ovenproof saucepan. Add the cornmeal, water, butter or oil, and salt and stir with a fork until blended. (It will separate, but don't worry—it won't come together for more than half the cooking time.) Bake uncovered for 1 hour and 20 minutes.

2. Stir the polenta with a long pronged fork, correct the salt, and bake 10 minutes more. Remove from the oven and let rest 5 minutes before pouring onto a wooden pizza peel or into a buttered bowl.

(continued)

NOTES TO THE COOK: To halve the recipe, use an oiled 8-inch-wide saucepan. Reduce cooking time to 45 minutes. Stir once and bake another 10 minutes or until the polenta is cooked.

The consistency of the polenta or cornmeal is a factor in deciding how much liquid to use. Here's a chart for using medium- or coarse-grind cornmeal:

For very soft polenta (*polentina*): . . . . 6 parts liquid to 1 part cornmeal

For soft polenta: . . . . 5 parts liquid to 1 part cornmeal

For medium polenta: . . . . 4 parts liquid to 1 part cornmeal

For very firm polenta: . . . . 3 or 3½ parts liquid to 1 part cornmeal

With thanks to Ed Fleming, owner of the Polenta Company, for permission to adapt their recipe.

Keeping Cooked Polenta What if you want soft polenta one day and firm the next? Use half as a "landing" for a stew or sauce, and set the remainder in a double boiler to continue cooking, uncovered, an additional 30 minutes. It will become thicker and can then be turned out and used for crostini, or, if allowed to become very firm, can be cut into dumplings for boiling (see page 319).

If well-wrapped, polenta made with water, cornmeal, and salt can be kept 3 to 4 days in the refrigerator. However, if you add some milk (for extra flavor) the resulting polenta won't have the same keeping qualities.

ONION JAM FOR POLENTA

❀

*S*ubtle additions to polenta during cooking will imbue it with special flavors. In this recipe, finely diced onions cooked until meltingly soft and golden (but not brown) are added to the cornmeal while it is still cooking. This "onion jam" will disintegrate as the cornmeal turns creamy.

Gayle Pirie, a former polenta "specialist" at Zuni Restaurant *and* Chez Panisse, told me that this onion jam improves texture in both cold and hot polenta: "You get better results for grilling or broiling because the slice caramelizes easier; it's tastier and also not as dense."

By adding this jam, you can also, if you wish, cut down on butter and cheese, while still creating a flavorful polenta.

3 tablespoons olive oil

2 pounds large yellow onions, finely diced

Pinch of salt

Heat the oil in a heavy saucepan, add the onions and salt, cover, and cook, stirring occasionally, 1 hour. Uncover, increase the heat to medium-high, and cook, stirring frequently, until onions are glazed and golden but not browned. Add 1 to 2 tablespoons to the No-Stir Polenta midway in the cooking.

NOTE TO THE COOK: Divide remaining onion jam into small dollops. Place dollops ½ inch apart on a tray and freeze. Pack in a freezer bag; keep frozen until needed

CARAMELIZED CABBAGE AND CREAMY POLENTA PIE (*Italy*)

Makes one 9– or 10–inch pie, serving 6

This winter dish of braised cabbage from the Italian Veneto looks as good as a lemon meringue pie . . . if you aren't wearing glasses. Anyway, it looks good enough to put on the table to accompany a winter dinner of a ragout, a stew, or grilled meat or poultry.

2 pounds green or white cabbage, outer leaves discarded, washed, quartered, and inner core removed

2½ tablespoons extra-virgin olive oil

2 to 3 tablespoons minced pancetta

2 cloves garlic, minced

1 small sprig rosemary, chopped

Salt

Freshly ground pepper

3 tablespoons dry white wine plus ½ cup water

A few drops of balsamic vinegar

½ cup coarse-grind cornmeal

½ cup fine-grind cornmeal

1 tablepoon butter, plus ½ teaspoon for greasing the ovenproof serving dish

2 to 3 ounces imported aged Asiago or a sharp pecorino cheese, grated (¾ cup)

1. About 2 hours before serving, preheat the oven to 350 degrees.

2. Thinly shred the cabbage.

3. Heat 2 tablespoons of the oil in a wide and deep saucepan over medium heat. Add the pancetta, garlic, and rosemary and sauté for a few minutes. Add the cabbage, salt, and pepper, and ¼ cup water; toss to coat thoroughly. Cook, covered, for about 1 hour, adding spoonfuls of water or wine whenever the cabbage turns too dry or begins to brown too fast. The addition of liquid to the pan must take place every 5 minutes or so. You want the cabbage to stew slowly and lightly brown. After about 1 hour you should have a meltingly tender, lightly caramelized, medium-colored brown cabbage that is somewhat dry to the touch and very delicious when corrected with salt and pepper and a few drops of balsamic vinegar.

3. While the cabbage is cooking, prepare the polenta in the oven. In a well-oiled heavy ovenproof saucepan combine the two types of cornmeal, 4 cups water, remaining ½ tablespoon oil, and 1 teaspoon salt and stir only once. Place, uncovered, in the oven and let bake 40 minutes.

4. Carefully remove the polenta from the oven, give it a good stir, and return to the oven to bake another 10 minutes. (If doubling the recipe, you will need to double the cooking time.) Fluff up with 1 tablespoon butter or oil. Pour into a 9- or 10-inch buttered baking dish, sprinkle with half the cheese, cover with an even layer of cabbage, and scatter the remaining cheese on top.

5. You can keep the "pie" hot over simmering water for up to 30 minutes. (It doesn't reheat well.) Return to the oven to bake until the tips of the cabbage are brown and crisp, about 10 minutes. Serve hot.

POLENTA TORTA WITH "APRON GREENS"

Serves 4

This polenta torta makes a very substantial side dish or may be served as a light supper dish on its own. "Apron Greens" are the wild and garden greens that Mediterranean women gather, tucked in the front pocket of their aprons. Often a woman's apron pocket will be divided into several compartments for "sweet" greens, "bitter" greens—and perhaps a third for wild mushrooms.

4 cups lukewarm water

1 cup fresh, organic, stone-ground, medium- or coarse-grind cornmeal

1 teaspoon salt

1½ pounds mixed tender greens: arugula, peppercress, spinach, kale, plus a few sprigs of dill or fennel

3 tablespoons olive oil

Freshly ground black pepper

¼ teaspoon crushed pepper flakes

1 clove garlic, peeled

½ cup grated pecorino Romano cheese

1. About 2 hours before serving, preheat the oven to 350 degrees.

2. Prepare the polenta: Place the water, cornmeal, and salt in a well-oiled, ovenproof saucepan. Set in the oven, uncovered, to cook for 50 minutes.

3. Meanwhile, wash the greens, cut away the thick stems, and chop the leaves coarsely. Heat the olive oil in a 10-inch skillet, add a pinch of black pepper, pepper flakes, and garlic and cook for 1 minute. Tilt the skillet and transfer half the oil to a 5- or 6-cup baking-serving dish. Discard the garlic. Brush the peppered oil over the bottom and inside of the serving pan. Tilt to recoup a tablespoon of "red" oil and reserve for sprinkling over the final dish.

(continued)

4. Add the chopped greens to the skillet, cover, and cook over moderate heat for 10 minutes or until they are tender, stirring from time to time so that the leaves cook evenly. Season with salt and pepper. Increase the heat at the end to evaporate any liquid. Makes 1½ cups.

5. When the polenta has cooked 40 minutes, stir in half the cheese and continue to bake 10 more minutes. Reheat the greens. Remove the polenta from the oven, quickly spread half the polenta into the prepared serving dish, distribute the greens on top, and cover with a layer of the remaining polenta. Let the torta rest for 5 minutes. Scatter remaining cheese on top and drizzle with the reserved "red" oil; return to the hot oven for 10 more minutes. Serve hot.

With thanks to Anne-Marie Lombardi for sharing this recipe.

SLICED POLENTA

*T*he traditional method of cutting a mound of polenta into slices is with a taut string, a wooden knife, or a knife dipped in hot water.

Michael Peternell, a young cook at Chez Panisse in Berkeley, told me how he learned to cut beautiful sliced rounds from a mound of polenta while he was living with a family in Tuscany:

> There was a thick, heavy cloth on the table. The polenta, cooked in the traditional manner, was poured right onto the tablecloth. Firm enough to keep its mound shape, it was allowed to cool. Then the father used a taut string to cut the cold polenta into quarters. After he cut it, he reached under the tablecloth and pushed up his fingers through the center of the mound. The four parts fell backward perfectly. He then took the string, stretched it tight between the thumb of his left hand and the forefinger of his right, and, holding a polenta quarter in his left hand, made a circular movement with the string. This way he cut off perfect slices of polenta, large ones for the adults and smaller ones for the kids.

Here's an alternative method suggested by another cook at Chez Panisse: Turn out your hot polenta on a large dampened white linen napkin set on a wooden board. With one swift motion pour the polenta into the center, fold up the corners of the napkin to cover and tie a knot. When cool, move the wrapped polenta to a table, untie, then use a wet knife to cut the ball into quarters and slices.

SAUTÉED POLENTA SLICES

❖

Pour hot dense polenta (see page 313) into a greased loaf pan or bowl. When cool, turn out, and slice with a taut string. Brush the bottom of a black iron skillet with oil, butter, or drippings from roast beef, pork, or chicken. Slip in a leaf of sage or rosemary and slowly heat to accentuate the aromas. Add garlic slices and stir around until just golden. Remove when ready to add the slices of polenta. Add polenta slices and fry until crisp, puffed, and golden. Turn, using a flexible spatula, and brown the second sides. Spread over crumpled brown paper to drain. Serve as an accompaniment to slices of sopprassata salami heated in olive oil and deglazed with vinegar, Shredded Red Radicchio and Smoked Fish Salad (page 144), or grilled chicken, quail, or lamb.

For grilling polenta slices, see page 110.

LEFTOVER POLENTA

POLENTA DUMPLINGS WITH MUSHROOMS, TALEGGIO CHEESE, AND SIZZLING BUTTER

❀

Serves 3 as a first course

As previously mentioned, if you cook your polenta with just salt and water, it will keep 3 to 4 days in the refigerator. It can then be grilled, fried, baked, or layered in a deep soup tureen with a sauce or fish soup. If you have leftover polenta to which you haven't already added butter and cheese, dice it into 1-inch dumplings, boil them, then top them with a sauce such as this delicious combination of mushrooms, Taleggio cheese, and sizzling butter.

In northern Italy in spring or autumn when there's lots of rain, the meadow mushroom is the mushroom of choice, but oyster mushrooms work well too. *(continued)*

2 cups leftover polenta cut into 1-inch dice

1 teaspoon extra-virgin olive oil

1 small clove garlic

5 ounces oyster mushrooms, brushed and cut into fine strips (about 5 cups)

Salt

3 tablespoons finely chopped flat-leaf parsley

¼ teaspoon freshly ground black pepper

1½ ounces Taleggio cheese, sliced (½ cup)

1½ tablespoons butter, melted

1. Preheat the oven to 350 degrees.

2. Drop polenta into salted boiling water and cook for 5 minutes. Drain and set aside.

3. Heat the olive oil in an 8-inch skillet and fry the garlic over medium heat until golden brown. Discard the garlic. Add the mushrooms and a pinch of salt and cook, stirring, for 3 minutes. If the mushrooms are dry, add a few tablespoons water to the skillet. Add the parsley and the pepper, cover, and cook for 15 minutes over reduced heat.

4. Grease a small shallow baking dish and spread a layer of mushrooms over the bottom. Cover with a layer of polenta. Top with the cheese and bake until hot all the way through, 20 minutes

5. Remove the pan from the oven and allow to rest 5 minutes before serving. In a small pan heat the melted butter to sizzling and pour over the polenta and mushrooms.

POLENTA IN THE MARCHES

✦

We always invite someone strong to come in and help when we're having polenta," my host tells me, describing the arduous stirring method used in his region, the Italian Marches on the Adriatic coast.

I've been invited to his country house to learn about Marches-style polenta. The cook, a tiny woman, has just ceded her place at the stove to the gardener, called in for additional stirring, which will take him a full half hour!

After much arduous work, the strong gardener, looking slightly haggard, pours the steaming hot polenta onto a wooden board about five feet long. It falls from the pot in soft, golden, undulating waves that hold their shape even as they span the board. Suddenly the kitchen is filled with the aroma of toasted corn. Immediately the tiny cook slathers rich tomato sauce over one half of the polenta and a ragù over the other, then the gardener carries the board to the dining room, where he sets it down lengthwise in the center of the table.

A wooden rectangular dish is set before each place. We sit down, then each of us scrapes polenta from the board onto our wooden plate. After a while, the board is lifted and turned so that diners who have been eating polenta covered with ragù can have a crack at polenta covered with tomato sauce and vice versa.

The polenta is delicious and hearty, the dining experience wonderfully homey. For me the best parts are the edges where there's just cheese and hot polenta, nothing else—a revelation of culinary simplicity. When I remark upon this to my host, he tells me the taste of a fresh shower of cheese on hot polenta is unreproducible, and never the same when leftover polenta is reheated.

An instant convert, I promise myself that upon returning home I will immediately go out and buy the largest Italian pizza peel I can find and make my own mini version of *polenta alla spianatora*.

POLENTA IN VENICE

✦

Venetians like white fine-grind cornmeal, with the result that their polentas are smoother than those in other regions of Italy. This works very well with their favorite polenta accompaniments—various forms of seafood such as crisp fried baby shrimps or stuffed soft-shell crabs. Among the most beautiful polenta dishes I found in Venice were those served in wine and coffee bars—little slabs of white polenta topped with warm, inky braised calamari, with a few chili flakes added on top.

The type of corn ground into white cornmeal is called pearl corn. If you decide to work with white cornmeal please keep a few things in mind. If you intend to chill, slice, and then fry your polenta, this cornmeal should be cooked drier than others, lest it turn gummy. Because of its fine texture, when allowed to harden it becomes very firm (and when fried it becomes lacy). On the other hand, if you want to eat it hot and creamy, use more water, in which case it will acquire the consistency of a loose pudding, the kind that literally trembles on your plate.

White corn has less of a corn flavor than yellow corn, tasting somewhat like farina except sweeter. The fine white cornmeal that's so beloved by Venetians usually isn't liked much by Americans or even Italians from other regions.

As you've probably inferred, I'm not all that crazy about white cornmeal polenta, but I do like white cornmeal very much as a coating or breading substance when frying food—another way it's used frequently throughout the Veneto.

Renato Piccolotto, chef at the world-famous Hotel Cipriani, taught me such a recipe. We were trading cooking techniques: I taught him how to make couscous and he taught me the secret of a dish of deep-fried stuffed *moleche,* or soft-shelled crabs, in which the crabs, to my amazement, had been stuffed with eggs. I couldn't imagine how this was done.

The secret turned out to be somewhat macabre, which is why I now call this dish "Death in Venice"! Here's the trick: While the crabs are still alive the tips of their claws are cut off! The crabs are then immediately soaked in a froth of eggs, which they absorb through their now open-ended claws. They are then dusted in white cornmeal and deep-fried. When presented on top of white cornmeal polenta, the effect is stunning and the crabs really do appear to have been miraculously stuffed. The dish, though "cruel," is utterly delicious.

9

SWEET GREENS
AND GRAINS

SWEET GREENS

Not surprisingly, I haven't found very many greens dessert recipes in my travels through Mediterranean countries. In Spain, borage leaves are dipped in batter, fried in olive oil, and served with a dusting of granulated sugar. Candied angelica, mint, and violets are used in desserts, especially in France. The most famous leafy green Mediterranean dessert is the Provençal *tourte de blettes*—a blend of Swiss chard, raisins, cheese, and sugar all wrapped up in a rich pastry shell, baked, then served cold or at room temperature (see recipe below).

In eastern Turkey, some leafy greens are dried in the sun, then used as the basis of a sweet winter soup along with raisins, figs, and plums. These same dried greens are revived and sweetened by being soaked in concentrated grape juice, then served as a sweet counterpunch to bulgur pilafs and fried *köfte* but not usually as desserts.

In the fruit and vegetable section of any "greens" market one can find dozens of candidates for sweet dishes. Dessert recipes using pumpkin, tomato, eggplant, and potato as well as all sorts of fruits are worthy of a book of their own.

PROVENÇAL CHARD, RAISIN, APPLE, AND CHEESE PIE

Serves 8

Swiss chard is the most popular leafy green eaten around the Mediterranean, and nowhere is it used more often than in Provence, where the residents are sometimes called, affectionately, *caga bléa* or "chard heads." Thus, it didn't surprise me when I heard they even make a dessert with it.

Chef Cathérine-Hélène Barale of the Niçois restaurant La Barale serves wonderful traditional Provençal dishes at remarkably fair prices. Though you might not savor the thought of dining at a long communal table, it's probably the best way to experience the most authentic Provençal cooking available in Nice today. There's no choice at La Barale; each day Cathérine-Hélène decides what she's going to serve. More likely than not, among your dishes will be a *tourte* similar to the one below.

I've long wanted this recipe, but it took a friend, food writer James Villas, to convince Cathérine-Hélène to share it for his book *The French Country Kitchen*. He was kind enough to pass it on to me. Actually, it isn't all that different from most traditional recipes for this dish . . . except for one item. The filling has a subtle creamy consistency due to the use of Gouda cheese.

Villas had noticed, when given the recipe, that the cheese wasn't the usual Parmesan. "So I asked her about the Gouda," he told me. "She confirmed that as long as she could remember, Gouda was the proper cheese for this *tourte*."

This is not the first time I've found recipes in Provence that employ Gouda or Edam (see Provençal Pistou with Aged Gouda, page 91). Such cheeses also turn up in quite a number of recipes in southwest French cooking, owing to the early brandy and wine trade with the Dutch.

Serve this wonderful sweet pie at room temperature as part of a buffet or picnic lunch.

(continued)

Pastry Dough

14 ounces all-purpose flour (about 2⅔ cups)

2 ounces cake flour (⅓ cup)

½ teaspoon salt

½ cup plus 1 tablespoon superfine sugar (8 tablespoons)

1 scant cup unsalted butter

2 large eggs, beaten

2 tablespoons ice water, approximately

The Filling

2 bunches Swiss chard

½ teaspoon salt

½ cup golden raisins, rinsed, drained, and macerated in 2 tablespoons marc, eau de vie, or dark rum until the liquid is completely absorbed

2 large eggs, beaten

½ cup plus 1½ tablespoons light brown sugar

1 teaspoon grated lemon rind

4 ounces Gouda or Edam cheese, finely cubed or grated

½ cup pine nuts

Freshly ground pepper

2 Granny Smith apples

[handwritten note in left margin: see version w. o.o.]

1. Make the pastry: Sift the flours, salt, and ½ cup sugar together into a large mixing bowl. Add the butter and work with your fingers until the mixture is mealy. Add the eggs and blend well. Add the ice water, blend well, and form the dough into a ball. On a lightly floured work surface, knead the dough for 30 seconds, divide into ⅔ and ⅓ portions, wrap each in plastic wrap, and chill for 1 hour.

2. Meanwhile, wash the chard; remove the ribs and reserve for some other purpose. Roll up the leaves and thinly slice. Toss with the salt and let stand in a colander until wilted, 15 minutes. Wash the chard in several changes of cold water until water is clear. Drain and squeeze dry. (You don't need to precook the greens.)

3. Roll out two-thirds of the dough to line a 10- to 12-inch round baking pan. Chill the dough in the pan while you prepare the filling. Keep the remaining dough chilled.

4. Continue preparing the filling. In a large mixing bowl, combine the raisins, eggs, and brown sugar and mix until well blended. Coarsely chop the sliced greens and add to the bowl with the lemon rind, cheese, pine nuts, and pepper and mix well. Let stand and "ripen" at least 30 minutes.

5. Core, peel, and slice the apples and add to the filling.

6. Preheat the oven to 375 degrees.

7. Stir the filling to be sure there are no juices settled on the bottom of the bowl, then spoon everything into the chilled pie shell. Roll out the remaining dough just wide enough to fit over the top of the pie shell and place it over the pie. Crimp the edges to seal securely, prick five or six times on top, and bake for 45 minutes, or until the crust is golden. Remove from the oven and sprinkle with superfine sugar. Let the pie cool on a rack.

NOTES TO THE COOK: To keep the taste of the greens vivid, prepare them for the pie without blanching. Roll up and slice very thin, allow to wilt, soak in several changes of cold water until the water runs clear, and squeeze dry.

If you prefer to use a pastry made with olive oil, follow the dough recipe for Field Greens, Rice, and Pumpkin Torta (page 56).

WHEAT BERRIES, DURUM, AND WHEAT STARCH–BASED SWEET DISHES

SHELLED WHEAT BERRIES, GRAPE MUST, AND BITTER CHOCOLATE ON VANILLA ICE CREAM (*Italy*)

❀

Serves 4

Scoops of vanilla ice cream, topped with a dark syrupy sauce made with *vino cotto* (cooked wine) and shelled wheat berries, are studded with bits of bitter chocolate in this restaurant version of a very old Mediterranean dish.

There are many desserts that use concentrated fruit juices instead of sugar combined with wheat berries. People have been eating this combination since the first century in Rome as documented in Apicius's book on Roman cookery. Turkish *bulumac*, Greek *melohondros*, Sicilian *cuccia*, and Armenian *bulghurapur* are all descended from the same ancient recipe, still prepared and eaten by those who like their sweets *very* sweet.

(continued)

Grape molasses (sold as "*pekmez*" in Middle Eastern groceries) can substitute for *vino cotto* in the following dish, which I discovered on a recent trip to the restaurant Le Arcate in the village of San Serveno in Apulia. For dessert I was enchanted with the notion of eating shelled wheat berries and concentrated grape juice over ice cream. I found it lighter and better at the end of a meal than the equally delicious and far richer *Pastiera di Grano*, the Italian Easter wheat pie made of cooked wheat, ricotta, and pastry cream served wrapped in a pastry shell.

⅛ cup shelled durum wheat berries, rinsed and drained

3 tablespoons grape *pekmez* (see "Mail-Order Sources")

A few drops of balsamic vinegar (optional)

4 servings of high-quality vanilla ice cream

1 teaspoon grated bitter chocolate

1. Place the shelled wheat berries in a heavy saucepan, cover with at least 2 inches of water, and bring to a boil. Let boil 10 minutes without stirring, then leave to soak for 1 hour. Cook the wheat berries for 20 minutes, cool, drain, and reserve.

2. Taste grape *pekmez* and thin to napping consistency (so it coats the spoon) with a few teaspoons of the wheat berry cooking liquid. Adjust sweetness, if desired, with a drop of vinegar. Spoon the ice cream into individual dessert dishes. Surround with some of the wheat berries, drizzle the *pekmez* over the ice cream, sprinkle with grated chocolate, and serve at once.

NOTE TO THE COOK: If you can't find shelled durum wheat berries (called "grano" in Italy), substitute any shelled wheat berry. See page 199 for more information on *grano*.

Milk Pudding with Pistachios (*Turkey*)

Serves 6

This unique Turkish milk pudding is unlike any other I know. The pudding is cooked and strained into a dish filled with cold water, which causes it to immediately shrink away from the sides of the dish. A few minutes later, more cold water is sprinkled on top to create a faint crackling and to keep the surface from developing a skin. After a night's chill, some of the water is carefully poured off, and diluted rose-scented syrup is added. The pudding is then cut into squares.

For a superior pudding, use wheat starch, available from candy or bakery suppliers or at Asian markets. If unavailable, use cornstarch, but be advised that you will get deep cracks as opposed to attractive crackling, which may detract from the visual perfection of the squares.

In Aleppo, this pudding is served with vanilla ice cream; in Gaziantep in its own syrup and some crushed ice, and with a sprinkling of green pistachios; in Istanbul at the Hotel Divan in a spoonful of rosewater-flavored syrup with an elegant dusting of confectioners' sugar on top.

This wonderful, refreshing dessert will keep 2 to 3 days in the refrigerator.

Do steps 1, 2, and 3 one day in advance.

1. Put ½ cup cold water into a 9-inch round or square shallow dish. Place a wide strainer next to the dish.

2. Put 3¾ cups of the milk, the salt, sugar, and bay leaves into a heavy-bottomed pan and slowly bring to a boil. Meanwhile, whisk the wheat starch with the remaining ½ cup milk to a smooth cream. Mix a little of the hot milk mixture into the cream, return it all to the pot, and heat, stirring constantly, over very low heat until the raw starchy flavor is gone and the mixture just comes to a boil, about 20 minutes. You can tell it is fully cooked when you catch a

Ingredients

4¼ cups whole milk

Pinch of salt

2 tablespoons sugar

2 bay leaves

½ cup plus 1 tablespoon wheat starch, powdery wheaten flour, farine de froment, or cornstarch

¼ teaspoon pure vanilla extract or more to taste

SUGAR SYRUP

1½ cups sugar

½ tablespoon lemon juice

½ teaspoon rosewater or more to taste

½ cup imported green pistachios, peeled and crushed (see Note)

glimpse of the bottom of the pan with the swirl of the spoon. Stir in the vanilla. Immediately strain the mixture into the prepared dish. Let cool for 5 minutes, then sprinkle ½ cup very cold water over the pudding. Cool, cover, and refrigerate overnight.

3. Make the sugar syrup: Place the sugar and ¾ cup water in a heavy saucepan and bring to a boil, stirring to dissolve the sugar. Skim the surface if necessary, then add the lemon juice and cook at a simmer until the syrup feels thick. Remove from the heat to cool. Add the rosewater to taste. Chill overnight.

4. The following day, when the syrup and milk pudding are both cold, carefully pour off the water. Dilute about 1 cup of the sugar syrup with ½ cup cold water, whisking until smooth. Pour the syrup over the pudding and cut into squares or diamond shapes. Serve chilled and garnished with pistachio nuts and a few spoonfuls of the diluted sugar syrup.

NOTES TO THE COOK: To preserve the flavor of *unsalted* imported pistachios, store in the freezer. When ready to peel, simply rub each nut in a coarse kitchen towel until the skin pops off.

Grape molasses may be purchased at Middle Eastern groceries.

Wheat starch or wheaten flour can be purchased in Asian markets or by direct mail from the Oriental Bakery (see Appendix).

VARIATION: Drizzle grape molasses or a dusting of confectioners' sugar on top of each square. If desired, serve with scoops of vanilla ice cream.

Adapted from a recipe of Mrs. Ulker Sacir of Gaziantep.

WHEAT STARCH

✧

*I*f there is anything truly "Turkish" in the repertoire of so-called Turkish delicacies and desserts, it is rahat lokum which, literally translated, means "a morsel of rest." These are the delicacies with which, for centuries, the ladies of harems passed their monotonous lives, fattening themselves for the greater pleasures of their lords and masters. For the Ottomans, like the Arabs, liked big, buxom women. . . .

—ARTO DER HAROUTUNIAN, *A TURKISH COOKBOOK*
(LONDON: EBURY PRESS, 1987)

Though some recipes for *rahat lokum* call for gelatin, the original and best recipes are always made with wheat starch, obtained by a long, arduous process of extracting starch from hard wheat berries. The wheat starch is then added to dishes to provide a voluptuous, creamy juice or liquor.

To acquire wheat starch, wheat berry kernels are soaked for a week in many changes of cold water, then pressed through a sieve to remove the skins (which can then be used to make a humble soup). The resulting liquid is then pressed through cheesecloth and boiled down till thick and unctuous. This thick liquid is then left to rest. After a time the starch falls to the bottom of the container and the water on top is ladled off. The starchy debris is then laid out on large pieces of cloth, exposed to the sun during the day, and taken in at night over a five-day period. It is then sieved again to obtain a powdery starch.

Commercial cornstarch has only recently arrived in the eastern Mediterranean. As soon as it did, women quickly started using it to avoid the arduous job of making wheat starch. Now that commerical wheat starch is imported from China, both types are readily available. Meantime, Turkish women are thinner, just the way the "new" eastern Mediterranean man likes them!

Buy wheat starch at Asian markets or by mail order (see "Mail-Order Sources"), as you will want to have some on hand for making Milk Pudding with Pistachios above.

See also the recipe for Anatolian Rice Pudding, *Zerde* (page 338) to learn how to use a natural starch with shelled wheat berries.

Moroccan Semolina–Yeast Crepes with Honey

Makes about 3 dozen 7-inch crepes, serving 8

These delicious, meltingly soft, and very light crepes served with a warm honey-butter sauce are traditionally eaten on *aid el seghir*, the so-called "little feast" near the end of Ramadan, the Islamic month of fasting.

The crepes are cooked on one side only; thus their uncooked tops display hundreds of tiny airholes. To achieve the proper lightness, Moroccan women work the dough for up to thirty minutes, a procedure you can duplicate in thirty seconds with a food processor. You want a smooth, velvety batter just thick enough to lightly coat a wooden spoon.

Moroccan women will cook their crepes on an unglazed earthenware pan set over live coals. (They use an onion half dipped into a dish of olive oil to grease their earthenware pans when making *beghrir*.) For best results in an American kitchen, use a good-quality nonstick skillet that will hold a steady high heat. And remember—as with all crepe and pancake recipes, your first few efforts will probably not be up to standard.

The easiest way to offer these crepes is to make them in advance, allow them to cool, brush them lightly with butter, then reheat them in a slow oven just before serving with the warm honey-butter sauce—a method I have adapted from one given in *La Cuisine Marocaine* by Latifa Bennani Smiras.

¼ teaspoon sugar

4 teaspoons (1½ envelopes) active dry yeast

2 cups plus 6 tablespoons fine semolina flour (13 ounces)

1 cup plus 2 tablespoons bread flour (5 ounces), sifted

1 teaspoon salt

1 cup milk, lukewarm

1 beaten egg

½ onion

1 tablespoon oil

8 ounces (1 cup) sweet butter, melted

Liquid honey to taste

1. Place ¼ cup lukewarm water and the sugar in a small bowl; sprinkle it with the yeast and stir to dissolve. Let stand until bubbly, 5 minutes.

2. Sift semolina and bread flours and salt into the work bowl of a food processor. With the machine on, slowly add the milk and 1 cup lukewarm water through the feed tube. Continue to process the dough 20 seconds. Then add 3 tablespoons of the egg and the yeast mixture and process for 5 seconds. Slowly add an additional 2 cups lukewarm water and process until smooth. (If your work bowl is small you may have to do this entire procedure in two batches.) Pour into a deep bowl, preferably plastic or earthenware, cover tightly, and let stand in a warm place until the surface is foamy and light, 2 to 4 hours.

3. Slowly heat an 8- or 9-inch nonstick skillet until it is medium to medium-hot. Dip the onion in the oil and grease the skillet. Stir the batter and ladle 3 tablespoons batter into the center of the skillet. Batter should be thin enough to spread and fill the bottom of the pan—if necessary make a quick twist of the skillet. Cook over steady heat until the crepe is covered with minute holes and the underside is colored pale golden, about 45 seconds. Do not turn crepe over. Transfer it, cooked side down, to a cloth towel. Stir the batter before making each crepe. Repeat until batter is finished. Do not stack the crepes until they are completely cold. (Up to this point the crepes can be made 2 to 3 hours in advance. Cover the crepes with a clean cloth and let stand at room temperature.)

4. Thirty minutes before serving, preheat the oven to 225 degrees. Place warm melted butter in a heat-proof serving bowl; lightly brush a crepe with butter and place it in an ovenproof dish. Place a second crepe, hole side up, over the first crepe without buttering. Continue alternating until all the crepes are stacked. Cover the dish and place in the oven to reheat for 20 minutes. Add honey to remaining butter and reheat gently. To serve, spread 3 crepes, slightly overlapping, on a dessert plate, drizzle with honey-butter, and serve at once.

LEBANESE SEMOLINA PANCAKES
STUFFED WITH CHEESE

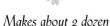

Makes about 2 dozen

In North Africa, semolina pancakes are cooked on one side only, then served in a pristine flat state (as in recipe above). In the Middle East, on the other hand, similar pancakes receive a far more lavish treatment—stuffed with a delicious cheese filling, broiled until crisp, then served warm drizzled with a perfumed sugar syrup.

1 teaspoon active dry yeast

½ teaspoon sugar

⅔ cup fine semolina

⅓ cup all-purpose flour

Dash of salt

1 cup milk or water at room temperature

1 teaspoon baking powder

½ teaspoon orange flower water

Oil for greasing the griddle

STUFFING

¾ cup well-drained ricotta cheese

2½ tablespoons shredded fresh mozzarella

2 tablespoons confectioners' sugar

5 tablespoons melted butter for broiling

¾ cup sugar syrup (recipe follows), cooled

1. Soften the yeast in ¼ cup lukewarm water and the sugar. Let stand 2 minutes, then stir and set in a warm place until the yeast is bubbly.

2. In the bowl of a food processor combine the semolina, flour, and salt. With the machine running, slowly add the milk, then the bubbling yeast, baking powder, and orange flower water in that order and process for 10 seconds. Pour into a bowl and let stand, covered, in a warm place for 2 hours.

3. Preheat the broiler.

4. Rub a large nonstick griddle or skillet with a cloth dipped in oil, then slowly heat until it is medium to medium-hot. Stir the batter and ladle 1 tablespoon batter onto the skillet. Use the back of a spoon to spread to 3 inches in diameter. (With a good-sized skillet you can make 4 or 5 pancakes at the same time.) Cook over steady heat until each crepe is covered with minute holes and the underside is colored golden brown and the top appears set, about 1½ minutes. Do not turn over. Transfer each pancake cooked side down to a cloth towel or wooden board. Repeat until all the batter is used.

5. In a bowl combine the cheeses and confectioners' sugar; mixing well. Place a teaspoon of stuffing on one half of the uncooked side of each pancake; fold and press to seal. Brush a baking sheet with butter and arrange pancakes in one layer. Dab tops with butter and broil until golden and crisp on one side. Turn and broil the other side. Spoon the sugar syrup over each and serve warm.

SUGAR SYRUP

Makes about ¾ cup

1 cup sugar

1 teaspoon lemon juice

1 teaspoon orange blossom honey (optional)

1 teaspoon orange flower water

Combine the sugar and ½ cup water in a small saucepan. Bring to a boil and boil slowly 1 minute. Reduce the heat, cover, and cook at a simmer 2 minutes. Add the lemon juice and honey, if using, and cook 1 minute longer. Cool slightly, then add the orange flower water.

TUNISIAN HOMEMADE COUSCOUS WITH GOLDEN RAISINS

Serves 6 to 8

*T*he smallest, finest couscous made with semolina is called *msfouf.* It is perfect for this haunting aromatic dessert in which it's freshly steamed, then served very simply—anointed with fresh butter, mixed with plumped golden raisins, then sprinkled with some delicate ground cinnamon. I know no other dessert quite like it.

See page 210 to learn how to make your own couscous. (If you use regular couscous for this dessert, your "grains" will be too big. You want your dessert couscous to be fine and very light.)

Serve warm with spoons.

(continued)

Fresh couscous (page 210)

Oil or butter for greasing the inside of the colander

1 cup golden raisins

6 tablespoons unsalted butter, thickly sliced at room temperature

3 tablespoons granulated sugar

Ground Ceylon cinnamon

Confectioners' sugar

1. Bring plenty of water to a boil in the bottom of a deep kettle or couscous cooker. Fit top onto bottom, checking for a tight seal. Pile the freshly rolled couscous into a lightly oiled colander or top container. Partially cover and steam 15 minutes.

2. Dump couscous onto a tray, sprinkle with ½ cup cold water, and rake the grains to keep them separate. Gradually add another ½ cup water while raking the couscous. When the couscous has absorbed all the water, repeat the steaming for 15 minutes.

3. Dump couscous onto a tray, gradually work in another cup cold water, and rake the grains to keep them separate. Allow to rest, covered, for 15 minutes. Fluff up the couscous and loosely cover with a damp towel. Up to this point the couscous can be prepared a few hours in advance. From time to time, rake the couscous to encourage fluffiness.

4. Twenty minutes before serving, bring the water back to the boil. Return the couscous to the colander or top container and steam uncovered. Meanwhile, soak the raisins in hot water for 10 minutes and drain. Spread butter and raisins over the steaming couscous. Dump couscous onto a wide shallow serving dish, mix in 1 cup water, and toss with the melted butter, heated raisins, and granulated sugar. Gently fluff the couscous; pile in a mound, decorate with lines of cinnamon, and dust the top with confectioners' sugar.

NOTES TO THE COOK: I suggest using Ceylon cinnamon for its delicate flavor. In my opinion, the stronger Cassia cinnamon is too pungent for this dessert.

If you want to make a lot of couscous, here's how to store it. Steam the couscous for 10 minutes, then spread it out on a dry cloth to dry; use a dehydrator at medium setting to dry the "grains"; store in cloth bags.

There's no need to line the upper steamer or colander with cheesecloth. With the water at a full boil, no couscous will fall through the holes.

To substitute store-bought couscous: Place couscous in a fine sieve and set under running water until completely wet. Dump it into a bowl and allow to swell for 5 minutes; then break up lumps. Steam as directed in the recipe.

MAKING SIMPLE STARCH JUICES
FOR TUNISIAN CRÈMES

✥

"You can make a good natural starch juice for a luxurious *crème* in about an hour," Tunisian chef Abdelrazak Haouari tells me when I describe the wheat starch made in Turkey (page 331). "During the Ottoman period, rich people here made it with semolina. You had to be rich to do that because semolina was so expensive and you ended up throwing away the residue or feeding it to animals."

Here's the Tunisian method: Soak coarse semolina in water for an hour, then strain through a fine cheesecloth. Boil the juice down to a good consistency along with sugar and your flavoring of choice.

One of the finest and most unusual of these *crèmes* is flavored with resinous black kernels, called *zgougou*, extracted from cones from the pine tree *(Pinus hale pensis)*. These black bitter-tasting kernels are crushed and pressed through a cloth to extract their dark syrupy liquid, which is then cooked down with semolina starch, sugar, and some milk, and, when thick, finally scented with some rose-geranium water. The resulting smooth, cooling *crème* is perhaps the most refined of all Tunisian desserts.

ANATOLIAN RICE PUDDING (ZERDE)

Serves 3 or 4

The lightest rice pudding I ever ate was this central Anatolian dish, made with a base of wheat starch and water rather than milk or cream.

"The purpose of making a rice pudding is so you don't have to eat another pilaf," my Turkish friend Ayfer Ünsal told me, an understandable statement when you consider that in Turkey pilafs are eaten nearly every day. In this version of rice pudding or *zerde*, the rice is sparse and the liquid soothing and refreshing. "You want to taste both the quality of the rice and the richness of the liquid," Ayfer explained.

½ cup shelled soft wheat berries,
rinsed and soaked overnight in 6 cups water

2 tablespoons rice, well washed and drained

Pinch of salt

2 to 3 filaments of dried saffron, crumbled

Sugar to taste, about 5 tablespoons

6 whole almonds, blanched, skinned, and sliced

12 pistachio nuts, blanched, skinned, and chopped

1½ teaspoons rosewater or more to taste

1. Boil the wheat berries in their soaking water until liquid becomes starchy, skimming occasionally, about 2 hours. Meanwhile, put the rice in a deep heavy saucepan, cover with 1½ cups water, add salt, and bring to a boil. Cook, covered, until rice is tender, about 17 minutes. Drain excess liquid, return rice to the saucepan, and hold.

2. Strain the wheat juice over the rice, pressing down on the wheat berries to extract as much starch as possible. Discard wheat berries. Add the saffron and sugar and bring to a boil, stirring. Boil about 3 minutes and remove from the heat. Stir in the rosewater. You should have about 2 cups. Pour into 3 or 4 individual ½-cup capacity ramekins and sprinkle each serving with nuts. Cool; chill without disturbing. The liquid will firm up as it cools. Do not touch the surface with your finger or with a spoon because this delicate pudding easily turns liquidy.

With thanks to Bahriye Hanim and Ayfer Ünsal for teaching me this delicious recipe.

BLACK SEA CORNMEAL WAFERS
BAKED ON COLLARD GREENS

Serves 4

*I*t wasn't that long ago that houses built along the Turkish Black Sea coast lacked ovens. Open fires, built beneath large concave stone bowls, were used to bake bread, wafers, and cookies, and even to grill vegetables. The heat was steady and intense, and often the bowl was lined with collard leaves to keep the bread, wafers, or cookies from sticking to the stone.

These leaves not only facilitated the turning of the wafer, which cracked easily, but also imparted a faint color and unusual markings. In this fascinating dessert recipe you can duplicate this process on top of the stove, or in an oven using an iron skillet first heated over a burner.

The Black Sea coast is famous for producing delicious hazelnuts (which replace pine nuts in pilafs and stuffings) and also the finest butter in Turkey (which replaces oil in the local diet). In the town of Trabzon the two are combined with the ubitiquous cornmeal in desserts such as these wafers.

Grape *pekmez*, a concentrated juice made from grapes often used in sweets in place of sugar, imparts its special delicious flavor and burnished color to these wafers. Grape *pekmez* can be purchased by mail order or at any good Middle Eastern market. There are many types, each made from a different type of grape. Two of my favorites are called Koska and Pyramid (see "Mail-Order Sources").

Serve these delicious wafers with fresh or poached fruit, or fruit sorbet.

1 tablespoon grape *pekmez*

¼ teaspoon grated lemon rind

1 8-ounce bottle soda water

1 teaspoon olive oil

½ cup unskinned hazelnuts or almonds,

¼ cup clarified butter, chilled and cut into small pieces

1½ tablespoons sugar

Pinch of salt

1 egg yolk

½ cup chapati or wholemeal flour

3 tablespoons fine cornmeal

2 to 3 tablespoons thick yogurt

4 to 6 large collard leaves

1. In a small bowl, mix the grape *pekmez*, grated lemon rind, 1 tablespoon of the soda water, and the olive oil, stirring until well blended. Set aside until step 3.

2. Boil the hazelnuts in the remaining soda water for 2 minutes; drain, rinse, and rub off the skins and dry well. In an iron skillet toast the nuts until golden, then set aside to cool.

3. In the work bowl of a food processor with the dough blade in place, cream the butter until light and fluffy. Gradually add the sugar with the machine on, then add the egg yolk and *pekmez* and pulse to combine. Scrape into a mixing bowl and carefully fold in the flour and cornmeal. Pulse the hazelnuts in the work bowl until finely ground; makes about ⅓ cup. Scrape into the bowl, gently fold in the hazelnut meal, and add enough yogurt to make a medium dough. Chill for 15 minutes.

4. Preheat the oven to 400 degrees, if planning to bake the wafer in the oven.

5. Set an oiled cast-iron skillet over medium heat. Spread the collard leaves one at a time in the skillet to soften. Spread the leaves, vein side down, and flatten them out to cover the pan without overlapping more than is necessary. With oiled palms, press the mixture into a 7-inch round, place in the skillet, and set on the middle oven shelf to bake until golden, 5 minutes; then reduce heat to 350 degrees and bake 20 minutes. Serve warm.

NOTE TO THE COOK: For stove-top cooking, flatten the mixture in a heated, greased nonstick skillet lined with collards. Cover and cook 10 minutes, turn, discard greens, and continue cooking, uncovered, for 8 minutes more. Serve warm.

10

SAUCES, CONDIMENTS, AND SEASONINGS

HOME-STYLE TOMATO SAUCE BASE

Makes 1 cup

This is one of my favorite tomato sauce recipes—the one I used in testing all the Italian recipes in this book. I often double the recipe and store half in the freezer.

2 tablespoons olive oil

2 tablespoons shredded prosciutto or pancetta (optional)

1 medium onion, finely chopped

1 clove garlic, chopped

1 small potato, pared and thinly sliced

¼ cup red or white wine

1 (20-ounce) can tomatoes, preferably organic

¼ cup sliced celery

¼ teaspoon dried rosemary

¼ teaspoon freshly ground black pepper

Salt

Sugar (optional)

Heat the olive oil in a small heavy skillet, and sauté the prosciutto, if using, onion, garlic, and potato over medium heat until onion and potato begin to caramelize, about 10 minutes. Deglaze with the wine and, when evaporated, add the tomatoes, celery, rosemary, pepper, salt, and sugar, if necessary. Simmer for 20 minutes. Press through a food mill for a smooth texture.

ONE-MINUTE *HARISSA* (*Tunisia*)

Makes 2½ tablespoons

This quick-to-make, spicy Tunisian spread is delicious on bread or may be used as a flavoring in any of the dishes that call for *harissa* in this book.

The beauty of this *harissa* recipe is not only its speediness but the fact that it's better than any bottled version you can buy.

I keep dried New Mexican chilies in my freezer and sun-dried tomatoes in the refrigerator solely to make this dish. With these ingredients on hand, I can make a small bowl of *harissa* in literally one minute from the moment the peppers and dried tomatoes finish softening in hot water.

After squeezing out excess moisture, rhythmically pound the peppers and tomatoes in a mortar for approximately one minute until you hear a thumping that signifies the ingredients have formed a paste. Smooth out with olive oil and the *harissa* is ready!

You can also make it in a food processor with excellent results.

1 clove garlic, peeled

2 dried New Mexican peppers, stemmed, seeded, and torn into 2-inch pieces, softened in warm water and squeezed dry

1 slice of sun-dried tomato, softened in warm water and squeezed dry

½ teaspoon salt

½ teaspoon Tunisian *tabil* (page 346)

⅛ teaspoon ground caraway

Olive oil

Lemon juice (optional, see Note)

In a stone mortar or the work bowl of a food processor, combine the garlic, peppers, tomato, salt, and spices and pound or pulse until pasty. Add the oil by the teaspoon until thick and spreadable.

NOTE: To serve as a dip, thin 2½ tablespoons *harissa* with warm water and olive oil to a dipping consistency. Correct the seasoning and if necessary add a few drops of lemon juice to round out the flavor.

ONION–RED PEPPER PASTE (HROUS)

Makes 1 cup

Hrous is a popular condiment in southern Tunisia, where women make it once a year, preparing a combination of lightly fermented onions with dried red peppers, then seasoning with plenty of spices.

I first published this recipe in the revised edition of my *Mediterranean Cooking*. I offer it again because it's so stunning and because it's needed for several recipes in this book.

2 fresh onions, peeled and thinly sliced

¼ teaspoon turmeric

3 tablespoons coarse salt

12 dried New Mexican chilies

1 teaspoon Tunisian *tabil* (page 346)

1 teaspoon ground caraway seed

¼ teaspoon ground cinnamon

¼ teaspoon ground black pepper

⅓ cup olive oil

If you make *hrous*, I promise you won't be disappointed. And if you make it and then forget to use it for a while, all the better! *Hrous*, you see, mellows beautifully in the refrigerator, reaching a truly glorious state after six months. For this reason I urge you to make it as soon as possible.

1. In a mixing bowl, combine the onions, turmeric, and salt and let stand until soft and wet, about 3 days.

2. Drain the onions and press out all moisture. Stem and seed the chilies. Grind to a powder in a blender or food processor with the spices and the onions, blending well. Pack into a sterile mason jar, cover with oil, and close tightly. Keep refrigerated.

ALI-OLI SAUCE (*Spain*)

❀

Making a garlic–olive oil sauce without eggs is not easy. You'll need a wooden pestle, an earthenware mortar, and, most important, a *juicy* clove of garlic. Winter is definitely not the season for making ali-oli, since winter garlic tends to be dry.

Ali-oli takes practice. What you want is a mound resembling a beautiful lemon pudding. But no matter what you do, sooner or later your ali-oli will "break." Some cooks choose to bind their sauce with an egg yolk. If you don't want to take that route, I suggest another solution: potatoes. Heresy—of course . . . but it works.

---

2 boiling potatoes (½ pound), peeled

4 cloves garlic or to taste

Coarse sea salt

Juice of 1 lemon

White pepper

Extra-virgin olive oil

Freshly boil the potatoes in water. Crush the garlic with sea salt in a heavy earthenware mortar until smooth. Drain the warm potatoes, reserving some of the cooking liquid. Press out all moisture, add to the garlic, and pound until smooth and elastic. Add the lemon juice and white pepper. Gradually drizzle in the olive oil in a slow, steady stream, about 3 tablespoons. Loosen with some of the reserved potato cooking liquid to develop a nice consistency. Set in a cool place to mellow.

NOTES TO THE COOK: The Spanish Table (see "Mail-Order Sources") sells beautiful Valencian yellow and green glazed mortars for making and serving the traditional ali-oli sauce.

Dense stale bread, soaked in water and squeezed dry, can substitute for the potatoes.

YOGURT–GARLIC SAUCE (*Turkey*)

Makes 2 cups

3 cups plain yogurt

½ teaspoon crushed garlic

Salt

Yogurt appears on the eastern Mediterranean table at every meal. Here's a simple sauce called *jajik* that will also go well with many of the Greek and Turkish recipes in this book.

Drain the yogurt to 2 cups. Beat in the garlic until smooth. Add salt to taste and chill for 1 hour.

TABIL (*Tunisia*)

Makes about 4½ teaspoons

1 tablespoon ground coriander seeds

1 teaspoon ground caraway seeds

¼ teaspoon garlic powder (optional)

¼ teaspoon ground red pepper

¼ teaspoon curry powder

This is a popular spice mixture used in recipes for Tunisian salads, stews, and couscous.

Mix and store in a tightly covered jar.

PRESERVED LEMONS (*Morocco*)

❊

Here's a quick 7-day method for preserving lemons: Scrub 2 ripe lemons and dry well. Cut each into 8 wedges. Toss with ⅓ cup coarse sea salt and place in a half-pint glass jar with a glass or plastic-coated lid. Pour in ½ cup fresh lemon juice. Close the jar tightly and let the lemons ripen at room temperature for 7 days, shaking the jar each day to distribute the salt and juice. To store longer, add olive oil to cover and refrigerate.

KITTINA'S *HERBES DE PROVENCE* (*France*)

✧

My friend Kittina Powers has a splendid garden in Marin County where she grows all sorts of aromatic herbs. Every year she makes up a batch of such exemplary *herbes de Provence* that I treasure the little jars she gives me.

She cuts handfuls of basil, winter savory, thyme, and lavender flowers when their flavors are strongest, just as they're beginning to flower. She lays the branches of herbs and flowers on a tray and lets them dry for several days until they're brittle to the touch, then she rubs the leaves off the stems. (She saves the stems to scatter over a grilling fire.) Next she rubs the resulting mixture through a coarse sieve. For every cup of herb mixture she adds 1 tablespoon of fennel seeds.

If you follow this procedure, you'll end up with a terrific herb mixture useful in Warm Scrambled Eggs and Aromatic Herbs with Baby Lettuces and Crispy Croutons (page 161), Grilled Treviso-Style Radicchio on Polenta (page 109), Watercress and Tomato Salad with Cured Tuna (page 134), grilled meat dishes, pasta sauces, on feta cheese, and so on. If you store it away from heat and light, in jars with tightly fitting lids, the flavor of the mixture will keep well for at least a year.

APPENDIX A: NOTES ON WILD EDIBLE GREENS POPULAR IN THE MEDITERRANEAN KITCHEN

Arugula, False and Wall (*Diplotaxis erucoides, Diplotaxis muralis*). Very spicy leaves used in salads or cooked with beans.

Bladder Campion (*Silene vulgaris*). The young leaves are tender and crunchy with the taste of sweet peas.

Borage (*Borago officinalis*). In Spain the shoots are added to shellfish and meat stews; the leaves are battered, fried, and sugared. In Italy the leaves are added to a stew of squid and greens, and to the Ligurian greens mixture *preboggion*.

Butcher's Broom (*Ruscus aculeatus*). The young shoots are tart and bitter, but when cooked they develop a bluish purple color and a well-balanced flavor. Used in risottos and frittatas.

Calamint (*Calamintha nepeta*). Ethnobotanist François Couplan writes that these leaves are used to aromatize fish soups in Corsica.

Carrot, Wild (*Daucus carota*). The leaves have the aroma of carrots and provide great flavor to stews. Cretans use the leaves to flavor their pies; Italians put the leaves in soups.

Chickweed (*Stellaria media*). Has a mild hazelnut flavor. Used raw in salads. In Italy it is added in large quantities to *minestras*.

Clematis, Wild (*Clematis vitalba*). Tender shoots with top leaves used for soups, risottos, and frittatas. Also known as Traveler's Joy.

Eryngo (*Eryngium creticum*). These furry sweet-tasting leaves and stalks, raw or cooked, are eaten in salads or dipped in batter and fried.

Fennel, Wild (*Foeniculum vulgare*). Aromatic leaves and stalks, raw or cooked; good in combination with other sweet greens, beans, and chicken.

Goat's Beard (*Tragopogon pratensis*). Stringlike, sweet-flavored leaves are mixed with other greens and used in stews and pies in Italy and Greece.

Ground Ivy (*Glechoma hederacea*). The bitter-flavored leaves keep their green color and strong aroma and are used in Italian risottos.

Horsemint (*Mentha longifolia*). A wild, thick-leafed mint that is very aromatic.

Kengar (*Gundelia tournefortii*). The root of this thorny plant is peeled, steamed, and mixed into a popular southeastern Anatolian bulgur salad.

Lemon Balm (*Melissa officinalis*). Very young shoots are added to salads in Italy and Israel to provide a lemony perfume.

Madimak, Turkish (*Polygonum cognatum*). Leaves are dried and used to flavor pilafs.

Mallow/Khobbeiza (*Malva sylvestris*). Dark curly leaves and tender shoots are cooked with olive oil and served in salads in the Middle East, North Africa, Turkey, and Cyprus. Larger leaves are stuffed with rice, parsley, dill, and onion and cooked in olive oil in central Anatolia.

Mallow, Common (*Malva neglecta*). The shoots and leaves are stewed with chicken in Greece.

Molokiah/Jew's Mallow (*Corchorus olitorius*). Young leaves are boiled with chicken, lamb, and rabbit for soups and stews. Powdered dried leaves are simmered in olive oil and used as a soup base in Tunisia.

Mustard, White (*Sinapis alba*). Leaves are boiled for salads or sautéed in olive oil and mixed with eggs to stuff in flatbread. A popular eastern Mediterranean green.

Mustard, Wild (*Sinapis arvensis*). Very bitter pungent leaves picked in early spring and boiled for salads dressed with olive oil and lemon.

Nettles, Stinging (*Urtica dioica*). Young nettle tops are not as acidic as spinach. Nettles are delicious in pies, risottos, and soups. The tops are delicious when paired with leeks, cream, butter, yogurt, bulgur, pasta dough, and eggs.

Oxtongue (*Picris echioides*). Very young leaves are sweet and tender and used in soups in France and Italy.

Pimpernel, Roman (*Tordylium apulum*). The aromatic leaves are used in combination with other sweet greens for Greek pies and stews.

Plantain, Buck's Horn (*Plantago coronopus*). In Provence young leaves are used in salads.

Poppy, Corn (*Papaver rhoeas*). In southeastern Turkey raw leaves are added to pies and bulgur pilafs, and stuffed into flatbreads. In Provence and Apulia the leaves are stewed with olives.

Radish, Wild (*Raphanus raphanistrum*). The leaves are sautéed quickly and folded into omelets in the eastern Mediterranean.

Salad Burnet (*Sanguisorba minor*). Delicious raw in salads with tomatoes, and cooked with greens such as spinach.

Salsify, Spanish (*Scolymus hispanicus*). In southern Spain the bitter root of the local *tagarinas* is blanched, sautéed, and seasoned with Spanish paprika and garlic.

Scorzonera, French (*Reichardia picroides*). The leaves of this spring green are crunchy and sweet, delicious raw in salads or mixed into the famous Ligurian greens mix *pre-boggion* for pasta and pies.

Sea Kale (*Crambe maritima*). Young stalks in the spring are blanched for salads. Also, a popular addition to northern Moroccan fish stews.

Shepherd's Needle (*Scandix pecten-veneris*). In Crete a handful of fragrant leaves is said to enhance the best wild greens pies.

Shepherd's Purse (*Capsella bursa-pastoris*). For *minestras,* frittatas, and cooked salads in Italy.

Sorrel, Garden (*Rumex acetosa*) Sourish leaves are stuffed with crushed shelled wheat, steamed, and topped with garlic-yogurt sauce in Turkey. In Italy the young leaves are steamed with fish.

Sorrel, Sheep (*Rumex acetosella*). Young leaves are eaten raw in salad in Turkey, cooked with fresh favas in Tunisia, lightly cooked for salad in Italy, and simmered with a few unripe plums in water and olive oil in Macedonia.

Thistle, Common Sow (*Sonchus oleraceus*). Sweet and tasty young green eaten raw or simply boiled and dressed with lemon and olive oil. A popular salad in the eastern Mediterranean.

Thistle, Sow-Field (*Sonchus arvensis*). These leaves add a sweet flavor to Tunisian vegetable dishes, Cretan salads, and Provençal soups.

Fresh Leafy Greens and Vegetables (In Season)

Bitter greens including chicories. Cardoons, cactus pads, chrysanthemum leaves or *shunkiyu*, garden sorrel, green garlic, mâche and pea shoots, purslane, stinging nettles, Treviso-style radicchio, Tuscan kale (also known as lacinata kale and dinosaur kale)—Greenleaf; Indian Rock Produce

Mallow leaves—Greenleaf; Stone Free

Live Plants

Borage, stinging nettles, chrysanthemum leaves (*shungiku*), mallow (*Malva sylvestris*), samphire (*Crithmum maritimum*), garden sorrel—Well-Sweep Farms

Sweet "wild fennel" (*Foeniculum vulgare*)—Southern Perennials & Herbs

Seeds for Leafy Greens and Vegetables

Arugula, *Chrysanthemum coronarium* (*shungiku*), cutting or European celery, mesclun, chicories, dandelion, lamb's-quarters, orach, purslane, sorrel—Cook's Garden; Shepherd's; Ornamental Edibles

Beans, long *(Vigna unguiculata var sesquipedalis)* #38395—B&T Seeds

Kale, Tuscan—Ornamental Edibles

Tenerumi/*Zucchetto Rampicante* (*Cucurbita moscata*)—Shepherd's

Grains, Beans, Spices, and Other Aromatics

Aleppo pepper—Dean & Deluca; Haig's; Kalustyan; Shallah's Importing Co.

Beans (cannellini)—Dean & Deluca; Phipps; Zingerman's

Basturma—E.K. Imports; Haig's; Kalustyan

Bread—Poilane's Finest Bread (fresh-frozen from Paris); Deborah's Country French Bread

Bulgur in all grades—Dean & Deluca; E.K. Imports; Haig's; Kalustyan; Shallah's Importing Co.

Capers in salt—Balducci's; Corti Brothers; Dean & Deluca; Todaro Bros.; Zingerman's

Cheeses: Italian *parmigiano-reggiano,* pecorino Romano, Gorgonzola Dolce, Galatea Pecorino Crotonese, ricotta Pecorino Roman-type, and ricotta salata—Dean & Deluca; Formaggio Kitchen; Todaro Bros.; Zingerman's

Italian Montasio—Mozzarella Company; Zingerman's

Greek feta, *kasseri, kefalotyri, manouri,* and *mizithra*—Dean & Deluca; Formaggio Kitchen

Chestnuts, roasted and vacuum-packed—Balducci's; Dean & Deluca; Williams-Sonoma; Zingerman's

Corn, toasted sweet (dried whole kernel corn)—John Cope's Food Products; The Great Valley Mills

Cornmeal—Gray's Grist Mill; Hoppin' John's

Polenta: Coarse, "Golden Pheasant"—Corti Brothers

Couscous—Dean & Deluca; Kalustyan; Shallah's Importing Co.

Flour, barley—The Great Valley Mills; King Arthur Flour

Flour, durum and fine semolina—King Arthur Flour; Kalustyan; Shallah's Importing Co.; Vivande

Fregula (Sardinian couscous)—Balducci's

Grano, see Wheat berries, shelled durum

Grape molasses (*pekmez*)—Haig's; Kalustyan

Green wheat (*frik, freekeh,* or *freekeh*)—Dean & Deluca; Haig's; Kalustyan; Shallah's Importing Co.

Lentils (very small brown lentils): Italian lentils—Balducci's; Dean & Deluca

Spanish pardina lentils—Phipps Ranch

Egyptian, Ethiopian, and Indian masoor dal—Kalustyan

Mastic—Haig's; Kalustyan; Shallah's Importing Co.

Mint leaves (dried)—Haig's; Kalustyan; Shallah's Importing Co.; The Spice House

Pancetta—Dean & Deluca; J. Pace & Son, Inc.; Zingerman's

Paprika: Spanish sweet, hot, and smoky *pimentón de la Vera*—The Spanish Table; Zingerman's

Pepper flakes, Turkish (Kahramanmaras pepper)—Zingerman's

Peppers, dried whole: *Ñoras*—The Spanish Table; Zingerman's

Peppers, dried whole: New Mexican—Tierra Vegetables

Pepper Paste (Turkish sweet and hot "Melis" or "Selim")—Dean & Deluca; Haig's; Kalustyan; E.K. Imports, Inc.

Peppers, piquillos—La Española; The Spanish Table; Zingerman's

Phyllo, fresh in one-pound packages—The Fillo Factor Inc.

Pomegranate molasses (concentrated pomegranate juice)—Dean & Deluca; Haig's; Kalustyan; Shallah's Importing Co.

Rice: Italian arborio, vialone nano and carnaroli—Balducci's; Corti Brothers; Dean & Deluca; Todaro Bros.; Zingerman's

Rice: Mediterranean-style Cal-Riso—Corti Brothers

Rice: Spanish—La Española; The Spanish Table; Zingerman's

Rice: Turkish Baldo—Kalustyan

Saffron—Dean & Deluca; Penzeys; The Spanish Table; Zingerman's

Sausage, black morcillas (blood sausage) and semicured chorizos—La Española; The Spanish Table

Sea salt—Dean & Deluca; Zingerman's

Semolina (coarse grain)—Kalustyan; Shallah's Importing Co.

Smoked fish—Ducktrap River Fish Farm

Snails (live)—Pennsylvania Snail Farm

Spices—Penzeys; Kalustyan; Shallah's Importing Co.

"Squid" ink—The Spanish Table

Sumac—Kalustyan; Shallah's Importing Co.

Taro root (Egyptian "Montana," frozen)—Nile Food Imports

Verjuice—Dean & Deluca

Wheat berries, shelled—Dean & Deluca; Haig's; Kalustyan; Shallah's Importing Co.

Wheat berries, shelled durum, "grano"—Balducci's; Corti Brothers

Wheat starch—Oriental Pantry

Equipment

Cazuelas (shallow and deep)—The Spanish Table

Chestnut knife—Williams-Sonoma and Sur la Table

Dehydrators—American Harvest; local hardware stores; Living Foods Dehydrators

Griddle to cover two burners for *arroces*: Lodge 21-inch grid-iron griddle—Sur la Table

Paella pans—The Spanish Table; Zingerman's

Parchment paper (five-pound minimum)—E.A. Dages Co.

Peking Pan-Pro for cooking polenta—Oriental Pantry

Steel Indian "tava" for stove-top bread baking—Kalustyan

Addresses for Mail-Order Sources

American Harvest (dehydrators)
4064 Peavey Road
Chaska, Minnesota 55318

Balducci's (Italian foods)
P. O. Box 10373
Newark, New Jersey 07193-0373
Telephone: (800) BALDUCCI
website: www.Balducci.com

B&T Seeds
B & T World Seeds
Route des Marchandes
Paguignan, 34210 Olonzac, France
Telephone: 011 33 04 68 91 29 63
Fax: 011 33 04 68 91 30 39
E-mail: B_and_T_World_Seeds@compuserve.com
Technical: R@thesys.demon.co.uk

The Cook's Garden (seeds)
P.O. Box 535
Londonderry, Vermont 05148
Telephone: (800) 457-9703

John Cope's Food Products (toasted corn kernels)
P.O. Box 419
Rheems, Pennsylvania 17570–0419
Telephone: (717) 367-5142

Corti Brothers (polenta, capers, rice, etc.)
5810 Folsom Boulevard
P.O. Box 191358
Sacramento, California 95819
Telephone: (916) 736-3800
Fax: (916) 736-3807

Deborah's (Poilane Bread)
4½-pound sourdough loaf, quick-frozen
954 West Washington Boulevard
Chicago, Illinois 60607
Telephone: (312) 633-4004
Telephone: (800) 952-1400
Fax: (312) 829-9671

E.A. Dages (parchment paper)
975 Bethlehem Pike
Montgomeryville, Pennsylvania 18936
Telephone: (800) 732-4377

Dean & Deluca (produce, grains, and aromatics)
560 Broadway
New York, New York 11101
Telephone: (212) 226-6800, ext. 269
(personal shopping service)
Telephone: (800) 999-0306 (store)
Telephone: (800) 221-7714 (catalog)

Ducktrap River Fish Farm (smoked fish)
R.F.D. 2, Box 378
Lincolnville, Maine 04849
Telephone: (207) 763-3960

E.K. Imports (Turkish imported foods)
171 Lombardy Street
Brooklyn, New York 11222
Telephone: (800) 783-3055
Fax: (718) 388-2737

La Española Meats
25020 Doble Avenue
Harbor City, California 90710
Telephone: (310) 539-0455
Fax: (310) 539-5989

The Fillo Factor Inc. (fresh phyllo)
56 Cortland Avenue
Dumont, New Jersey 07628
Telephone: (800) OK-FILLO

Formaggio Kitchen
244 Huron Avenue
Cambridge, Massachusetts 02138
Telephone: (617) 354-4750
Fax: (617) 547-5680

The Great Valley Mills (toasted corn kernels and flour)
1774 County Line Road
Barto, Pennsylvania 19504
Telephone: (800) 688-6455
Fax: (610) 754-6490

Greenleaf (fresh produce)
1955 Jerrold Avenue
San Francisco, California 94124
Telephone: (415) 647-2991
Fax: (415) 647-2996

Gray's Grist Mill (cornmeal)
P.O. Box 422
Adamsville, Rhode Island 02801
Telephone: (509) 636-6075

Hoppin' John's (cornmeal)
30 Pinckney Street
Charleston, South Carolina 29410
Telephone: (800) 828-4412

Indian Rock Produce (fresh produce)
530 California Road
Quakertown, Pennsylvania 18951
Telephone: (800) 882-0512
Telephone: (215) 536-9600
Fax: (215) 529-9447

Kalustyan
123 Lexington Avenue
New York, N.Y. 10016
Telephone: (212) 685-3888
Fax: (212) 683-8458

Living Foods Dehydrators
P.O. Box 546
Fall City, Washington 98024
Telephone: (206) 222-5587

Mozzarella Company (fresh mozzarella,
montasio, and ricotta)
2944 Elm Street
Dallas, Texas 75226
Telephone: (800) 798-2854
Fax: (214) 741-4076
E-mail: mozzCo@aol.com

The Oriental Pantry (pot for cooking polenta)
423 Great Road
Acton, Massachusetts 01720
Telephone: (508) 264-4576
Telephone: (800) 828-0368
Fax: (617) 275-4506
Website: www.orientalpantry.com
E-mail:oriental@orientalpantry.com

Ornamental Edibles (vegetable seeds)
3622 Weedin Court
San Jose, California 95132
Telephone: (408) 946-SEED
Fax: (408) 946-0181

Penzeys, Ltd. (quality herbs and spices)
P.O. Box 1448
Waukesha, Wisconsin 53187
Telephone: (414) 574-0277
Fax: (414) 574-0278

Pennsylvania Snail Farm
Kenneth Ohler, President
236 North Street
Meyersdale, Pennsylvania 15552
Telephone: (814) 662-2253

Phipps Country (beans and lentils)
P.O. Box 349
Pescadero, California 94060
Telephone: (800) 279-0889
Fax: (415) 879-1622

Shepherd's Garden Seeds
30 Irene Street
Torrington, Connecticut 06790
Telephone: (860) 482-3638

Southern Perennials & Herbs (live plants)
98 Bridges Road
Tylertown, Mississippi 39667
Telephone: (800) 774-0079
Fax: (601) 684-3729

The Spanish Table (Spanish imports)
1427 Western Avenue (Pike Street Hillclimb)
Seattle, Washington 98101
Telephone: (206) 682-2827
Fax: (206) 682-2814
E-mail:tablespan@aol.com

Sur La Table
1765 Sixth Avenue, South
Seattle, Washington 98134
Telephone: (800) 243-0852

Stone-Free Farm
P.O. Box 1437
Watsonville, California 95077
Telephone: (408) 761-7222
Fax: (408) 761-7217

Tierra Vegetables
13684 Chalk Hill Road
Healdsburg, California 95448
Telephone: (707) 837-8366
Fax: (707) 433-5666
E-mail: evie@tierravegetables.com

Todaro Brothers (Italian imports)
555 Second Avenue
New York, New York 10016
Telephone: (212) 679-7766
Fax: (212) 689-1679

Vivande Porta Via (Italian imports,
including vegetable seeds)
2125 Fillmore Street
San Francisco, California 94115
Telephone: (415) 346-4430

Well Sweep Herb Farm (live plants)
205 Mt. Bethel Road
Port Murray, New Jersey 07865

Williams-Sonoma (kitchen supplies and tableware)
P.O. Box 7456
San Francisco, California 94120–7456
Telephone: (415 421 4242

Zingerman's Mail-Order Department
(quality imported foods)
422 Detroit Street
Ann Arbor, Michigan 48104-1118
Telephone: (313) 769-1625
Email: zing@chamber.ann-arbor.mi.us

BIBLIOGRAPHY

Alexiadou, Vefa. *Greek Pastries and Desserts.* Salonika: Alexiadou, 1995.

Alford, Jeffrey, and Naomi Duguid. *Flatbreads and Flavors.* New York: Willim Morrow, 1995.

Al-Jabri, Lamya. *Shahiyya Tayyiba* (Delicious, Good-Tasting). Damascus: Tlas, n.d. (in Arabic).

Alonso, Francisco G. Seijo. *Gastronomia de la Provincia de Alicante.* Alicante: Editorial Villa, 1977.

Anderson, Pam, and Karen Tack. "How to Quick-Cook Strong-Flavored Greens." *Cook's Illustrated,* January 1995.

Andrews, Colman. *Flavors of the Riviera.* New York: Bantam Books, 1996.

Ansky, Sheri. "Musbacha." *Ma'ariv,* Jerusalem, May 17, 1997.

Baytop, Dr. Turhan. *Türkçe Bitki Adlari Sözlü.* Ankara: Türk Tarih Kurumu Basim Evi, 1994.

Bernaudeau. A. *La Cuisine Tunisienne d'Oummi Taïabat.* Tunis: Imprimerie Saliba, 1937.

Bittman, Mark. *Leafy Greens.* New York: Macmillan, 1995.

Caceres, Angeles, and Bonet Rafael. *Comer Como Dios Manda.* Alicante: Editorial Aguaclara, 1993.

Canetti, Elias. *The Voices of Marrakech.* New York: Continuum, 1978.

Coon, Nelson. *Using Wild and Wayside Plants.* New York: Dover, 1957.

Corriher, Shirley O. *CookWise: The Hows and Whys of Successful Cooking with Nearly 150 Great-Tasting Recipes.* New York: William Morrow, 1997.

———. "Keeping Fresh Produce Really Fresh." *Fine Cooking,* February/March 1996.

Couplan, François. *La Cuisine Sauvage.* Volume 2. Flers: Equilibres Aujourd'hui, 1989.

———. *Les Plantes Sauvages Comestibles*. Paris: Editions Sang de la Terre, 1995.

Couplan, François, and Marc Veyrat. *Herbier Gourmand*. Paris: Hachette, 1997.

Crett, Giorgio. *Erbe e Malerbe in Cucina*. Milan: Edizioni Sipiel, 1987.

DeSilva, Cara. "The Many Joys of Soffrito." *Newsday*. June 1, 1994.

Dosti, Rose. *Mideast & Mediterranean Cuisines*. Tucson: Fisher Books, 1993.

Ducasse, Alain. *Méditerranées, Cuisine de L'essentiel*. Paris: Hachette, 1996.

Emery, Carla. *The Encyclopedia of Country Living*, 9th edition. Seattle: Sasquatch Books,1994.

Evans, Alan, and Beatrice Evans. *La Cucina Picena*. Padua: Franco Muzi, 1991.

Facciola, Stephen. *Cornucopia: A Source Book of Edible Plants*. Vista, Calif.: Kampong Publications, 1990.

Field, Carol. *In Nonna's Ktichen: Recipes and Traditions from Italy's Grandmothers*. New York: HarperCollins Publishers, 1997.

Food and Agricultural Organization of the United Nations (FAO). *Traditional Foods in the Near East*. Rome: FAO Food and Nutrition Paper No. 50, 1991.

George, Nora. *Nora's Recipes from Egypt*. Fresno, Calif.: 1995.

Gobert E., "Usages et rites alimentation tunisiens." Tunis: Archives de l'Institut Pasteur de Tunis. T. 29, pp. 475–589, 1940.

Gold, Jonathan. "Basturma Boss." *Los Angeles Times,* April 4, 1996.

González Pomata, Antonio. *Cocina Alicantina*. León: Editorial Everest, S.A., 1996.

Gray, Patience. *Honey from a Weed*. New York: Harper & Row, 1986.

Hal, Fatéma. *Les Saveurs & Les Gestes: Cuisines et Traditions du Maroc*. Paris: Stock, 1995.

Hamlin, Suzanne. "Farro, Italy's Rustic Staple: The Little Grain That Could." *New York Times*. June 11, 1997.

———. "Giant Squash Turns Briefly into Belle of the Harvest Ball." *New York Times*. September 18, 1996.

Haroutunian. Arto der. *A Turkish Cookbook*. London: Ebury Press, 1987.

Hayward, Vicky. "The Grain of Life." *Gourmetour Magazine*. Madrid: ICEX, 1993.

Hubert, Annie. *Le Pain et L'Olive*. Paris: Editions du Centre National de la Recherche Scientifique. 1984.

Jordan, Michele Anna. *Polenta: 100 Innovative Recipes, from Appetizers to Desserts*. New York: Broadway Books, 1997.

Kalças, Eveyln Lyle. *Fresh from the Fields*. Izmir: Telif Hakki Mahfuzdur, 1984, third printing.

Kazmaz, Suleyman. *Rize Yemekleri ve yemek Kultura*. Ankara: Basim Tarihi, 1992.

Kimball, Christopher. *The Cook's Bible*. Boston: Little, Brown, 1996.

Kremezi, Aglaia. *The Foods of Greece*. New York: Steward, Tabori & Chang, 1993.

Kremezi, Aglaia. "The Case of Kythera." Oxford Symposium. 1994.

Larkcom, Joy. *Oriental Vegetables*. New York: Kodansha America, 1991.

———. *The Salad Garden*. New York: Viking Press, 1984.

Louis, Diana Farr, and June Marinos. *Prospero's Kitchen*. New York: Evans and Company, 1995.

Luard, Elisabeth. *The Flavours of Andalucia*. London: Collins & Brown Ltd, 1991

Maffioli, Giuseppe. *La Cucina Trevigiana*. Padova: Franco Muzzio, 1983.

March, Lourdes. *El Libro de la Paella y de los Arroces* Madrid: Allianza, 1985

Onstad, Dianne. *Whole Foods Companion*. Vermont: Cheslea Green Publishing Company, 1996.

Paoletti, Maurizio, A. L. Dreon, and G. G. Lorenzoni. "*Pistic,* Traditional Food from Western Fruili," *N.E. Italy Economic Botany* 49 (1) pp. 26–30, 1995 (New York Botanical Garden, Bronx, N.Y.)

Parsons, Russ. "I Ain't Stirrin'" *Los Angeles Times*. April 2, 1997.

———. "A Stirring Tale of Italian Polenta" *Los Angeles Times*. January 13, 1994.

Perry, Charles. "A Funny Thing Happened on the Way to the Noodle." *Los Angeles Times*. April 21, 1994.

———. "Grain Cooking: Tales from the Bulgur Belt." *Los Angeles Times.* January 27, 1994.

———. "Splendors of the Grass." *Los Angeles Times.* November 5, 1992.

Phillips, Roger. *Wild Food.* Boston: Little Brown, 1986.

Pla, Josep. *El que hem Menjat,* Barcelona: Edicions Destino, 1972.

Poulain, Jean-Pierre, and Jean-Luc Rouyer. *Histoire et Recettes de la Provence et du Comté de Nice.* Toulouse: Privat, 1987.

Roden, Claudia. *The Book of Jewish Food.* New York: Knopf, 1996.

Santich, Barbara. "Testo, Tegamo, Tiella, Tian: The Mediterranean Camp Oven." Oxford Symposium on Food and Cookery, 1988.

Sandri, Amedeo. *La Polenta nella Cucina Veneta.* Padova: Muzzio, 1985.

Sass, Lorna. *Cooking Under Pressure.* New York: William Morrow, 1989.

Schneider, Elizabeth. *Uncommon Fruits & Vegetables, A Commonsense Guide.* New York: Harper & Row, 1986.

———. "Whole Grains Explained" Parts 1, 2, and 3. New York: *Food Arts Magazine.* July-August 1994, October 1994, March 1995.

Schoenfeld, Bruce. "Paella as a Way of Life." New York: *Saveur* magazine, July-August 1996.

Schwartz, Arthur. "Love Me, Tendril." *New York Daily News.* August 17, 1994.

Sevilla, Marie José. "Vegetables with Personality" Madrid: *Spain Gourmetour,* Issue 43, November 1997.

Simeti, Mary Taylor. *Pomp and Sustenance, Twenty-Five Centuries of Sicilian Food.* New York: Knopf, 1989.

Stark, Freya. *Letters from Syria.* London: John Murray, 1942.

Steingarten, Jeffrey. *The Man Who Ate Everything.* New York: Knopf, 1997.

Stobart, Tom. *The Cook's Encyclopedia, Indgredients and Processes.* New York: Harper & Row. 1981.

Thompson, Sylvie. "How Green Was My Garlic." *Los Angeles Times,* May 6, 1993.

Torgersen, Susan. *Flavors of Egypt: From City and Country Kitchens.* Cairo: Maidi, 1992

Ucer, Mujgan, *Sivas Halk Mutfagi* (Sivas People's Cooking Sivas: Dizgi, 1992. (In Turkish)

Villas, James. T*he French Country Kitchen.* New York: Bantam Books, 1992.

Willinger, Faith. *Red, White, and Greens. The Italian Way with Vegetables.* New York: HarperCollins, 1996.

Wolfert, Paula. *The Cooking of the Eastern Mediterranean.* New York: HarperCollins Publishers, 1994.

———. *Mediterranean Cooking,* revised edition. New York: HarperCollins Publishers, 1994

INDEX

baby, and purslane with cucumber and shredded cabbage, 138–39

with barley, beans and tomatoes, 167–76

and barley with pan-fried prosciutto, 167–68

in best-ever *bugulama,* 293–94

bitter, best-ever *bugulama* with, 294

bitter, pasta with tomatoes and, 196–97

Black Sea soup with cornmeal, mushrooms and, 63–64

blending of, 3

boiling of, 7

braised cabbage with glazed onions and sautéed mushrooms, 306–7

chiffonade of wild and not-so-wild edible, 132

and clams with potatoes *à la importancia,* deep-dish, 247–48

collard, Black Sea cornmeal wafers baked on, 339–40

Cretan mixed, and tomatoes with black-eyed peas, 168–69

and crispy potatoes with smoky paprika and whipped eggs, gratin of, 164–65

"dragged," with potato, garlic, peperoncino and rosemary, 291–92

dried, 298

edible wild, 159–60

and eggs, 159–64

farro and potato soup as prepared in the Marches, 66–67

field, rice and pumpkin torta, 56–57

frozen, cooking of, 9

garden, and herbs with tomatoes and green olives, 133

garden, sautéed yard-long beans and walnuts with, 147–48

garlic, yogurt, red pepper swirls and, 150–51

garlic soup with, 82

with golden raisins, pine nuts and sherry vinegar, 300

in green dumplings tossed with diced tomato, toasted walnuts and fresh herbs, 200–201

mallow leaves with Tunisian spices, 296

measures for, 5

in Middle Eastern chard and lentil soup, 85

mixed, flavored with lamb, 299

mixed, potato strudel stuffed with, 122–23

mixed, with garlic and balsamic vinegar, 291

mixed wild, salad with preserved lemons and olives, Moroccan, 152–53

mustard, with black-eyed peas and rice, 170–71

mustard, young, with pomegranate molasses, 301

North African steaming of, 8

pan-wilting and sautéing of, 7–8

pea shoots with tomato and egg, 304–5

and pomegranates with cheese crisps, 142–44

potato cake stuffed with Tuscan kale and Taleggio cheese, 307–8

preparation for the skillet of large amounts of, 9

Provençal braised celery hearts with scallions, 310

"scrambled" with eggs on polenta, 112

skillet, with garlic and anchovies on grilled polenta, 111

snails with, 177–79

sorrel, spinach and artichoke ragout, 308–9

steamed lamb with winter vegetables and, 256–57

stewed, with basturma chips, 297

stewed, with tahini, Moshe Basson's, 93

storing of, 5–6

Stravoula's Cretan snail and fennel stew with, 178–79

stuffed, 116

sweet, 324–27

sweet garden, and toasted bread cubes with roast chicken, 248–49

tender, and sheep's milk cheese, 290

tender young, with tomato and onion, 304–5

Tunisian fish couscous with pumpkin, 205–7

Tunisian-Jewish wedding *pkaila* with beef and, 275–77

with wavy frico and grilled polenta, 143–44

wild, *al pomodoro,* 302

wild, Cretan "scarf" pies with, 55

wilted, handkerchief pasta with wild mushrooms and, *mandili de sea,* 192–93

green wheat:

Egyptian-style baked squab stuffed with garlic, lemon and, 254–55

Gaziantep-style triangles of Swiss chard stuffed with lamb, pine nuts and, 120–21

griddle bread, Turkish, stuffed with green garlic, 48–49

grills, sautés and gratins, 105–15

ham and parsley sauce, asparagus *à la parilla* with, 105

handkerchief pasta with wilted greens and wild mushrooms, *mandili de sea,* 192–93

harira, summer, with purslane and spices, 80–81

harissa:

cactus and cilantro salad, 149

one-minute, 343

harpout köfte with fresh mint and egg salad, 264–65

herbes de Provence, Kittina's, 347

herbs:

aromatic, and warm scrambled eggs with baby lettuces and crispy croutons, 161

fresh, green dumplings tossed with diced tomato, toasted walnuts and, 200–201

fresh, medley of wheat berries, lentils and rice with, 68–69

and garden greens with tomatoes and green olives, 133

honey, Moroccan semolina-yeast crepes with, 332–33

hops tops frittata, 163

pine nuts:
escarole stuffed with capers,
anchovies, golden raisins and, 124
Gaziantep-style triangles of Swiss
chard stuffed with green wheat,
lamb and, 120–21
greens with golden raisins, sherry
vinegar and, 300
mussels stuffed with rice, currants
and, 128–29
pistachios:
carrots and chestnuts, glazed, rice and
chicken with, 252–53
milk pudding with, 329–30
pistou with aged Gouda, Provençal, 91
pizza with pan-seared cabbage, the
monk's, 44–45
polenta, 311–13
buying of, 312
caramelized onions and cheese on, 110
crostini, 108
crostini, shredded red radicchio and
smoked fish salad with, 144–45
dumplings with mushrooms, Taleggio
cheese and sizzling butter, 319–20
grilled, leafy greens with wavy frico
and, 143–44
grilled, skillet leafy greens with garlic
and anchovies on, 111
grilled Treviso-style radicchio on, 109
keeping of, 313
keeping of cooked, 314
leafy greens "scrambled" with eggs
on, 112
leftover, 319–20
in the Marches, 321
no-stir, 313–14
onion jam for, 315
pie, creamy, caramelized cabbage and,
316–17
sautéed slices, 319
slicing of, 318
torta with "apron greens," 317–18
in Venice, 322
pomegranate(s):
and escarole, warm, with sherry and
sherry wine vinegar, 135
and leafy greens with cheese crisps,
142–44

molasses, young mustard greens with,
301
pork:
Alicante-style rice with pig's hand,
sausage and celery, 232–34
broccoli rabe risotto with, 189
ground, Provençal "meat loaf" with
cabbage, artichokes, chard, spinach
and, 269–70
in Provençal-style stuffed cabbage,
272–74
sausages, crusty rice with chicken and,
234–36
in stuffed Swiss chard on a bed of
taro root or potatoes, 270–71
potato(es):
cake stuffed with Tuscan kale and
Taleggio cheese, 307–8
crispy, and leafy greens with smoky
paprika and whipped eggs, gratin
of, 164–65
"dragged" greens with garlic, peperoncino, rosemary and, 291–92
farro and leafy greens soup as prepared in the March-es, 66–67
greens with barley, beans and, 167–76
à la importancia, deep-dish leafy
greens and clams with, 247–48
strudel stuffed with mixed greens,
122–23
or taro root, stuffed Swiss chard on a
bed of, 270–71
young turnip shoots and tops with
Spanish paprika and, 165–66
prosciutto:
beans with arugula and, 176
pan-fried, greens and barley with,
167–68
Provençal:
braised celery hearts with scallions,
310
chard, raisin, apple and cheese pie,
325–27
creamy cardoon potage, 90
"meat loaf" with cabbage, artichokes,
chard, spinach and ground pork,
269–70
pistou with aged Gouda, 91
-style stuffed cabbage, 272–74
tian with creamed spinach, 303

Provence, herbes de, Kittina's, 347
pudding:
milk, with pistachios, 329–30
rice, Anatolian (zerde), 338
pumpkin:
field greens and rice torta, 56–57
Tunisian fish couscous with leafy
greens and, 205–7
purslane:
and baby greens with cucumber and
shredded cabbage, 138–39
crunchy, with garlicky yogurt sauce,
151
and samphire salad with tapenade
toasts, 140–41
or samphire with taratour sauce, 141
and spices, summer harira with,
80–81

radicchio:
marinated Treviso-style, with crumbled eggs, 146–47
pasticcio, 197–98
red risotto with Barolo wine and, 186
shredded red, and smoked fish salad
with polenta crostini, 144–45
Treviso-style, on polenta, grilled, 109
ragout, sorrel, spinach and artichoke,
308–9
raisin(s), golden:
chard, apple and cheese pie,
Provençal, 325–27
escarole stuffed with capers,
anchovies, pine nuts and, 124
greens with pine nuts, sherry vinegar
and, 300
hoshaf, Zeliha Güngören's scallion
bulgur pilaf with, 286
Tunisian homemade couscous with,
335–36
ratatouille, Madame Saucourt's fabulous,
106–7
relish, green chili-cilantro (zhug), 22–23
ribollita from Sienna, crunchy-topped,
84
rice:
"Alexandria Quartet" of brown
lentils, pan-crisped pasta, browned
onions and, 180–81

[handwritten notes:] perol – deep flat-bottomed
2 handed rolled steel perol

mastic

veijuia
earthenware flameproof dish
or 10–12 cup casserole